John P Jeffries

The Natural History of the Human Races

John P Jeffries

The Natural History of the Human Races

ISBN/EAN: 9783337367398

Printed in Europe, USA, Canada, Australia, Japan

Cover: Foto ©ninafisch / pixelio.de

More available books at **www.hansebooks.com**

CAUCASIAN.

AFRICAN.

MALAY.

MONGOLIAN.

INDIAN.

THE

NATURAL HISTORY

OF THE

HUMAN RACES,

WITH

THEIR PRIMITIVE FORM AND ORIGIN, PRIMEVAL DISTRI-
BUTION, DISTINGUISHING PECULIARITIES; ANTIQUITY,
WORKS OF ART, PHYSICAL STRUCTURE, MENTAL
ENDOWMENTS AND MORAL BEARING.

ALSO,

AN ACCOUNT OF THE CONSTRUCTION OF THE GLOBE, CHANGES OF ITS
SURFACE; ELEVATION OF ITS MOUNTAINS AND SUBSIDENCE OF
LAND; TOGETHER WITH OTHER INTERESTING MATTER,

Illustrated by Colored Plates of each Type,

WITH NUMEROUS ENGRAVINGS REPRESENTING THEIR
VARIED FORMS.

By JOHN P. JEFFRIES,
WOOSTER, OHIO.

NEW YORK:
PRINTED FOR THE AUTHOR,
BY EDWARD O. JENKINS, 20 NORTH WILLIAM STREET.
1869.

PREFACE.

HAVING long been convinced of the necessity of a work such as is presented in the following pages, I imposed upon myself the labor of the undertaking. The principal object was to bring within the smallest compass a general outline of the natural history of the Human Races, and, at the same time, be sufficiently comprehensive as to give the ethnological student and general public an historical account of the Types of Mankind.

THE AUTHOR.

Wooster, Ohio, *August*, 1869.

CONTENTS.

(v)

vi CONTENTS.

INTRODUCTION.

NO subject is more replete with interesting story and specu-
lative fancy than that of the Human Races; yet comparatively few seem to consider it worthy of reflection.

"Know thyself!" was an inscription placed by the Greeks
over the door of the Temple of Apollo in letters of gold, to re-
mind the worshippers at the shrine of that god that they were
required to know themselves, in order to become worthy of his
favor.

Man, created as he was, but "little lower than the angels,"
with intellectual endowments capable of comprehending the
universe, has, thus far, it would seem, been unable to discover
his origin or write his own history, though inhabiting the earth
for many thousands of years.

Learned ethnologists have made repeated efforts to solve the
mystery of Man's first advent upon the globe by the philosophy
of reason; in all their labors, however, they have most signally
failed. It is not a subject susceptible of solution by any system
of philosophy based upon human reason alone, else man would
attain to the intellectual eminence of the Deity.

Man had a beginning, but when that beginning was has been
the perplexing question since the first dawn of civilization. The
origin of the several races of Man, too, has been almost, if not
quite, as hard to solve as to find the date of his creation; yet
distinct races have existed from the earliest historic period—at
least the four leading types, White, Yellow, Red and Black, were
the same thirty-three hundred years ago as they are to-day, as

shown by Egyptian paintings and sculpture; and it has been asserted that they so existed five thousand years ago in Egypt.

The Human Races, though originally confined to particular localities, are now spread over nearly the whole earth—as well where their bodies are exposed to cold occasioning congelation of mercury, as where they sustain heat at which ether boils; and the same peculiarities that existed among them in the earliest ages are still manifested, as well where the Races have been removed from their original seat, as where they continue indigenous.

The subject of man has long been a theme of wide-spread discussion and profound research by learned and accomplished scholars, among whom, Buffon, Blumenbach, Cuvier, Lawrence, Prichard, Smith, Humboldt, Morton, Bryant, Lyell, Lepsius, Owen, Moffatt, Gliddon, Nott, Agassiz, Van Amringe, Latham, Pickering, Hale, St. Hilaire, Wells, Pouchet, Huxley, Barth, Livingstone, Du Chaillu, Gastaldi, Schoolcraft, Catlin, Brace, and other distinguished authors.

Dr. Prichard was the great expounder of the question of the original unity of the Human Races; and, however erroneous his views may have been, they, to a measurable extent, have been adopted by the public at large. Still the question is far from being satisfactorily settled, and recent developments in ethnological science has materially shaken the Doctor's theory, if not, indeed, completely overthrown it. Connected with his idea of original unity is that of the equality of Races as a part and parcel of the same system of philosophy.

No portion of Man's natural history is entitled to greater consideration than that which brings all the families of mankind upon a common level, socially and politically. The subject has not, generally, been considered with the view of learning their fitness for equality upon philosophical principles under ethnological rules, but upon the abstract question of political economy—the right of individuals, by the law of nature alone, being regarded. Each Race was created to fulfill its destiny; and, in this respect, their status is unalterable. Mental power is the true standard of equality when the safety, stability and harmony of communities and governments are considered. Discordant elements can never be made to harmonize with profit; and forced Equality of Races is a system of tyranny intolerable in civilized governments that cannot be sustained upon any principle of political economy, law or morals.

Abandoning all old theories in regard to equality of the Races I have considered the subject upon the broad principles of right and justice, giving to each its appropriate position according to respective endowments, physically, mentally and morally. By the order of Providence they were created to fill allotted spheres, in distinctive orders and grades. This is nature, and cannot but be apparent to the commonest observer. All things prove the fact—from the smallest insect crawling upon the earth to the mightiest constellation circling in the heavens above.

" The noblest study of mankind is man." To make that study of interest, Man should be presented as he is in all his varied peculiarities. With that view each race, family, nation and tribe has been, as far as practicable, separately discussed in this work, with the design to present the Races as they existed before and since the historic period, giving their natural history, antiquity, physical characteristics, mental capacity and moral standard.

It is generally believed that the Races of Man originated in Asia; and it is claimed, with much plausibility, that they can still be traced to their original seats by their several distinguishing characteristics. In western Asia, on Mount Caucasus, dwell Caucasians bearing the full impress of the primitive type, and in whom are witnessed the perfections, purity and superiority of the White Man.

Though the term Caucasian is given as a designation of the race having fair complexion, it by no means follows that all are white; some indeed are found who are almost as dark-skinned as the African, but at the same time have none of his features. Whatever complexion Caucasians may bear, they may be, by every characteristic, traced to their original type, much as it may seem to have been modified. Not so, however, in regard to the Mongolian, Malay and American, in whom there is such similarity of form and feature in the modified families as to make it quite difficult to trace in them the original type; and hence it is, that the Malay has, by some authors, been regarded as descendants of the African, and the American of the Mongolian.

The Indo-Europeans, or Japetic family, constituting the Aryan group, seem to have originated in Iran, where the type is still well preserved by the Hindoos, Persians, Afghans, Baluchi, Kurds, Assetens and Armenians.

The numerous nations of higher Asia, of nomadic habits, of which the Ugrians are chief, include the Tartars, Kalmucks, Tungusians, Finns, Lapps, Tschides, Osticks and Siberian tribes. The Tartars seem to display two types, not so much in physique as in peculiar habits; yet there is some resemblance between the nomadic and Mongolian nations; but the other family, the Turks of Europe, are literally Caucasians. Dr. Prichard considered these two families as not of the same type; he was evidently mistaken, though the nomades are doubtless tainted with Mongolian blood. The Kalmucks are good representatives of the nomadic Tartars, and so strongly resemble the Mongols as to warrant their being classed with the Mongolian. Among the Tungusian group of Tartar peoples are found almost every shade of complexion, from the fair-skinned Mandrichies to the dark hue of the Kalmuck, and sometimes those having blue eyes and aquiline nose.

The aborigines of India are distinct from the Hindoos, and inhabited the country now occupied by their descendants before the Hindoos crossed the Indus river. Though attached to their native country at the present day, they were once of a wandering character, as some of this family first peopled the valley of the Nile. The Fellahs seem to be the posterity of the earlier people of Egypt; and, although considered kindred of the Polynesians, are nevertheless Caucasians. Classing them with the Malay does not make them such, or change their character.

The old system of ranking all dark-skinned people with the Negro has been exploded since it has become manifest that there are Black Caucasians, and that the Gallabes, Fellahs and Hottentots are not Negroes.

The main and prominent features of the Races consist in the color of the skin, quality and quantity of the hair, structure, or rather shape of the skull, their habits and general capacity of body and mind. The color and quality of the hair of the African is different from all others, and by it alone he may be readily recognized. Caucasians are frequently found with dark curling hair, but never of the woolly texture of the Negro. The hair of the African is not wool, as generally supposed, but hair of a coarse texture kinked or curled. It has the appearance of a cylinder with a smooth surface when examined microscopically. The hair of the Mulatto and Abyssinian has also a riband-like band running through the middle of the tube, while the hair of the Caucasian is almost transparent, like an empty tube.

The American race is less adulterated by amalgamation than any of the types; but yet are two distinct orders of people: one is of Malay origin, the other Mongolian. These two orders of the American seem to have first met upon the plains of Mexico —the former, it is presumed, reached the Western Continent by way of the Pacific Ocean, the latter by Behring Straits.

The Toltecs and Aztecs were preceded in Mexico by the Tarascas, Othome, Talanacs and Huaxtecas. The Othome had a dialect resembling the Chinese, being monysyllabic, whilst that of the other tribes was polysyllabic.

At the time of the discovery of America, the Algonquin-Lenape and Iroquois or Huron occupied the northern and central part of the country as far west as the Mississippi river, and the Mobilian nations the southern slope of the Alleghanies from Virginia to the Gulf of Mexico. Between the Mississippi and the Rocky Mountains dwell the Dacotas (or Sioux), Pawnees, Osages, Blackfeet, Crows, Asinboins and kindred nations. Upon the Rocky Mountains and their western declivity are the Shoshones, Nez-Perce and Flat Heads. In the northern portion of the continent are the Chippeways, Athapascas, Kaluchi and Esquimaux. In Texas are the Apaches and Comanches; in New Mexico the Pimas, Moquis, Navajos, and some civilized nations passing under the name of Pueblos. In California, Oregon and Washington are many tribes the chief of which are the Californians and Chinooks.

In South America there are three leading families of Indians. The Andians or Alpines, including the Peruvians, Antisians and Araucanians; the Brazilian Guarani and Mediterranians in the southern part of the continent. The Incas were known as " the Children of the Sun," and occupied Peru at the time of its conquest by the Spaniards under Pizarro. The Aymaras were the earliest inhabitants of Peru, and much resemble the Incas, both having very large chests, which is owing to the rareness of the atmosphere. Their chief city was Tiaguanuco, the most ancient of South America, and where the arts, sciences, and religion of the Incas originated.

The Araucanas occupy the western slope of the Andes, and the Changos the plain along the coast. The Antisians reside on the eastern declivity of the Bolivian and Peruvian Andes. They are almost white. The Araucanians occupy the mountains of Chili, the passes of which they defended against Pizarro. The Terra del Fuegas are of this family.

The Mediterranians comprise the Patagonians and other tribes in the vicinity of the Straits of Magellan. Their complexion is darker than the other tribes of the country. The regions east of the Parapia river is inhabited by two great families, the Guarani and Topi, and the Caribbes of the region bordering on Central America and the Mexican Gulf. Their complexion is yellowish brown and their eyes obliquely set and raised at the outer angles.

As a matter of ethnological convenience the Races have been grouped into four great families, viz: Turanian, Semetic, Aryan, and Hamite. The Hamite, however, is virtually included in the Semitic. The most ancient of these families is the Turanian. Yet the Hamites appear upon the stage about the same period. The Turanian appear in history at the founding of the Babylonian Empire. Their capital was founded, and their government flourished and fell before Nineveh was known in history. Its duration was supposed to date from 2458 B. C. to 2234 B. C.

The Turanians were the first nations to migrate westward from the original seat. The Chinese were the first people to move as a nation. They migrated in two directions. One portion gave rise to the Tai tribes, the other founded the Tungusic families; another family pushed south to the sea and the islands in that direction; a second to the north originated the Mongol Tartar tribes; and a third to the north produced the Turks; and another to the south brought into being the vast people of India. The last migration to the north produced the Finnish tribes including the Basque and Samoides. These migrations can only be traced by the structure of language. By this means each family and tribe may be traced. When the Turanians left their native mountains they had no literature or any system of laws. They were virtually savages, as low in the scale of barbarism as any of the savage tribes of the present day. Whilst these migrations were progressing a well regulated government was in existence in China, and also one in Hindoostan, at least 2000 years B. C. The Turanian language includes that of the Finns, Lopps, Magyars, Turks, Tartars, Mongols, Thibetians, and the Aboriginal Indians.

The Turanian is better defined by dividing the group into the Mongols, Tungusians, Turks, and Ugrians. From the Ugrians the Magyars derive their descent, and this is the reason they have been said to be of Finnish stock.

Before the historical appearance of the Turanians, the Hamite tribes, it has been claimed, had established the Egyptian Empire.

The term Hamite, it should be borne in mind, does not necessarily mean people of dark complexion, hence the terms Hamite and Semitic may be considered one and the same thing in many particulars. The Hamites, like the Semitics, were some of light and some of brown complexion, but ever having the European features. Both stocks of people were of Asiatic origin.

It is pretty generally believed that before the historic period the Hamite or Cushite tribes of dark complexion resided in Asia along the whole southern coast.

The Bible version of the peopling of Ethiopia (Africa) by Hamitic people is sustained by the monuments of Egypt, her paintings and preserved skulls. All show the Egyptians to have been of Asiatic origin and not Negroes, but of the Semitic family of the Caucasian race.

The Greeks doubtless believed in two branches of the Hamites—Asiatic and African. Herodotus also understood there were two branches of Hamitic stock, the Asiatic and Egyptian Cushites. Bible history would even sustain that the Babylonian Empire was erected by a Cushite chieftain named Nimrod. As late as 600 B. C., the Hamites were a powerful element in the Babylonian Empire. They made their way into Egypt through lower Babylonia, Arabia, and by Suez to the Nile. When they entered Egypt is not known. The invasion of the Hyksos or Shepherd Kings is fixed at 2167 years before Christ by Lepsius. He says Menes founded the United Kingdom of Egypt 3892 B. C., or 112 years after the creation according to his system of chronological reckoning. At that time the Hamites had consolidated the two Egyptian kingdoms into one and built up an empire whose works of art astonished the world.

There were in Egypt, at an early day, three leading nations of people of definite characters. One had prominent cheek-bones, swelled lips, broad flat nose, protruding eyebrows, and crisped hair and dark colored skin. They were the Ethiopians so-called. Another had a long narrow nose, receding forehead, eye-lids short, thick body, long legs, and flowing hair of reddish color. The third and most common had a short chin, full voluptuous lips, large prominent eyes, slightly curved nose, and full cheeks, the hair thick and braided. The present Copts are the true representatives of the ancient Egyptians proper.

The Hamites, it appears, invaded Babylonia before the historic period, and drove out the Turanians, taking possession of the government. They brought with them at their invasion a system of picture-writing and introduced a system of astronomy at Babylon. The first historical date of this Cushite empire is fixed at 2234 years B. C. They held the government down until 1976 years B. C. One of the line of Kings of this dynasty was Chedo-Loamer, a Hamite prince of Elam, who built up a vast Empire. He marched an army of many thousands from the Persian Gulf to the Dead Sea, a distance of 1200 miles, and held Palestine and Syria in subjection twelve years. At the close of this Hamite dynasty, 1976 B. C., another Hamite tribe from Susiana invaded Babylonia, and established the second great Chaldean Empire, which lasted until 1518 B. C. The Arabs then took possession of the Empire and governed it for a period of 245 years. This Arabic dynasty put an end to the Chaldean government, and the Chaldeans themselves became absorbed in the Arabic people. The Hamite nation have also become absorbed and have long since disappeared as a distinct people. Upon their ruins the Aryans and Semites proper have built up kingdoms, nations, and empires, which have given laws to the civilized world. It is claimed that whilst the Turanians were barbarians, the Hamites were enjoying refined civilization—had alphabetic writing, were learned in astronomy, history, sculpture and navigation.

The Semites, though less in number than the other families, produced greater results than all others combined. They originated commerce, invented the alphabet and numeral characters, and through them have sprung the religions of the world. They revealed to man the will of God upon the tablets of stone, and diverted his attention from the Christian faith to Mohammedanism ; and they crucified the Savior as an impostor because he did not reveal himself to them in the pomp and splendor of their refined civilization.

Their first migration from Central Asia occurred before the historic era. The first record of them is about 2000 years B. C. When Abraham journeyed from Ur in Chaldea to Egypt he found Semitic tribes in Canaan ; before that period the Phœnicians had established themselves upon the Mediterranean, and the descendants of Joctan had spread themselves over the Arabian peninsula.

The chief countries occupied by the Semitics were Syria, Phœnicia, Palestine, Mesopotamia, Chaldea, Susiana, and Arabia. The Hebrews, Canaanites, Phœnicians, and Syrians, were the leading tribes of this family. The Hyksos or Shepherd kings were descendants of the Canaanites. They were a distinctly marked race. The forehead was straight but not high, the brow was full, eyes large and almond-shaped, nose aquiline, mouth strong and firm with somewhat thick lips, chin full and well formed, abundant hair and ample beard.

The Aryans constitute the white race, but include the leading families of dark complexion, following, viz : Spaniards, Iberians, Basques, Celtic Finns, Hindoos, and Siamese.

The Aryans occupied, as their original place of abode, a district at the source of the Oxus river. From where they spread over upper Asia and drove out of Europe the Turanian tribes, who had settled there, and occupied the country themselves. The several Aryan tribes thus entering Europe are known by the name of Kelts, Teutonians, Sclavonians, Lithuanians, Pelasgians, and Phrygians.

The Indian Aryans, at a very early period, according to the Vedic hymns, drove out the Turanians, and spread themselves over the country to the Ganges. From them have sprung the Bromatic Hindoos ; and from the Irans the Persic Aryans, the

Medes, Carmanians, Bactrians, Logdians, Hyrcanians, and others
of lesser note.   Their migrations have not been definitely fixed ;
but M. Bunsen supposes that the Aryans occupied the valley of
the Indus from 4000 to 8000 years B. C.   Rawlinson fixes the
emigration of the Aryans to the south of the Caspian at about
640 years B. C., at which time they established the empire of the
Medes.   The Aryan language shows they had passed the state
of barbarism before they began their emigrations, having built
dwellings, constructed boats, trained domestic animals to labor,
worked in metals, and did weaving and sewing.

During the latter part of the 7th century B. C., the Aryans
and Semitics of southern Asia were subdued by vast hordes of
Turanians from the north, among them were the Cimmerians,
who were Irans and Scythians.   The Cimmerians occupied the
country between the Danube and the Don, north of the Black
Sea, from 800 to 600 years B. C.   They were driven out into
Europe by the Scythians 600 years B. C.   They occupied the
Crimea and are supposed to be identical with the Cimbri and
the ancestors of the Kelts or Celtic families.

The Pelasgians were a leading people of Aryan Stock, and
were the common ancestors of the Greeks and Italians.   The
Aryans are traced by their language and works of art.   The
Turanians also made history in the same mode.   All over the
western continent, in Europe, Asia and Africa, monuments of
these families are to be found.   Tumuli, holes excavated in the
ground for dwellings, pottery, knives of bone, axes of stone, flint
arrowheads, and ornaments of bronze, are found in great profusion.   Also their ruined dwellings are discovered in the bottom
of the lakes in Europe.   They seem to have entered Europe and
America from the north.   The Mongolian Finns were perhaps the
first people of Europe.   They were there at least when the Celts
entered the country and occupied it in the Stone age.   The
Celts held it in the Bronze age, and the Teutons in the Iron age.

The Celts were the oldest Aryan family and the first to emigrate from Asia to Europe after the departure of the Turanian
hordes.   They are traceable by their language, which is considered older than the Sanscrit.   In the time of Julius Cæsar the
Celts were described as a tall race, with ruddy complexion, bland

temperament, light hair and blue eyes. They then possessed the art of writing and had an alphabet.

The Etruscans were Aryans. They called themselves Tyrrhenians, and were virtually the founders of the Roman Empire. They have been supposed to be a branch of Finnish stock; but this supposition is based upon a very limited foundation. The Latins and Umbrians constitute the Italicans, all of whom were Aryans and closely allied with the Greeks.

The Teutonic family, consisting of the German tribes, were the most powerful of all the nations of Europe. They were Aryans of extraordinary prowess and energy. The old Roman Empire was overthrown by them; and they built up on its ruins a new refined civilization, thereby changing the whole policy of Europe. Their original seat was in Asia, from where they commenced their emigration westward 1200 years B. C.; but they halted north of the Black Sea until the 7th century B. C., when they entered Europe, and spread over Germany.

Although it would appear that the several races of man originated in Asia, except the Negro, the common origin of the races is not by any means determined. Whether there was an original diversity of races, or not, the permanence of the types will not be doubted.

The whole Indo-European, Semitic and Hamitic families may be grouped in one family or individual mass. All can be traced to their original abode; so with the Turanian family, which may be traced to their home in Asia. These three great families have made the greater portion of the history of the human races. But, whilst they were performing their great deeds, the other three Types were in comparative inactivity, enjoying their uncivilized privileges. Strike out of the world's history their record, and nothing would be left to admire as regards the actions of man.

If there was unity of origin of the races, there has certainly been no unity of action, or unity of design, among them, especially between the white and black.

It is difficult, if not impossible, to trace to their source the origin of the types and physical differences of the families of man, there being no data upon which to predicate a probable period. For aught we are advised, they may have existed for many

2

thousands of ages. As far back as history leads us, the same types have been in existence; and, though there may be physical differences in families, the original type remains the same, and may still be traced.

Various shades and hues of complexion are found existing among the Caucasians and Africans, and indeed in all the Races, but still the original type is always traceable in each individual case.

The five Races we have enumerated are considered permanent types, neither having originated from the other, all being original orders of mankind.

Though their descendants to some extent have been modified in particular instances, such as the Albinos, and present various subdivisions of types, in particular families, color has been permanent in the original races for ages. No cause has been in existence to make black white, or white black, permanently so.

It is noteworthy that the several Types have occupied the same Zones where they were first discovered, and which are presumed to be their native places. But since the discovery of the marine compass, during the last hundred years the Caucasians have colonized almost every portion of the globe. This disposition of enterprise, however, does not change the law of the human race. The Creator has placed the several races in the locality best suited to their nature.

It is most natural to conclude diversity of origin for all animated nature. Agassiz upon this subject remarks :

" Under such circumstances we should ask if we are not entitled to conclude that these races must have originated where they occur, as well as the animals and plants inhabiting the countries, and have originated there in the same numerical proportions, and over the same area in which they now occur; for these considerations are the conditions necessary to their maintenance, and what among organized beings is essential to their temporal existence, must be at least one of the conditions under which they were created.

" We maintain that, like all organized beings, mankind cannot have originated in single individuals, but must have been created in that numerical harmony which is characteristic of each species. Men must have originated in nations, as the bees have originated in swarms, and, as the different social plants have covered the extensive tracts over which they have naturally spread.

.   .   .   .

" The coincidence of geographical distribution of the human races with that of animals, the disconnection of climatic conditions where we have similar races, and the connection of climatic conditions where we have different human races, shows further, that the adaption of different races of men to different parts of the world must be intentional, as well as that of other beings; that men were primitively located in various parts of the world they inhabit, and that they arose everywhere in those harmonious numeric proportions with other beings which would at once secure their preservation and contribute to their welfare.

" To suppose that all men originated from Adam and Eve, is to assume that the order of creation has been changed in the course of historical times, and to give to the Mosaic Record a meaning that it was never intended to have. On that ground we would particularly insist upon the propriety of considering the Genesis as chiefly relating to the history of the white race, with special reference to the Jews."

The law of the human race has proved that the natives of one zone will not admit of being transferred to another without producing a material physical deterioration of the race. Such seems to be the great mysteries of human nature.

Ethnologists have greatly disagreed in regard to the number of the races of man. Buffon enumerated six races; Hunter, seven; Metzon, two,—white and black. Viery divided mankind into three races; Blumenbach, into five, viz: Caucasian, Mongolian, Malay, African, and American; Barry de St. Vincent reported fifteen races or species, but made only three primitive types; Martin classified man into twenty-two families;· Pickering gives eleven races; Luke Burke, sixty-three; and Jacquenet divides man into three, viz: Caucasian, Mongol, and Negro.

The various classifications rather tend to embarrass the student of ethnology than enlighten him on the subject of the race of man.

Some have contended that the races not only proceeded from a common parentage, but that in their origin they presented physical differences of types which are still manifested as distin-

guishing characteristics; for instance, the four leading races may
be recognized by the shape of the skull; that the oval form presents
the Caucasian; the round form, the American; the square form,
the Mongolian, and the oblong form the Negro. These are peculiarities which exist and detect the races to which they several-
ly have reference. These forms of skulls have existed since the
various families of man were known to each other, and though
the races have passed through various phases, the same shaped
skulls are still presented as in the original or primitive types.

The diversity of the race is not accidental. Such an idea is
inconsistent with man's natural history. No one ever knew of
an instance where a Negro was accidentally born of Caucasian
parents; nor of a case where the white man was accidentally
born of Negro parents.

Dr. Prichard advanced the idea that the whole human family
did not only spring from Adam and Eve, but that Adam was a
Negro. He based his theory upon the idea of Albinos (white
Negroes) being derived from black parents, and in no instance
did a Negro spring from white parents. He also argued that the
dark races were better fitted for savage life than the fair-com-
plexioned families, as if man was, in all instances, to be a savage.

It is a general rule in natural law, that deviation from the
original types will correct itself and assume its original form.
This is manifest in the Mongrel and Mulatto, who will soon become extinct unless kept near the parent type. Accidental
freaks of nature do occur, but they are never transmitted.
Esau was a hairy man, yet no hairy men arose from him.

There is no accident or chance about the human complexion,
or races. They were produced by design of the Creator, and it
is too late now to assume they were freaks of nature, or that of
chance; and it is unreasonable to claim that the complexion of
the races originated with the three sons of Noah—Shem, Ham,
and Japheth. The races did not create themselves, nor did they
invent their complexions or their peculiarities or characteristics,
and no one is to be called to account for color or physical
deficiencies. The Races are as God made them. If they are
deficient, man is not responsible for it.

MONTEZUMA.

HYPERBOREAN.

NOJAI TARTAR.

CHAPTER I.

ANTIQUITY OF MAN.

EARLY history of Man.—Barbarous age.—Stone, bronze, and iron periods.—Scotch firs, oak, and beech of Denmark.—Peat deposits.—Lake dwellings.—Bones of domestic animals in deposits with bronze and stone instruments.—Submergence of Europe and North America.—Geology.—Mountains hove up.—Ancient canoes.—Skeleton of a whale in alluvium.—Exhumed human skulls.—Ancient hut discovered in the drift.—Ruined town discovered seventeen feet under ground.—Wakey hole.—Engis cave.—Human skulls found in oyster beds.—Shell mounds.—Elevation of land in Chili, on Baltic coast, Scotland, England and Wales.—Mount Nuevo.—Jourillo.—Subsidence of land on the Columbia River.—Denmark.—Temple of Serapis.—Sindree.—Volcano of Sumbewa.—Submerged forests.—Coal strata.—Dead Sea.

MAN'S early history is buried in obscurity—in the gloom of ages. His origin, save the brief account thereof contained in the Genesis, is unrecorded. His antiquity, though interesting to the ethnological student, is at the same time the most perplexing feature of his history.

In the absence of historic data, the mind readily seizes upon the next best means for the solution of the mysterious problem. His works of art and physical and mental developments enable the ethnologist to trace man back to a comparatively early period of his existence. These, with his language, are the only safe guides to follow in tracing out the origin of races and families of mankind.

Considering man in his natural state, there seems to be but little doubt about all the races at one time being in a state of the rudest barbarism, from which they slowly emerged by force of their mental qualities, and in proportion to the degrees of intellectual endowments of the several types.

The first record of his emergence from the savage state is discovered in the stone implements wrought by him for domestic purposes, and for weapons of war and self-defence. These imperishable relics are found in every habitable portion of the globe. Next in order appears the bronze implements, and finally the iron, each proving an advance step in the progress of civilization. How long the first people of the globe existed before the commencement of the stone period is not even susceptible of plausible conjecture, though in regard to the stone, bronze, and iron periods, by the aid of geology we may approximate their probable eras. After their emergence from these several periods they can more readily and certainly be traced by their monuments of art, sculpture, and paintings.

The age of stone dates with the period of first vegetation in Denmark.* The Scotch fir seems to have been the first vegetation of Denmark, as the trunks of these trees are now found buried in the peat deposits at the depth of thirty feet, some of which being three feet in diameter. This tree is not now a native of Denmark, but must have been indigenous subsequent to the stone age, as stone implements, the workmanship of human hands, have been found underneath their buried trunks.

The oak was the second vegetation of this region, which coincides with the bronze period, swords and shields of this metal having been found in the peat deposits of that age. Iron was first made use of by the people of Denmark when the beech was the prevailing timber of the country, implements of iron being found buried in the peat bogs with the beech trees of that period.

The age of these peat deposits cannot be definitely ascertained, but Sir Charles Lyell supposes the time required for their deposition at about fifty thousand years. However remote the period may have been, it is well established that man was inhabiting the country before the age of the formation of peat. The bronze instruments not only show the high antiquity of man, but his advanced condition in civilization and in arts. The bronze instruments are composed of nine parts of copper and one of tin ; the former is often found in its native state but the latter never ; and

------

* Lyell's Antiquities of Man, p. 10.

it requires skill to detect it and disengage it from its ore and mould it in proper proportion with copper. The vast number and variety of instruments discovered show most clearly the age of long duration.

Bronze was a great stride of improvement over stone, as much so as iron was over bronze. How long an interval existed between these several ages is impossible to tell; or how long the natives or peoples of the countries where they are found continued without them, or used the stone before resorting to the bronze and iron, is beyond the knowledge of man.

In the departments of the Somme and Seine, stone instruments have been discovered in the diluvian beds at great depth. These are supposed to be the implements of the earliest peoples of Europe (Celts), the authors of the upright stone, a circle of which, called Stonehenge, is an illustrious example. They have been conjectured the work of the celtic Druids, but by whom, when or for what purpose erected, has not been revealed. They have no inscriptions or marks of origin, hence must have been built and abandoned before the invention of written language. Even when the Romans first visited the British Isles, the origin of these stone monuments was unknown to the natives by history or tradition. The people who erected them had passed away without leaving any other record of their existence, unless the works of art found in the same soil at considerable depth below their foundation be theirs also.*

In the diluvian gravel pits of Menchecourt, numerous axes and other instruments of stone have been discovered, associated with the bones of the elephant, rhinoceros, hippopotamus, bear, hyena, stag, ox, and other mammalia. The axes were found ranging from thirteen to twenty-seven feet below the surface of the ground. They were of flint, and very similar to those found in the mounds of North America, which fact has given rise to the absurd notion that the Indians are of Celtic origin, the stone axes of Europe being considered of Celtic construction. The Celts, it will not be denied, were early in Europe, but they were not the first peoples, at least of Caledonia, as two types had successively dwelt there before the advent of the Celts, but who, like the constructors of Stonehenge, are unknown in history.

* Types of Mankind, p. 356.

These two types are recognised by their peculiarly shaped skulls, the Kumbe-kephali being boat-shaped,* and the Brachy-kephali, short heads. The former lived in the country in the primeval or stone age, the latter in the close of that era, both being displaced by the Celts in the bronze period, who were forced to give way by the Teutons in the iron period.† These two primitive types also were the first peoples of Denmark and Scandinavia.‡

In connection with the first peoples of Europe may be considered the lake dwellings recently discovered in Switzerland and the British Islands, which seem to have been constructed in the stone period, though extending into that of the bronze.

The first of these dwellings was discovered in 1854, in Lake Zurich. In dredging the lake the workmen came upon rows of piles driven into the bottom, the foundations of dwellings. They also found stone instruments and one small bronze hatchet, portions of rude pottery, charred wood and decayed timber. As many as three hundred wooden huts were comprised in one settlement, and supposed to have contained a thousand inhabitants. At Wangen forty thousand piles were used.§ These dwellings, it would seem from recent investigation, existed in nearly, if not quite, all the lakes in Switzerland.‖ In the small lake near Berne, instruments of stone, horn and bone have been found; the stone (flint) is not a native of the country, but of France, and from which it was brought and worked near the lake, where spawls and chippings of the flint are still existing in great abundance. Hatchets of serpentine and granite, and arrow-heads of quartz have been discovered in great profusion in Lake Constance. In the vicinity of New Moges, on Lake Geneva, there was a large collection of dwellings of the bronze age. No less than forty hatchets of bronze have been found there recently.

---

* The Neanderthal skull is of this race; at least from the very pertinent descriptions of it, it seems to be of the same order, and also very similar to the Engis cranium.—Evidence of Man's place in Nature.—Huxley, p. 160.

† Types of Mankind, p. 360.   ‡ Indigenous Races of the Earth, p. 20.

§ Lyell's Antiquity of Man, p. 20.

‖ They are also found in Italy, with the flint and bronze instruments, and bones of domestic animals.—Pre-Historic Remains in Italy, by Prof. Gastardi, pp. 121–122.

The bones of animals found with these remains of dwellings show that the inhabitants had several of the domestic kind, such as the ox, sheep, goat and dog. Much conjecture has been indulged in in regard to these lake dwellings. The most plausible theory is, they were so located to shield the inhabitants from the wild beasts and savage tribes of the forests. During the stone period it has been estimated by M. Troyon that 31,875 persons dwelt upon the lakes. In Switzerland alone over one hundred and fifty of these lake dwellings have been discovered. This author fixes the period of the lake dwellings at about two thousand years before the Christian era. Mr. Lyell, however, calculates the lake dwellings' era at about 6750 years ago. M. Morlot on the other hand assigns to the bronze age a date of between 3000 and 4000 years, and to that of the stone period an age of from 5000 to 7000 years.*

The Irish lakes abound in lake dwellings of the stone and bronze periods. At Sagore a space of 520 feet in diameter was found inclosed by timbers and divided into compartments, in which were found bones of swine, goats, deer, oxen, sheep, foxes, dogs, horses, and the ass. Overlying these bones was a bog of sixteen feet in vertical thickness. Instruments of stone, bronze, and iron were found in these ruined dwellings.

Very marked changes have taken place in the surface of Europe since the stone and bronze eras, as it is quite evident the glacial period was of prior date. Had man existed in the country in the glacial era, whilst the elevation and subsidence of land was in progress, and perished by the floods, his remains would doubtless be found with those of the lower animals and plants deeply buried in the earth.

It is evident there was a time when the greater portion of Europe was under water and unfitted for the habitation of man. Scandinavia during that period remained above water; England and Scotland were marked by a few islands along the western coast; Ireland by a few elevations at the corners of the islands; France had a few elevations above water; Bohemia was a vast island; portions of the Vosges and Black Forest, and some portion of the country now occupied by the Alps between Toulon and Milan and the Tyrol, composed an Archipel-

* Lyell's Antiquity of Man, pp. 28-29.

ago; all the regions of Southern Europe, except Spain and Turkey, were submerged, or had not yet been elevated. Then North America was mainly under water, the Alleghanies forming an island, and a vast sea lying between this chain and the Rocky Mountains, as also between Nova Scotia and Newfoundland. None of the lands along the Gulf of Mexico existed; Florida was at the bottom of the sea, and the gulf extended up the valley of the Mississippi, almost if not quite its whole length. M. Guyot asserts that at that period the Rocky Mountains, the table lands and the high snow-capped chain from California to the frozen ocean, were still at the bottom of the sea.* These changes of surface are visible in every part of the earth. Elevations and subsidences of land are constantly going on, though not to the extent of former ages. They are as a book of recorded facts of the antiquity of man. By these changes not only man's works of art have been preserved for ages, but also his fossil remains. Geology has fully revealed that the mountains are hove up to their present heights by internal force, and that the same cause is still existing, as there are recent cases where large bodies of land have been raised up even in the sea and still remain. It is not impossible that the bottom of the Atlantic may be elevated and the Continent of Europe become a sea. In such a case we would have presented to view a vast ruined world upon the floor of the ocean, as no portion of the globe contains more buried treasure and remains of man and his works of art.

The changes of surface of the coast near Naples, noticed in another place, is an apt illustration of this subject. The strata is raised about twenty-five feet above the level of the sea, forming a terrace skirting the eastern shore of the bay of Baiae. This elevated strata contains fragments of sculpture, pottery, and buildings.

In Cashmere, India, fragments of pottery have been found at the depth of fifty feet beneath the surface of the ground. On a table land in the valley two buried temples have been discovered, one of which has a colonnade of seventy-five pillars. On exposing three of the pillars to view they were found fresh and the architectural ornaments as perfect as when first executed.

In South America, in the island of San Lorenzo near Lima,

* Earth and Man, by Guyot, p. 108.

Peru, Dr. Darwin found, at the height of eighty-five feet above
the sea, pieces of cotton thread, plaited rush, and the head of a
stock of Indian corn, with shells similar to those now existing in
the sea. The whole region shows that the bottom of the sea had
been elevated eighty-five feet since man was an inhabitant of the
country.*

Near Glasgow, Scotland, above the banks of the Clyde, within
the last century have been found buried in the silt and clay, in
what are called the flat lands, no less than seventeen canoes,
five of them being found under the streets of the city. The
other twelve were discovered about a hundred yards back from
the Clyde. They were buried in the soil to the depth of about
nineteen feet, and were seven feet above high water mark.

These canoes showed the grade of mechanical skill from the
rude dug-out to the ornamental barge, constructed in many respects like the skiffs or yawls of the present day. In one of
these barges was found a beautifully polished celt of greenstone,
such as would indicate the workmanship of the bronze period.
These ornamental canoes being made of plank, with ribs, pins
and metal nails, would show them to have been built in the
bronze period, if not indeed in that of iron. Though no evidence
of iron is now visible, the metal nails used in the construction of
the canoes having all disappeared, the places where they were
driven were still plainly visible when the buried vessels were exhumed. In one of these canoes was found a plug of cork, from
which fact Mr. Geikie, the geologist, argues they were not of
the latitude of Glasgow, but of Spain, Southern France or Italy.†

At Dunmore, a few miles below Stirling, the skeleton of a
whale eighty feet long was found about twenty feet above high
water mark. Seven miles above the estuary above Stirling, at
an elevation of about thirty feet above the sea, skeletons of three
whales were discovered as late as about the year 1824, and near
these were instruments of deer horn, one of which retains a portion of a wooden handle. This instrument is preserved in the
Edinburgh museum.

In the Parish of Dundonald an ornament of cannel coal was
exhumed from gravel and marine shells fifty feet above the sea
level.

* Lyell's Antiquity of Man, p. 46. † Geikie, Geo. Quart. Journal, vol. 18, p. 224.

On the coast of Cornwall more remarkable discoveries in regard to man have been made. At Pentuan and Carnon human skulls have been exhumed in mining for tin at a depth of from forty to fifty-three feet beneath the surface. The strata overlying these skulls contains sea-shells, the bones of whales and those of animals. In the vicinity of Stockholm, whilst digging a canal in 1819, the workmen, in cutting through a marine strata containing fossil shells of the Baltic species at the depth of sixty feet, came upon the remains of a wooden hut, the lower part, which stood upon a level with the sea, was in a tolerable state of preservation. On the floor was a rude fireplace constructed of stones, in which were found cinders and charred wood. Near the hut lay limbs of the fir tree having the appearance of being severed from the trunk by an axe or sharp instrument.[*] In the strata overlying the hut were found vessels of rude form, but fastened together with wooden pins, showing them to have been constructed before the age of iron, or perhaps bronze.

In India, near Behat, a very ancient town was discovered in the year 1833 underlying a stratum of river sand five feet thick, and a bed of alluvial clay twelve feet in thickness. Coins of silver and copper, articles of metal and earthenware have been found in this subterranean place.

Dr. Buckland with considerable minuteness describes human skeletons found in the cave of "Wakey Hole," near Wells, in the Mendips, in connection with mud and clay, some of them even united by stalagmites into a firm osseous breccia.

Near Liege, on the banks of the Meuse, Dr. Schmerling discovered in caverns human bones in the same mud and breccia with those of the elephant, rhinoceros, bear and other quadrupeds of extinct species.[†]

M. Tournal found in the cavern of Bize, in the department of the Aude of France, human bones with fragments of rude pottery in the same mud and breccia cemented by stalagmite in which were also shells of living species imbedded.[‡]

Dr. Schmerling, of Liege, discovered in the Engis cave near that city several human skeletons. He preserved a skull of one

---

[*] Phil. Trans. 1835, Part I. pp. 8–9.   [†] Principles of Geology, p. 727.
[‡] Annales des Sciences Naturales, Vol. XV. p. 48.

which he found buried five feet deep in the cavern in breccia
with the tooth of the rhinoceros, the bones of the horse and reindeer. In this cavern the learned naturalist also discovered some
rude flint instruments dispersed through the cave mud. He also
found in the cave of Chakier, a few miles distant from Liege, a
jointed and polished needle-shaped bone instrument having a
hole pierced through it obliquely at the base. The preserved
skull above referred to was Caucasian, and, though very ancient,
approaches the highest order of that race.*

This Engis skull has given rise to a wide range of discussion
on account of the perfectness of the type it represents and tending to prove that man has been true to the original design of his
Creator and constant in his osteological character; proving, to
a measurable extent at least, the absurdity of the progressive and
gradation theory of Lamark.†

In the Brigham cavern of Devonshire, discovered in 1858, was
found numerous flint knives in connection with the bones of the
elephant, rhinoceros, lion, hyena, reindeer, horse and ox. Also
the hind leg of a cave bear was found in the same deposits, and
in close proximity to which was one of the flint instruments.
It is quite clear this bear lived subsequent to the manufacture of
the flint tools. This limb of the bear was deposited in the alluvium when it was clothed with flesh, or at least when the
ligatures bound the bones in contact.

It has been shown by incontestable proof that the flint hatchets
of St. Acheul were exhumed from the lower beds of diluvium
and that their owners existed coeval with the mammoth and
rhinoceros.‡

Flint implements similar to those already mentioned, have
been found in great abundance in not only the British Isles, but
also upon the Continent, especially in Germany and Scandinavia,
as well in the boulder strata as the diluvium.

In Sardinia, at an elevation of nearly an hundred metres, over
300 feet above the level of the sea, oyster shells imbedded in

---

* Two skulls were found in the vicinity of Modena, Italy, of very high antiquity. They were discovered in the earth about thirteen feet beneath the
surface. One was of Caucasian type. Pre-Historic remains in Italy, p. 10.

† The Engis skull was found deposited with the bones of the Elephant and
Rhinoceros. Evidence of Man's place in Nature.—Huxley, p. 140.

‡ Antiquity of Man, p. 104.

breccia, in which fragments of limestone and pieces of course pottery, have been found. In the same mass was also found a flattened ball of baked earthen ware, through the centre of which was pierced a small hole. This portion of the island has undoubtedly been elevated from the bed of the sea to its present position in all probability in the post pliocene period. The shell-mounds of Denmark are, as would seem, depositories and antique works of man; indeed the shells themselves show him to have occupied Denmark at a very early period. Scattered through these mounds are innumerable flint knives, hatchets and instruments of stone, horn, wood and bone; also fragments of pottery in connection with charcoal and cinders. These mounds vary from three to ten feet high; some of them are one hundred feet long and two hundred wide, and generally elevated about ten feet above the level of the sea.

Similar heaps of oyster shells are found on the sea shore in the states of Massachusetts and Georgia, in the United States, known to have been deposited by the native Americans. In these beds are found the stone implements of the natives similar to those found in the beds of shells in Denmark. The Danish shell-mounds were accumulated before the bronze period during the age of stone. These shell-mounds of Denmark from their vastness must have required many centuries in their accumulation. Their site is on the most ancient portion of the globe; and, though the coast has been somewhat changed, there is no evidence of the country having been materially disturbed, so as to molest the people inhabiting it, in the locality of these mounds.

There is ample evidence, however, that the globe has undergone many very marked changes since man's first advent upon its surface, and such changes as have proved detrimental and often destructive to his race. These changes of surface have been brought about by several causes, such as subsidence and elevation of land, and by earthquake and volcanic force, also by the glacier process, and other submergences.

The most remarkable instance of elevation of land occurred in South America in 1822; the shock of the earthquake producing the elevation was felt along the coast of Chili the distance of 1200 miles, and the coast for more than an hundred miles was in an instant elevated from three to four feet, and so remains. The elevation is estimated as containing an area of 100,000 square miles.*

Along the coast of the Baltic, a distance of a thousand miles, the country has been raised up from 100 to 700 feet above the sea ; and the movement is still in progress at the rate of about four feet in a century.†

In Scotland, England and Wales the coasts have been elevated in many places from a few feet to that of thousands. This is manifest by the various shells found on these elevations. This is also the case in several locations in the United States, where beaches are covered with sea-shells; in some instances the elevations being five hundred feet above the level of the sea. Instances of the kind may be seen in Portland, Maine ; Brooklyn, New York; Vermont, and at Boston, Massachusetts.

Dr. Darwin has very conclusively shown that the eastern part of South America has been for many centuries quietly rising (without in the least disturbing the horizontality of the strata) from 1000 to 1400 feet, and that the elevation has reached 1180 feet since the drift period. He also has shown that in many instances portions of the islands of the Pacific are being elevated.

In the northern part of Norway beds of sea shells have been found 400 feet above the level of the sea. These shells are the same as those of the living species now inhabiting the contiguous ocean. In volcanic regions the elevations of land are much more marked and definitely determined than those just mentioned. Volcanic agencies always leave the evidences of internal force. The elevation of Monte Nuovo and Jourillo, are very striking examples of volcanic agencies. The former was elevated in the space of forty-eight hours in 1538 ; the latter in about twenty-four hours. The first indication of Nuovo's elevation was presented in the rise of the bottom of the sea near Puzzuoli, several hundred square yards in extent. On the second day at noon, the earth was hove above the water, and kept on gradually rising

* Wonders of Geology—Vol. I., p. 112.

† In August, 1868, Peru, Chili and Ecuador were almost literally overwhelmed in ruins by an earthquake. The sea rose forty feet high and rolled its fearful tide over the coast. Towns and cities were wholly destroyed, and 300,000 persons perished in the general disaster. The whole face of the country is changed.

until the summit stood 440 feet above the level of the sea. Its circumference was about one and a half miles. As it was being elevated, fire, stones and ashes were ejected from an opening in its summit. It now stands 437 feet above the sea's level, with a crater 420 feet deep. During the time of the eruption of Nuovo the coast on the north of the bay of Baiæ was permanently elevated to the height of 20 feet, and formed a tract 600 feet of land, upon which stands the temple of Serapis.*

Jourillo was elevated in 1759. It rose from the plains of Mexico, as if by magic, to the height of 1600 feet, and still remains at that altitude.† A very extraordinary amount of matter was ejected from the apex of the cone, which overspread the country about its base. So intense was the heat of the lava, which was piled up to the depth of 500 feet, at the base of the volcano, that as late as the year 1780, according to Humboldt, a segar could be lighted by it at the depth of a few feet from the surface. Fifty years elapsed before this lava became cooled.

In the vicinity of the Azores, in 1811, an island, a mile in circumference, was heaved up in the sea to the height of 300 feet. It remained in that position a few weeks, and then sunk beneath the waves. During the progress of its elevation, solid matter was thrown up from the bottom of the sea to the height of 800 feet.

In India, during the great subsidence of the country, at Sindree, presently noticed, a large mound was raised to the height of about ten feet, fifty miles in length, and about sixteen miles in width. This mound turned the tide of the Indus in a new direction to the sea.

These instances of elevations of land are not more wonderful than numerous occurrences of subsidences which have taken place in various portions of the globe.

The Rev. Mr. Parker notices a subsidence of land just above the falls of the Columbia river, in Washington Territory, U. S., of twenty miles in extent, and about one mile wide. For the whole distance the trees are still standing erect in the bottom of the river which has made its way into this subsided district. The water is about twenty feet deep—the height of the trees— the remaining portion, which once stood above the water, having

* Wonders of Geology, Vol. I, p. 109.   † Ibid., Vol. II., p. 836.

been destroyed. This subsidence is the result of volcanic action, the whole region in its vicinity being volcanic.*

Dr. Pingle, a Danish naturalist, has clearly shown that the coast of Greenland, for the distance of 600 miles, north and south, is gradually sinking.

In treating upon this subject, Robert Chambers has shown that, whilst one portion of this coast may be subsiding, another may be rising. He gives as an instance a district of forty geographical miles in extent, which subsided fifty-eight feet at one extremity, and became elevated ninety-six feet at another.†

The subsidence of the coast upon which is located the Temple of Serapis, is a remarkable instance of the changeableness of the crust of the earth. The temple was located upon the northern shore of the Bay of Baiæ. The roof was supported by twenty-four granite columns, and twenty-two marble, each formed of a single stone. Only three remain standing, the tallest being forty-two feet in height. It is very evident that these columns have been immersed in the sea at least twenty-three feet. The perforations in the marble columns, made by the lithodomi, whilst they were submerged, were twenty-three feet above high water-mark in 1838, when examined by Sir Charles Lyell. At that time, the platform of the temple was about one foot below high water-mark, and still continues at that level. It is difficult to say when the subsidence of this temple took place, but it was doubtless before the Christian era. About eighty years prior to that date, when the mosaic pavement was constructed, the pavement was about twelve feet above where it stood in 1838, when examined by Mr. Lyell. Its submergence in the sea, however, was gradual, and may not have reached its greatest depth until several centuries after our era. Septimus Severus, between the years 194 and 211 A. D., adorned the temple with precious marbles; and as late as the year 235 A. D., Alexander Severus added to its adornment. From that date it passes from history, except the mere notice of Puzzuoli being sacked in 456 by Alaric, and in 545 A. D. by Genseric. It doubtless subsided to its lowest depth in the early part of the Dark Ages, as

* Wonders of Geology, Vol. I., p. 390.
† Edinburgh New Philos. Journal, January, 1850.

3

the pierced columns by the lithodomi show they remained stationary under water for a long period.

The date of the elevation of the temple is not definitely fixed, but no doubt it was during the time of the formation of Monte Nuovo. The ruined temple was discovered in 1749, covered with rubbish and volcanic tufa. But, strange as it may seem, over the top of this rubbish and tufa is a deposit of fresh-water-limestone, of perfectly even and flat surface. Overlying this is another bed of volcanic ashes and eruptive matter. The temple, though considered now stationary, is not so, but seems to be gradually sinking—not the edifice alone, but the coast upon which it is located. We learn, from the writings of Niccolini, that since the beginning of the present century the temple has subsided more than two feet. He estimated its subsidence at about one inch in four years.

About a mile northwest of Serapis are the ruins of the Temple of Neptune, and also those of the Nymphs, now under water. The columns of the former stand erect, their summits just rising to the surface of the sea. The sinking of the coast upon which these ruined temples rest, it would seem, is to a great extent controlled by the volcanic action of Vesuvius.* When that volcano is active the subsidence goes on, but when it is dormant for any great length of time, its upheaval takes place. Its dormant state for nearly five hundred years caused such internal heat in and around the Bay of Baiæ as to produce Monte Nuovo and the upheaval of the country at Puzzuoli and where the temple of Serapis is located.

A most extraordinary subsidence occurred in India in 1819. Two thousand square miles of country sank, and formed the bed of an inland sea. The village of Sindree was so far submerged that the tops of the houses only were visible above water. The fort of Sindree was, to a measurable extent, destroyed by the subsidence. The inhabitants of the village made their escape from the top of the tower of the fort in boats. The fort was left in the midst of a lake, which has become a salt marsh.†

---

* During the present time (1868) an alarming eruption of this volcano is going on. Even the villages in its neighborhood are threatened with destruction.

† Quart. Geological Journal, Vol. II., p. 103.

In the vicinity of New Madrid, in the State of Missouri, in the valley of the Mississippi, remote from all volcanic regions, during the shock of an earthquake, in the year 1812, large lakes were formed, and the country in many places covered with water, for miles, to the depth of three and four feet. The graveyard at New Madrid was precipitated into the river, and the ground upon which the village stood sunk eight feet below its former level. The trunks of large trees are still standing in the subsided districts, especially along the course of the White Water and its branches, several feet in the water.

During the progress of the earthquake the earth rose in waves in places to a fearful height, and when they were at the greatest altitude the soil burst open at their summits, from which issued " vast volumes of water, sand, and pit-coal, as high in the air as the tallest trees."

During the frightful eruption of the volcano on the island of Sumbawa, in April, 1815, the town of Tomboro, on the west side of the island, was submerged by the sea. The land upon which the town was situated sunk to such an extent that the water remained permanently eighteen feet deep where the dry land existed before the subsidence. So frightfully destructive was this eruption, and fatal in its consequences, that, out of a population of 12,000, in the province of Tomboro, but twenty-six individuals remained alive. The concussions were heard at Sumatra, 970 miles distant ; and so dense were the ashes during the eruption in Java, that the most profound darkness prevailed in the daytime. The ashes and cinders collected two feet thick upon the sea for several miles in extent, rendering it difficult for vessels to sail through the floating mass.* This darkness commenced about eight o'clock A. M., but did not reach its maximum intensity until noon, when it continued a pitchy darkness until after six o'clock A. M., next day, at which hour light began to appear.†

A volcano called Papandayang, the largest one in Java, located on the southwestern part of the island, on the 12th day of August, 1772, after a violent paroxysm, entirely disappeared in the earth—not only the cone, but the country around about it to the extent of six by fifteen square miles. About forty vil-

* Principles of Geology, p. 464.   † Geological Observer, p. 142.

lages were virtually destroyed, some wholly swallowed up. Not less than 2,900 inhabitants perished in this catastrophe.[*]

There is no better evidence of the submergence of land, perhaps, than the "Submarine Forests" of Europe and America. Those of Europe are found along the Western Coast, from Scandinavia to Spain and Portugal, and in the British Islands. In what has been called the Bridgewater Levels, the oak, fir and willow trees, of large dimensions, have been discovered, partly rooted in their native soil, twenty feet beneath the surface of the ground, some of these trees, or portions of them, remaining rooted as they grew.

A submergence of great extent occurred in Cornwall after the introduction of man into the country, and whilst the red deer was in existence in the district. Human skulls have been found at the Carnon tin steam works, beneath the bottom of the estuary, with trees and other vegetable remains, many feet beneath the surface.[†] In the Pentuan tin steam works, at the depth of forty-eight feet below high water-mark, trees, partially in their places of growth, with their roots descending among the tin stratum, were found. At the Happy Union Works, the vegetable accumulation, where the roots of the trees pass down to the "tin ground," is about thirty feet below the level of low water-mark. The skulls and bones of the deer, above alluded to, lay buried fifty-two feet beneath the surface of the soil, the overlaying mass consisting of fifty feet, in vertical thickness, of silt and sands, with shells, and about two feet of vegetable accumulation, consisting of wood, leaves, nuts, etc., immediately resting upon the skulls and remains of the deer.[‡] The trees had oyster shells attached to their trunks, which show that they, at one period of their submergence, were covered by the open sea. Mr. Colenso states that the shells are commonly discovered in the mass overlying the trees and skulls, in such condition of layers as to "present the appearance of the animals having lived and died in the places where their remains are now found." This author also states that a row of wooden piles had been dis-

---

* Daubeny's Description of Volcanoes, 2d. Ed., p. 406.

† Geological Observer, p. 436.

‡ Henwood, Trans. Geological Society of Cornwall, Vol. IV., p. 58.

covered in this accumulation, sharpened at one end, and appeared to have been used in the construction of a wooden bridge or footway across the valley. They were six feet long, their tops being on a level with the present low water or spring tides, and at the depth of twenty-four feet from the present surface of the overlying ground.[*]

In regard to the British submarine forests, they seem to have existed erect at a period before man became an inhabitant of the country, especially those found in South Wales, as, in the clay intervening between the stumps of the trees, and in which their roots are punctuated, foot-prints of beasts and animals are plainly discerned; among others, those of the deer and the gigantic ox. The stumps of the trees, with the roots standing as they grew, together with their prostrate trunks, and other vegetable substances, show this portion of Wales, in many ages past, to have been a forest of stately trees.

The coal strata of the north of England is 3,000 feet in vertical thickness; the aggregate thickness of the coal, however, does not exceed sixty feet. In South Wales, the coal measure is found 12,000 feet in vertical thickness. In one section, near Swansea, where the total thickness of the stratas is only 3,246 feet, there are no less than ten principal beds of sandstone, one of which being 500 feet thick. The coal beds, sixteen in number, are from one to five feet thick, one only attaining to six feet in thickness. In these coal beds ferns and trunks of trees abound.

In the Swansea valley the trunks of the plant Sigillaria were found erect in the coal beds; two stood close together; the largest was 5½ feet in circumference. These plants not only pierced through the coal and shale, but the sandstone also, which were so arranged around the stem as to show the manner in which the sand had been washed around the trees by the waves. These Sigillaria had the appearance of being in their native place of growth, and to have been gradually submerged, by reason of the subsidence of the soil where they stood, and eventually surrounded by the several deposits in which they were entombed. Prostrate stems of this plant, full thirty feet in length, and of proportionate diameter, have been found in these coal fields, as

* Geological Observer, p. 437.

well as their stumps, apparently in the places in which they grew.*

In the coal fields of Nova Scotia and Cape Breton the stems of these plants are still standing in their place of growth. But, wonderful as it may seem, ten forests of this kind are reported by Sir Charles Lyell as occurring above each other in successive growths in the cliffs at the head of the Bay of Fundy. The coal measure containing the upright stems or trunks is 2,500 feet in thickness. The plants or trees vary from six to twenty-five feet in height, one of them being twenty-five feet high, and four feet in diameter.†

Sir Roderick Murchison has pointed out vertical trunks, apparently in their native soil, not only in shale and sandstone, but also, at the distance of forty miles from the coal beds of the coast, in the Yorkshire moorlands, where the forests of plants were gradually submerged and quietly entombed in the mud and sand.‡

Instances of inclining or slanting positions of the trunks of trees are not unfrequent in coal fields and quarries. One was discovered in 1830, in Craiglieth quarry, near Edinburgh, Scotland, sixty feet in length, of diameter at the top, seven inches, and at the butt, five feet diameter. § Hugh Miller mentions four huge trunks of trees in the Edinburgh quarries, one of which was sixty, and another seventy feet in length, the larger one being six feet in diameter. They lay diagonally across the strata, at an angle of about 30°.

The depression of the country around the Dead Sea and the Caspian would lead to the inference that they result from subsidence. The Dead Sea was doubtless formed by volcanic action, and the same remark will also apply to the Caspian. Neither of these seas have an outlet, both being depressed. The former is 1,312 feet beneath the level of the Mediterranean ; the latter eighty-three feet below it.

Lake Ontario, also, is based upon a subsided district, and there are evidences tending to show this subsidence of volcanic origin. Indeed, all the lakes of North America seem to be resting upon

---

* Elements of Geology, p. 467.   † Geological Observer, p. 489.
‡ Murchison's Proceedings of the Geological Society, Vol. II., p. 41.
§ Dawson's Geological Journal, No. 37.

subsided strata. The basaltic rocks in the Lake Superior district tend to prove its origin to be volcanic, at least the basin in which its waters rest to have been produced by such agency.

The submergence of the district wherein the coal deposits are found in Cape Breton has been so wonderful as to be almost incredible. The Sydney beds show that there were over forty periods in the accumulation of the several stratas and coal, during each period sufficient time having intervened for the deposit of soil and the production of the Stigmaria and other vegetable matter producing coal, the upright trunks of this tree being found in the coal strata rooted in the ground beneath.

The Bristol coal measure shows fifty periods in the descent of the accumulated mass, in each of which the roots and trunks of the Stigmaria were discovered as at Sydney. Each vegetation required atmosphere in their growth, and must have been produced upon the surface of the ground. The series of the strata are about 5,000 feet thick, and based upon a sandy deposit of about 1,200 feet in vertical thickness.

The Glamorganshire coal fields are of still greater magnitude, containing the same kinds of vegetable deposits and trees. The accumulations of these fields reach the vertical thickness of about two miles, thus presenting a subsidence at successive periods, the time of which not being susceptible of plausible conjecture, but many thousands of years must have intervened in the deposition of this overlying mass.* These deposits of vegetable matter, and at such great depth, seem to indicate very marked changes of the crust of the globe, even after it was fitted for the habitation of man, and very clearly show the action of water at each successive period.

The water seems to have drowned the entire globe, even since the mountains were brought forth. The condition of the earth before the beds of the seas were formed, or the hills and mountains elevated, was doubtless a vast ocean, as it has been estimated that, if the waters now upon the earth were equally spread out over its surface, they would stand 3,280 feet deep upon every part of it. Mountains, being of much greater altitude, were, doubtless, the first dry land. Their elevation, and the breaking in of the earth's crust, gathered the waters into their present ba-

* The Geological Observer, pp. 487, 488.

sins. Afterwards, after an eternity of years, other changes took place, such as produced the state of things above described in the coal fields. The water swept over these regions, depositing the several stratas over the coal deposits, each intervening period being marked by an elevation and submergence, of great length of time. To even conjecture the date of the first subsidence or vegetable growth would be an absurd presumption. Geologists, however, seem to be to some degree shedding light upon the subject. They may approximate the several eras of vegetation and submergence, but nothing more.

CHAPTER II.

WE have already referred to the stone, bronze, and iron implements, discovered in the peat bogs and lakes of Europe,
as being the works of man in very remote ages; and now purpose
giving geological and other evidences tending to show that the
human race existed upon the globe for many thousands of years before the historic period, and more remote even than established by
the stone and other implements referred to, or the quartz instruments of India or Italy.*

The Book of Genesis, according to Biblical scholars, fixes the
creation at about 6000 years ago. The Genesis, however, gives
no date. Moses's object seems to have been to present man in
his two-fold character: perfect as he was created, and dwelling
in Paradise; and then, falling from his holy estate, under God's
displeasure driven from Eden and compelled to subsist by the
"sweat of his brow."

The age of the globe, therefore, has not been determined by
authentic history; and we are entirely left to conjecture as re-

* The implements of quartz recently found in southern India, are of the
same order as the stone instruments of Europe.—Man, where, whence, and
whither, p. 133.

gards the time when it was cast into the boundless space of the universe. Proofs of its vast antiquities multiply daily.

The unprejudiced mind of man is beginning to look at things as they are, and not as they may desire them to be, as has been too long the case upon this important subject. The sciences are making such demonstrative developments as are tending to prove most clearly, that the globe has been in existence many thousands of years prior to the supposed days of creation, as recorded in the Genesis, and that the human family has been on the earth many thousands of years before that supposed era.[*]

Past time may be considered an eternity. Even the Egyptian monuments, it is claimed and believed, date far beyond the deluge; yet they do not seem to have been disturbed by that catastrophe, or the people molested in their pursuits in life in the valley of the Nile.

All calculations of time are arbitrary in geological and ethnological science, but vast epochs of time are shown by geological facts, such as organic remains of plants and animals, and also of man.

It has been asserted by a learned ethnologist [†] that the remains of man will yet be found in the fossil state, as low down as the eocene period, and that he walked the earth with the Megalonyx, and Pollatherim. Until very recently it was denied that the monkey tribes were found in the fossil state; but they have been discovered in the Himalayas and in Brazil; also in England within the last few years.

Geology has disclosed to us, that the crust of the earth has undergone several very marked changes since its formation. At first the globe was a mass of soft matter glowing with heat. During the process of cooling, the plutonic rocks, granite, porphyry and basaltic, were formed. These underlie all others when not interfered with by volcanic agencies. In many instances, however, these rocks have been pushed up through the other strata, and rest upon recent formations, and even upon the surface of the ground. The internal force of the globe is of in-

---

[*] Plato in his *Critias*, mentions the island of Atalantis as having been buried in the ocean 9000 years before his time.

The Chaldeans records place the origin of society at a period dating **437,000** years ago. Plurality of Races, by Pouchet, p. 122,—*note.*

[†] Dr. J. C. Nott.

calculable power. The upheaval of the primitive rocks, and elevation of mountains, fully attest this fact. The volcanos are, doubtless, the vents from the internal fires of the nucleus of the globe, or the chimneys of the central fire.

The metamorphic rocks were formed in gulfs, low lands, and seas from the deposition of various fragments and disintegrations of primitive formations. The principal range of mountains belong to this system. They generally rest upon granite, but were thrown into their present position by internal force. The upturned edges of the broken strata, may be seen in any of the ranges, showing most clearly the manner of their elevation. That the formation of these various strata required vast periods of time all readily admit; indeed none will deny it, as the same process is still going on in rivers and lakes, bogs and marshes, as all can bear witness. The primitive rocks give no date of formation, nor indeed the secondary either. It is not so with the aqueous rocks, known as the fossiliferous strata, they being of more recent formation, and still forming. Geologists can approximate to the period of their origin. These rocks, or strata, are found in some instances, to be composed almost entirely of corals; others are made up of shells; others of plants and vegetable matter, turned into coal; whilst others contain neither of the above substances. However improbable it may seem to the common observer, it is a well established fact that many of the highest elevations (mountain peaks) were once at the bottom of the ocean. This strata is not always found in this elevated position. In Sweden one of the oldest formations of fossiliferous rock remains undisturbed, as if formed of the delta of a great river. The same is the case with a large bed of this strata in the lake districts of North America, in extent several hundred miles. The Table Mountain of the Cape of Good Hope is another example of unbroken elevated fossiliferous rock of high altitude and of 3,500 feet in thickness.

The fossiliferous rocks, such as contain the remains of animals and plants, are six miles in vertical thickness, and composed of alternate layers. The principal rocks of this order are the Silurian (Greywack), old Red Sandstone, Carboniferous Limestone, and Stone coal measure.

Thus far the great mass of organic remains prove to be of marine origin. In rocks of the Alps organic remains are found from six to eight thousand feet above the level of the sea; in the Pyrenees about as high; but in the Andes they are found at the height of 16,000 feet above the level of the sea. It has been estimated that two-thirds of the surface of the globe is composed of fossiliferous rocks, and often several thousand feet in thickness.[*]

The upheavals and subsidence of land have not only produced the fossiliferous record, but severed the globe into fragments, cutting off communication between the inhabitants.

There was evidently a time when the strata of the surface of the globe was unbroken; a time when the straits of Behring, and the great ocean between Europe and America, did not exist; and when the waters of the Black Sea poured their floods into the Northern Ocean; when the waters of the Potomac and James rivers set back to the Gulf of Mexico, or flowed down the Mississippi valley. The whole face of the country along these rivers shows the action of water high above their banks. The drift of Cincinnati, Ohio, is over eighty feet in perpendicular thickness. Indeed, the great mass of the surface of the entire valley is alluvium, and in many places much greater in thickness than at Cincinnati.

In this drift, or alluvium, man's remains have been found at great depth, as will presently be shown. The age of the alluvium has been ascertained in the Mississippi valley, at the mouth of that great river, by Agassiz, Lyell, and other distinguished geologists.

Drift, or diluvium, differs from alluvium in this: the former is composed of deposits of clay and sand—erratic boulders, from pebbles to masses of stone many thousands of tons in weight, and is found at all elevations, even on the summits of the highest mountains, where no agency now in existence placed them. The latter is deposited along the margin of rivers and at their mouths, and consists of loose gravel, sand, and mud.

The Gulf of Mexico is five hundred feet deep. At New Orleans borings have been made to the depth of six hundred feet, and the bottom of the alluvium not then reached. Five hundred feet is believed to be the thickness of the delta of the Mississippi,

---

[*] Hitchcock's Elements of Geology, p. 102.

which extends over an area of 30,000 square miles. The time for its formation has been fixed by geologists at 100,000 years, calculating it to have been deposited whilst the river occupied its present bed.*

Bennet Dowler, an eminent geologist, has made a calculation which proves pretty satisfactorily the age of the delta to be 158,-400 years. He based his calculation upon the time required to form any considerable portion of delta by accretion. In the drift at Cincinnati, Ohio, in digging a well in 1826, the workmen, at the depth of eighty feet, came upon the stump of a tree three feet in diameter rooted in its native soil, which had the appearance of having been cut with an ax or sharp instrument. Iron rust was found on the top of the stump, as if the ax had been decomposed during the time the incumbent mass of earth rested upon it. This drift has every appearance of being as ancient as any portion of the Mississippi valley.

In July, 1868, on the line of the Union Pacific Railway, 450 miles west of Omaha, in digging a well for the Railway company, the workmen, at the depth of sixty-eight feet, came upon a deposit of human bones, among which the skull, jaws and bones of the extremities were plainly visible. This is a remarkable discovery, one not yet fully investigated, but opens a new page in the geological and anthropological records, and field for speculation of ethnologists. The grave question is at once presented as to when were these bones thus deposited, and also of what race are the antique remains. In the sand strata the workmen also found the bones of elephants and tigers. During the same month the skull of the Mastodon was exhumed on Camp Creek, Pike County, Ohio, three feet in length, two feet eight inches in width, and two feet across the nostrils, weighing one hundred pounds. The largest tooth is six inches wide, eight inches long, and weighs six pounds.

In excavating the foundation of the gas works at New Orleans, at the depth of sixteen feet the workmen came upon burnt wood and the skeleton of a man. The head lay under the roots of a cypress tree belonging to the fourth forest,† as there are ten

---

* Lyell's Principles of Geology, chap. xv.
† Dr. Dowler estimates the age of this skeleton at 50,000 years. *See* Man's Origin and Destiny, by Lesley, p. 65.

similar growths buried in the delta below the present upright
forest. The skeleton was that of the American type. The cypress trees of the delta average in diameter about ten feet, and
each growth had existed about 5,700 years. From this delta
it would appear that the human race existed in Louisiana 57,000
years ago.[*] Also, these facts establish that an exuberant flora
existed in Louisiana 100,000 years prior to the age when man
first became an inhabitant of the country.

Cypress trees are noted for their antiquity. Baron Humboldt
considers the one in the garden of Chapultepec, Mexico, to be
over six thousand years old. According to his measurement,
this tree was forty and a half feet in diameter.

Professor Agassiz in his lecture at Mobile, in 1853, presented
the remains of a human being, consisting of a foot, and jaws with
teeth, taken out of the coral reef limestone at Lake Monroe.[†]

This accumulated strata is of an average height of seventy
feet, which must have begun to form a thousand years or more
before the supposed days of creation. What is known as the
Florida Reefs is the work of corals, their foundation being laid
in the bottom of the sea, whose construction required not less
than 14,000 years. The bluff on the main land in their vicinity
also being the work of corals, required a much longer period in
its construction. Still further inland the same formation exists;
indeed, the southern half of the peninsula is considered post-ter-
tiary; and according to the estimate of Agassiz, 135,000 years
were needful for its formation.[‡]

These startling facts tend to show the globe to be much more
ancient, at least this portion of it, than is generally supposed.
These facts, however, do not stand alone, but many others of
equally conclusive character on the subject also exist.

The stalagmite caves of Brazil, which contain fossils of man
and the lower animals, show, by the growth of the stalagmites,
which can be as easily counted as the growth of trees by the annual ring-fibers of the wood, overlying the fossils and bones, that
these caves have been in existence twenty thousand years since

* Types of Mankind, p. 338.
† By Agassiz's estimate of the deposition overlying these remains, the fos-
sil had been buried in the rock 10,000 years. Types of Mankind, p. 338.
‡ Man's Origin and Destiny, by Lesley, p. 65.

the carbonated waters from their roofs begun the deposition of the stalagmites.*

In the valley of the Nile, borings have been made in the delta to the depth of seventy-two feet, where Egyptian works of art were discovered in the Nile mud.   According to the estimate of M. Rosiere, 30,000 years have intervened since their deposition. Burnt brick was found in the delta at the depth of sixty feet, which has been considered 14,000 years old.   The mass of deposit in which these remains were discovered is modern, compared with the diluvium of the Mississippi and France, Italy, Switzerland, Denmark, Sweden, and of the valleys of the Indus and Ganges.

The discoveries made in the marl-beds, turbaries and lakes of Italy fully show the great antiquity of that portion of the globe, as well also the high antiquity of man.†

The question as regards fossil man, to some extent remains unsettled, which is mainly owing to the innocent desire of mankind to cling to what have been old and well established opinions regarding the age of the world and creation of Adam.   This is not at all surprising, although recent geological and ethnological discoveries have doubtless shown that the earth is much older than generally conceded, and that it was occupied by man many thousands of years before the supposed days of creation.

If the fossil remains of man do really exist, all should know it, as well as that of the age of the globe.   We have already, in a former chapter, shown a very high antiquity of man, by his works of art and exhumed remains, and also that the earth is by no means of recent origin.   And even without the discovery of fossil man, there are ample evidences of his early advent upon the globe, such as to satisfy any unprejudiced mind that he occupied the earth many thousands of ages past.

Dr. Dickeson found a human pelvis near Natchez, on the bank of the Mississippi river, in a fossil state.‡

Dr. Ildefonso, a distinguished naturalist of Rio Janeiro, found a fossil bone of man in the stalagmite cave in that vicinity.   The fossil was deeply buried in the bone clay underlying the stalagmite floor of the cave.   His estimate of the stalagmite covering

---

* Man's Origin and Destiny, p. 65.   † Pre-historic Remains in Italy, p. 80.
‡ Antiquity of Man, p. 194.

the fossil was that it had existed in the cave twenty thousand years since the commencement of the formation of the floor by the carbonate waters of the cave.*

A fossilized body of a man was discovered at Gibraltar, by workmen engaged in blasting rocks, in 1748. The fossil was found fifty feet above the level of the sea, imbedded in the solid rock, showing it had at first been buried in a plastic substance, which eventually became formed into solid rock, enclosing the fossil. Unfortunately for the sciences of geology and ethnology, the workmen who discovered this precious treasure, without knowing its great value, blew it into fragments with the rock in which it was encased.

Fossil human skeletons were discovered embedded in limestone rock on the coast of Guadaloupe. One of them, that of a female, the head of which being absent, is preserved in the British Museum. In the bed of rock where these skeletons were discovered were found teeth of the crocodile, stone hatchets, and pieces of wood having rudely sculptured on one side a mask, and on the other figures of an enormous frog.† The skulls of these skeletons showed them to have been of the Peruvian family, and not Caribs, as was at first supposed.

At Quebec, in Lower Canada, a fossil human skeleton was found entombed in the solid chist rock, the same formation underlying the city.

There was found in a cave in Neanderthal, near Dusseldorf, in 1857, a human skeleton having a remarkable skull, unlike that of any of the existing races.‡ Dr. Fuhlratt, an eminent naturalist of Bonn, upon a careful examination of the skeleton, pronounces it fossil. The form of the skull, and other remarkable features of the skeleton, and the circumstances connected with its preservation and location, enabled Huxley and others to conclude that the native to which it belonged occupied the country at a period antedating the eras of the Celts and Germans.

A human fossil was found in Brazil, enclosed in the body of a large sand rock, which was overgrown with large lofty trees.

In the post-pliocene deposits on the bank of the Rhine, in 1853, at Lahr, a small village in Baden, parts of a skeleton of a human

---

* Man's Origin and Destiny, by Lesley, p. 65.   † Ibid.
‡ Evidences as to Man's Place in Nature, Huxley, p. 149.

ANTIQUITY OF MAN, AND WORKS OF ART. 49

being were found deposited in the lower portion of a bed of loam, eighty feet in thickness. This deposit of loam was similar to that of the adjoining plain, and shows it to have been accumulated by the Rhine.*

The bones of a man were found at the depth of ninety feet in the delta of the Ganges.†

There was discovered, in the third soil strata overlooking Lake Geneva, at considerable depth from the surface, a human skeleton, having a small, round and very thick skull, of the Brachykephalous type, of the stone age of Denmark. This skull, though small, was well proportioned, the intellectual portion being well developed. Similar skulls have been found in France, Ireland and Scotland, and they are so similar to the Laplanders as to warrant the conclusion that they were of that family, and the last survivors of the age of stone. There were found in the strata, overlying this skeleton, Roman relics 1,700 years old; those of the bronze age, 4,000 years; and those of stone, from 5,000 to 7,000 years. And M. Morlot estimates the delta at 10,000 years, calculating the time required to accumulate the entire mass of the surrounding delta 100,000 years.‡

Within the last few years a human skull, well preserved, was found in the strata of Bald Mountain, near Altaville, California, one hundred and twenty feet below the surface of the ground. Overlying this remarkable relic were formations of basalt, and strata of lava. This discovery has been verified by Prof. J. D. Whitney, who was upon the ground and made a careful examination of the whole subject.§

In Egypt, it has been ascertained, by excavations in the valley of the Nile, that 36,000 years have intervened since civilized man occupied the country. His works of art, such as burned brick, underlie even the foundations of the Pyramids.

In the marl beds of Torre del la Maina, in Italy, two human skulls were discovered.‖

* Elements of Geology, p. 117.   † Van Hoff, Vol. I., p. 379.
    ‡ Elements of Geology, pp. 113–121.
§ This skull is doubtless that of the lost race of America—the mechanics and people who have left such stupendous structures of stone, now in ruins, in Mexico, Central and South America. Geology places this skull's deposition at a very remote era—at a much earlier period than has been allotted to the creation of man.
    ‖ Pre-Historic Remains in Italy, p. 96.

4

Forty human skeletons were found, in the fall of the year 1856, near Modena, in cutting through an eminence for the construction of a railway. The skeletons were buried about nine feet below the surface of the ground, and were not placed there by accident, but seemed to have been buried by their comrades or friends. They lay in two parallel rows, all with their heads turned toward the south; by their sides were arms of bronze and stone; each skeleton had on its right side a lance-head of copper, and on the left an arrow-head of flint stone; some, also, had cuneiform lance-heads of bronze, whilst others had similar lance-heads of green serpentine. One of the skeletons also had on its right side a large lance-head of elaborate workmanship.*

These skeletons are supposed to be those of Roman warriors, and the place of their deposit the remains of a burying-place, as works of Roman art were found in the same deposit, such as the tear bottles, coins, lamps, and fragments of tiles.

The early Roman nations were not artistic people; they seemed to have no taste for the fine arts. To them, therefore, we need not look for very early relics of new inventions or national ornaments. They were not inventors, but to a great extent imitators, until they had reached a tolerable degree of civilization. Even as late as the conquest of Græcia Magna, the monuments and works of art adorning the capitol were the work of foreigners, even to their coins, bronze vases, and house furniture.† When the empire became extended, and foreigners became Roman people, wealth and national pride made the Romans glory in their great national works of art, many of which were robberies from the treasuries of art of Greece. Roman nationality was eventually impressed upon marble and bronze, upon which historical events have been preserved with wonderful fitness and artistic skill: the Celtic Gaul in the dying gladiator, and the ancient German upon the triumphal arch, are plainly visible. In these and other works of art, not only the Roman physical development is preserved, but also those of other nationalities.

The Etruscans of northern Italy, a very ancient people, preserved their early nationality by the construction of magnificent

---

* Pre-Historic Remains in Italy, pp. 6, 7.
† Indigenous Races of the Earth, p. 173.

tombs and depositories for their dead.* They were a powerful
nation long before the founding of Rome, and before that éra
had attained to a high degree of civilization. They entered
Italy from the north, and established their civilization in the
provinces of the barbarous Pelasgians and Tyrrhenians, even
wrested from the Umbrians part of their territory.† They were
unlike the present Italians; their countenances were large and
round, their eyes large, nose short and thick, heads large, body
small and clumsy. They have preserved representations of
themselves in the coverings of their sarcophagi, even to the color
of the hair, which is of yellowish brown.‡

Similar sepulchral depositories of the dead are found throughout northern Europe, northern Asia, and northern Africa, and
were the remains of people whose descendants cannot now be
readily traced in any of the existing races, except the Caucasian
and Mongolian types.

The earliest system of burial was doubtless merely the depositing of the dead bodies in caverns, or, it may be they were consumed by fire.§ In the age of stone, however, there was an advance made in the system; tumuli were erected over the dead
at least some of them were at a very early day buried in this
way. Every habitable portion of the globe seems, at one time,
to have been occupied by people adopting this system. Step by
step, from the stone, bronze, and iron periods, this system was
followed by the early nations of the globe. Man may yet be
traced throughout the continents and islands of the sea by this
system of burial, from the rude mounds of the Mississippi valley,
to the gigantic pyramid of Ghizeh. But it is difficult now to
designate the particular peoples who constructed the tumuli of
the old and new world, though the constructors of the tombs
and pyramids, at least those of Egypt, may be traced.

The mounds of Denmark, according to Professor Eschricht's
description of the skulls found therein, would entitle their builders to be considered northern Asiatics, if not, in fact, Mongolians,
or Esquimaux. The skulls are round, almost spherical, and are,

* Prichard's Natural History of Man, Vol. I., p. 188.
† Ancient and Mediæval Geography, p. 250.
‡ Prichard's Natural History of Man, vol. I., p. 188-9.
§ Pre-Historic Remains in Italy, p. 80.

no doubt, those of the ancient Cimbrians, as they had the spherical shaped head.

The tombs of Egypt almost rival the great temples and pyramids. Those of Thebes surpass all others in magnitude and grandeur. Near every ancient Egyptian city is found a tomb corresponding with the size and wealth of the city, and these cities of the dead seem to be as densely populated by dead bodies as the city above is with living subjects. These sacred places contain vivid representations of the character, type, and peculiarities of the Egyptians, as well as of the nations with whom they had intercourse. Here, also, is preserved, in the sculpture and paintings, the temple, tomb, and pyramid constructors, plainly showing to which of the races they belonged.

Greece also has preserved in her sculpture and paintings her ancient history, and furnished a record showing the type to which her people belonged.

So also the Assyrians, Persians, Hebrews, Chinese, Hindoos, Phœnicians, and Germans.

The Persian palaces and tombs preserve numerous representations of the ancient Persians. The rock sculpture at Murghab, near Persepolis, represents a man with four wings, bearing upon his head the Egyptian crown; above the crown is a cuneiform inscription, which, being interpreted, reads, "I am Cyrus, the King, the Achæmenian." * There are other representations also, showing the pure Aryan type of the Persians. Xerxes's portrait is given, representing the Aryan family with the greatest accuracy. But the most interesting specimen of historic nationality of the Persians is the relief group of the sepulchre of Darius. In this group the Lydian, Scythian, Chaldean, and African negro are represented. This rock-hewn tomb was executed 490 years B. C. Four types are here represented, as plainly as they could be sculptured to-day, viz: white, yellow, brown, and black.

The Hindoos have preserved for themselves in their architecture, cave-temples, colossal tanks, and huge buildings, a distinct history, as well upon the adjacent islands, as upon the continent. The most finished Hindoo sculpture extant is found in the

---

* Indigenous Races of the Earth, p. 148.

ruined temples of Baro Bado and Barandanum in the isle of
Java.   The most distinguished cave-temple of India is called
Elephanta upon an island of the same name in the vicinity of
Bombay.   It is entirely excavated in the rock in the side of a
mountain.   The entry is by three magnificent avenues, skirted
by four rows of massive columns.   The interior of this temple is
220 feet long, by 150 feet broad, the ceiling about fifteen feet
high.   The caves of Kenneri, on the island of Salsette, and others
of similar character on the opposite shore of the continent, are
almost as wonderful as Elephanta.   The Kenneri caves seem to
be a city hewn out of the rock, and capable of containing thousands of human beings.

The Chinese, like the Hindoos, have been the inventors of
their own arts, as well as their own civilization and social qualities.   They differ materially from the Hindoos, having no affinities, and being two distinct races.   They have some striking
works of art, chief of which is the porcelain tower of Nankin
and the great wall along the Tartar frontier.   The tower consists of nine stories, the upper one being reached by 884 steps.
The material of which it is constructed consists of white tile,
which being painted various colors, presents the appearance of
porcelain.*   The whole is so skillfully united as to seem one
entire shaft.   No doubt there are many ruins in China, relics of
the early inhabitants; but thus far the Chinese have had so
little intercourse with the rest of mankind that their country is
comparatively unknown to Europeans or other foreign nations.

The new world also presents many evidences of man's early
advent upon its surface.   This, in several instances, has been
already shown by his remains, consisting of skeletons and fossils.   His works of art, discovered and existing upon this continent are wonderful and immense.   The tumuli, similar to those
of the old world, are scattered throughout the entire country,
showing at an early day the same system of burial of the dead
in the western world was almost universal.

Two mounds of this class are upon the author's premises
within the limits of the city of Wooster, Ohio.   They are situated upon an eminence, and constructed of fine gravel and sand;
and not of the same material of the surrounding country.   The

* Encyclopædia of Geography, vol. II., p. 422.

gravel and sand composing these tumuli were brought from some other locality. On opening one of these mounds, fifteen years ago, and reaching a point on a level with the surrounding plain, the workmen came upon a deposit of black loam, in which were found two stone axes, one of which was granite, the other flint. The granite had a deep groove, or crevice, extending around the main body of the axe, near the pole, evidently designed to sustain the handle. The pole was flat, with edges rounded ; the other end shaped like a common axe, and sharp, as much so as stone could be made. The other instrument had a pointed pole and sharp axe bit, the whole surface being smooth. It was originally, when discovered, about six inches long, the axe end being about two and a-half inches wide. Both of these instruments were of symmetrical proportions. Several arrowheads of flint were also found in the mound. The aborigines occupying this valley, when the whites first settled here, had no knowledge, by tradition or otherwise, as regards the builders of these mounds. Their constructors had passed away long before the Shawnees, Delawares and other Indian tribes had entered the country.

On the high lands overlooking the city of Wooster, at the south, is an ancient fortification, enclosing several acres of ground ; only part of it now remains unobliterated, the main portion being in cultivated fields. That part uncultivated, lying in the woodland, is still visible, though the embankment is greatly worn down and the trench nearly filled up. Thirty years ago the whole enclosure was easily traced, even through the plowed fields, and across the public road, which was cut through the banks of the enclosure. The fort was not fully circular, that portion of it overlooking the Kilbuck river to the west being an obtuse angle. About four miles up the Kilbuck, situated upon a high bluff, at the junction of the little with the big Kilbuck river, is located a small fortification enclosing a large mound. The south embankment is close upon the precipice of the bluff, which is very steep, and about seventy feet above the plain. This embankment foundation consisted of a stone wall, the stone being regularly laid upon a straight line, but not in mortar. South-west from this, about three miles, are several small mounds similar to the ones already described.

The Mississippi valley is full of small tumuli, with occasionally some of great magnitude. Judging from the vast number of mounds and other works of art discovered upon this continent, it must have been densely populated at a very early period. The Mississippi valley, it would seem, was peopled by another and different race than the American Indians; but whether they had perished, or been exterminated before the present race occupied the country, or were absorbed by them, is unknown to history and tradition; and whether the extinct people were relapsing into barbarism, when they erected their monuments of art, or advancing in civilization, is equally uncertain. All that is now known of this last people are their monuments of art, ruined cities and mouldering bones. Their record otherwise in this valley is an entire blank.

At Piqua, Ohio, on the western side of the Miami river, is located a circular wall of stone, enclosing about twenty acres. The wall is built of silicious limestone taken from the bed of the river. The stones were laid in mortar, but no marks of tools are found upon any of the stones composing the wall.

Lower down the river, near the mouth of Hale's Creek, are extensive ruins upon the plain. The wall of the fortification is composed of earth; is twelve feet high and encloses 160 acres. Near Hamilton, at considerable distance from the great Miami river, is situated, upon the crest of a high hill, a fortification enclosing fifty acres; near to this stands a mound twenty-five feet in diameter and about seven feet in height. On the highlands, near the mouth of the river, are extensive ancient military works of great strength.

On the bank of the little Miami, six miles above Lebanon, upon the summit of a ridge two hundred feet above the river, are two forts, or as they have been termed, "Figures of trapezoidal form." The walls are of earth and from six to ten feet high, except where one crosses a ravine, or plain, and is 18 feet high. There are about eighty gateways in the walls, placed at irregular intervals.

Near Chillicothe, Ohio, on the bank of Point Creek, are extensive ancient ruins, located 250 feet above the bed of the stream. The wall of the enclosure is of stone laid in mortar, and is about a mile in extent. The stones were taken from the stream below. The wall is in ruins and appears to have been shaken down by an earthquake. Four wells were discovered on this stream, which had been dug through a solid, pyritous stone rock in the bed of the creek. When discovered they were covered by stone lids about the size of mill-stones, and of the same shape, and had evidently been wrought with tools of some hard substance. Each of these stones had a hole in the center four inches in diameter. Near Portsmouth is an extensive ruined fortification, which contains walled roads.

At Circleville, Ohio, are remains of vast works of military character. Two of the fortifications, the main ones, one round, the other square, of extraordinary proportions, and laid out with great engineering judgment. The circular fort was surrounded by two walls twenty feet high, also by a deep ditch. Eight gateways led into the square fort; in front of each gateway stood a mound forty feet in diameter and four feet high. Near the round fort was a fortification ninety feet high overlooking the whole country. The square fort was set with the cardinal points, and eight small mounds were within its walls.*

At Newark, Ohio, very extensive ruined fortifications exist. The main fort is of horse-shoe form, and about 600 rods in circumference, or nearly two miles in circuit. On the side next the stream flowing by the forts, is a wall of earth of 400 rods in length, built upon the brow of the hill above the stream. Several other forts are in its vicinity, some of which being round, others square; one of them is surrounded by a wall twenty-five feet high, on the outside of which is a deep ditch, and on the south side of the main fortification a covered roadway leads to the country.

Five miles from Somerset, Perry County, Ohio, is a ruined fortification enclosed by a stone wall. The stone are not built in wall form, but piled up without any evidences of masonry; in the center of the fort is a stone mound fifteen feet high.

Near the village of Miamisburg, south of Dayton, are ancient ruins very similar to those at Newark. On an elevation 100

* The town of Circleville is on the site of these ancient fortifications, and but few if any vestiges of them remain. In removing the mounds human bones in great quantities were found; among which a skull having a high forehead, bold features, and containing all the phrenological marks of daring and bravery.—Historical Collections of Ohio, p. 411.

feet above the great Miami river, is situated the largest mound of the valley. It is 800 feet in circumference at the base, and when first discovered was 67 feet high and wholly overgrown by forest trees. The Indians had no knowledge of its builders, or of the people who constructed the work in ruins near the village. They were antiquated structures when their forefathers first entered the country. Extensive ruined fortifications exist upon the Muskingum. One of them encloses sixty acres by an earth wall six feet high, by from twelve to twenty feet broad. On each side are gateways; leading from the one next the river is a covered way formed by two parallel walls of earth one hundred and thirty feet distant from each other. These walls are about twenty feet high, or were of this height when first known. Within the enclosure is a mound 180 feet long and 130 feet broad and nine feet high. There are other mounds of similar character within the enclosure. Fragments of pottery, composed of shells, gravel, clay and sand, have been found in these ruins.*

In Fairfield County, is a large mound in which was a large earthen vessel placed upon a furnace. It was eighteen feet long by six feet broad, and contained the skeletons of twelve persons, which were at the depth of fifteen feet below the surface. It is often the case that the tumuli contain the bones of the human race. In the great mound at Circleville, many skeletons were found, all resting with their heads towards the center.

Here also was discovered, in the ruined fortifications, pottery, and stone implements, such as hatchets and arrow-heads and earthenware.

In the vicinity of Wheeling, Virginia, on both sides of the Ohio river, are extensive ancient fortifications and mounds. What are called the Grave Creek flats have been the site of a very ancient city, of what nation it is not known. When the country was first occupied by the whites, the traces of the an-

---

* Dr. John Locke, of Cincinnati, Ohio, in 1838 described an extensive fortification located upon the crest of a high hill in Highland County, Ohio. It is elevated 500 feet above Brush Creek. The works are enclosed by a wall which is surrounded with a ditch one mile and five-eighths in circuit. The ditch is 64 feet wide. The wall at the base is 40 feet in width, and from 4 to 9 feet high composed of stone and earth.—*See* Second Annual Report of the Geological Survey of Ohio, p. 268.

cient city were quite visible, especially a large circular enclosure
and seven mounds. Above these works, upon the hill, was a
ruined tower or lookout. It had been constructed of stone,
which must have been conveyed the distance of a mile up the
hill. Similar works are on the right bank of the Ohio, directly
opposite those above described. The Great Mound, at Grave
Creek, is one of the largest of the Mississippi valley.* It is
three hundred and thirty-three feet in circumference, and seventy
feet in height. When discovered it was bearing large trees.
The mound was opened and explored by Mr. Abelard B. Tomlin-
son, about the year 1838, and found to contain two vaults; in
the lower one were found the osseous remains of two human
skeletons, in a state of decomposition. One was ornamented
with six hundred and fifty beads. The upper vault contained
but one skeleton, and a great number of trinkets, among which
were seventeen hundred bone beads, five hundred sea-shells, one
hundred and fifty pieces of mica, five copper wrist and arm
bands, and a small flat stone with engraving upon it.† These
discoveries have given rise to much discussion among archæolo-
gists and ethnologists. Dr. George Morton, of Philadelphia, Pa.,
has given a full description of the skull of the skeleton found in
the upper vault. The posterior portion is largely developed, the
facial angle being 78°. His description would class this skull
with the Southern type. It is evidently not Mongolian. The
inscribed stone was taken to Washington city by Dr. Willis D.
Hass, in 1850, but thus far no new light has been shed upon the
mound mysteries by the deciphering of the engraved characters.

At Brownsville, Pa., were discovered ruins of an ancient fortified camp, enclosing thirteen acres, in circular form. The
walls were of earth, seven feet high; within the enclosure was a
pentagon, with walls four feet high, having a passage way between them and the main wall of three feet in width. It had
few openings, for in the outer wall was but one gateway. In
the center of the camp stood a mound thirty feet high.‡

Mr. Scott, in his Gazetteer of 1806, states that in Wheatfield
Township, Westmoreland County, Pa., is a remarkable mound,

---

* Silliman's Journal, Vol. VI., p. 166.
† Schoolcraft's Indian Tribes of the U. S., p. 121.
‡ American Antiquities, p. 84.

from which several strange specimens of art have been taken.
One was a stone serpent, five inches in diameter; part of the
entablature of a column, both rudely carved in the form of dia-
monds and leaves ; also an earthern urn with ashes.*

Indian mounds, such as are considered of Indian construction,
are very numerous in Kentucky, New York, Virginia, and in
the Western States, and in the Southern States to the Gulf of
Mexico. They are most numerous on the Mississippi and its
tributaries, and along the great lakes, and only extend to the
ocean at the southern extremity of Florida; from which it is
supposed the great mound builders entered the country at that
point from Mexico, and were the same race that constructed
Cholula and Teotihuacan.†

Some of the mounds and fortifications found in ruins in the
State of New York were immense. One in Onondaga County
enclosed within its walls more than five hundred acres ; the tri-
angular forts, situated at about eight miles distant from each
other, constituted its outposts.

The ruined works found in the State of Georgia are also of
great magnitude. On the banks of the Little River, near
Wrightsborough, are the remnants of a gigantic pyramid, large
pit, or excavated area, of a cubical form ; also, the remains of a
town. Near Savannah, among other ruins, is a conical mound,
truncated, fifty feet in height, and eight hundred feet in circumference at the base. Others of similar character are frequent in
Georgia, Florida and Alabama.‡

In the State of Wisconsin are extensive ancient ruins and tumuli. Those upon the west branch of Rock River, in Jefferson
County, are of great extent. The main ruins are one-half mile
distant from the village of Aztalan, but its site is amid a cluster
of ancient mounds.§

The walls are about four hundred yards long each. Near the
western wall was an oblong mound, which was opened some fifteen years ago, and found to contain human bones, pieces of
pottery, fragments of burnt brick, or clay, mixed with straw or

* Historical Collections of Pennsylvania, p. 680.

† Another theory is that the aborigines peopled Mexico from the north, by
way of Behring Straits, halting on the way at Aztalan, and on the Gila, before
reaching Tula. American Antiquities, Bradford, p. 202.

‡ Bartram's Travels, p. 37.   § American Antiquities, Bradford, p. 46.

grass; * pieces of rope matting, and several rope strands, made
of grass or some similar fibrous substance; also a fabric resembling coarse cloth was found in this mound. Within the fort
was situated a large mound of square form, about twenty feet
high, with a flat summit; from it extends a ridge or wall, connecting it with another mound of similar character. Several
smaller ones were also within the enclosure, some of which, on
being dug into, were also found to contain human bones, brick
and pottery. The walls of the citadel or fort were composed of
brick, and were about twenty-five feet wide at the base, and five
feet high, according to the account of them published in Silliman's Journal of 1840.† The brick walls of the fort were not
regularly laid walls of brick, such as is generally understood by
the term, but presenting the appearance of a mass of burnt clay,
evidently prepared out of brick clay, mixed with straw, in such
a manner as to be hardened by fire.

West of Madison, on Sugar river, at the foot of a pine bluff,
is an ancient breastwork of about two hundred and twenty yards
in length, but in the center is interrupted by a gap, opposite to
which is a buffalo shaped mound. About three miles below,
back from the river, are seven tumuli. In the vicinity of the
Four Lakes of Wisconsin, are numerous mounds, conical and animal shaped also.‡ In one opened in 1837, at the depth of about
five feet from the summit, broken glazed pottery, agate arrow-
heads, and the skull part of the skeleton of a human being, were
found. The material of the mound is not of the vicinity
where it is located, being composed of reddish brown soil, clear
of rubbish, and as devoid of gravel as if it had been sifted. The
animal-shaped mounds also contain human bones. They were
not the only way of disposing of the dead; as, in Tennessee, the
graves of the dead of an ancient walled village were found in
abundance three feet deep; and, in other localities, evidences of
the bodies having been burnt have been frequently witnessed;

* The brick composing the wall is not such as is generally understood by the
term, but presents the appearance of a mass of burnt clay, containing straw,
after the Egyptian mode of brick-making. History of Wisconsin, by W. R.
Smith, Vol. III., p. 237.

† Silliman's Journal, Vol. I., p. 322.

‡ Dr. David D. Owen's Survey of Mineral Lands in Iowa, Wisconsin, and
Northern Illinois, Document No. 239, 26th Congress, 1st Session, House of Representatives, Executive, p. 136.

whilst some mounds contain no evidences of human bodies having been buried in them.

The explanation in regard to the animal-shaped mounds is,
that they are the burying places of the several Indian tribes
bearing the names of the animals they were known by, such as
Fox, Snake, Deer, Wolf, Turtle, etc.

In Illinois, nearly opposite St. Louis, within a circuit of a few
miles, are the remains of more than a hundred and fifty ancient
tumuli. The largest one of the group is ninety feet high, and
nearly a half a mile in circumference.* In the vicinity of this
group of mounds are the remains of two ancient cities of vast
proportions, situated upon the right bank of the river, in Missouri.† At the mouth of the Missouri there stood a pyramid,
with three stages or landing places, similar to those of the Tower
of Babel. Fifteen miles west of St. Louis, on the Maramec river,
is a group of ruined tumuli; in one of them were found stone
coffins, containing human bones. The skeletons were those of
men whose lower limbs had been disjointed at the knees, which
at first made the impression upon the minds of the discoverers,
that the bodies were of a pigmy race, the coffins being about
four feet long; but the disjointed limbs being found in the coffins, soon dispelled the delusion.

What is known as "Mount Joliet,‡" on the banks of the river
Desplaines, in Illinois, is one of the most gigantic mounds of the
West. Mr. Schoolcraft gives its height at sixty feet; length, four
hundred and fifty yards; width, seventy-five yards. It is erected
upon a bed of secondary limestone formation. In its construction eighteen millions two hundred and fifty thousand solid feet
of earth were required.

The ancient ruins and pyramids of Mexico, Central and South
America, are upon a much more extensive scale than those above
described, and show their builders to have been enjoying a high
degree of civilization. The pyramid of Cholula rivals some of

---

* This mound is truncated, and was at one time occupied by some friars of
the order of La Trapp, hence called the "Monk Mound." Breckenridge's
Views, p. 173.

† The one located in Gasconade County was regularly laid out in streets and
squares. Foundations of stone are found in different parts of its ancient pile;
and west of it, sixteen miles, exist other stone works of similar character, regularly laid. American Antiquities, Bradford, p. 47.

‡ Beck's Gazetteer, p. 140.

the greatest of Egypt in magnitude.* It is 177 feet in perpendicular height, and its base 1,023 feet long, and covers forty-four acres of ground. The top is level, and contains about an acre within its area. When first discovered by Europeans, the summit was occupied by a sumptuous temple, dedicated to the worship of the "god of the air." It was the great resort of the religious worshippers of the country, and where six thousand human beings were annually offered up as sacrifices to this imaginary deity by the superstitious Mexicans. The pyramid, though used by the Aztecs, was not constructed by them, but was an ancient ruin when they first entered the country. The Toltecs were, in all probability, its builders,† though the Almecas have been considered its founders.‡

The pyramids of Teotihuacan are the most remarkable antique monuments of American semi-civilization, and were dedicated to the sun and moon. The one dedicated to the sun, called Tonatiuh, is six hundred and eighty-two feet long at the base, and one hundred and eighty feet high. It is divided into four stories of about equal height; upon the summit stood the temple, which contained the colossal statue of the sun, made of a single block of stone. It was in existence during the early part of the Spanish invasion, but demolished as a heathenish deity by Bishop Zumarrago.§

The pyramid upon which was erected the temple called "Leacalle," constructed by the Aztecs, and dedicated in the year 1486, with the sacrifice of 70,000 human victims, was 300 feet square at the base, and 100 feet high. The top was reached by 114 steps, constructed after the manner of those of Egypt. Upon the top of the pyramid the sacrifices were offered, an account of one of which will be subsequently noticed.

About five miles from the city of Curriavaca, are the ruins of Xochicalco, considered of very high antiquity. The stones facing the outside of the pyramid are covered with mortar. The structure was originally five stories high, of terraced form. The

---

* The Pyramid of Mycerinos is 280 feet long at the base, and 162 feet high. The Pyramid of Cheops is 728 feet long at the base, and 448 feet in height.

† Indigenous Races of the Earth, p. 213.

‡ Prichard's Natural History of Man, Vol. II., p. 509.

§ Ibid, p. 388.

stones are of porphyritic rock, dressed and carved with singular figures and hieroglyphics, skilfully executed.

Near the village of Popantla, is the temple and pyramid of that name. From the mass of ruins strewn over the plain in their vicinity, it is very manifest the ruined city must have been over a mile in extent. The pyramid is seven stories high, each story terminating with a frieze and cornice, all composed of solid sandstone, neatly squared and jointed, and covered with a cement three inches thick. Remains of colors are visible upon the walls, as if they had been painted. The pyramid is 120 feet square; in front are fifty-seven steps, by which the top of the sixth story is reached. This is a very ancient structure; large trees are growing upon its sides; yet it is tolerably well preserved. The natives call this pyramid El-Tajiu.

Near Jalap, on a lofty ridge, the ruins of a very ancient city are located; stone walls, ruined buildings and pyramids are still visible. The stones are large and dressed, and united by a cement. In the center of the main inclosure there is a pyramid, eighty feet high, and forty-nine feet front, by forty-two feet back, and consists of three stories. In front a stairway leads to the second story; the top of the third is reached by steps cut in the corner edge of the wall. On the top stood a gigantic tree, so firmly rooted upon the spot where once existed the sacred temple, as to defy the whirlwind. North of these ruins are others equally extensive. Near those of Teotihuacan, by an able system of engineering, the water from a brook had been brought in conduit pipes the distance of three miles; in one place it was conducted over a ravine a hundred feet deep. The pipes were raised to the proper level on stone mason work of very substantial character.

The ancient ruins of Yucatan and Central America are very extensive, and show much mechanical skill and refined taste. The house of the Governor, as the ruins of Uxmal are called, consists of a hewn stone structure, 320 feet in front, by forty feet deep, and about twenty-five feet high. In the front are eleven doorways; also one in each end. The building is divided into various apartments; one of the rooms is sixty feet long, and twenty-three feet from floor to ceiling. The upper portion of the edifice is rich in ornamental finish, with elaborate carving, upon which traces of colors are visible. It had evidently been painted. Every room had the arch peculiar to the country, but the lintels were wood, now decayed. Over the central doorway was a seated figure, the head-dress decorated with feathers, but the whole so much defaced as to obscure the design ; well sculptured hieroglyphics are visible upon the outer wall. The cornice represents the coil of a serpent, and extends round the entire building. The edifice is located upon three terraced walls, the lower one being three feet high, fifteen feet wide, and 575 feet long ; the second, twenty feet high, 250 feet wide, and 445 feet long ; and the third, nineteen feet high, thirty feet wide, and 360 feet long ; all constructed of stone, and laid with skill.

Mr. Stephens describes a building at Uxmal, of oblong form, built upon an artificial elevation. It was 240 feet long at the base, and 120 feet broad, protected all round by a wall of square stone from the base to the top. On the east side, was a broad range of stone steps, about nine inches high, and so steep that the utmost care must be observed in ascent and descent. Mr. Stephens counted 101 of these steps, still in their places ; nine had been displaced at the top ; and he estimated that twenty were concealed by the rubbish at the base. The whole building is of stone ; the inside walls are of polished smoothness. Above the door is a rich cornice, extending around the building. All the walls from above the door line are covered with elaborately sculptured ornaments, some strange and grotesque, others tasteful and beautiful. Among the ornaments were busts of human beings, heads of leopards, and compositions of leaves and flowers. Every combination of ornament is carved upon a single stone. From the front door of the edifice is a hard cement pavement, twenty-two feet long, by fifteen feet broad, leading to the roof of another building, seated lower down on the artificial base.*

There are other ruins in the vicinity of these singular edifices ; no doubt but an ancient city was located at Uxmal by peoples whose history is buried in the night of ages. Neither the Toltecs nor Aztecs were the founders of this city, or constructors of the singular building above described ; and the native Indians have no knowledge of their authors.

The temple of Chi-chen is an interesting ruin, as much so as any

* Travels in Central America, Chiapas, and Yucatan Vol. II., p. 421.

of Yucatan. The walls, which are of stone, stand upon an elevated foundation of 16 feet. The building is about 450 feet long. The stone composing the walls are hewn, and laid in fillet and moulding work. The structure was evidently ornamented with sculptured stone pillars, as such lie broken around the base. These ruins are covered with rank vegetation, including large trees, which have fastened their roots amid the ruins of the temple. Part of the right hand wall is still standing to the height of fifty feet. The stones of the walls of the building are all cut to the size of two feet square. In the center of the walls are large stone rings, carved from an immense block. These rings are four feet in diameter, and two feet thick. Their sides are beautifully carved.

The ruins of Zayi are also quite singular and extensive. The main building is an immense structure located upon a natural eminence. The foundation is a parallelogram consisting of stone; length, 268 feet; width, 116 feet; and is 20 feet high. The ruined building stood in the center of the foundation. Only the wall of its western end remains standing, with a portion of the steps leading to the top. Corridors lined the front, each having been supported by two pillars, the spaces between the main pillars being occupied by smaller ones beautifully ornamented. The front over the corridors is ornamented by a carved cornice moulding. Above this moulding is a finish of small round pillars interspersed with squares of fine ornamental carvings. This temple was entirely different from Chi-chen.

The ruins of Copan and Palenque are very extensive. Mr. Stephens describes a statue, found at Copan, to be eleven feet nine inches high, which stood upon a pedestal seven feet square. It was placed at the foot of a wall which rises in successive steps, to an elevation of thirty feet above the statue.

Near Palenque are the remains of the ancient ruined city of Culhuacan. In 1787, Don Antonio del Rio traced the boundaries of the city, and found fragments of fallen buildings for several miles strewn along the mountain. Fourteen large stone houses, almost entire, were then standing amid the ruins. The buildings are rude and massive, the principal apartments of which are adorned with numerous figures in relief, representing human beings of strange form, and variously

5

adorned. The ancient ruins of Guatemala are not of so great extent as those of Mexico and Yucatan, though it seems that the peoples of that portion of Central America were in advance of the Aztecs in point of refinement and polished civilization, as their works of art fully attest.*

The tombs of Mitla are magnificent ruins; elegantly ornamented by paintings representing warlike trophies and sacrafices.† The sculpture and architectural designs are of refined order, and in good taste. The ruins of South America, in some respects, are more extensive, and evincing a higher degree of architectural skill in their design and construction than those of Mexico, or any of those already described.

The successive steps of human progress are visibly manifested in the works of art of the early peoples of South America, from the age of stone until that of iron. The greatest development of mechanical skill manifested among the peoples of the country before the invasion of the Spaniards, was in the bronze period. During that age the splendid ruined edifices, found scattered throughout the country to-day, were constructed. Though unacquainted with the use of iron, the early nations of the country invented a material of equally hard consistency, such as to dress and to work the hardest stone, to the same degree the Anglo-Saxons of the present day dress and carve the granite rock with the hardest steel instruments.‡

Peru, Bolivia, and Brazil are distinguished for their ancient ruins. The Peruvians as a nation have been noted for their architectural taste and refined civilization before the advent of the Spaniards, though unknown to the civilized world until the conquest of Pizarro. Until then the "children of the sun" were unknown beyond their own boundaries.

In the vicinity of the lake "Titicaca" are antiquated ruins, referable perhaps to an age antedating that in which were constructed the pyramids of Egypt. The buildings, now in ruins, were doubtless fortresses, and, though built with great skill, were constructed without the aid of iron implements. They were composed of stone, some of the blocks of which being thirty feet

* Indigenous Races of the Earth, p. 185.
† Encyclopædia of Geography, vol. III., p. 328.
‡ Prescott's Conquest of Peru, Vol. I., p. 152.

long, by eighteen feet in width and six feet thick. These huge stones were cut out of the solid rock of the mountain, and transported many miles over hills and valleys from their native beds to their final resting-places in the walls of these buildings.* How they were transported and laid in their places is unknown. Modern science, with all the improvements in the arts combined, would fail to accomplish such a herculean undertaking; yet the semi-civilized original people performed the great feat, and the Peruvians acknowledged these ruins to be of older date than the pretended advent of the Incas, and to have furnished them the models of their architecture.†

In the great basin of lakes Titicaca and Aulagas, at an elevation of 12,900 feet above the sea, are situated the splendid ruins of Tiahuanaca, presenting in the ruined edifices the evidences of the greatest advancement in civilization of any other portion of the western continent. The recent survey of Mr. E. G. Squier has placed these ruins in their proper light before the public. They are not mythical, or entitled any longer to be considered the work of the Incas; but are, perhaps, more ancient than those of lake Titicaca, and in all probability the work of the same people. They consist of mounds; terraces walled with stone; upright stone rudely worked, others of finished workmanship constructed in walls; piers, portions of stairways, blocks of stone with mouldings and cornices, monolithic doorways bearing symbolical ornaments in relief; and are, as Mr. Squier remarks, scattered in confusion over the plain. The destruction of these ruins has been made the more complete by the peoples who succeeded their builders, who converted them into quarries from which to procure stone for modern constructions. Mr. Squier minutely describes the several structures readily traced; among which the Fortress, Temple, Hall of Justice, Stonehenge, Monolithic doorway, Cemetery, Symbolical slab, arches, columns of stone and statuary. The whole covers a square mile of surface, and presents an aspect similar to that of Thebes. All the buildings were complete in their architectural designs and finish; all constructed of stone, some of the blocks being of huge proportions. What Mr. Squier denominates the symbolical stone is 13 feet 4 inches square and 20 inches thick.

* Prescott's Conquest of Peru, Vol. I., p. 18. † Ibid.

The building in which it was placed stood upon stone piers, some of the blocks being 14 feet in length and of corresponding width and thickness.

The monolithic gateway consists of a huge block 13 feet 5 inches long, 7 feet 2 inches high above ground, and 18 inches thick. Through the center is cut an opening 4 feet 6 inches long and 2 feet 9 inches wide, which doubtless was the passage way through it to the interior of the Fortress, or Temple, though its precise location has not been definitely determined upon, as where it is now located is evidently not its original position. Above the doorway are rows of sculpture in low relief, but immediately over the entrance are sculptured figures in high relief. The whole block is the hardest trachite of dark color. Its workmanship is of the finest finish. The face is polished and of the utmost regularity and precision. The lines and angles are those of the greatest geometrical accuracy. The reliefs have human figures each holding a scepter. The upper and lower tiers have human heads wearing crowns. The principal and central figure is a bold representation and of singular design. The head is surrounded by what Mr. Catherwood calls rays, in which, at their extremities, are the heads of the condor and tiger. In each hand he holds a scepter, the lower end of that of the right representing the head of a condor, and the upper that of the tiger, whilst the upper end of that of the left hand scepter represents the head of the tiger and the lower end two heads of the condor.

The monolithic doorway, now used as a gateway of the cemetery of the village of Tiahuanacu, near these ruins, was evidently one of the original doorways of the temple, or hall of justice. It is similar to the one above described, but not so ornamental or massive, being 7 feet 5 inches high, 5 feet 10½ inches wide, and 16½ inches thick. The door passage is 6 feet 2 inches high by 2 feet 10 inches wide.

That which is termed the temple seems to be the most ancient structure of the group; as shown by the character of the workmanship displayed by its builders, and the frayed appearance of the stones which composed its walls. The space occupied by the temple is of rectangle form, 388 by 445 feet, the lines defined by upright stone (red sandstone) of irregular size and height, and are, in the main, from 8 to 10 feet high, from 2 to 4 feet,

and 20 to 30 inches thick.   These upright stone seem to
have been about fifteen feet distant from each other, the spaces
between them filled up with unwrought stone, forming a wall
supporting a terrace line of earth raised to about eight feet above
the level of the plain.   On the eastern side was a platform terrace, of lower grade, eighteen feet broad, along the edge of the
central part of which were located ten great stone pilasters fifteen feet apart, which are still erect with a single exception, one
being prostrate.   They varied in height and thickness; the one
fallen down is 13 feet 8 inches long, and 5 feet 3 inches in width,
and thirty-two inches in thickness, appears above ground—how
much below ground has not been ascertained.   One standing, as
measured, was found to be 14 feet high, 4 feet 2 inches wide, and
2 feet 8 inches thick.   At the top of the tallest pilasters are
shoulders, as if to receive a finish, such as architraves; these not
appearing upon the shorter ones it is inferred they have been
broken off, and that all one day supported a proper finish, if not
a roof.

The Fortress consists of a great mound of rectangular form
620 feet in length by 450 in width and about 50 feet high.   It
was terraced in three stages.   Cieza de Leon, who visited these
ruins soon after the conquest, describes the fortress as being
supported by great walls of stone.   Upon the summit of this
mound are the remains of stone walls and the foundations of rectangular buildings.   Modern barbarians, in search of treasure
supposed to have been secreted in hidden vaults in the mound,
have made the ruins of the fortress quite complete.   The treasure hunters made an excavation in the center of the fortress 300
feet in diameter and sixty feet deep.

When the Spaniards first visited these ruins, they found, in
the vicinity of the fortress, two stone idols of human shape, of
giant stature, executed with skill, and, as was remarked by Cieza
de Leon, by very able masters.   They were broken in pieces
by modern vandals, except the head of one of them upon the
roadside on the way to La Paz.

The stone composing the ruined building and works of Tiahuanacu, consisting of red sand-stone, slate-colored trachite, and
a dark, hard basalt, are not of the vicinity of the ruins, but must
have been brought from quarries ranging from five to forty miles

distant. The sand-stone was obtained at the distance of five miles; the others upon the isthmus of Yunguyo, forty miles.*

The native Indians have no knowledge as regards the author, of these ruined structures, and told the Spaniards that "they existed before the sun shone." The Peruvians also were entirely ignorant as regards their origin; but had a tradition, that many ages before the invasion of the Spaniards, a large vessel landed at St. Helen's point, manned by giants having no beards, but long hair hanging loosely upon their shoulders; their eyes were wide apart, bodies very large, represented to have been taller from the knees downward, than the height of a man's head. The probability is, the people here represented were Tartars or Chinese on horseback or on some other animals; though it was not pretended that they were the earliest people of the country, as the Incas were then occupying it.

There are many other ruins in what was known as Peru at the time of the Spanish conquest, but those already described are sufficient to show their antiquity and character.

In many places are found ruins of massive aqueducts, constructed of hewn stone, laid in cement, and which would do credit to modern mechanics.

The question remains unsettled as to who constructed the ruined buildings, mounds and tumuli found upon this continent. Though it may be admitted that the Indians reared the tumuli, it is hardly probable that they constructed the vast fortifications, pyramids, temples and cities, now found in ruins, in various parts of the country. These are doubtless the works of an extinct people, who evidently had to contend against desperate foes; otherwise such vast forts and places of safety would not have been required. They were doubtless engaged in a struggle for life, but finally overcome, and extirpated by their enemies, in all probability the Red Indians, who never, as far as history leads us, had adopted the mode of life the lost people seem to have enjoyed. Many of the buildings in ruins seem to have been destroyed by violence. This may have been done by foes during the contest for the mastery; at all events, the Red

---

* For a full and interesting description of these antique works the reader is referred to Mr. Squier's account of them in No. 216, Harper's Magazine of May, 1868, p. 681.

Indians would have no need for them, civilization being antagonistic to their savage nature. The age of these ruined works and institutions cannot even be guessed at, or hardly a reasonable approximation be made as regards the time when their foundations were laid, or the periods required for their construction. As no iron tools have been found of an age cotemporaneous with the period of their construction, the reasonable inference is, their builders were ignorant of the use of that metal. A singular instance of iron tools being discovered, enclosed in the solid rock at Salem, Ohio, has been reported.* In dressing a rock for a mill-stone the workmen found at the depth of three inches, holes which had been made in the rock by art: upon further examination they found two iron wedges driven into the rock, and on each side of the wedges was a thin piece of iron, showing the wedges were driven for the purpose of splitting the rock. Three inches of solid mass of rock of the same texture as that in which the wedges had been driven had been formed over them after they had been abandoned by the owner.

This is not perhaps so strange an occurrence as reported by Professor Silliman, from Count Bournous' Mineralogy, of stumps in columns and fragments of stone half wrought with cones and handles of hammers, at the depth of fifty feet beneath layers of eleven beds of compact limestone. At the same place in France, was discovered a board seven feet long and one inch thick, which had been formed into agate, as well as the wooden instruments found in the same locality. The edges of the board were rounded the same as those used in quarries at the present day.

Another evidence of the antiquity of man upon the western continent is presented in petrified bodies, being discovered under circumstances showing an eternity of time has intervened since the flesh and bones became a solid. One case demands our notice here: In the Cumberland Mountains of Tennessee is a vast cave in which was found the petrified bodies of two men and that of a dog. One of the men was standing erect with a spear in his hand in a balanced position; his attitude evinced surprise, as if he had just started upon a fast walk. The other was in a sitting

* Delafield's Topographical Description, p. 28.

† The iron wedge above described found in Salem, Washington County, Ohio, has been considered to be not of ancient origin.—American Antiquities, Bradford, p. 38.

posture. The dog was crouched by their side upon a flat rock, as if in terror, or about to make a leap. The place they were was one hundred and twenty-five feet from the mouth of the cave. The men seem to have been in a nude state, at least, no evidences of clothing are visible about their bodies.

The Old world has quite the advantage over the New, as regards monuments of art now in ruins. Their authors have left the impress of their own character so indelibly stamped upon them, that it is no difficult task to prove the people to which each belong. The ruined structures of Greece, Rome, Carthage, Persia, Assyria, Arabia, China, Hindoostan, Asia Minor, and the eastern continents are generally referable to particular eras in the world's progress, and traceable to the nations and peoples who constructed them. The pyramids of Egypt which bear date before the time of the erection of the Tower of Babel, have preserved the character and history of their builders, in stone, paintings, and parchments, as well as by mummified bodies. And so with Nineveh, Balbeck, Palmyra, Ecbatana, Persepolis, Idumea and Jerusalem, each having their preserved history; Balbeck attests the advance of civilization during the dark ages; China and the Chinese have remained the same for thousands of centuries. Their ruined edifices are of the same order of their subsequent and present structures. The renowned "city of the Great King" is a monument attesting the character and refinement of the Jews. The Celts marked their course in Asia, Africa, Europe, America, and the isles of the sea by erecting upright stone, such as those of Stonehenge in Europe and similar monuments in South America.

One remarkable fact connected with the stone and bronze age, is the similarity of the implements and peoples of the old and new world during these respective periods, which admits of the probability of their being of the same race of peoples. The similarity of the pyramids and ancient building are evidences tending to show that the same race of people constructed the pyramids of Egypt, Mexico, Peru, Central America and the Mississippi Valley.

The buried cities of Pompeii and Herculaneum, still retain the evident impress of the national character of their authors, as fresh as if recently erected, and showing there has been no material architectural changes in Italy for the last eighteen hundred years. Marked changes during that period have taken place on the coast where these cities stood when they were overwhelmed by the eruptions of Vesuvius 1800 years ago. Pompeii then stood upon the sea shore ; now it is a mile distant from the sea.*

* Lyell's Principles of Geology, p. 390.

CHAPTER III.

DISTRIBUTION OF MAN.

THE distribution of mankind over the earth is not governed by the same laws controlling animals and plants, as these are ruled by the degrees of heat and cold, and other stimulating agencies, the law of physical order. As regards mankind, they are not controlled by climate—existing even where the cold is so intense as to occasion the congelation of mercury, as well as where their bodies sustain heat higher than that at which ether boils.

The law of man's adaptation to climatic conditions seems to be of moral order, climate having little or no effect upon the races.

The tropical man is so organized as not to experience want; he lives at ease; his daily food provided for him by the spontaneous products of the earth. The polar man is in a constant state of want—ever laboring to prevent starvation. The man of the temperate zone is the perfect type of the human race, physically and mentally; he toils and thinks, and reasons and toils—makes full development of his physical, mental, and moral nature.

The center of the animal kingdom is in the tropics; passing from thence north and south, they decrease in beauty and numbers. But man, being perfect in the temperate zone, shows

his development, is stimulated by the climate and other surrounding agencies. His type becomes less energetic and less
intellectual as he passes north or south from his central seat.
As we go from this great geographical center, north and south,
the regularity and harmony of the races disappear, and new
orders of men are presented, suited to the localities in which
they reside. This is the case in the old and new world, and is a
universal law of the human races. Mental culture always bears
a proper proportion to the perfection of the race, and has always
been the case. The extreme northern races have no time for
mental culture, it all being employed in providing for their daily
wants. The extreme southern races of the tropics are very
indolent, and see no necessity for mental culture; they eat,
drink, and indulge in pleasure, such seeming to be their highest
aim.

The idea of the superior race being modified by passing from
the geographical seat, north or south, may be questioned, yet the
most indubitable evidences exist in its support. Take the Esquimaux of the extreme north—the true representative of the polar
man—and compare him with the European. The contrast will
be very manifest; no one will doubt the superiority of the
European. The same striking contrast exists in regard to the
natives of Southern Africa, and Northern Asia, and the Caucasian race. But it is not to be denied that the superior race will
stand pre-eminent over the others in any of the zones, though
not possessing the same intellectual energy or vigor as in their
natural latitude. The white man is a cosmopolite; the whole
earth, indeed, appears too small for his range; he pines to
advance to other worlds, and to explore the whole universe.

Western Asia is not only the center (geographically,) of the
races, but also the place from whence have radiated the influences
of man's moral nature.* The ideas we have of mankind issued
from this locality. Here it would seem was man created, and
from whence the world was peopled.

Sacred history gives us a short detail of the peopling of the
globe, at least part of the old world, by the descendants of Noah.
Before the flood, 1656 years had elapsed since the creation of
Adam, as computed by biblical scholars. Some of the antede-

* Natural History of Man, vol. I., p. 120.

luvians lived more than half this period; even Noah himself was a witness to many of the important events of the antedeluvians, being 600 years old when the floods came, but failed to give any history of the people who lived before the deluge, deeming it proper rather to let their crimes and wickedness remain buried in the past, than reveal them to coming generations.

If the deluge was universal, all the human races, save Noah and his family, perished by direction of the Deity; but if it was not universal, we may have other parentage to look to for the present races of man, besides Noah and his posterity; and, hence, an important feature in man's distribution would at once be presented. Was the deluge universal? is a very important subject of inquiry, and one we shall not dispute or attempt to solve.

As we said in a former chapter, geology has demonstrated that much of what heretofore has been the best evidences of a universal deluge of waters, was produced by other causes than "rain from heaven." The highest peaks of the mountains were once at the bottom of the sea, and were brought up from thence to their present positions by the internal force of the globe.[*] All show the action of water, even to their very summits. The mighty waters of the ocean now rest upon mountains, hills, and plains, miles below the wind-driven waves upon which our ships steam and sail—but when, if ever, a new continent shall arise from the depths, or ours be submerged, is far beyond human reason to decide.

The first location of man upon the earth, as regards place, is very uncertain, as well as the era when he became an inhabitant. It is very easy to imagine that before the subsidence of the land between America, Africa, and Europe, the same people inhabited the whole country, from the Red Sea to the Pacific Ocean, in the west, and under these circumstances, the sameness of the pyramids, temples, and ruined cities, could readily be accounted for.

The distribution, therefore, of the races over the globe, may have been accomplished whilst the land was united, or before the Atlantic Ocean was formed; at least, this is probable, though the approved theory is, that America was peopled by way of

* Lyell's Principles of Geology, p. 163.

MAP

SHOWING THE PRESENT DISTRIBUTION OF
THE
VARIOUS RACES OF MANKIND.

EXPLANATION.

Caucasian Race.
Mongolian "
Americans "
Malay "
Negro "
Lands in Red Sea

NOTE.—Where the Lines are Striped, it
denotes that the People are of
Different Races.

See opposite page.

the straits of Behring, and the Pacific, in boats and canoes, upon the assumption that the original seat of the human race was in Asia, as recorded in the Genesis.

It is worthy of note, that all the races are not of migratory character. The Esquimaux are contented in their ice dwellings, and in their snow huts. It is only the Caucasians, as a general rule, who are restive and disposed to wander. The Mongolians are now rivcted to their country, unless compelled to emigrate. The Chinese, and indeed the people of Asia, other than white nations, are domestic in their habits. The term Caucasian, in this connection, does not simply mean peoples of white complexion, but also embraces all the grades of this race, including the Egyptians, Jews, Celts, Teutons, Gauls, Pelasgians, Sclavonians, Iberians, Romans, Berbers, and other families of mixed blood of this type. The mixed stock of the primitive races, is now found in almost every clime; often the inferior type predominating, as is the case with the Hottentots, Bushmen, and other tribes now classed with the African; yet in all these families, the Caucasian blood is still visible. The adaptation of the races to the zones, as before remarked, is always governed by the law of the races; hence, the Caucasian will not be perfect in the tropics or polar regions. Some have even gone so far as to affirm that the Anglo-Saxons would become extinct if cut off from intercourse with families of the same type.

The population of the United States is not so strong as the original stock of Great Britain or Germany. Each continent has its mixed races, showing that the disposition of mankind to distribute themselves has been universal. The distribution is not of recent date, but antedates authentic history. When nations first became known, there were mixed races, but no new orders or types seem to have been produced.

It is worthy of remark, that however scattered and mixed the races have become, the original abode of each is yet plainly visible in the several zones, where the Creator seems to have assigned them to reside.

It cannot be denied, therefore, that the human races have their geographical locations as well as the lower animals, and where they thrive better than in any other locality. They appear to be adapted to extreme conditions and influences that cannot be changed by them. The polar man cannot subsist in the tropics, nor the tropical man in the polar regions, not being physically organized for these several localities. By the universal law of origin, the Negro's place is in the tropics, and the Esquimaux in the polar regions; to these several localities they have been assigned by the Creator, by his immutable laws of distribution.

These differences of adaption of races to geographical zones, are as ancient as the races themselves. History proves it to be so, and traditions, monuments of art, and geology—confirm it. The great works of art, from the founding of Babel to the erection of the monument on Bunker's Hill, are of the Caucasian family of man.*

The great plain north of the Himalayas, very early in the history of the races, swarmed with Caucasians of primitive stock. Some of their bold adventurers climbed to the top of the mountains which environed them, and beheld from thence vast hosts of people inhabiting the plains of Iran and Bactriana; the scene was inviting—soon the bold white emigrants of the north issued through the gates of the Himalayas, and mingled with the dark-skinned tribes of the Ganges and Indus. Here, in all probability, was the place and the time the white and black races first came in contact with each other.

The whole of Southern Asia was soon overrun by these bold adventurers, who also passed into Africa, and peopled Egypt by the way of the upper Nile, where they built the Pyramids, and other astonishing works there existing. The same order of peoples passed into Europe by several emigrations, founding kingdoms and empires on the way thither, such as those of Persia, Media, Babylonia, and smaller states of that region, and in Asia Minor among which that of the Trojans. The leaders of these emigrations were the Pelasgians, Celts, Iberians, Huns, Finns, Teutons, and Goths. The Celts were very early settled in Europe, and came in two families, one by the north-east, the other by the way of southern India; the latter were of darker complexion than the former, which resulted from their connection with the Semite nations on their way. Some of them not only had the dark colored skin, but the black curly hair. The amalgamation of races in Europe has produced several new

* Earth and Man, Guyot, p. 228.

families, such as the Anglo-Saxons, the French, Swedes, Norwegians, Polanders, Welsh, Irish, Spaniards, Portuguese, and Hungarians.

The distribution of mankind over the islands of the sea, is governed by the same rules as those already stated. The natives are all of the same races found upon the continents, and derived from the same primitive types.

Australia, though far distant from the continents, has no distinct race. The natives have the color of the Negro, and hair of the Mongolian, but crisped. They have the Negro features to a high degree, and are classed with them; but one family doubtless is of the Malay race.

Of late, some ethnological authors have been disposed to treat the Australians as a new race; such is not the fact, in the true sense of the term, as they are doubtless only a cross between the Malays, Mongolians, and Negroes, elements of each being very manifest in their composition. Whether they were produced in Australia, or transported thither, cannot now be ascertained. As to their distribution, we are compelled to leave them where we find them; and, if they are a new race, the purpose of their creation has not yet been disclosed, unless to present the lowest type of mankind, as they are scarcely intellectual animals.

In what is termed the glacial period, mighty changes of the surface of the continents of Europe, Asia, and North America, took place. If man was an inhabitant of the regions of the glaciers, he had either to flee the country, or perish in the general catastrophe. His sagacity would most likely enable him to foresee the approaching danger, hence his distribution in families in this way may be accounted for. In such contingencies, man will make desperate efforts to save life. Those living along the coasts, of course, would take to their water crafts as a place of safety, and, as the mass of ice and rock moved on, would escape to the open sea, and be at the mercy of the waves, liable to be driven across the Atlantic, or far out into the Pacific.

There is no doubt about the glaciers having performed a very important part in forming the present surface of Europe, Asia, and the northern part of North America. If man did then exist, and perished in the general inundation, his remains are deeply buried in the drift produced in that period, so far down in the earth or in the sea as to make their discovery very doubtful. One fact is prominent in this connection, that if man did occupy these several continents, or either of them, before the glacial period, he has left no history, and very few, if any, works of art to tell of his existence.*

The lake dwellers doubtless inhabited Europe after this period.† The elephant and rhinoceros had disappeared from the country before man entered it. They had sought a warmer climate, as the glaciers had very materially changed the temperature of the country. Remains of these animals have been found even as far north as Siberia.

It is not at all strange that the remains of man have not been discovered of the glacial age, even if he was inhabiting the country at that epoch, as they are readily decomposed, unless in bog, or undergo a speedy petrifaction.

M. Boucher de Perthers, who, for over thirty years, devoted his attention to the early works of mankind in France, asserts to have found indubitable evidence of his existence at a very remote age, antedating even the glacial period. He has claimed to have discovered rough implements of flint, fashioned by art, in the undisturbed beds of clay, gravel and sand, near Abbeville. The beds alluded to vary from ten to twenty feet in thickness, covering the chalk hills in the vicinity. With these flint instruments were also the bones of extinct mammalia, such as the mammoth, the fossil rhinoceros, tiger, bear, hyena, stag and horse. They were discovered in the undisturbed beds of clay and diluvial deposits known as drift.‡ These flint instruments are very rude, showing them to have been fashioned in the first ages of the stone period.§

The conclusion to be derived from these developments is, that man existed in Europe coeval with the elephant and rhinoceros,

---

* The drift at Cincinnati, overlying the stump; the works of art, and remains of man, found elsewhere in the Mississippi valley, may have been deposited during the glacial period.

† Though it is now claimed by Boucher de Perthers, as subsequently noticed, that man inhabited Europe before the glacial era.

‡ It has been claimed that these remains were antediluvian ; even their discoverer so considered them, as by reference to his great work, entitled " Antiquities Celtiques," will fully be shown.

§ Antiquity of Man, pp. 94, 95, 122–150.

6

and at a period reaching back many thousands of years before any received date of creation. *

These great facts seem to mystify the early distribution of man over the globe, and tend to establish different creations. The rudeness of the stone implements rebuts the presumption of the people of that era emigrating to Europe, by water, at least. They were doubtless too low in the scale of civilization to have constructed even a canoe. The early distribution of man being conceded, the next important inquiry is as regards the type or types first occupying the various portions of the globe where mankind have existed. We have already made a general survey of the subject, and pointed out the great central seat of man, showing the native zones of the several races, and causes tending to their distribution; but as yet their indigenous character has not been defined, though in a subsequent chapter we shall endeavor to show to what race or type each family belongs.

All mankind, springing from the five leading types presently named, it might seem comparatively easy to trace the present families to their original form and source. The task might be readily performed, had not ethnologists confused the subject by increasing the number of the primitive types. One great error of the early authors consisted in resorting to language as the chief source in tracing out the primitive race, which is shortlived compared with the physical and mental qualities of a race. One race may readily adopt the language of another, and thus become, by language alone, one people; whilst, at the same time, in physical and mental qualities, they may differ as widely as the Caucasian and African. Indeed, here is a proper test, as the Negro has adopted the English tongue in the United States, and knows no more about his native dialect or language than if it never existed, yet the types are as distinct as they possibly can be. The language of a nation or type may be entirely forgotten, still the type remains; such, for example, was the case in Europe. The Roman invasions of Gaul and Britannia almost completely dispelled the Celtic dialect; no traces of it now remain, with the exception of a few Celtic words found incorporated with the French tongue. The Celtic man, however, still exists as perfect in form and character as when he made his first

* Brace's Races of the Old World, p. 439.

advent in Britain. Many other instances of like character might be cited. That language may or may not be permanent, is no longer doubted, being controlled by circumstances entirely. The predominant tongue will always prevail. The early German settlers of Pennsylvania and New York for a century endeavored to preserve their native German dialect, and transmit the same unimpaired to their posterity ; yet their descendants are now as thoroughly Anglo-Saxon as any of the people of the United States, many of them being even wholly unable to speak a single word of the German dialect.

The Pelasgic language, the root of the Greek and Latin, is no longer spoken by a single tongue, and if we were to attempt to trace present nations by the idioms which follow it, we should come in contact with a boundless débris of tongues, as from this language have originated an endless variety of tongues and dialects, adopted, too, by people as remote and foreign from the Pelasgic stock of people as the Germans and French are from each other.

The peoples who have been sufficiently national to preserve their dialects and language have also preserved their physical and mental type ; for instance, the Greeks, Jews, Chinese, Japanese and Italians, all preserve not only their language, but their characters, physical and mental.

The Sanscrit, the oldest language of Central Asia, is the root of nearly all the dialects of the early peoples of Europe, except the Germanic, which are more readily traced to the Zend and Persic dialects of the Iranian languages. The Gothic, Flemish, Dutch, Icelandic, Danish, Swedish, and Anglo-Saxon, all belong to the Germanic branch of the Zend and Persic languages.

The Finnish and Basque languages are of Hindoostanic origin, though the Basque seems to be a distinct dialect. They are a distinct family of people, allied with the Tartars, having preserved their tongue and type for over 2,000 years in Europe. Under the name of Iberians, they, at a very remote age, occupied Western Europe. Of the Finns it may be remarked, that their language partook of the Aryan, Iranian and Turanian dialects.

The Semitic tongue was spoken by the Semitic family proper and the Phœnicians, the latter spreading it over Northern Africa, especially Numidia and Mauri. Like that of the Egyptian and Hamitic, the Semitic was not confined to the original family, but spread broadcast throughout Western Asia and Northern Africa, and the eastern portion of the continent. Even the Galla, of Abyssinia, seem to have the Semitic pronoun. The Hamitic and Semitic dialects were very similar, if, indeed, they were not substantially the same.

The Egyptian (now the Coptic) is very ancient, and seems to be based upon the Aryan and Iranian languages. The Fellahs and Berbers spoke branches of the Egyptian tongue. We thus far have been unable to discover any satisfactory evidence warranting the conclusion that there is any new race of mankind; and it is equally true that there are no indigenous races in Africa, Europe or America, nor upon any any of the isles of the seas. Outside of Asia, all are, as races, emigrants. It may, therefore, with safety, be asserted, that the five races all had their origin in Asia, and from these primitive types are derived all the families of man existing upon the globe.

The innumerable families of man now dwelling in the various countries of the earth, though considered indigenous, are referable to the primitive races, white, yellow, and black, of Asia, the Malay and American, even, being derived from the Caucasian, Mongolian, and African.

CHAPTER IV.

THE EARTH'S CRUST.

THE causes now disturbing the crust of the globe did not, it would seem, produce the wonderful revolutions it has undergone since it became a solid mass. Whether the earth was disrupted by sudden convulsions occasioned by internal force, or torn in fragments by deluging waters, has not been revealed; but that it has been wrought upon by mighty forces is very manifest.

Asia, a very ancient portion of the earth, seems to be held in position by a great volcanic trunk, which, in very remote ages, brought forth, and still holds her vast mountains in position. In the east there are two ranges, between which lies the great Gobi Desert. These mountains were hove up, in all probability, as soon as any portion of the globe, except Africa, yet late in the calendar of time, compared with the formation of the general body of the earth. Oysters were in existence when these mountains were brought up, as is shown by their numerous beds found on the sides of the Himalayas, some of them three miles above the level of the sea. In Thibet beds of oyster shells have been found upon the mountains at an elevation of 17,000 feet above the sea level.

Tradition, historical records, and physical facts, fully attest that vast and mighty changes have taken place in the surface of the earth in Asia, since the mountains were elevated. The Arctic shore has been for many centuries gradually rising, whilst whole regions in the southern part of the continent have been subsiding. In the Chinese and Japanese seas, vast regions of land have been submerged—entirely disappeared. In remote ages, by upheavals, lakes have been dried up, and rivers absorbed. Cashmere and Nepaul are instances of the kind remembered by the inhabitants of the country in traditionary story. The western Gobi was drained into the upper Irtish, and Lake Balcach, of the same district, was absorbed in the sand. Very heavy concussions have been heard in Asia, and so great was the convulsions in some instances that buildings and cities were destroyed and many human lives sacrificed. In Japan the convulsions have been still more severe and violent. In the north of Asia the mountains dip into the ocean, and then rise again, producing vast desolation.[*]

The Straits of Babel Mandeb present indisputable evidences that the time was when the waters of the Red Sea did not flow into the Indian Ocean. These Straits are of volcanic origin, "the volcano having torn the principal chain of Central Africa from the old crest of Southern Arabia."[†]

Before the giving way of the barrier above referred to, and that which divided the waters of the Mediterranean from the Atlantic Ocean, the countries lying east and west, and Northern Africa, and Southern Asia Minor, and regions in that vicinity, were covered by the waters of the Mediterranean. The Straits of Gibraltar were probably formed when the waters of the Black Sea broke through the Hellespont.

The Greeks and Romans were well satisfied that some great internal power tore Sicily from Italy, Cyprus from Syria, Euboea from Boeotia Atalante, and Mocris from Euboeœ and Leucosia from Sirens.

We learn from Pliny, that in the reign of Tiberius, no less

* Natural History of the Human Species, p. 106.
† Johnson's Physical Atlas, p. 5.

than fifty-seven earthquakes occurred in a single year, during which time, by one extraordinary concussion, twelve cities of Asia were laid prostrate in a single night.* Rome even vibrated under these mighty convulsions. During these paroxysms the face of the country was materially altered—whole districts became seas and lakes, and islands were hove up at the same time. During such convulsions Delos and Rhodes were brought forth; also Anapha, Nea, Serpho, Theria, Therosia, Heira and many others.

Plato reports that the Atlantic Ocean covered over a vast portion of the land along its coast; and more recently, according to Pliny, great changes had taken place of like character. He notes:

"Acarnania has been overwhelmed by the Arabian Gulf; Achaia, by the Corinthian; Europe and Asia, by the Propontus and Pontus; and besides these the sea has rent asunder Leucas, Antirrhum, the Hellespont and the two Bosphori.

"The sea, near the Palus Mæotis, has carried away Pyrrha and Autissa, also Elice, and Bura in the Gulf of Corinth. In Sicily, also, the half of the city of Tyndaris, and all the part of Italy which is wanting, was in like manner carried away."†

This author also described a percussion, at which time two mountains, in the district of Mutina, rushed together, falling upon each other with a very loud crash, and then receding, while in the day time flame and smoke issued from them.‡

The River Indus now runs nearly due south, yet it is manifest, from the face of the country and its delta, that it originally flowed south-east from the terminal point of the Lukkee mountain, being a space of nearly ten degrees. Thus, a vast region of country by this river was rendered uninhabitable, and then left dry land in course of time. The delta, however, as the whole region encroached upon appears to be such, may have been covered by the river at the same time. This is probable, though not very likely.

Ceylon was once joined to Asia, but severed by volcanic agency, or some other internal cause. The early people of India consider Ceylon the original abode of man—the Garden of Eden. The spot designated as the Garden of Eden, is on the top of a

* Pliny's Natural History, Vol. I., p. 116.   † Ibid., p. 120..   ‡ Ibid., p. 115.

mountain which rises 7720 feet above the sea. There is no doubt about the very remote peopling of Ceylon, and probably long before it was rent from the continent. Ruined cities fully attest the submergence of this Island. These ruins are perhaps as ancient as any upon the globe.

Australasia is composed of fragments of the continents of South America and Asia. The islands present the ruins of a submerged region which one day was high above water, but now at the bottom of the sea, which lies between the two continents. Every one passing over this region is struck with the vestiges of a ruined world.

The eastern portion of Asia is subject to volcanic convulsions, of extraordinary character. * The country came up from beneath the sea since the Mongolians occupied central and northern Asia. They start off in their fabulous history with the story that they expended great toil in endeavoring to rid the country of lakes and marshes. The waters, even recently, spread over the territory to the great destruction of life and property. The Yellow Sea in 1845 rose and swept the land to the destruction of several thousand lives.

The Marian islands are now low and small, but they were one day doubtless large and elevated. The great city of Tamen stands so far out in the water that it can only be reached by boats. Lord Anson in his voyage, found upon one of these islands a row of upright stones, in form of obelisks, each surmounted by a coping block. These were constructed by a race of people other than the present population. Dr. Darwin says these islands are the remains of lands of much greater extent than now presented, which have sunk beneath the sea. The group is composed of volcanic cones and low coral reefs. Northern and north-western Asia has been less disturbed by internal agencies than any other portion of the continent. The chief rupture appearing to be the straits of Behring, a channel about forty miles wide and of no great depth. There are no very marked evidences of any great percussion where the straits were formed, and no evidence that the level of either sea was al-

---

* In the year 1845, the waters of the Gulf of Pechee-lee, rose to such height as to destroy several hundred thousand human lives, and ruin all the houses of the province, effecting the total ruin of 16,000,000 of the population.—The Natural History of the Human Species, p. 116.

tered in the least, when the waters of the two seas became united. But since the arctic regions have been rising in Asia and Europe there is a current in the straits, and, as northern Asia is still rising, the current is increasing.

The Caspian sea, which has no outlet, was once connected with the Black Sea. At that period the latter inundated a large portion of southern Russia, and set back its tides to the Baltic, White Sea, and Arctic Ocean, by the Gulf of Finland and Bothia.

The continent of Africa has but little evidence of having undergone any very marked changes by any known causes. It stands out in the tabular form as if hove up from amid the waves in mass, some of its mountain peaks being crowned with limestone. Africa is, perhaps, the oldest of the continents, its age is not fixed by any date of human circulation; all is surmise; but the continent is so aged as to be worn out and exhausted to a measurable extent.

Volcanoes exist in Abyssinia and along the south-east coast; also on the west coast; but they do not appear to have disturbed the main land materially, except the tearing away of Madagascar on the east, and the islands on the south-west, from the continent. The mighty volcano of Teneriffe has frequently shaken the earth and sea for hundreds of miles, but has not altered the continent since the historic period. Etna also has frequently shaken Sicily and Italy.*

The western continent has undergone marked changes by volcanic influces; yet there are strong indications of alterations of surface of the country not attributable to such agencies. The neighboring islands were doubtless once a part of the continent, as the whole region, from Barbadoes to Vera Cruz, presents many indications of a violent disruption during the present geological superficies of the earth. The event may may have been since the deluge, and, if so, the ruined buildings and pyramids may be readily accounted for.

The boulders are ample witnesses of the submergence of the northern portion of the country. If they were brought to their present resting-places by floating ice it is hard to tell how high the stage of water in which they floated thither may have been.

---

* The beds of lava that have issued from Etna, prove it to have been in activity over 14,000 years.—Pouchet's Plurality of Races, p. 122, note.

For aught that appears to the contrary, it may have covered every hill and filled every valley.

These boulders are not confined to this continent, but are strewn over Europe and Asia in great profusion.* Those found in England are granite, syenite, and greenstone. They came not from the north, but from the land where is now the British channel. One of these boulders at Pagham measures twenty-seven feet in circumference. They were drifted in the ice and dropped to their present position whilst England was submerged, during the glacial period, as now supposed.

Boulders are found 5000 feet above the ocean in Europe, and in the United States equally as elevated. In New England they are very massive. One is upon the side of Hoosac Mountain, 1000 feet above the valley, over which it was transported, weighing 680 tons. They have been often brought several hundred miles. Those found in the state of Ohio, lie scattered over the the state as far south as the Ohio river, some of enormous bulk. They were taken from their beds in Wisconsin—four or five hundred miles distant from where they are now.

Boulders are also existing in Switzerland, Germany, France, Spain and Italy, and show an overflowing of the country after the mountains had been elevated, being found upon their sides, even on the Himalayas. Their course can be traced by the marks upon the rocks over which they were drifted. Had the countries where these boulders drifted been populated, the people would either have perished by the floods, or been driven from their abodes.

No record of the boulder era is known to be in existence. If the countries were then peopled, and the people perished, their remains will no doubt yet be found under or in the drift deposited in that age. The boulders were most likely deposited in the glacial era, in those regions at least.

The submergence of the countries in the boulder period, must have destroyed the vegetable products, as it is not possible such a flood of waters as floated these rocks would pass over the country without materially changing its physical character. During this time, it has been supposed, the foundation of coal was depos-

* There is a large boulder in the plain near Mount Sinai. It is a block of granite nearly twenty feet square.—Wonders of Geology, Vol. I., p. 210, *note*.

ited. In some places these boulders are so located as to almost warrant the conclusion that they were, in geological sense, deposited recently.

The submergence of Wales, to the extent of 1400 feet, as proved by glacial shells, would require 56,000 years at the rate of two and a-half feet per century.* If these rocks were of the glacial period, they are certainly not recently deposited. They are taken from the Alps, and carried across the deepest and most rugged valleys of the globe, a distance of fifty miles, and many of them of such enormous bulk as to be incredible. One resting on the hill 900 feet above Lake Neufchatel is forty feet in diameter. Some contain 50,000 cubic feet of stone. One of limestone, at Devens, near Bex, which was drifted thirty miles, contains 161,000 cubic feet. Those resting on the Jura and opposite Lake Geneva, are from Mont Blanc.†

The United States contains many other evidences, besides the boulders, of having been under water since the upheaval of the mountains. Her great mountains, it will be observed, all run in transverse direction to the course of the rivers; and that the rivers have cut their way through these barriers to the sea. Such has been the case of the Potomac, Susquehannah, Juniata, Delaware, and James River. The Ohio, on its way, cut through an almost interminable barrier near Silver Creek. Before the Potomac made its way through the Blue Ridge, or the James River ruptured the mound which hemmed in its waters, a vast lake must have existed in the Shenandoah valley, and in that of the Conecocheague, extending from Staunton to Chambersburg, and filling the several valleys in the vicinity of the North mountain and Blue Ridge, to the Alleghanies, and beyond the Susquehanna to the Schuylkill and Delaware. The Blue Ridge is a geological curiosity. Unlike others of such magnitude, this huge mountain range is a vast heap of detached blocks of different magnitudes mixed with vegetable mould, all having the appearance of being deposited there as drift. It is very obvious that the

---

* The submergence and re-elevation of the country, according to Prof. Ramsey, would require 224,000 years.—Antiquities of Man, p. 285.

† The Alpine erratics are found at an altitude of 3450 feet above the sea. The granite blocks found at this elevation, being 2015 feet above Lake Neufchatel, were torn from the east shoulder of Mont Blanc.—Lyell's Antiquities of Man, p. 300.

draining of this vast lake would materially change the face of the country.

The valley of the Hudson also was one day crossed by a high barrier above West Point, near Newburg, which dammed up the waters of the Hudson to the rapids at Fort Edwards. At the time the water of the Ohio river was set back from the barrier at Silver Creek, its tides reached to the base of the Alleghanies, at least to Pittsburgh. This being the case, a vast extent of the western country must have been under water. The Silver Creek barrier would not only set the waters of the Ohio back to Pittsburgh, but extend them beyond Lake Erie, and to the north of Lake Superior. During this period the coal beds of the regions covered by the waters were supplied with the vegetable matter which formed the stone coal.

The regions of country referred to give strong indications of having been under water since their upheaval. The boulders seem to have been brought thither since the draining of these vast oceans, as they generally are located upon the surface of the ground.

There is no evidence that man existed in the regions bordering these lakes when they broke through their barriers, other than his remains found in the Mississippi Valley, and other physical indications, such as the stump found at Cincinnati. If he dwelt east of the Alleghanies, he must have been swept away by the overwhelming floods of the Shenandoah, and other valleys where the water had been confined.

There was no place of escape on any of the lowlands. The same was the condition of things west of the Alleghanies. At that time the human remains found in a fossil state at Natchez, may have been buried in the drift and the eighty feet of earth piled upon the stump at Cincinnati, though it would seem otherwise, and that these vast accumulations were deposited after the manner of the delta of the Nile, and other great rivers.

CHAPTER V.

PHYSICAL MAN.

MAN'S physical body, a solid composed of gases.—Living animalcules in the blood.—The nervous system.—Brain the organ of the mind.—Circulation of the blood.—Animal life.—Unity of the races.—Types of mankind.—The Deluge.—Turanian, Semitic and Hamitic orders of man.—Origin of the human species.—The Book of Genesis.—Caucasian, Mongolian, Malay, American and African races.—Families and groups.—Four distinct races existing 3,300 years ago.

PHYSICALLY, man is the most perfectly organized being in creation. He possesses many superior qualities not enjoyed by any of the lower animals, yet breathes of the same atmosphere, is composed of the same kinds of material matter, and lives by virtue of the same laws of animal life; only differing from the lower animals in this respect by his organism. By his five senses he derives all his knowledge of the external world. His body is a solid, composed of various substances, namely: carbon, hydrogen, oxygen, and nitrogen gases; phosphorus, sulphur, iron, earth and saline matter. These are organized by imperceptible parts or atoms, and globules, all of the same size, each being 75-100 parts of an inch, and all cohering by attraction; but having at the same time no connecting texture.

In the blood of man, in his adult state, there are living animalcules, so minute that they cannot be detected without the aid of the microscope. Ten thousand of them may exist in a space not larger than a grain of sand. Man is, indeed, "fearfully and wonderfully made."

The idea that all things were made out of nothing will be readily comprehended, when it is understood of what man's body is composed. The gases, which enter so largely into his composition, are as nothing; we can neither see nor feel them, yet they exist, pervading all space; the air we breath is but gas; our food is mainly of the same elements, in an organized form; by attraction our bodies are held together; remove this agency and they would at once return to their original nothingness.

"All are but parts of one stupendous whole,
　Whose body nature is, and God the soul."

The bones constitute the frame work of the body, and are a wonderful display of mechanism. They are 245 in number, composed principally of lime, hard as limestone and nearly as imperishable. Each individual of all the races has the same number of bones, though differing in many other particulars.

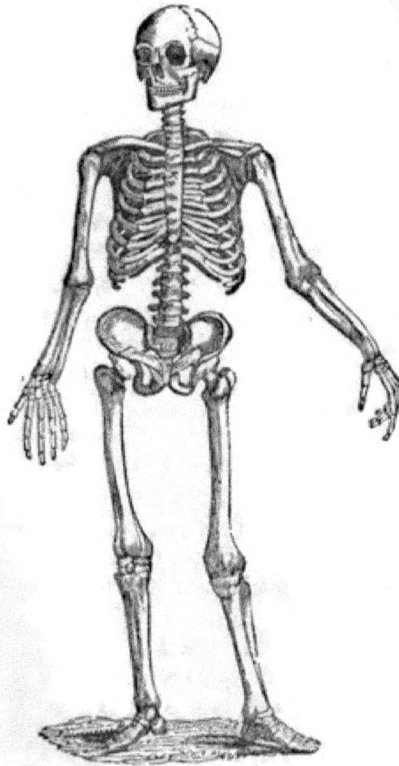

The nervous system is the most interesting and mysterious portion of man's physical constitution. The brain is the center of the nervous functions, nerves constituting the galvanic battery of the human system, and by means of which the lightning of the soul is conducted to the seat of thought.

The blood is the great nourisher of the body, and generally conceded to be the life of man; but it is not any more so than some of the other fluids of the system. Though every individual can feel the action of the blood at each pulsation, its circulation as a physiological fact was unknown until in the early part of the 16th century, when Hervey discovered it. Its temperature is the same in each individual, in all climates, being 100° Fahrenheit. It is claimed, with much plausibility, that the heat of the human body is generated in the blood by means of oxygen taken into the lungs, and carbonic acid discharged therefrom by respiration. Heat in this way may be induced, but animal life cannot in such mode be restored, or for a moment prolonged. Heat and life depend upon a proper organism; and if this is destroyed, life at once becomes extinct. Were it otherwise, life could be prolonged indefinitely by the introduction of this gas into the respiratory organs. Another theory is that the iron of the blood is the source of animal life; that the iron becomes heated by the process of breathing, by which means electricity is generated in the lungs. Iron being a conductor, and electricity heat, so long as there is iron in the blood, it is claimed there will be heat in the system. It is a fact well established that the subject may be warmed up to the proper degree of animal life and heat, by electricity, yet vitality will not be restored.

What is life? is the most perplexing subject connected with man's physical organism. He lives, glows with life and animation; but why, no mortal has been able to tell. The living principle has not yet been revealed to man. The principle of life is peculiar to each individual; were it otherwise, the life of one subject (if the life be in the blood) might be transferred to another. Old age, by this process, could be restored to youth, and the dead subject quickened and revived to life. The time may come when this fugitive principle of animal life may be discovered. We are not without hope upon the subject, even if the process of discovery be slow.

FRANKLIN.

We should not despair of success, when we consider it required nearly six thousand years to discover the circulation of the blood; and an equal period almost, to convince the world that the lightnings of the heavens were but electricity. By the genius of Franklin the "Immortal Jove," who for so many ages appalled the world by his terrible voice and fiery glances, was compelled to leave his celestial habitation and submit to the will of man on earth.

> " Nature, and nature's laws, lay hid in night;
> God said, let Franklin be—and all was light."

The unity and common origin of the several varieties of the human species have been so generally received by the public at large for the true exposition of these subjects, as to make it almost sacrilegious to assume any other hypothesis. It has seemed sufficient to simply affirm that in very remote ages only two persons dwelt upon the earth, and that from them all the races and families of man derive their descent. No one should dispute the Bible History of the creation; it is not at all necessary to do so, in order to show the origin of the races and types of mankind. The author of the book of Genesis, it is very plain, did not intend to give a detailed account of the creation, or the history of man, any further than to show the line of the descent of the Hebrews, and assign the reason for the overthrow of the antedeluvians by the deluge, and repeopling of the earth by Noah and his family.

If there was only one race of mankind the vexed question of common origin would be put at rest by the Genesis. There being several distinct races, and many marked differences in their physical aspect, it is impossible to trace them to a common parentage by the ordinary rules of descent. They may be traced, to a limited extent, to their origin by their physical development and mental capacity. These, in the absence of authentic information, are the only safe guides to follow in discovering the lines of descent and origin of the types.

Ethnologists have not all agreed upon the number of the races. Cuvier divided man into three types: Caucasian, Mongol and Negro. Pickering reports eleven races; Morton, Gilddon and others five, viz.: Caucasian, Mongolian, Malay, American and African, whilst others divide the families of man into

many more races, as we shall notice in a subsequent chapter.
Five types are even more than we think justly warranted by the
strict rules of ethnology. The red, white and black are evidently
the primitive races. We shall, in this work, however, adopt the
popular theory of five races, standing in order thus: Caucasian,
Mongolian, Malay, American and African, each distinguished
by the color of the skin, and other marked peculiarities.

In the year of the world 1656, as computed by biblical
scholars and chronologists, the whole population of the globe
perished by the deluge, save Noah and his family. From this it
is forcibly impressed upon the mind that Noah and his sons were
the ancestors of all the races and families of man now existing
upon the earth; hence all are traceable through these channels
to a common origin, if the premises be correct. If there were
but one distinct race, this would be a rational conclusion; but
when several distinct types are presented with very marked differences of physical aspect, the question of common origin and
unity of the races becomes one of doubtful probability.

Until recently the ethnological authors appeared embarrassed
in the investigation of man's physical history by the Hebrew
narration of his origin; but now, since ethnology is being better understood, great facts are being evolved upon the subject of the races; and what has heretofore remained mysterious
in their history, is beginning to be satisfactorily explained. To
facilitate the investigation of the subject, the races and families
of man have been classified under four leading heads, viz.:
Aryan, Turanian, Semitic, and Hamite. The Aryans are derived from Japeth, Semitic from Shem, Hamite from Ham; and
the Turanian receives its name from Turan the country beyond
Iran.

The Turanian family embraces the Mongolian race and mixed
peoples of that type, in which division are the Chinese, Japanese,
Tartars, Finns, Lapps, Mongols, Calmucks, Samoieds, Esquimaux,
some of the American tribes, and other less noted peoples of
Asia and Africa.

The Semitic family embraces the Hebrews, Phœnicians,
Carthagenians, Iberians, Spaniards and other kindred tribes.

The Hamites include the Canaanites and other kindred nations. They were so closely allied with the Semitics as to be

7

literally one and the same family; not Negroes or black persons, as has been generally claimed.

The Aryan includes all families of fair complexion and those of Caucasian blood, whatever may be their color.

Though it is admitted there are five distinct types, it is worthy of remark that the red, white, and black are the primitive complexions, and have never changed. The Ethiopian has not changed his skin; the white man has not yet put on the color or adopted the features of the Negro, nor has the red man become a Caucasian. They are all the same as they were 4500 years ago.* The Negro had then his thick lips, black skin, protruding jaws, woolly hair, flat nose and curved legs; the Semitic had then his tawny skin and bent nose; and the Turanian is still what he was 3000 years before the Christian era.

We are not informed by the Genesis what the complexion of the original race was, but Josephus, a learned Jewish author, affirms that Adam was red and gives as his reason for so determining, that Adam was made of red earth. This being the case, by the law of nature his descendants would be of his complexion; consequently Noah and his sons would be of the complexion of their great ancestor Adam. This theory would only account for the red or copper-colored race, if the offspring will always prove true to nature, and bear the complexion of the parent.

For want of a better theory, it has been claimed that the three sons of Noah had different complexions; that Ham was black, Shem red, and Japeth white, and that their descendants bear their complexions. There are several prominent facts in support of this theory. Shem and his sons occupied the country from the Euphrates to the Indian Ocean; and from them Chaldeans, Assyrians, Syrians, Lydians, Hebrews and Arabs derive their descent. Ham and his sons occupied Philistia, Canaan, Ethiopia, Lybia, and from them it is claimed all people of dark complexion derive their descent. Japath and his sons occupied the country between the Taurus Mountains and the river Don, and Europe to Cadiz; and from him Greeks, Medes, Persians, Egyptians, Sythians, Gauls, Celts, Hindoos, Turks, Gomerians, and Iberians derive their descent. These several families were doubtless the roots of at least a portion of the present popula-

* Plurality of Races. p. 87.

tion of the globe. But when the other varieties of mankind originated is the all important question for solution, and which can only be determined, if at all, by the mode already intimated —their physical and intellectual development.

The doctrines of La Marck and others on the subject of grada-tion, are of very doubtful probability, to say the least; * and the theory that food and climate will produce a race different from the original type, is equally unfounded. Marked changes may take place in the appearance of a race by food and climate, but the type will never be so far altered in any degree as to be a dif-ferent race from the original.

The several races are known by the following characteristics:

The Caucasian, by fair complexion, large oval skull, the interior portion being finely formed, full and elevated; the hair is of various colors, fine, long, and frequently curling; beard heavy; features well-proportioned; chin full; nose prominent; teeth vertical; eyes full, bright, and spark-ling. The skin of this race, in some cases, is quite dark, as is the case of the Hindoos and Nilotics. The leading families of this race are the Germanic, Celtic, Nilotic, Libyan, and Hindoostanic.

CAUCASIAN GROUP.

The Mongolian, as having a sallow, olive-colored skin, long straight, dark hair; scanty beard; broad short nose; black eyes, set obliquely in the head; arched eyebrows; oblong skull, and wide frontal head. The Chinese, Japanese, Mongols and Esquimaux, are most prominent families of this type.

The Malay, by a dark brown complexion; black, coarse, lank hair; square forehead; long jaws; large mouth; broad nose and

* The Thibetians believe that mankind descended from the ape. The Pelas-gians believed they sprang from the ground ; and the Chaldeans believed that from the blood of Belus, which mingled with the dust, he having cut off his own head, man was formed.—Man—Where, Whence, and Whither, p. 139.

MONGOLIAN GROUP.

MALAY GROUP.

AMERICAN GROUP.

vertical teeth. The Malays proper, the Siamese, Cochin-Chinese, Polynesians, and some of the Indian tribes of North and South America, are leading families of this race.

The American, as of reddish copper color complexion having black, long coarse hair; scanty beard; tumid lips; large mouth; aquiline nose; black eyes, deeply set; small skull, with receding forehead. The race consists of many tribes, with no very marked difference in physical aspect.

The African, by having a black complexion, with black curling hair; large prominent eyes; thick, flat nose; low, receding forehead; thick, heavy skull; large mouth; thick, pouted lips, and long, protruding jaws. There are many families of this race, the chief of which seem to be the Mandigoes, Jolafs, Guineas, Ashantes, Dahomians and Australians.

Type is a term used to designate those original or primitive forms of mankind, which are independent of physical or climatic influences. For instance, the white man is a type, as his physical constitution remains the same under all circumstances. It has never become transformed—remains the same as originally created. Type is synonomous with species, though not with race. The term race is applied rather indifferently to families, groups, and types; for instance, in speaking of the Australians, authors call them a race; so also the Arabians, Ethiopians, Negrillos, and indeed, all the subordinate varieties of mankind.

This classification tends to confusion; but it is perhaps too late now to change the public mind in regard to the proper classification of the several orders and varieties of the races. To avoid confusion in these pages, we shall use the

AFRICAN GROUP.

term type in designating races or the primitive stock, such as Caucasian, for the white race. The subordinate varieties will be included in the terms families, and groups, nations, and tribes. Keeping in mind that the terms type, race, and species are used in the same general sense as meaning the same thing.

Some of the leading families of the Caucasians and Mongolians, for instance the Jews, Egyptians, Arabs, Mongols, and Japanese, have so long retained their definite characters, as to enable them almost to be called types; some of them have indeed been thus designated.*

The Red, White, Black, and Yellow races have been in existence, according to the Egyptian records, for at least 3,300 years. They are plainly represented upon the Egyptian monuments thus early in the world's history; and though it has not yet been fully ascertained, it is strongly conjectured that they have so existed for more than 5,000 years. If the geological facts presented in this volume can be relied upon as even an approximation to the truth, man's existence upon the globe was at a period

* Types of Mankind, p. 81.

far more remote than any historical or chronological reckonings fix it.*

Geology, doubtless, shows the globe to have existed many thousands of years, and as compared with man's advent upon it, almost from eternity, as countless periods have seemed to precede one another, in its geological history. The primitive rocks, as regards their origin, as far as man's knowledge goes, may be considered eternal. No vestiges of history exists pointing to their formation in regard to time. They were not all produced in the beginning of things, in the condition they are now found, but in the night of ages have undergone marked changes. The term primitive, however, is not so comprehensive in a geological sense as generally supposed. The granite class are doubtless of igneous origin like the volcanic; yet geologists have failed to detect the plutonic granite in process of formation. They are vastly different from the volcanic, being of crystalline texture, and do not contain tuffs or breccias, nor any traces of organic bodies. Their place, as a general rule, is beneath all other rocks, though they have been found protruding up through other formations, but never repose upon the volcanic.†

The metamorphic series, consisting of mica-schist, clay, slate, chlorite-schist, marble, etc., contain no organic remains, and is said to be stratified, though some of the class are as crystalline as granite. Their origin is even more uncertain, in a geological point of view, than the plutonic.

The stratified rocks, including the various orders of calcareous formations, and in which organic remains are discovered, are supposed (as has been noted in another place,) to be formed under water, among which the coral may be noted as a leading class. The great mounds of the rapids of the Ohio river, at Louisville, Kentucky, are considered by Sir Charles Lyell to be a coral reef.‡

This system of rocks has been formed subsequent to the granite and metamorphic, though the date of their formation has not been ascertained; but in some instances, such as the coral reef of Florida, has been forming since man became an

* Evidences of Man's Place in Nature, by Huxley, p. 140, 141.
† Principles of Zoology, by Agassiz and Gould, p. 216.
‡ Elements of Geology, p. 545.

inhabitant of the earth. Because organic remains do not exist in unstratified systems of rocks, is not proof positive that man did not exist coeval with their formation, though most probably he did not then occupy a place in nature, as these systems doubtless were produced by heat, and at a time when the globe was unfit for the occupancy of the human race. There is no foreign matter in the composition of the unstratified rocks, each series being composed of its peculiar elements: the essential ingredients of granite, being feldspar, quartz, and mica. If animal or vegetable matter had at any period been mingled with the constituent elements of the igneous rocks, it was absorbed by the heated mass. It is in the rock system of non-igneous character we must look for organic remains, and there is where they are to be found, and in great abundance, animal and vegetable, with fossil man. The tracks of animals, now discovered upon the solid rocks, show them to have been in existence in full life, whilst the rocks were in their plastic state.

CHAPTER VI.

NATURAL HISTORY OF MAN.

HOWEVER scattered and confused the races of mankind
may now appear, the original purpose of the Creator is
still quite apparent. He doubtless designed each race to occupy
its appropriate sphere, and fill its destiny. The place of each
was designated by Him, as the primitive types can still be traced
to their original places of abode.

It is a universal law of nature, that creatures will propagate
and multiply their own kind : this is self-evident in regard to
man. From white men and white women spring white descendants, and from black parents originate black offspring. It is just
as evident that cohabitation between the whites and blacks will
produce a different offspring from either parent, yet partaking
of the nature of both ; though this offspring is not a new race,
as hybrids never become races. Each offspring of this order is
referable to the primitive types.

Keeping in view the great fact that the five races have existed
as far back into the past as history and tradition lead us, and
that during that period no race has become extinct, or a new one
been produced, and the primitive types remaining intact, we are
not quite at open sea in regard to the origin of the various

nations and families of mankind now found broadcast over the earth. Though scattered as they now are, their location seems to be not a matter of necessity, but of choice ; and, wherever located, the leading physical characteristics of the primitive races remain unaltered.

There has been much controversy among naturalists on the subject of the origin of races. Some have assumed that they were created in distinct orders, whilst others affirmed that they all sprung from one common source ; and to sustain the latter view, the Scripture passage, " Eve was the mother of all living," has been quoted. Whatever weight this passage may be entitled to, it does not disprove that there were several orders of men created, at least such do exist, and existing, they must be presumed to have been created, and not by themselves, but by their great author, God.

Physically, man, at his birth, is much inferior to the lower animals. His advent into the world is fraught with many disadvantages ; whilst not wholly inanimate, he is entirely helpless. Nature obliges him, alone of all animated nature, to clothe himself, whilst to all the rest she has given various kinds of coverings. But thus helpless and neglected as he is at his birth, he, nevertheless, brings with him into the world the germ of thought, and his body, feeble as it may be, is the tenement of the soul.

To a very great extent man is a vicious animal, more savage than the lower animals. The latter live in peace with their own kind, but mankind appear to delight in the destruction of their own species. His greatest misfortunes are occasioned by his own race.

> " Man's inhumanity to man
> Makes countless thousands mourn."

The physical peculiarities and differences in the several species of mankind give strong reasons, if not conclusive ones, to doubt their common parentage. So strong have some of the peculiarities impressed themselves upon the mind, that learned ethnologists have been bold to aver that all mankind do not derive their descent from Adam, and assert that there were different creations, in which the more prominent of the species had their origin ; and that these, amalgamating with those of other creations, produced the several subordinate varieties now found scattered throughout the globe. Some have even gone so far as to assume that man is the offspring of the lower animals, and that his original type is visible in the monkey tribes.* However unfounded this theory may be, the idea of gradation of the races is plausible to the common observer, who only looks to the lower animals for proof of this theory. That there are grades of the races is very evident, and orders and degrees in the animal kingdom, and hence, when it is observed that there are marked differences in the human species, the mind, for a better reason, adopts the theory that there are different creations and orders of mankind, and that these, like the lower animals, may be recognized by their physical development and general characteristics.

No cause as yet, as before observed, has been found capable of changing the primitive types of man. Amid the constant changes and succession of individuals, and of the character of the surface of the earth, there can be traced to the earliest ages the form and character of the several types first impressed by the Creator, uninterruptedly transmitted from parent to offspring. " One generation passeth away, but another cometh, like in form and every other particular : and however man may become modified by education or other influences, is born the same helpless, dependent being, with the same predominant passions and faculties, as first bestowed upon the original parent, and is cast upon the world without having any control over his origin or place of his birth."

Historically, we know but little of man's origin, except what is contained in the Genesis, and there is a remarkable silence in that sacred record on the subject, his creation and fall simply being announced. Nothing is said of his physical constitution, or extent of his mental capacity, after he was expelled from Eden.

The history of man teaches that his origin was wisely designed. The work of creation would not have been complete without his production, as the head of all animated nature.

Man differs very materially from even the most perfectly or-

---

* The man-like Apes and the Chimpanzes walk erect as man by times ; but the great Orang-Outang goes on all fours. His arms are longer than his legs. —Evidences as to Man's Place in Nature, by Huxley, pp. 16–20–45–46–47—48 49–50.

ganized of the lower animals,* aside from his capacity to reason. The power of speech, erect position, and elevated head, makes him the superior of all animals. But when he is considered clothed with the power of reason, and as capable of considering the works of the universe, and as an accountable being, the pretended comparison between him and the most intelligent of the lower animals becomes chimer-ical in the extreme. None of the latter are capable of walk-ing erect. The chimpanzee and gorilla are the nearest approach to the human species, yet they fall far short of reaching the lowest grade of mankind ; they are not bipeds, but animals cre-ated to run upon all fours.†

THE GORILLA.

The human head and face show a marked difference between man and the lower animals. Man alone has the ca-

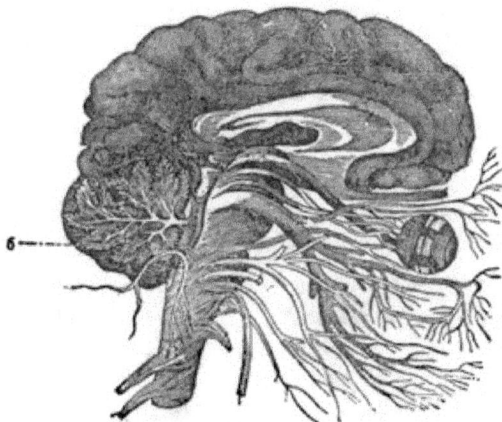

THE HUMAN BRAIN.

* Agassiz considers that animals have an immortal principle, the same as man, and the capacity to reason.—Essay on Classification, pp. 96–7. London. 1859.

† The gorilla does not walk upright, generally, but can stand erect and walk like man.—Evidences of Man's Place in Nature, by Huxley, pp. 62–3.

pacity to reason; and no quadruped has such magnitude and convolutions of brain in that part of the cranium known as the intellectual seat.

The size of the human brain varies in volume in the several types. It being the organ of the mind, the greater its volume the more highly will be the display of the mental manifestations, as size is admitted to be a measure of power.

Dr. Morton, after great research, presented the public with a chart of the internal capacity of the skulls of the several races and leading families of mankind. During his researches, he measured no less than an hundred Egyptian skulls, taken from the ancient tombs and temples of Egypt. Below is a copy of the Doctor's chart:

	Cubic Inches.
Teutonic Group	92
Pelasgic "	84
Celtic "	87
Semitic "	89
Malay "	85
Chinese "	82
Negro "	83
Hindoo "	80
Fellahs "	80
Egyptian, Ancient, Group	80
Toltec Group	79
Hottentot "	75
Australian Group	75 *

The following is another of the Doctor's charts, which includes many other families and groups:

Races and Families.	No. of Skulls.	Largest I. C.	Mean I. C.
Teutonic Family—German,	18	114	90
" " English,	5	105	96
" " Anglo-American,	7	97	90
Pelasgic—Persians,	10	94	84
" Armenians,	10	94	84
" Circassians,	10	94	84
Celtic—Native Irish,	6	97	87
Indostanic Bengalees,	32	91	80

* Types of Mankind, p. 454.

Semitic—Arabs,	. . .	3	98	89
Nilotic—Fellahs,	. .	17	96	80
Ancient Pelasgic, Tombs, Egypt,	18	97	88
Nilotic,	" "	55	96	80
Chinese Mongolians,	. .	6	91	82
Malay Group,	. . .	20	97	86
Polynesian,	. . . .	3	84	83
American Group—Peruvians,	155	101	75
Toltec Family—Mexicans,	22	92	79
Barbarous Tribes—Iroquois,	161	104	84
Native African Family,	.	62	99	83
American-born Negroes,	.	12	89	82
Hottentots,	. . .	3	83	75
Australian Family,	. .	8	83	75

From this table it is shown that there is no difference in the volume of brain of the ancient Pelasgic family, being eighty-eight cubic inches in both instances. The ancient Egyptians and their modern representatives, the Fellahs, are also the same —eighty cubic inches. The Hindoos present the same volume as the Egyptians. The civilized Toltecs measure seventy-seven cubic inches, and the barbarous tribes eighty-four cubic inches, being seven inches in favor of the savage.

The average size of the brain of the white race of America is twenty-two and a half inches in circumference, the aboriginal American's being nineteen and a half inches. Dr. Morton's chart gives the largest volume of brain (internal capacity of the skull) at 114 cubic inches. Dr. Wyman, upon his post-mortem examination of Daniel Webster, found the internal capacity to be 122 cubic inches. The average weight of the brain of the European is about forty-four ounces, troy weight; but Cuvier's brain weighed sixty-three ounces, Abercrombie's sixty-three ounces, Dr. Chalmers' sixty-three ounces, and Dupuytren's sixty-four ounces.

The development of the brain is not always a proper test of mental capacity, as often the smaller brains will surpass the larger in mental power. To make size the true measure of power, the whole physical organism must be perfect. A large brain may be often prevented from activity by some unknown disability. This is manifest, as we see, almost daily, in persons with large heads who make no display of mental endowment, and who are but little more than intellectual animals. Little reliance can therefore be placed upon the fact that a person has a large brain, unless his physical and mental organism is perfect.

Intellect is the creature of organism, and its development mainly depends upon the vital energies of the several individuals of each of the races for its proper manifestations. No one doubts but that the intellectual force of nations and people control their destinies. The superior endowments of the Caucasians have always kept them far in advance of all the other types and families of man, and the inferior mental capacity of some of the other types has kept them in a state of degradation. Man cannot create himself, but may improve the talents God has given him.

All the races are governed by the same immutable laws of life; but, however much a race may desire to rise to eminence, there can be no particular advancement unless there is the proper physical and mental developments.

The history of the world shows that but little advance in civilization has been made, except what has been accomplished by the white man. The Chinese, it is true, within their dominions have made considerable progress in the arts and sciences; also, the Japanese, who equal, if not surpass, the Chinese in the fine arts. And the Malays have made some advance in civilization, also. But the black man has remained in low barbarism, except where the whites have, in some instances, lifted him from his savage degradation, and brought him under the rules of European civilization. The Indians, with few exceptions, remain savages. The Toltecs and Aztecs had attained to a tolerable degree of refinement in Mexico. The Creeks and Cherokees, and other tribes, are now enjoying, to some extent, a refined civilization under the protection of the Federal Government.

The Africans inhabiting the regions south of Egypt have been in constant intercourse with the civilization of that country for more than four thousand years, without making any apparent advance above their native barbarism.* Like the Indians, they

* The Mandigos and Grebos, Caffres, Hottentots and Negroes, of Central Africa, had no idea of God before the advent of the missionaries; neither had the Australians.—Plurality of Races, p. 68.

despise refinement. The American Indians prefer their forest life, where they skulk, prepared to scalp the first white man, or Indian foe, who may chance to cross their path. This disposition to destroy each other, manifested among the Negroes and Indians, is a strong argument against the unity of the races.

The Mosaic record is the only written history we have of mankind, except what is preserved in the hieroglyphics of Egypt. Adam's creation took place 4000 years before the birth of Christ. He lived 930 years. Noah was born Anno Mundi 1056, and died A. M. 2006, having lived 950 years, 600 of which he passed in the old world before the deluge, and 350 years in the new world. He was born 126 years after the death of Adam, and 14 years after the death of Seth. Methusala, the oldest of the antedeluvians, lived until the year of the deluge, and his father died only five years prior to that event. Noah, therefore, must have been cognizant of the important transactions of the ante-deluvians. He lived in Canaan's time 129 years, in that of Enoch 86 years, in Methusala's time 600 years, and in Lamech's time 595 years.

As to the degree of intellectual culture of the antedeluvians, we have but little account. Adam was, doubtless, a botanist and zoologist, otherwise he would not have been capable of giving names to all the animals and plants, or distinguishing the "green herb" and "seed-bearing fruit trees."

The question of antedeluvian literature has greatly perplexed biblical scholars. . They generally concede that they were without alphabetic characters or writing; yet it is hardly probable that the genealogy of the people of that age, so minute in detail, found in the fifth, tenth, and eleventh chapters of Genesis, would have been preserved without being in writing. It is hardly possible it could be retained and transmitted by memory for nearly a thousand years, and given to the Hebrew author in such minute detail as is reported in the "Book of Genealogy."

The Book of Job is supposed to be the most ancient written document extant. He lived before the exode of the Hebrews, about 200 years. He speaks as familiarly of writing and books as an author would at the present day. He exclaims, "Oh! that my words were now written! Oh! that they were printed in a book, that they were engraved with an iron pen and lead in the rock for ever. Oh! that mine adversary had written a book." From this it is quite evident that writing was in use before the giving of the law from Sinai. Before that, Moses was commanded to write the important transactions of the Hebrews as they journeyed from Egypt to Canaan. "And the Lord said unto Moses, write this for a memorial in a book." Moses did write as they journeyed, his first journal being a description of the battle between the Hebrews and the Amalekites, at Diber, a city of Canaan, also called Kirjath-Sephar, which name means city of books.*

Adam, it would seem, had predicted that the world would be destroyed at one time by fire and another by water. This prophetic announcement induced the Sethites to build two pillars, one of brick the other of stone, and to inscribe upon them discoveries. These, according to Josephus, were still extant in his day at a place called "Siriad." The authorship of writing by the Jews was ascribed to Seth.

It is claimed that there were distinct races of man existing upon the earth coeval with Adam. Berosus, a learned Chaldean priest, who lived 270 years B. C., gathered from tradition, that before the flood there was a great city of giants called Aeno, situated in Libanus, and that these giants governed the whole world. Cain, after the murder of Abel, left the vicinity of Eden, and dwelt in the land of Nod, and there took him a wife.

The Genesis informs us that there were persons living before the deluge denominated the "sons of God" and "daughters of men," who were "fair," and that the "sons of God" took them wives of the "daughters of men," all which they chose. The sons of God alluded to were said to be of the family of Seth, and the daughters of men to be descendants of Cain. The marriage of the sons of God with the daughters of men, it has been claimed, produced such a wicked stock, that Jehovah, to get rid of them, brought on the deluge.

Abraham was of the tenth generation in the line of descent from Noah, being born 292 years after the flood, hence was fifty-eight years old when Noah died. About this period Abraham visited Egypt. He found it teeming with millions of people, a refined king upon the throne. Around Abraham stood the

* Moses and his Times, pp. 50-57.

temples and monuments found there in ruins to-day; and the
annals of the Egyptian nation as a civilized people, antedated
his birth more than 2000 years.   The shepherd kings were then
in power in Egypt, having wrested the government from the
Egyptians.   These rulers were of the Hyksos family, being
Semitic Arabians, hence they knew their kindred, the Hebrews.
After their expulsion, a "king arose that knew not Joseph," being
of the old Egyptian stock who had repossessed the throne.

As early as the fourth dynasty, which dates 3500 years B. C.,
Egyptian sculpture and painting show the arts and sciences to
have been then little short of what they were in her Augustan
age.   The Greeks learned the fine arts from the Egyptians.
Before the Greeks had written any of their history, Egypt had engraved hers upon stone and painted it upon canvas.   The
Egyptians were a people of dark complexion, though not black.
They were not Negroes as before intimated, and had none of
the African features. When the Hebrews went down into Egypt
to see Joseph, they did not know him, but supposed him to be an
Egyptian.   Had the Egyytians been Negroes, Joseph would have
been readily recognized.   Had the Egyptians been Negroes, the
wise Solomon would not have married one of the females, and
brought her into the "Holy temple" as a mother in Israel; nor
would it have been tolerable among the Hebrews for him to
have introduced a Negress into their family.

In support of the unity and common origin of the races, it has
been asserted that the New Testament boldly avows it to be the
case; and the passage, "God hath made of one blood all nations
of men for to dwell on all the face of the earth,*" is presented as
conclusive evidence upon the subject.   This passage may be
literally true, and still there may have been distinct creations;
there is nothing in it to the contrary, or that disproves distinct
orders or separate creations. All must admit that the whole
human family was not the work of a day, and that nations were
not brought forth at one birth. The blood of all the races, as a
physiological fact, is the same.

There is no force in the expression that "Eve was the mother

* Owing to the controversy among Biblical scholars in regard to this expression in the original, nothing can be considered proved by it.—Indigenous
Races of the Earth, pp. 587-8-9.

of all living." She was not naturally the mother of all living, but may have been the mother of the original types. The term has been extended to include all those who have been born. It proves too much, and does not ignore the idea of separate and distinct creations.

No one doubts different creation in the lower animals. The elephant and mouse are not of common origin; nor is there any unity between the eagle and the owl; yet they were all created by the same power that spoke the human races into existence, and live by virtue of the same principles of animal life. Pairs of each were saved from the flood in the ark with Noah and his family.

The place of the creation of man is claimed to be in Cashmere in the Himalaya mountains; this range, as is supposed, was the first dry land appearing above the water after the formation of the globe, the rivers of Eden being the Ganges, Indus, and Brahmapootra, all which have their source in this range. These are only learned conjectures, having no substantial facts in their support. The precise location is unknown, and will ever so remain, as also where the Ark rested after the deluge, though Mount Ararat is claimed as the very place where Noah made his descent from the ark. And Berosus affirms, that pieces of the decaying ship's timbers were found there during his time.

Much controversy has taken place between ethnologists on the subject of the human complexion, some affirming it to be the result of food and climate, whilst others assert it to be permanently and indelibly fixed by the Creator. The dark color of the African's skin is claimed not to be of the skin itself, but under the cuticle in the pigment cells or epidermis only, and is the result of an admixture of pigment cells with the ordinary epidermic cells.* Here the coloring matter is withdrawn from the blood, and elaborated in these cavities producing coloring matter of various shades. This is all good in theory, but it is a fact that the negro still retains his black color; no change of climate or food having made the least alteration in his complexion from the earliest known history of the race. His complexion is not artificial. He cannot change or alter it. The same may be said in regard to the complexion of the other races;

* Natural History of Man, by Prichard, Vol. I., p. 80.

. they have also retained their color since the earliest period of their existence.

The hair is a peculiar mark of the several types, it being of different texture in each. There are variations, however, in the same type; in some instances the parent may have short black hair, and the offspring's be curling and of a different hue. This is the case only when the primitive blood has been tainted by amalgamation.*

We do not pretend to dispute that all the primitive types may not have been created during the six days of creation, but there is no proof that they were then produced; on the contrary, the Genesis is clear that but two persons, Adam and Eve, were then created. They of course could not bear the several complexions of the present types of mankind. We, therefore, gain no light from the Genesis as regards the human complexion, or common origin of the types of mankind.

* Natural History of Man, Vol. I., p. 88.

CHAPTER VII.

THE CAUCASIAN RACE.

TO this branch of the human family belong the nations of
fair complexion, also including all individuals of whatever
complexion of Caucasian blood. It is difficult to classify the
several nations of this race, but the type may be traced in all
the families of mixed and pure blood, for a period of 5,000 years
as readily as the European type is recognized now. It has been
fully established that distinct races, the white man included, existed in Egypt 3,400 years B. C., though the Jewish chronology,
according to Usher, reaches only back to the year 2348 B. C.
This Hebrew record, even giving full credence to the Septua-
gint, dating 3245 B. C., falls far short of the records preserved
by the Egyptians. They enjoyed a refined civilization during
the IVth dynasty, which dates 3400 years before the birth of
Christ. How long they were civilized, or an existing nation,
before that period is unknown, but it is very evident they did not
become a refined people in a day. Centuries must have intervened before they became civilized.

The researches of Mr. Wilson in the peat bogs of the British Isles, have shown that the human race existed there at a very remote period; long before, it is supposed, the construction of the Egyptian pyramids, or any known date of man's existence elsewhere upon the earth. The people of Europe, as far back as history extends, were of Caucasian blood, unless the early Finns were Mongols. The Celts, Etruscans and Basques were prominent families of Europe, among the first to wake up the

DANIEL WEBSTER.

people to civilization. They were not, however, the first people of the continent, but had been preceded by other families, perhaps Finns, who had made but very little advance from abject barbarism.

The Gauls and Celts were of the same stock of people, each of whom have so indelibly stamped their respective characteristics upon their posterity that their type is preserved in almost all its purity. The Basques, Irish, Scotch, French and Italians present the Celtic and Gallic blood as worthy representatives of their illustrious ancestors.

The successive invasions of the barbarians of the North consisting of Vandals, Huns, Goths, and other hordes, who overran the country, had but little effect, and made no lasting impression upon the Celtic and Gallic nations. Of the barbarians no vestige now remain in Europe, except Lombards and Hungarians, the former occupying a district in Upper Italy, the latter possessing Hungary.

CAUCASIANS IN DETAIL.

The Teutonic family embraces the whole German population. The ancient Slavic and Cimbric were the leading Germanic groups. The former were the ancestors of the Prussians and Tyrolese, and the latter those of the Saxons, Frisians, Hollanders and other lesser nations of Western Germany. The Scandinavian family was a mixture of the Suevi and Goths belonging to this family; and the Vandals to the Suevic group. The Anglo-Saxons, though of Teutonic stock, did not derive their descent from that group, but from the Angli and Saxons, two powerful Germanic tribes who occupied the country between that of the Cimbri and the Baltic. They became masters of Britain as early as 449 B. C. They subdued the Celts, who then occupied the islands, and became the rulers of Britain. The country was then peopled by a mixed multitude, consisting of Anglo-Saxons, Celts, Pelasgians, and Teutons; these, blended and combined, produced in Britain a population of vigorous, strong-bodied and intellectual men, the English still, to a great extent, retaining their Teutonic type; the Irish, Scotch, and Welsh presenting that of the Celtic.

The European Finnish family were doubtless of Caucasian origin,[*] and were the earliest people of Scandinavia who had fair complexion and light or red hair. They occupied the country before the Teutons possessed it. The present Finns seem to be of Mongolian type, and will be noticed in another place.[†]

The Sclavonic family did not appear in Europe until after the

---

[*] Natural History of Man, Vol. I., p. 206.

[†] The present Finns of Russia have the reddish hair, gray eyes, scanty beard, and sallow complexion.—Sear's Illustrated Russian Empire, p. 47.

Christian era. They are descendants of the ancient Sarmatians. The Russians, Poles, Lithuanians, Bohemians and Moravians, belong to this group.

The Pelasgic family constitute the original peoples of Greece, but were eventually called Hellenes, under which name they became the most noted people of ancient times. They had a refined civilization when the most of the other nations of Europe were yet barbarians. The Pelasgians entered Europe at a very remote period, having emigrated from the interior of Asia—of fair complexion, with classic head; were the founders of Grecian refinement, and formed the nucleus of European civilization.

` The Celtic family, once so powerful, is not now known as a nation, being broken and scattered throughout Europe. The Scotch highlander may be considered a good representative of the primitive stock of the Celtic family. The jovial Irishman is also of Celtic stock.

They were a very sprightly people. Under the name of Gallo-Celts they passed through a most brilliant career in Europe, Asia, and Africa, during which period they vanquished the Romans and burnt Rome; wrested Macedonia from the veteran legions of Alexander; forced Thermopylæ, and pillaged Delphi; pitched their tents on the plains of the Troad in Miletus, and on the banks of the Nile; besieged Carthage; menaced Memphis, made tributary to them the most powerful monarchs of the east, and created and enforced civilization throughout their dominions. Their advent in Europe was made at a very early period.

The Indostanic family presents a vast diversity of groups and shades of complexion, yet in some districts the original Hindoo type remains unchanged. The Aryans were a people of very fair complexion, of the sanscrit tongue. Their original seat was in eastern Persia. The Persians may be considered as good representatives of the ancient Aryans. Some of the Hindostanic families are of dark complexion; but, having none of the Negro features, have by some been classed with the Mongolians; they are not of Turanian but of Aryan stock. The Hindoos boast of a very high antiquity. Their annals date thousands of years before the first period of sacred history, but are not reliable, though they may have been a distinct people and exercised the privilege of civil government before the founding of the Egyptian empire. Although intercourse was had between the Hindoos and western nations at a very early date, little was known concerning them before the expedition of Alexander. The Phœnicians dealt with the people of India, and brought Indian goods to Tyre by way of the Persian Gulf and Euphrates river, and then across the Syrian desert. Both Ptolemy and Pliny give accounts of numerous families and peoples inhabiting India, but do not give any satisfactory report of the country or people. The Sanscrit language was familiar to the Hindoos, if not their own in point of fact. Their sacred writings were recorded in this language. The Aryans in personal appearance resemble the Spaniards, and are divided into five great castes according to language. Those of Persia are of fairer complexion and a more perfect physical development than the other families.

The Semitic family includes the Chaldeans, Assyrians, Syrians, Lydians, Arabs, and Hebrews. They emigrated from central Asia westwardly before the historic period, and came from the mountains of Armenia and regions of the lower Euphrates. The first notice we have of them is in the Babylonian records, which give them an history ante-dating the Christian era 2000 years. About that period Abraham, a leading Semitic, emigrated from Ur in Chaldea, to Canaan. When he

ARAB.

entered that country he found it occupied by his kindred, the Semitic peoples. The probability is that, long before his emigration, the Phœnicians had settled on the shores of the Mediterranean.

The countries occupied by the Semitic family were Chaldea, Syria, Phœnicia, Assyria, Palestine, Mesopotamia, Susiana, and Arabia.

The Jews have preserved their early history in the Scriptures,

Abraham was their great ancestor, and doubtless retained the type of Shem and Noah. No nation has so well preserved its primitive type as the Hebrew. The days of Abraham have been fixed at from 1500 to 2000 years B. C. His son, Ishmael, whose mother was an Egyptian maid, was the first instance we have upon record of the amalgamation of the races, or rather families of man. Ishmael was the great ancestor of the Bedouin Arabs.

The Semitic group has been divided into three families: Arabian, Hebrew, and Aramæians. The latter occupied Babylonia after the Hamite dynasty had ceased.

The Arabs are of swarthy complexion, occupying an extensive district in south-western Asia, but take a wider range, extending their periodical migrations from the Red Sea to Persia. The Arabs, at a very early day, sent a colony into Egypt, which located opposite Yemen, where their descendants continued to reside. In their earlier history they were more disposed to dwell in cities and towns. Petra was one of their most noted cities. Pliny describes it as a city two miles in extent, with a river running through the midst of it, situated in a vale enclosed by steep mountains, by which all approach to it was cut off. It was so impregnable as to defy the power of Rome. Petra was the capital of Idumea, forming the great entrepot between Palestine, Syria, and Egypt and was a flourishing city seventeen centuries before the Christian era. Balaam, the soothsayer, was a native of Petra, and the Ishmaelitish merchants, to whom Joseph was sold by his brethren, resided there.

After the decline of the Roman Empire, Petra, it seems, passed from the page of history, and remained concealed until 1812, when the celebrated traveller, Burkhardt, discovered it enclosed in the mountain desert. The entrance to the city is by a passage between perpendicular and overhanging rocks, not more than sufficient for the passage of two horsemen abreast. The ruins of Petra are grand beyond description; some of the most magnificent buildings are hewn out of the side of the mountain's solid rock, among which is a superb temple, described by Mr. Burkhardt as the most elegant remains of antiquity found in Syria. The desolation of Petra is complete; the prophecy concerning Edom has been literally fulfilled; "My sword shall come down on Idumea; thorns shall come up in her palaces; the screech owl also shall rest there and find for herself a place of rest."[*]

The Arabs are really two nations; those who dwell in cities and towns, and those who follow a pastoral and predatory life.

Moses married a daughter of one of the pastoral Arabs, Zipporah. She fed her father's flocks in the desert of Horeb. She was called an Ethiopian, or native of Cush.

The early history of the Arabs is fabulous, they having no annals of their origin, or exploits of any reliable character, prior to the Mohammedan era. One point among themselves seems to have been settled, in regard to their descent, which they claim to derive from Joctan, the son of Heber.[†] The old Arabic stock has become extinct; at least this is asserted in the Koran. The present pure Arabs claim their descent from Kohtan, a noted patriarch, whose sons founded Yemen, and Jorham, and Hejaz. A studied distinction is kept up between the descendants of these two sons by the Arabs, dividing this branch of the family into two tribes. The other family consists of the Ismaelites, or, as they have been termed, the Saracens, descendants of Abraham and Hagar, the Egyptian slave, Sarah's handmaid. Ishmael was taken by his mother to the wilderness of Paran, where they took up their residence. There, it seems, Ishmael married a wife of his own kindred on the side of his mother. The place Paran, where they dwelt, is claimed by the Arabs to be Hejaz and Mecca the very spot where Ishmael was preserved from death by the angel, and the place where his mother died and was buried. They had other noted cities also, among which were Bagdad, Racca, Balbec, Cufa, and Bussoro; some of them even surpassed Petra in point of architectural display. The famous Queen of Sheba, or Saba, was an Arabian, though the Abyssinians claim her as one of their queens. She married King Solomon of Jerusalem, in the twenty-first year of her reign, as some authors have claimed.

The Arabs are entitled to the credit of many of the inventions which have so greatly advanced civilization and embellished human life. They invented our numeral characters; also gunpowder, and taught the use of firearms. But that which dis-

---

[*] Isaiah. Chap. xxxiv., verses 5, 13, and 14.
[†] Natural History of Man. Vol. 1, p. 73

tinguishes them most was their literature. When the successive waves of the barbarians of the north had nearly quenched the last ray of literature in Europe and Asia Minor, and the world at large seemed buried in the gloom of the dark ages, the Caliphs and learned Arabians preserved the arts and sciences, and a refined literature that has never been surpassed.

Mahomet was an Arabian, and the most distinguished man of his time, if not, indeed, of any age. He established a religion and an empire which still prevail. His religion is the most extended of any upon the globe, and the worshippers of that faith more numerous than any other sect.

The Phœnicians were a branch of the Aramæan, Semitic stock. They once occupied the shore of the Persian Gulf. There is no record of their migration to the Mediterranean, but it must have been at a very remote era, as Sidon, one of their chief cities, was a distinguished emporium in the days of Solomon. Sidonians and the Phœnicians generally were noted for their commerce. The Greeks give to the Phœnicians the credit of the invention of letters. They were a people of great enterprise—sent colonies to various regions of northern Africa. Carthage was founded by them. According to Herodotus, they circumnavigated Africa. They attained to a very high state of intellectual culture. Tyre, their capital, was for a long time the most noted city of the country, and Sidon was a place of great distinction in the age of Homer. The Tyrians supplied King Solomon with all kinds of artificers to aid him in the construction of the Holy Temple at Jerusalem.

The Jews, or rather Hebrews, sojourned in Egypt over four hundred years. The greater portion of that long period they were degraded to abject vassalage; yet they made an impression on the country that was lasting. Though their religion was not adopted by the Egyptians, their civilization had much to do in the advancement of the former in refinement.

The Jews have preserved their family type unimpaired; and though they number over five million souls, each individual retains the full impress of his primitive typical ancestors.*

* Jews having blue eyes and flaxen hair, reside in England. In some parts of Germany they are seen with red hair. Those of Portugal are very dark; and those in Cochin are as black as the dark-skinned Hindoos.—Natural History of Man, vol. I., pp. 131-2.

The Nilotic family consists of the Egyptians proper, and the Fellahs. They were an intelligent and enterprising branch of the Caucasian family, that entered the country from India, as is supposed, by the way of the upper Nile, at a period long ante-dating the historic era. They doubtless had established an extensive civil government, and enjoyed a refined civilization long before Europe was inhabited by man. Their history it would seem was coeval with that of China and Hindostan. Egypt was the great seat of learning when the Greeks were yet barbarians.

The temples, monuments, pyramids, tombs, and other works of art in Egypt, present effigies and portraits of sovereigns and citizens which date back 5760 years, corresponding with the heads and features of the mummified bodies taken from the tombs at Ghizeh, and other places on the banks of the Nile. Lepsius fixes the date of the first Egyptian monarch, Menes, at 3893 years, B. c; and at that remote era, the people had attained to great proficiency in the arts and sciences.*

The works of the Egyptians are stupendous and magnificent. The pyramids at Ghizeh are the most massive stone structures reared by man. The largest of the group, called Cheops, has a base 767 feet square, and is 480 feet nine inches high. It is built of huge blocks of stone, and is of conical form, being smallest at the summit. The top is reached by 200 stone steps, located on the outside of the pyramid.

All the ancient temples, tombs, pyramids, and sculpture of the Egyptians, exhibit a wonderful display of human genius, skill, and completeness of the mechanic arts. The Sphinxes alone, are such a display of gigantic sculpture as to astonish the world. One of them is 125 feet in length, and otherwise in proportion.

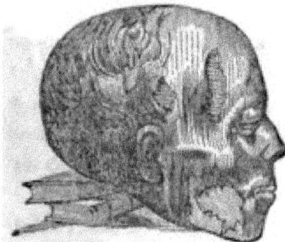

EGYPTIAN HEAD.

The Fellahs are the descendants of the ancient rulers of Egypt, and now the working people of the country. They resemble the Arabs and Berbers, but are a different family. Their skulls are of the Egyptian mould, complexion a greyish brown. They are the only people

* Lepsius' Chronologie der Egypter, p. 196.

of the whole valley of the Nile who have become acclimated, except their ancestors, and the Kopts. The other races, it seems, have not been successful in transmitting their descendants beyond the third generation. It will not be claimed that the Egyptians of the present day are a perfect representation of the primitive stock,* but as they were after they became acclimated in the valley of the Nile. The Danes occupied Denmark at a very early period, but in what era history does not disclose.

The classic historians give a very limited account of the Danes. About 320 years before the Christian era, the shores of Denmark were visited by the Greeks. At that time an adventurous navigator, named Pytheas, after sailing round the coast of Spain, Gaul, and Albion, entered the Baltic, and explored that region as far as the mouth of the Vistula. He describes the people of that region as savage, and subsisting by hunting and fishing.

The Danes were described as a people of fair complexion, with light flaxen hair, who occupied Jutland and Sleswick, and were a branch of the great Scythic famliy of Goths, leaving their abode on the Araxes 2000 years B. C., and passing into northern Germany and Scandinavia. They were not the first people of the regions they first occupied, having been preceded by the Finns and Lapps, and are known in classic history as a family of the Cimbri.

Their historic period, as a distinct nation, commences about seventy years B. C., when the divine Odin became supreme ruler of the country, and were first known to civilized Europe as a band of pirates. France and England suffered severely from their piracies. In the year 781 they made a descent upon Southampton, with seven piratical ships, pillaged the country, and escaped unmolested with their booty. Encouraged by the apparent timidity of the British, they subsequently plundered the whole coast from the Thames to the Mersey, during which incursions they took and plundered Chester and London, keeping up their piracies until the year 1002 A. D., when they overthrew the Anglo-Saxon government, and annexed the English provinces to the Danish crown.

---

* The Egyptians were an indigenous race created to people the valley of the Nile.—Types of Mankind, p. 241.

They overrun Gaul, crossed over the mountains into Spain, fought and defeated the Arabs at Seville, and demolished their fortifications. They founded the kingdoms of Naples and Sicily, and established the Duchy of Normandy in France, from whence issued the rulers of England under William the Conqueror.

War and plunder seemed to be the first objects of the ancient Danes, which they conducted for a thousand years with very marked success. Their course of policy, however, tended, in the end, to stimulate the nations with whom they contended to a more vigorous degree of self-protection and defence, resulting in the expulsion of the Danes from their conquered provinces, prescribing them to their own peninsula with a limited power over Iceland and the Faro Islands.

The Danes have long since ceased their piracies, and become an upright and industrious people, and have long cherished science and literature, education being an object of primary importance with the government, the poor children being educated at public expense. There are many distinguished learned men among the Danes. In this respect they stand very prominent among the European nations. The celebrated traveler and historian, Niebuhr, was one of their number. The Danes have well preserved their primitive type; are tall and robust, with regular features, florid complexion, and hair inclining to yellow or red, which was the complexion and color of the hair of the ancient Scandinavians.

Red hair is common among the Anglo-Saxons, very distinguished Europeans; also, Anglo-Americans have had red hair, among whom were the Marquis Lafayette and Thomas Jefferson, both of whom seemed to have not only inherited the complexion of the Danes, but also their vigor of thought.

The Swedes and Norwegians are the descendants of the ancient Scandinavians. Their ancestors were described by Tacitus as a people of "robust bodies, compact limbs, blue eyes, stern countenances, and fierce, warlike disposition." Procopius, in his description of them, says "they are all of fair complexion, having red or yellow hair, and a tall, manly stature." Those upon the highlands were savages, subsisting upon game and fish. The lowlanders had made some advance in civilization; they "produced grain, reared bees, and brewed hydromel, their favorite drink."*

Sweden was occupied by the Hilleviones, Gutæ, Suiones and Finni. The Gutæ were the Goths. The Finni were described by Tacitus as a savage race, without arms, horses or iron, with arrows pointed with bone.

The Swedes were known to civilized Europe at as early a day as the Danes, if not earlier, under the name of Goths, as, indeed, were all the people of Scandinavia. They were long in subjection to the Danes, but achieved their independence from that power in the year 1528, under their great leader, Gustavus Vasa. In the reign of Charles the Twelfth, Sweden was shorn of her foreign conquests by the Russians, and driven within her own barren limits.

The Swedes are described as a most amiable and innocent people, having light flaxen hair, and ruddy countenance, the face of every one expressing docility and good humor. They have made a distinguished literary record. Their Linnæus, as a botanist, has had no rival ; Bergman and Shiell stand prominent in chemistry, and Jenny Lind continues unrivalled in vocal music.

The Norwegians are the descendants of the ancient Sitons, of Scandinavia. Their early history, like that of the Swedes and Danes, is fabulous. They became known to civilized Europe about the latter part of the ninth century A. D., though their civil history dates as early as the year 640 A. D., at which time commenced their heroic dynasties.

About the close of the ninth century A. D., by the aid of the Danes, the Norwegians placed a king upon the throne of England, and established a permanent government in Normandy. But, by the defeat of their prince, Haco, in Scotland, and Harold III., in England, in the eleventh century, their power in those regions ceased.

Since the year 1814, Norway has been united with Sweden, though the Norwegian constitution has not been abrogated by the union of the crowns.

The people are frank, robust and brave; of fair complexion, blooming countenance, and light hair; of middle stature, and well shaped; the men are genial, and have a joyous appear-

* Pliny's History, Lib. IV., 12, *notes* 13, 16.

ance, and the women are tall, remarkably fair, and handsome; their whole bearing is noble; even the peasant acts wth gentility and courteous demeanor.   They cannot boast of literature, and it is doubtful if there is a single bookstore in the kingdom.

The Spaniards derive their descent from the Iberians, who are also called Basques, known to the ancients as mariners, and were closely allied to the Phœnicians, whom they much resembled.   They have been grouped with the Turanian type, but erroneously, as they are evidently Aryans.   The present Spaniards seem to preserve the primitive type, though they are strongly tinctured with Celtic blood.   No country has more variety of population than Spain.   The people are a mixed multitude; remnants of all the races, and many leading families of antiquity are represented.   The Spanish authors trace their descent back to Noah, through the Iberians.

The Celts occupied Spain long before the Iberians ; and, when the former entered it, found some native tribes in the country, who were, perhaps, Phœnicians or Carthagenians.   The former were acquainted with the country long before the founding of Rome and Carthage.

It has been claimed that the Celts were of Spain, and that the Iberi were the aborigines.*   Prichard was of opinion that the latter occupied the country before the Celts entered it.†

The Iberians were an intelligent family, acquainted with the art of writing at a very early period.   They sacrificed human victims to their divinities, and their priests pretended to foretell future events from an inspection of the palpitating entrails.

The Celtiberi, a mixed family, composed of Celts and Iberians, were the most numerous people of Spain.   They were the mountaineers, and more rude than the Iberians proper.

The present Spaniards, as well as the Portuguese, are derived from an intermixture of Celts, Carthagenians, Romans, Goths, Saracens and Moors.   Their general appearance is that of an intelligent people; form delicate, though commanding; head finely formed, eyes quick and animated, complexion swarthy, varying, in degrees of shade, even to the olive hue.   The Castilians seem to be the most perfect Spanish type.   The females are generally

* Strabo, Vol. III., p. 162.
† Natural History of Man, Vol. I., pp. 182-264.

small and slender, and well formed. Their complexion also varies from fair to brown.

The Portuguese, who occupy the western part of the Spanish Peninsula, are not, in general, so tall as the Spaniards, or so well made; complexion swarthy, black hair, and dark eyes. The women are small, with brown complexion; dark, sparkling, expressive eyes, and regular features. They have none of that maritime spirit which so distinguished them in the fifteenth and sixteenth centuries, during which time they discovered the coasts of Guinea, the Cape of Good Hope, and the passage by sea to the East Indies.

The Gauls * were a family of the Celtic group; a tall, large-bodied, blue-eyed, yellow-haired people; but have long since become absorbed, as a distinct family, in the great commingling of nations in Europe; yet the type is often met with in individuals, as distinctly as first impressed upon the primitive stock. The French have, in many particulars, preserved the Gallic features, though not generally so; yet the Gallic-Celtic characteristics are plainly manifested in many of the French people.

The early inhabitants of Gaul were Finns, who were reduced to subjection by the Celts. At the invasion of Cæsar, the Celts were divided into three great families; the Celts proper were in the center; the Belgæ to the north; and the Aquitani to the south. The tribes Cæsar called Celts were the Gauls, and occupied then the middle, western and southern portions of the country.†

The Franks, a German family, or rather confederation of families in the 4th century, occupied the country on the right banks of the Rhine, from the junction of the river Mayn to the sea. They preserved their independence, though each tribe had a separate king. It is difficult to trace the Franks to their origin, and equally so to give the origin of the French. They are considered a new family springing from Celts, Teutons and Romans.

The ruins in France show the country to have been inhabited by several distinct orders of people, such as the Goths, Celts and

---

* The Gauls were tall of stature, very fair, and had red hair.—Natural History of Man, Vol. I., p. 192.

† The houses of the Celts were round, covered with thatch.—Pre-Historic Remains in Italy, p. 25.

Romans. The French people show in their composition the combination of the characteristics of these three orders of people.

No people can surpass the French in display of brilliant military evolutions, courage, celerity of movement and prowess. They seem to consist of different tribes; in the north the Teutonic blood prevails, where the men are of taller stature than in the other provinces. These Teutonic French have blue eyes and fair complexion. In the south the Roman and Celtic blood prevails—people here have darker complexion and dark hair. They are active and gay; much more so than the Teutonic branch. In the west the pure Celtic blood prevails. They have small bodies, but strong and elastic; complexion darker than the other families.

As a nation, the French stand unrivaled. No people have passed more trying and exciting scenes than they have witnessed, and no nation has had a more brilliant career. Theirs is a bright and conspicuous page of history. Their Napoleon taught the world a new lesson in brilliant feats of arms. By his great deeds his name has become immortal; it required Europe combined to stay his gigantic power; the world seemed to be his field of conquest; and though long since dead, there seems to be more power in his ashes than in all living heroes.

The Italians, like the French, are a new family, though preserving to a high degree their primitive type. The primitive Italians occupied Italy before the Etruscans; they comprised two families, viz.: the Japygions and Italicans. The latter were the Latins proper, and Umbrians, and embraced the Volskians, Marsians, and Samnites. The greater portion of Italy was originally inhabited by the Pelasgians, who were of the great Sclavonic group. The Siculi family dwelt in the regions of the lower Tiber, the Tyrrheni, in Etruria, and the Aborigines in the neighborhood of Reate.*

The Umbri, who occupied northern Italy, have been by some considered the most ancient people of Italy, though they were probably of the same stock as the Siculi; as a nation they have long since become extinct.

---

* The early Italians are of the Tuscan family, except those considered the Aborigines, called Rasemians, who were not of the Greek, or Palasgic stock, but Aryans.—Natural History of Man, Vol. I., p. 181.

The north-west of Italy was inhabited by the Ligurians, whose history is very obscure, nothing definite being known of them until about the time of their dissolution as a nation.*

The Etruscans occupied the country between the Tiber and the lower sea, and as far north as the Rætian Alps; they were known by the name of Rasena. They invaded the country from the north, subdued the Pelasgians and Tyrrhenians, and occupied their provinces.

The Sabines occupied the regions about Amiternum, in the Alps.

The Celts and Gauls were numerous in Italy before the invasion of the barbarians from the north. Tuscany was peopled by Lydians, Umbrians, and Tyrrhenians. The Tuscans subdued the latter and dwelt there, and also on the banks of the river Po.

The Sabines were an early indigenous nation of Italy, and one of the few families that preserved their primitive type.† Their name, according to Cato, was derived from the god Sabus, an original deity of the country. They, for a long period, refused to hold intercourse with the Romans.

The Romans proper did not consist of one single tribe or nationality, but were a heterogeneous compound of many families, among which the Trojan element prevailed to some extent. The Julian family constituted the nobility, and was of indigenous origin. Although mixed with fair-haired tribes, the Romans were more of the Persic type than the Celtic; but the Roman head was much oftener the order of the Grecian mould; and in any point of mental power they were equal with the Greeks, and their history is equally as brilliant.

The Teutons were the ancestors of the great Germanic families of Europe, hailing from central Asia, entering Europe at an unknown period; but it was not until a few centuries B. C. that they made their power felt there. In successive waves they extended over Europe from north to south, and from south to

---

* The Ligurians were of the Iberian family, and occupied Piedmont before the Gauls entered the country. They and the Umbri were the most ancient peoples of Italy.—Pre-Historic Remains of Italy, by Gastardi, p. 92.

† The Sabines occupied a district north-east of Rome. Dionysius supposed them to have been a colony of Lacedæmonians in the age of Lycurgus.—Anthon's Classical Dictionary, p. 1178.

north, until the whole country seemed to be within their control—swept away the Roman empire, and laid the foundation of a refined civilization in Europe ; not only creating civilization but enforcing it with the sword throughout their dominions.

It is impossible to tell at this late day what induced the Teutons to leave their home in Asia and take up their abode in the wilds of Europe amid swamps, marshes, and bogs. Their advent in Europe is supposed to have been about 1200 years B. C. They entered it by the way of the Baltic and Black seas. The great mass, however, did not reach Europe until about the fourth century B. C., when they entered it by the Dnieper to the countries of the Baltic, including Scandinavia, some even then passing to the lowlands along the Danube and the valley of the Rhine. They mingled with the Celts and produced the Belgic family, and forced the Cimbri down upon the Romans. The typical Teutonic stock consisted of the Germans proper, Saxons, and Swiss, the latter being partially of Sclavonic blood. The main families of the latter were Goths, Langobards, Vandals, Burgundians, Rugians, Herulians, and many other tribes of lesser note. The Goths include the Gepidæ, Danes, Swedes, and Herulians. The Goths very anciently occupied the southern part of Sweden. In 375 B. C., they appeared as West-Goths, on the lower Danube and Thrace, and Gaul, where they founded the West-Gothic kingdom. The East-Goths, in the fourth century B. C., passed over the lower Danube to Bulgaria ; thence to Italy, where they ruled the Romans for nearly a hundred years, until the empire was overthrown by the Byzantine army.[*]

The Gepidæ, of Gothic origin, appeared in Hungary, but were subdued by the Langobards in the latter half of the sixth century B. C. The Bavarians are first mentioned in the early part of the sixth century B. C., and then occupied Swabia.

The Goths were the first branch of the Teutonic family ; the Vandals, of mixed blood, being largely Sclavonic ; and perished in Africa under Semitic civilization. The Burgundians were classed by Pliny with the Vandals. They warred successfully with the Romans, and preserved their primitive type quite as long as any of the Germanic tribes, being eventually known as

---

[*] Linnæus described the Goths as a nation having smooth, fair hair, and the iris of the eye of blue color.—Plurality of Races, p. 102.

Kelts or Sclavonians. The destruction of the Roman empire materially changed the status of the Teutons; some of the families remained in Italy, others took up their abode in Spain, others in Belgium, others in Holland, whilst a portion settled in France, Austria, Bohemia, and Hungary.

Denmark, Sweden, and Norway, and indeed all northern Europe, seems to be mainly peopled by Teutonic and Germanic peoples. The primitive Germans were a tall, powerful family, with light hair, blue eyes, and blonde complexion, and were remarkable for personal dignity.*

THE BRITONS.

The British people are of Celtic stock. The term Briton is derived from the word Brith, supposed to refer to the custom of the early Britons staining their bodies a bluish color by a substance extracted from woad.

The Celts crossed over from Gaul to Britain, in all probability before the islands were known to the Phœnicians or Carthagenians. Cæsar describes several tribes of Britain, all of whom stained their bodies with woad. The Druids were the priests of Britain, and conducted religious exercises.

The Roman conquest brought a new element into Britain, and from that time the general character of the people began to undergo a change.

The conquest of William the Conqueror brought the Norman element into the country, which became engrafted upon the Celtic-Gallic stock. Then came the Angli and Saxons, who made a permanent and lasting impression upon the British character. A new stock of people sprung up, which now constitutes the English nation. The Celtic stock is still preserved by the Irish, Scotch, and Welsh, and is frequently visible in the English.

THE IRISH.

The Scoti were the rulers of Ireland in the beginning of the Christian era. They were closely allied with the Belgæ, if, in fact, they were not of the same stock of people. Nothing is known of the Irish family, as a distinct nationality, until long after the conquest of Britain by the Romans. There is a long,

* The Races of the Old World, p 96, 108.

fabulous history of the Irish people, in which it is boldly asserted that the country was very anciently peopled by the Phœnicians, Carthagenians, and Scythians. Many ancient structures are found in the country which are not the works of the Irish, but supposed to be constructed by the Phœnicians. Some, however, suppose them to be Persian fire temples, whilst others claim them to have been constructed by the Danes.

Irish tradition has it that the Scoti * came from Spain, and spread over all the country. Whatever may have been the early history of the country and the Irish nation, the people of the island were not designated by the Romans. They had several kingdoms; indeed each province seemed in early days to have its king. When the Danes invaded the country it was full of kings. Two hundred, we are told, perished in battle.

The Irish nation has passed through many exciting scenes, especially so before they became established as an independent nationality—seeming incapable of retaining independence—lost their freedom as a nation by the treachery of their own people, who bartered away their liberty to the English sovereign. The present Irish population is mainly made up of Celtic stock, though there is not a general uniformity in their physical aspect, in all localities. The red hair, also black and curling, is often seen in the same family, and the complexion is not uniform, though it is generally fair.

THE SCOTCH FAMILY.

The first inhabitants of Scotland were a tribe of the Cimbri, who entered it from Denmark, their original seat, about 200 years B. C. The name of Scots is derived from the Scoti of Ireland. The Picts were early settlers in Scotland. The Scoti emigrated from Ireland in the 6th century, where they kept up almost constant hostilities with the Picts for two or three hundred years; but in the year 839, A. D., Kenneth wrested the sceptre from the Pictish king. Since then the Scots have been the ruling people. They are a mixed family, being made up of the Anglo-Saxons, Picts, Celts, and descendants of the ancient Britons; also Gauls and Scandinavians. The Scotch are a sprightly and intelligent people, very similar to the Irish. They have

* The Scoti, by their own traditions, came originally from Scythia.—Anthon's Ancient Mediæval Geography, p. 209.

spare bodies and high cheek bones; and generally large front teeth. The highlanders are a brave, hardy people, and noted for their military prowess. Their complexion is fair, though like the Irish, there is a great diversity in their physical aspect. Their country was called Caledonia.

The Picts were probably of Gothic descent. They were called Picts by reason of their staining their bodies before going to battle. Some supposed them to have been Caledonians; the latter being descendants of Celts and Goths.

The Persians' early history is wrapped in profound obscurity. The reliable features of their antiquity are gathered from the Hebrew scriptures, and the writings of Herodotus, Strabo and Diodorus. The first civil government of the Persians was founded 747 years B. C. Before that period the people seem to have been nomadic, and divided into as many as ten families, of which the Pasargadæ tribe was the head. Cyrus, a descendant of this family, became the leader of a vast horde of Persian adventurers, and eventually greatly distinguished as a bold, daring captain. His advent in public life was made 561 years B. C., and at the time the Median and Babylonian kingdoms were in their decline. He was remarkably successful in military exploits, and by conquest built up the kingdom of Persia upon the ruins of those of the Medes and Babylonians, yet unsuccessful in his wars with some of the tribes of central Asia. Herodotus and Justin state that Cyrus was taken prisoner and put to death by Tamyris, Queen of the Messagetæ. This is doubted by others, who claim he was killed by the javelin of an Indian warrior whilst making war upon the Dervishes of that country. Xenophon informs us that he died in his bed 529 years B. C. His successors made the Persians a daring, warlike nation, capable of conducting vast armies and waging gigantic warfare. They undertook the conquest of Egypt and Greece; and, for a time, were successful against both these great powers. Under Cambyses, one of their great leaders, they invaded Egypt, took Memphis, and set themselves down as conquerors in the very heart of the country. A revolt of the people at home compelled Cambyses to quit Egypt. He did not reach Persia, having died on the way by an accidental wound from his own sword, as Herodotus advises us.

Darius, another great Persian general, made extensive conquests. He entered Scythia with an army of 700,000 men.[*] but meeting with no success against the Scythians, was forced to quit the country in disgrace, being virtually defeated in every engagement.

His failure in this quarter did not seem to diminish his desire for conquest. He turned his attention to the nations of India and the people of the west; subdued the Babylonians, tore down the walls of Babylon, and founded Susa upon its ruins; ruled in great splendor at Susa, though he had Ecbatana and Persepolis also as capitals. His expedition against the Greeks greatly perplexed Darius. The battle of Marathon turned the tide of war against him. After the death of Darius, Xerxes sought to take vengeance upon the Greeks; mustered a host of several millions of fighting men;[†] bridged the Hellespont; cut a channel through the isthmus of Mount Athos, and successfully invaded the Grecian empire; but in the end was compelled to quit the country in disgrace, after the battle of Salamis. This disaster brought him into disrepute, and resulted in his assassination by his own people. With the defeat of the Persians at Salamis commenced the decline of their empire, which eventually was incorporated with that of Macedonia, under Alexander who, in the third century B. C., after rescuing it from foreign sway, established the Parthian government in Persia. About the year 220 B. C., the Parthian empire was subverted by the Sasanides, who restored the name of Persia and re-established its ancient religion and laws. In the seventh century it was subverted by the Saracens, and the Mohammedan faith imposed upon the people. After this, it became the theatre of war for several centuries, during which time the Tartars and Turks supplanted each other, but finally the native Persians repelled every foreign yoke. Abbas the Great, in the year 1586 A. D., raised himself to the throne of Persia and restored the country to its original prosperity. Two centuries afterwards the Afghans desolated Persia by fire and sword to her utmost extremities, even reducing the capital to ashes. About fifteen years there-

---

[*] Strabo, Vol. VII., p. 305.

[†] Xerxes' army was set down at 5,283,220 men. This no doubt includes women, allies, and camp followers. Herodotus, Vol. III., Book VII., Cha-xlix., p. 126.

after Nadir Shah restored the independence of Persia, but the government did not become permanent until the year 1796, under Fulteh-Ali-Shah.

The Persians are the living representatives of the Persians of antiquity. Their complexion does not differ materially from that of the European. The face is long and oval, features regular, eyes large and black. They are of the Aryan type, but some of them are tainted with Turanian blood, having amalgamated with the dark-skinned Indians.

The early history of the Persians is preserved in their sacred book, called the Zendavesta, composed, at least compiled, by Zoroaster in the mountains of the Elburz, whence he carried the sacred volume to Darius, in Balekh, who was so well pleased with the composition of the Zendavesta, that he caused it to be transcribed upon 1,200 cowhides, prepared for the purpose.*

AFGHANS.

The family bearing this name are descendants of the ancient Aryans, and are close relatives, by family ties, of the Persians; and, in the highlands, their complexion is as fair as the Europeans.† Yet they present almost all varieties of shades, from white to black. Those on the Indus are quite dark-skinned, though having none of the features or characteristics of the African.

This family is divided into several leading tribes, of whom the Duranis of the west are the most accomplished, being to some extent versed in Persian literature. The Ghilzyes, another prominent tribe, occupying a vast region eastwardly of the Duranis, extending northwest to the Parapamisan and eastward to those of Soliman, including Cabul. They have a much more liberal government than the Duranis. The sovereigns of Cabul have patronized the arts and sciences, and the people have made considerable advance in literature. The Berdironis are an important family equal almost to those already described; Peshawer, their capital, is one of the most noted places of Afghanistan. Besides these there are several other tribes of this great family, some of whom are almost in a state of barbarism, whilst others

* Frasier's History of Persia, pp. 108-9
† Natural History of Man, Vol. I., p. 193

are enjoying a tolerable system of civilization. The Khyberis are a dark-skinned tribe, occupying the regions of the famous Khyber Pass. They are an independent tribe, who depend much upon plunder. But few travellers escape them who deign to cross the mountains lying between Cabul and Peshawer.

The Afghans are properly divided into two groups, one dwelling in towns and cities, and the other roving about and dwelling in tents. The Afghans number at least six millions of people, and their dominions comprise three hundred thousand square miles. Their origin is very obscure, though they claim to derive their descent from the ancient Hebrews, and pretend to be able to trace their genealogy back to Saul, king of Israel. The probability is they are descendants of the Arabs.

THE BELOOCHES

Occupy the country known as Beloochistan, which lies south of Afghanistan, extending to the Indian Ocean and to Hindoostan.

Ancient history is almost silent in regard to this region. It was no doubt one of the one hundred and twenty-seven provinces ruled by the Persian monarch mentioned in the Book of Esther, where he is described as ruling over the country extending from India even unto Ethiopia.*

Alexander the Great passed through this territory on his return from India to Persia. At that time it was sparsely populated by a rude, barbarous people, who lived upon fish, and dwelt in huts formed of shells and fish bones.

The present population comprises several tribes, but seems to be properly divided into two families, the Belooches and Brahoes—the latter are the Tartars of the country, being nomadic in their habits. Those who approach nearest Hindoostan are civilized, but those of the west are freebooters, and almost wholly uncivilized, seeming to have a natural taste for plunder and robbery.

The civilized Belooches are brave and hospitable; and, though addicted to plunder, are considered honorable robbers. They resemble the Afghans in some particulars, but have also some resemblance to the Jews. They are doubtless Aryans,

* History of all Nations, by S. G. Goodrich, Vol. I., p. 492.

though within their territory are dark-skinned tribes, supposed to be Turanians. They are a family of Persian Iliyats and speak a dialect of the Persian language.*

The Kurds are divided into two classes: one the nobles, resembling the Greeks, the others having some of the features of the Tartars. They are a high-spirited people, yet much given to war and its spoils. They were accidentally called Karduchians, with whom Xenophon contended and fought his way through, in his famous retreat with ten thousand Greeks. They are, as they were then, the boldest people of Asia, living to a great extent by plunder, but honorable in their robberies, preferring to take from those who have to spare. They often extend their incursions into the plains and carry off much booty, preying upon the caravans passing through the regions within their range. The Yezidis belong to this family. They have not adopted the Mohammedan faith, and continue to enjoy their ancient religion, and worship the sun. They are robust, of dark complexion, black hair and small eyes.

The Nestorians occupy a district in Kurdistan; are a Semitic family, and a relic of the ancient Nestorians, who, as a Christian sect, date back as early as the fifth century A. D. Their language is Syriac, with a mixture of Persian, Kurdish and Turkish words. Their ancient tongue was pure Syriac. They are a pastoral people, of handsome features, blond complexion, and light beards, strongly resembling the Jews.

THE TURKS.

This family descended from the Hiung-nu tribe, an ancient people, inhabiting a district on the northern borders of China. They were known as early as the middle of the third century B. C., commencing their migrations in the first or second centuries A. D., a portion of them having been driven westward by the Chinese. One of the tribes, called Tukiu, established a government in the sixth century A. D., between the Altai Mountains and the Caspian Sea. As early as the year 568 A. D., they had established themselves west of the Volga and the sea of Azof.†

On their way westward, the Turks built up a vast empire,

---

* Natural History of Man, Vol. I., p. 174.
† The Races of the Old World, p. 126.

including Persia and Bokhara.   The Osmanli Turks are the ancestors of the present Turkish people of Europe, who were forced out of Persia by the Mongols in the year 1224 A. D. Othman was their great leader, and from him they derive the name of Ottomans.   They were the Caucasian Tartars.

The Turkish Empire was begun remotely by the white Huns of Scythia, but its permanency, as an empire and stable government, is credited to Solyman, chief of the Soljukian Turks, who settled in Asia Minor, in the thirteenth century.   In the year 1453 A. D., they took the city of Constantinople, and made it their capital, which it still remains.

The Turks are of fair complexion, with Caucasian features. The Toorkies are of Semitic origin; have dark complexion, lofty stature, an abundance of beard, and are, in all respects, Caucasians of Yuchi family. The Toorkies are more hyperborean than the Turks, the former being tinctured with Finnish blood, whilst the latter only seem to have amalgamated with the Parsees, Armenians, Greeks, and other Caucasian families. The Toorkies once inhabited Mongolia proper, and possessed a vast empire, which was in its Augustan age in the third century B. C.

The Georgians occupy the southern declivity of the Caucasus mountains.   They are tall, well-proportioned; have handsome features, fair complexion, and are, in every way, Caucasians. Their history is that of their type, which they have well preserved, though having passed through great tribulation and many changes of fortune as a nation.   They suffered much degradation from their own race, who carried many of them as captive slaves to Egypt; and, even now, the Turkish harems are supplied with some of their most beautiful females, who are taken thither by their own kindred and sold as slaves.

Whilst in Egypt, under the title of Mamelukes, they did the drudgery, until their expulsion from Egypt by Mohammed Ali.

The Circassians are also of pure Caucasian stock.   Like the Georgians they have long been celebrated for the beauty of their women, and symmetry of their form.   They are good representatives of the ancient Caucasians; their most beautiful females also become the inmates of the harem.   They have kept no annals of their early migration or settlement in their present locality.

Some suppose them descendants of the ancient Medes; others that they are a branch of the Arabians. They themselves have a tradition that makes them the descendants of Ishmael; but are not such, however, as they, in no particular, resemble the Ishmaelites. The Greeks hailed from the regions occupied by the Caucasians and Georgians; also, the Cossacks.

The Hungarians are descendants of the ancient Huns, Sclavonians, Germans, Turks, and Gypsies; are tall and well shaped— as perfect in form almost as the original Caucasian race.

KOSSUTH.

The Armenians originally occupied the country on the southeast of the Euxine Sea. According to Strabo, it was bounded on the north by Iberia and Albania, east by Media, south by Assyria, and west by Pontus. Herodotus considered them descendants of the Phrygians. Most likely they were of the same stock of people as the Syrians. Berosus, of Chaldea, who wrote a history of the Armenians, says their first king was Scytha, who was succeeded by his son Barzanes. Upon his death the government was divided into small kingdoms. In the sixth century B. C., Astyages, king of the Medes, subjected Armenia to his kingdom. At a subsequent date it became a province of Persia. When Alexander built up his Eastern Macedonian Empire, Armenia was incorporated with it. Under Tigranus, they conducted successful war against the Cappadocians, of whom he carried as captives into Armenia, three hundred thousand, whom he employed in building him a city, which he called Tyranocerta, in honor of himself. He was successful against the Greeks and Parthians, but was unable to cope with the Romans, who, under Lucullus, invaded Armenia, and took the capital, A. D. 68. Plutarch states that one hundred thousand of the Armenian cavalry were killed in one engagement, and on the part of the Romans only five men were slain. Shortly after this the Romans became masters of Armenia, and Pompey, the successor of Lucullus, bestowed the crown upon Deiotarus of Galatia. It next fell under Persian rule; then became coveted by the Romans and Turks, and finally by the Tartars under Zingis. The Turks soon overthrew the Mongolian authority; Egypt became partner with the Turks in devastating Armenia. The Egyptians carried vast hosts of their captives into slavery. In 1375 A. D., the Armenian kingdom was destroyed, and Cilicia made a province of Egypt.

The Armenians are not known as a nationality, but as individuals. Like the Jews they are scattered throughout all lands.

The Armenians are Aryans, and in physique are a handsome people, well made, and of dark complexion, though not black. They resemble the Persians; number three million souls, and cling to their ancient religious faith.

The Welsh are a branch of the Celtic family, being descendants of the Ancient Britons, who took refuge in the mountains of western England, to escape the destroying sword of the Saxons. The ancient Welsh called Wales Cymry, and their language Cymraig. From the former is derived Cambria, an ancient name of Wales. They long had an independent kingdom, but, after a gallant resistance, were forced to yield to the power of England, under Edward I., since which period the Welsh have been subjects of Great Britain, though for a long time very refractory; so much so, that the English were obliged to erect strong and numerous fortifications in Wales, to prevent the Welsh from assuming their independence. For the last three hundred years they have been most willing subjects.

The ancient Welsh consisted of two families; one called Ordovices, and the other Silures. The Britons, unable to defend themselves against the invading Picts and Scots, called to their aid the Angli and Saxons, two renowned German tribes, who repelled the Scots and Picts, but seized upon the country themselves, and drove the Britons into the mountains of Wales, where they added great strength to the Welsh nation. The name Welsh was first applied to the people of Cambria by the Saxons in the sixth century A. D. When the Romans invaded Britain, Wales was occupied by three separate tribes, viz.: Ordovices, Silures, and Dimetæ, who had a well-disciplined army, divided into charioteers, cavalry, and infantry, and a regular organized civil government. They were far advanced in refined civilization, raised corn and stock, such as sheep, cattle, and swine. Their money consisted of rings, and small plates of iron strung together. Wales was the chief seat of the Druids. The great High Priest of druidical religion resided in the island of Anglesea, then called Mona. Here they sacrificed human victims, mostly of prisoners taken in war, and criminals condemned to death for crime. The bodies of the sacrificed victims were burned in wicker cages before the altars. Mercury was their chief deity.

The Druids had unlimited powers over the people, much more indeed than the king. He even dared not dispute the decrees of the druidical high priest with safety, not at least without the punishment of excommunication.

The Romans, under Suetonius Paulinus, waged a war of extermination against the Druids in Wales, and drove them into the Island of Mona. Thither they were also pursued by the Romans, who cut down their sacred groves, and put the Druids to the sword. The Romans, having subdued the Ordovices, invaded the provinces of the Silures. They made a gallant resistance, but were defeated by the Romans, at the battle of Caer-Caradoc, under Agricola. The kind and generous treatment of Agricola toward the Welsh won their affections to such a degree that they willingly became Roman subjects, and the dominions of the Welsh were made a Roman province under the name of Britannia Secunda.

After the decline of the Roman power, the Welsh assumed their original forms of government, each tribe having an independent king. In the year 650 A. D., Maelgwyn, king of North Wales, made himself supreme ruler of the country. This government lasted until the year 703 A. D., when the Saxons made successful inroads into the country, and established their power to a great extent throughout the kingdom. The Danish invasion of England gave repose to the Welsh, having called away the invading Saxons. The Danes themselves sought to establish their power in Wales, without success; but William the Conqueror brought them under subjection to his power. From this period the English monarchs claimed Wales as part of the dominions of the British crown. This claim was the occasion of almost constant wars between the English and Welsh, until the reign of Edward I., A. D. 1277, when the Welsh king, Llewellyn, and his barons were compelled to do homage and swear fealty to the British crown. Peace was of short duration. The Welsh revolted, rose in arms against the English, and were soon defeated, with the loss of their king, Llewellyn, and Prince David, his successor, the former being slain in battle, the latter captured by the English, tried for treason, hanged and quartered by order of Edward I. This virtually ended the kingdom of the Welsh, which deserved a better fate.

The Welsh are an unmixed family, having to a great extent preserved unchanged their primitive type, and adopted the manners and customs of their ancestors. Their language is a dialect of the Celtic tongue. The Welsh were a learned people at a very early period, and furnished the Anglo-Saxons with an alphabet.

The Welsh, in person, are generally short, with stout limbs. Their complexion is fair. The females have round faces, and dark, expressive eyes. Some of the Welsh have considerable display in literature, the higher classes generally being well informed. They are a religious people, and pay the strictest attention to the Sabbath. The lower classes do the labor of the field, whilst the aristocracy engage in drinking and sports. The Welsh are litigious, supporting more lawyers than any other country of Europe.

RUSSIANS AND POLES.

The Russians and Poles are of the same stock of people, being descendants of the ancient Sarmathians and Scythians. They were first known in history as nomadic tribes, occupying the country between the Don and Dneiper. The Sclavi family seem to be the stock of people from which the Russians and Poles derive their direct descent.

The Sclavonic tribes in the fifth century crossed the Danube, and passed down the Vistula, and up the Dneiper, and founded the two cities, Novgorod and Revel, which may be considered the founding of the Russian Empire, as the people in a considerable degree abandoned their roving and pastoral habits, and cultivated the ground.

Prior to the ninth century the Poles consisted of a multitude of independent tribes, each headed by a chief. They founded the kingdom of Poland in the year A. D. 1001. Among the Russians and Poles may be witnessed the higher and most perfect development of the Caucasian type.

10

CHAPTER VIII.

THE MONGOLIAN TYPE.

THIS type comprises many families and nations, of which the Chinese and Japanese are the most prominent representatives. The other leading families are Mongols proper, Finns, Lapps, Tartars, Basques, Esquimaux, Coreans, Kalmucks, Gypsies, Kamschatdales, and some of the families of the American Indians.

The Chinese are the leading branch of this race. They number over four hundred millions, and possess a territory of five millions four hundred thousand square miles, being twice the extent of the United States of America.

The Chinese empire is the most ancient government in the world. Other great empires, such as those of Babylonia, Assyria, Egypt, Greece, and Rome, have all passed away, and the oldest empire extant is but as yesterday, compared with that of China. Like the early nations generally, the Chinese have a fabulous history, which dates far back in the gloom of ages— placing the origin of their government at a period antedating authentic history many thousands of years. They constitute a world by themselves. For thousands of years they have been civilized, and enjoying the benefits of the arts and sciences, all which they discovered and wrought out themselves. Their early annals trace their history, as a nation, back ninety-six millions of years.

Their authentic records begin in the year 2989 B. C.; before that period their history is lost in the history of the past. They discovered the arts and sciences at least 2000 years before they as a nation became known to Europeans. Some of the arts they have brought to a perfection not yet reached by any other people.

As early as the year 450 B. C., they had reached a high degree of mental and moral refinement. Confucius in that era promulgated a system of moral philosophy and code of laws almost equal to any produced since his time. It is their great system of morals that makes them so distinguished as a nation and induces the people to submit to the powers of the government. They are capable of performing great deeds, their celebrated wall in northern China fully attesting this. It was built in the year 214 B. C., and extends fifteen hundred miles in length, separating China from Tartary, and was erected to prevent the Tartars from invading the Chinese provinces, which they were in the habit of doing before its construction. The wall is carried over deep rivers, and high mountains, and in height was about thirty feet, the top paved, and so broad that a carriage can be driven along it. The main wall is of earth, but faced with brick and stone, and contains sufficient materials to construct a wall several feet high around the globe.*

The Chinese were learned in the arts and sciences before the days of Homer. They invented printing type, firearms, and gunpowder before any other people; computed time upon a system nearly as accurate as that of the Europeans, and calculated the eclipses and phases of the moon with equal certainty.

One striking feature of the Chinese is the sameness of physique throughout the empire. The female and males also resemble each other to that degree, as often not to be distinguished. Their primitive type is well preserved.

The complexion of the Chinese is of a yellowish hue, but the females are almost a sickly white, or pale yellow as the faded leaf of autumn.

* Murray's Geography, Vol. II., p. 416.

It has only been a few years since the Chinese have been known to the world at large, having remained sealed up within the limits of their own world, until the English and the Federal Government of the United States, forced them to open their ports to foreign trade.

China has not always been governed by its own people; the Tartars have on several occasions given them emperors. Their government is described as a patriarchal despotism.

Their language is a dialect peculiar to themselves, and has no resemblance to any other. It consists of about 330 monosyllables, and the characters in which the language is written number 40,000.

In their persons, the Chinese are of middle stature; have small, elongated eyes, placed obliqely, the nose turned upwards and broad at the base, face broad, cheek bones high, and chin pointed. They shave the whole of the head except the cranium, where the hair is suffered to grow long, which is generally plaited in a long cue, and hangs down the back, frequently extending to the calf of the leg.

THE JAPANESE.

The Japanese occupy a group of large islands in the Pacific Ocean east of China, their whole territory consisting of about 260,000 square miles. The people of Japan are representatives of two types: the Mongolian and Malay, the Mongolian being very largely in the majority. They resemble the Chinese, but are of better form and larger. · Their complexion is yellow;* nose short and flat; head broad; hair thin and black. This is as the Mongolian Japanese appear. The Malays are different, resembling the Siamese and people of Malacca more than the Chinese, their complexion being as dark almost as the Sandwich Islanders. Mr. Pickering classes the Japanese with the Malay types, considering he discovered sufficient in their appearance to warrant that conclusion.†

Until recently the Japanese desired no intercourse with other nations, but now seem to invite social intercourse, especially with the people of the United States.

* Their hair according to Siebold, in many instances is red.—Natural History of Man, Vol. I., p. 255.
† Pickering's Races of Man, p. 117.

They were entirely unknown to the Europeans until Marco Polo discovered them in the year A. D. 1298. Their history like that of the Chinese, is fabulous, though they claim very high antiquity for their government, averring that they were ruled by seven celestial spirits for 6,000,000 of years. According to their annals their second dynasty commenced 15,000 years before the days of creation as recorded by Moses.

In the year 1542, Mendez Pinto, a Portuguese navigator, was cast upon one of the Japanese Islands. His discovery induced a Portuguese settlement upon the island; but the colonists were banished by the Japanese in 1585 by reason of the colonial priests interfering with the Japanese religion. The Dutch, after much difficulty, in 1600 opened a limited trade with Japan, under very restricted rules.

The Japanese are an ingenious people, as much so as the Chinese, whom they seem to imitate in almost everything, except they have more vigor of thought and power of execution. In some respects their mental powers assimilate much nearer with those of the Europeans than the Mongolian race. Their language is peculiarly their own—nothing like it in Asia. It is most allied to the Eastern Tartars, but unlike the Chinese. They pay a high regard to literature, which is widely disseminated. Their religion is Polytheism; the sun, moon, and stars, and the spirits of departed saints all coming in for a goodly share of worship.

The Japanese are described as intelligent, polite, upright, frank, faithful and brave.

THE FINNS AND LAPPS.

The ancient Finns were closely allied with the Mongols and Huns, though they eventually became mixed with the Yeto tribe of Sweden. The western Finns to a great extent have preserved their primitive type, being identical with the ancient people of Scandinavia; but the other Finnish families have become so far corrupted by amalgamation as to almost lose their identity.

The ancient Finns were of Asiatic origin.* When they first

---

* The Finns were a family of the Ugrian group.—Prichard's Natural History of Man, p. 204.

entered Europe is unknown. Their original seat was supposed to have been in the Ural Mountains, and are of the same family who founded the kingdom of the Magyars in Hungary. The primitive Finns, it is believed, had red hair. Tacitus describes them as a nation of extraordinary ferocity. However this may have been, they seem to have been readily subdued by the Swedes, and easily held in subjection. The Lapps and Samoieds are supposed to be kindred nations. The present Finns are a diminutive people. Their complexion is of a yellowish tinge, and their hair yellow or flaxen. The western Finns, to a high degree, present the features of the Aryan and the eastern the Turanian type.

The Lapps are a diminutive people, with swarthy complexion, dark, straight lank hair, and narrow dark eyes; are wholly ignorant of their origin, and which, to the rest of the world, is unknown. They, however, are supposed to be descendants of the eastern Finns, and of the same original family as the Woguls and Ostiacs of Siberia. They were originally a band of hunters and fishers, which still seems to be their employment. Though within reach of refined civilization, they continue to be the most degraded people of Europe. All efforts to induce them to adopt a system of refinement have been almost in vain; yet some of them have become Christians.

The Lapps are divided into several tribes who are known as Esthomans, Livonians, Bulgarians, Permains and Votiacs; the latter are a red-haired people, and much resemble the western Finns.*

THE SAMOIEDS

Inhabit the great northern promontory of the Siberian coast, and are spread on both sides along the shores of the Icy Sea. They are divided into numerous tribes who wander from place to place in search of game or fish, which constitute their principal food. Their country is the bleakest and most inhospitable portion of the earth. They eat human flesh, hence are called " man-eaters." In stature, complexion and general habits they much resemble the Lapps.

* The Finns and Lapps were residing in Europe long before the arrival of the Germans and Slavic nations in it.—Prichard's Natural History of Man, Vol. I., p. 204.

The Samoieds are divided into two divisions; the Yurak, Tawgi and the Ostiak of the north; and those of the south, known as the Soiot Kamas, Koibal and other tribes of the Altai range and Sayan Mountains.

They are Russian subjects. Before their subjection some of the tribes were powerful and warlike, but now all are weak

SAMOIED.

savage nomads. The great mass of the Samoieds are pagans, only a comparative few have become Christians. Pallas was of opinion that the Samoieds originated from the southern tracts of the country bordering on the Yenisei and the chain of Sayan; but they themselves declare that they came from the east, and that Siberia is not their original country.

THE TARTARS.

This great Turanian family are descendants of the Scythians, and a primitive family of high Asia,* at an early day were

* Milman's Gibbon's Rome, Vol. III., p. 3, note.

termed Bhotiga ; not confined to any fixed habitation in their
early history, but then wandering nomads, spreading themselves
over Asia and Europe almost at will.

The primitive Tartars were of medium height, and, though
thin, were strong and athletic, their complexion of light olive
hue.   They consisted of two families, one as above described,
the other being of lighter complexion, and bearing the Caucasian features generally, the same displayed in the modern Turks.
They occupy two divisions of country, one called Independent
Tartary, the other Chinese Tartary, and consist of numerous
tribes.   They have not been confined to any particularly defined
locality, but have passed almost from one extreme of Asia to the
other, east and west, and north and south.   In all ages they were
a wandering people, renowned for their courage and prowess.
China, Hindoostan, Persia and Europe have felt their power, and
been to a measurable extent subject to their arms.   Their great
captain, Tamerlane, who had no superior as a commander, lead
the Tartars through successions of conquests unparalleled in ancient or modern history.   He placed no less than twenty-seven
crowns upon his head during his conquests.   As a general rule,
they neither sow nor reap, nor gather food for the flocks or herds,
but wander from place to place, and pitch their tents in every
green spot and rich pasturage.   They do not all thus wander,
only the shepherd tribes ; others dwell in cities and towns, and
cultivate the soil.

SCYTHIANS.

The people bearing this name, according to Herodotus, were
Mongolians, who were driven from their home in Asia by the
Massagetæ, to the north of the Araxes, from whence they passed
into Europe about the year 640 B. C.   The Scythians were a very
active people, and made a brilliant history for themselves in
Asia in the seventh century.   Under their great leader, Madgis,
they broke the power of the Medes, and overrun what was then
known as the civilized world ; not only ravaged the kingdoms
of Asia Minor, Palestine, and Lower Egypt, but planted colonies
in Upper Egypt and Abyssinia.   The Parthians, who set bounds
to the Roman Empire, and bid defiance to the conquering legions
of Pompey and Crœsus, were Scythians, the Tartars, their offspring.   The Scythians are referred to in the Hebrew records.

Some claim they ruled over Egypt for several hundred years, and desolated all Northern Asia. They, it would seem, were of two types, one Mongolian, the other Aryan; hence the fair Tartars, called Turks. The Scythians did not long enjoy their conquests, and were eventually compelled to yield their own dominions to superior force. The Getæ and Sauromatæ possessed nearly their whole territory, and gave it the name of Sarmatia. As early as the time of Pliny they had become extinct as a people.

The Kalmucks are a Mongol family, though classed with the Tartars, and much resemble the American Indians, except that their color is darker. They roam all over Asia, north of India; differ materially from the Tartars; are athletic, and strongly built; have coarse black hair; nose prominent; face broad; cheek bones high; eyes dark, and set obliquely; chin full and prominent: and complexion dark, though not black. They boast of their

KALMUCK.

country as being the place from whence issued the Huns, and even claim the great Genghis-Khan as their countryman.

At the close of the seventeenth century, the Kalmucks had made themselves masters of Central Tartary, but were forced to yield up their power over that region to the Tartars and Chinese, who combined against them.

The skin of the Kalmucks is said to be naturally white, but assumes a dark hue by exposure to the sun in summer, and smoke of the cabin in winter. The females have handsome figures and fair complexion. They are, in fact, white Tartars by nature, and Mongols by habit; Turanians in name, and Aryans by nature. They are sociable and fond of society, and dress like the Poles.

THE MONGOLS.

This family, so celebrated in the annals of conquest, under

their own name and that of the Huns, occupy a district of country bordering on the desert of Shamo. They were, originally, a tribe of Tartars. In the time of their great chief, Genghis-Khan, they numbered about 400,000 tents. He made the name so illustrious, that after his great conquests, many nations, who theretofore had despised it, adopted the name of Mongols.* The title itself means " brave and proud." The name first appears in history in the tenth century.

Genghis-Khan began his military exploits by feats of arms against his own refractory subjects. His success was wonderful. His fame and great deeds brought him legions of soldiers; his policy made him successful in all his undertakings, and astonished the world by great deeds in arms. In a short space of time he established an empire extending from the Indus to the Danube; in one battle he slaughtered 160,000 of the enemy. Genghis-Khan could neither read nor write, yet he promulgated a system of laws humane and wise, equal to any legislator of his time. His talents were of such high order that his origin has been doubted, but he claimed to be a Caucasian.

The Mongols are described as being diminutive compared with the Tartars, though very muscular and active. Their faces are broad; cheek bones high; nose depressed; small, piercing, black eyes, bending obliquely towards the nose; lips thick; hair scanty and black; complexion light brown, about the same as the Tartar's, being a shade darker than the Chinese.

THE GYPSIES.

None of the families of man have so well preserved their primitive type as the Gypsies. Though classed with the Turanians, they doubtless are Aryans; have none of the features or physical caste of the former, being almost a transcript of ancient Hindoos.

Their complexion is tawny, hair black, eyes black and piercing, cheek bones high, and head pyramidal. Their language is peculiar to themselves, has no poetic element or neuter gender, and there is no alphabet to it. Until recently their language had no word to express the term God or immortality. They have no literature, and no abiding city or fixed habitation; neither sow

* Travels of Marco Polo, p. 224.

nor reap, nor, as a general rule, do any labor; like the wandering Jews; subsist by trading in horses, and fortune-telling, which is largely indulged in by the females, whilst the males speculate in horses.

The Gypsies were originally Hindoos, but, owing to their peculiar habits, most likely were forced out of their native country. They first appeared in Europe in the early part of the fifteenth century; are now scattered all over Europe and America; and, wherever they go, seem to be detested and shunned. They refuse to mingle with the other races; hence their type is the same it was when they first became known to Europeans.

THE BASQUES.

The Basques are descendants of the ancient Iberians; are of dark complexion, but not black. The Iberians were among the first inhabitants of Europe, having preceded the Celts, Finns and Tartars in Gaul, Britain and Spain. Their language is Turanian.

A remnant of the Basques exists in Europe, and one hundred and thirty thousand reside in France. "They are believed to be the most southern of the Finnish stem in Europe."*

It has been remarked that there is hardly a province in Europe that does not contain remnants of Finnic and Iberian types. Not only the living subjects preserve such evidences, but their works of art also attest this fact most fully. Their implements of stone, bronze, iron, pottery, and tumuli are found profusely scattered. Also, "knives of bone, flint arrow-heads, stone hammers, necklaces of teeth, and ornaments of amber or of coal, of barbaric form, canoes burnt out of trunks of trees,"† are found in Europe.

THE MAGYARS

Are a branch of the Finnish family, and the only Turanians who have effected a permanent settlement in Europe. They originated near the Ural Mountains, and were originally called Ugri, or Hungri. In the 9th century A. D., they, in alliance with the Khazars, appeared upon the plains between the Dnieper and the mouth of the Danube, entering Hungary through

---

* Natural History of the Human Species, p. 305.
† The Races of the Old World, by Brace, p. 78.

Transylvania; after which overrun and plundered Europe, for at least an hundred years. During their ravages they invaded France, Germany and Italy, and menaced Constantinople. Being pressed by the people of the invaded kingdoms, and tired of conquest, the Magyars quietly settled down in Hungary, where they still remain the ruling spirits of the country. The other tribes of the region, except the Slavonic, have become absorbed in this nationality. The Magyars are Aryans in spirit and vigor of thought, though they have been generally considered as Turanians. The Finns of Sweden are their only near relatives, except the Turks. Their complexion is about as dark as the Spaniards, but their general appearance is European; are tall and well shaped; quite as refined as the French and equally polite. They constitute three-fourths of the population of Hungary.

THE KAMTCHATDALES

Occupy a peninsula near the eastern extremity of Asiatic

KAMTHCHATKAN.

Russia. They are a diminutive people, resembling the Samoieds.

Their heads are large, faces flat, eyes small, lips thin and beard scanty; complexion tawny; but the females generally of fair complexion and very handsome. They are of mild disposition and noted for their hospitality, and live principally upon fish, and dwell in huts, but formerly made their dwellings in the ground. They train dogs to draw their vehicles, six constituting a full team. They have no annals, and since the Russians put an end to the wars among themselves, have become an indolent, drunken people, not disposed, as a general rule, to make any particular advance in civilization.

ESQUIMAUX.

THE COREANS

Occupy a peninsula on the east coast of Asia. They much resemble the Chinese, but are taller and stouter, and speak a different language. Their mode of writing is also different. They are Mongolians in every sense of the term; are almost, if not quite, equal with the Chinese in civilization; yet no country is more shut out from intercourse with the world than Corea. Europeans are not allowed to come into, or remain in, the country.

The earliest people of Corea were the Sinapi, who were merged in the Turkish and Tartar families, and occupied the country 400 years B. C., under the Chinese Emperor, to whom they paid tribute, though allowed to have their own king. Their complexion is the same as the Chinese.

THE ESQUIMAUX.

This family differs from the American Indians in several particulars. Their complexion is sallow, hair thick, long and black, stature low, and constitution feeble. They are very timorous, and resemble the Samoieds not only in their physique, but also in their mode of life. They have no annals, nor literature, and seem to have no desire to change their mode of life; live in huts of ice and snow, subsist upon animal food, and dress in skins; have no commerce; seem to pay little or no attention to agriculture, and are one of the lowest orders of mankind upon the American Continent. By some Ethnologists they have been considered a family of the American type.

As a family, hold a very prominent position in China. They occupy a very extensive territory of the Chinese Empire, fill many of its offices, and are its ruling military power. The Mandchus, a tribe of Tungusians of remarkable intelligence and energy, occupy the garrisons, and constitute the soldiers of the Empire.

The Tungusians have an alphabet of their own, which was invented by order of the Emperor in 1599 from the Mongolian language. They are of fairer complexion than the Chinese, and larger in person, more beard, and a more intelligent face. Some of them have the Caucasian features, such as the blonde complexion, brown beard, blue eyes, and aquiline nose. The Mandchus dwell in cities, and are not nomadic like the other tribes of this family, the latter presenting to the fullest extent the Turanian type of features and general characteristics.

The Tungusians, as early as eleven hundred years B. C., brought to China arrows made of the hoo-wood, and arrow-heads of hard stone. At that time they consisted of seven tribes; the Y-liu, Moo-ky and the Khi-tan were the most prominent. The Y-lius, in their early history, had neither chiefs nor princes, dwelt in caverns, kept many swine, upon which they fed, using their skins for garments, in winter greased their bodies with the fat of their swine, the better to endure the cold; in summer went naked, except a piece of skin about the loins. They had neither salt nor iron, their implements of warfare consisting of the bow and arrow; had no writing, their word being their bond. They were wicked and of cruel character, yet reverenced justice. All thieves were put to death without regard to the article stolen, value being of little consequence.

The Moo-kys were a brave warlike tribe, the most powerful of the Tungusians, and lived on the mountains and along the streams. They had no cattle or sheep, but raised horses, and cultivated wheat and some other grains.

The Khi-tans were a powerful nation. In the year 553 they invaded China, but were defeated, a hundred thousand of their forces taken prisoners, and many cattle taken from them by the Chinese. They eventually became civilized, built cities, fortified and dwelt in them, and established an extensive empire. In the commencement of the seventh century, the Chinese Emperor united the seven Tungusian tribes into one nationality, and at the end of that century, they had founded a kingdom of vast extent, including a part of Corea. They were then so far civilized as to have a civil government and the use of letters. This kingdom ended in 925, when it fell under the power of the Khi-tans, who eventually became rulers of China for two hundred years, when they were deposed by the Yu-tchins, one of the Tungusian tribes, who, in turn, subdued all northern China, as far as the Hoang-ho. The government thus established, continued until it was overthrown by Genghis-Khan.

THE TIBETANS.

This family of Turanians resemble the Chinese and Mongols, but are a more powerful people. They have a brown complexion, but frequently the Aryan type is plainly presented. The white skin is not seen, but the pale brown complexion often presented. They are nomadic cultivators, only a few of them having become permanently located. Their language resembles that of the Chinese.

TURANIANS OF INDIA.

There are several tribes in India which have been recognized as belonging to the Turanian group. These have been designated as the Vindhya mountain tribes, and those of Dekkan. Of the former are the Bhilla, Mina, Mera, Kalus, Poharia, and Kandos. The Bhilla are a wild tribe living near the rivers Tapti and Nerbudda, and on the northern extremity of the eastern Ghats. They are of short stature, thick lips, and curly hair. The Mina and Mera tribes very much resemble the Bhillas. They occupy the mountains of Kalikho from Agmir

to Jumna.   The Kolos consists of two tribes—one of the
Dekkan, the other of the aboriginal stock of Vindhyas.

They are a bold people, and represented as presenting the
perfections of physical beauty.   The Paharia were described in
early ages as robbers and murderers, but have been to a great
extent civilized by the English.   They are of dark complexion,
having small eyes, broad face, and thick lips.

The Dekkan or Tamulic tribes are recognised by their high
cheek bones, lozenge contour of the face, short, wide nose, large
ears, thick lips, and brunette complexion.   Nearly all the tribes
are superior to the Vindhya peoples.   The Gonds are in the
lowest state of barbarism; have dark skin, black hair, small
eyes, deep set and reddish; in some instances they are found
with red hair, but curling.   The Tuluvas and Malabars are
black tribes, and are descendants of the Tamuls.   The
Telinga, Kornata, and Malabars of Ceylon belong to the Tamul
family.   The Tuda, in the Nilghiri mountains, are of brown
complexion, of tall athletic bodies, with features and countenance resembling the Romans.*   They have heavy beards and
dark hair.   Females wear long tresses of black hair.

THE TAI FAMILY.

This family consists of several tribes, all of whom present the
Turanian type, except the Siamese, who seem to be of the order
of the Malay race.   Their complexion is yellow, skull oval, with
a full forehead, and strongly marked Mongolian features.

THE TAMULIANS

Are described as being of lower stature than the Aryans; as
having large cheek bones, long jaws, large mouth, round face,
and large in proportion to the head; short, thick nose, round
open nostrils, and complexion of brunette color.   They inhabit
the northern portion of Ceylon, and the southern part of Dek-
han.   Their early history is unknown, but it is thought they
were enjoying civilization and the art of writing before the conquest of the Hindoos.   They are considered of kin to the Telinga;
but, according to J. R. Logan, who has given a concise history
of this family, they differ in some respects from the Aryans.

* Natural History of Man, vol. I., p. 253.

They have a pointed, and frequently what is termed the hooked, pyramidal nose.

The Ainos, or Kurelians, occupy the Kurelian Islands, and a part of the Asiatic coast, as far southward as the mouth of the Amur and island of Jesso. They resemble the Kamtschatdales, but their features are more regular, their countenances approaching nearer to the Caucasian than Mongolian, except in color, which is a reddish brown. Their stature is about five feet, and they are the most hairy people of the world. Their hair is bushy, and the men wear long beards. The females comb their long, black, glossy hair down over their faces, and down their backs. They are an intelligent people, in this respect surpassing the Chinese.

THE BHOTIYA FAMILY

Comprises several tribes dwelling in the villages of the Brahmapootra and Ganges. They are closely allied with the people of the Tibet and Tamulians of India. They seem to be of the same stock of peoples as the Polynesians and are looked upon as the first settlers of India. They do not materially differ from the Tamuls. Their complexion is pale brown, yet there is found among them individuals of Aryan features and Aryan type.

There are other families residing in India besides those above mentioned, among whom a great variety of physical differences are presented; but between them there still seems to be a connecting family link. Dr. Prichard, in his researches into the physical history of mankind, has fully presented the physical differences and peculiarities of those several nations. These nations, as well as the people of India, generally do not belong to the Mongolian type, but are Aryans, having, as a general rule, well retained their native character. The great variety of complexion found among them is attributable to local causes, such as those which produced the various shades of color in Egypt. Some of the nations of the high lands are fair and handsome, whilst the Brahmans are as dark as negroes. The Rajputs of northwestern India are tall and well formed people, with fine features, arched eyebrows, hooked nose, and fair complexion. The Hindoos, in the neighborhood of Jumnotri and Gongotri fountains, are very fair, with auburn hair, and often, blue eyes.

11

The Tudas, already referred to, may be considered good representatives of the Hindoos in color and general features. Their appearance is prepossessing—have bold expressive countenances, are athletic, well made, and in stature above the common height. Their hair is jet black, which is parted on the forehead, and worn in bushy ringlets six or seven inches long. They have a large, full, expressive eye and Roman nose; have a religion of their own, which has no resemblance to that of the Buddhist; are susceptible of culture, though to a great extent barbarous; salute the sun on its rising, and believe that, after death, their souls go to a country of which they have no knowledge.

MALAY.

CHAPTER IX.

THE MALAY TYPE.

THE Malay type of mankind stands the third in order in point of intelligence and mental endowments. Though called a distinct race, and such we shall consider them, they, nevertheless, seem to be so closely allied with the Caucasian and Mongolian, as to lead to the inference that they are the offspring of these two races, corrupted by the blood of the African. Malays are found in Asia, the East Indies, in Australasia, Polynesia, Madagascar, and in North and South America. They seem to be almost amphibious, preferring to dwell nearly exclusively upon the islands of the Pacific and East Indies.

There is a general uniformity in the physique of the Malays, though in some cases their complexion is but a little darker than the Europeans. They are a bearded race, and their hair more abundant perhaps than any of the others. The aquiline nose is often witnessed among them. Some of the tribes are of large stature, but the race, as a general rule, is less than medium height, the average of stature being about five feet, especially those of Asia and the East Indies.

The Polynesians are generally of large stature, but are not above the average size of Europeans.

We have no authentic account of the origin of the Malay race. It is claimed by some that they originated in Sumatra, as there, probably, they were first recognized as a distinct type. From here, it is supposed, they spread over Malacca, Borneo, Java, and eventually became the ruling peoples of the East India seas, as well as of Polynesia.* They were not the original people of Sumatra, but are of the Pacific Islands; the Papuan family seem to have preceded them in these several regions, the interior being occupied by them. The regions of the Pacific called Malaisia consists of numerous islands inhabited by this race. They occupy Siam, Cochin-China and Malacca in Asia, and some families are doubtless residing in the interior regions of Indo-China, others reside on the coasts and lowlands of Sumatra, Java, Borneo, Madagascar and Australia. The people of the Sandwich Islands are true representatives of the Malay type.

Having no annals makes it difficult to trace them to their original place of abode. Ethnologists seem to feel warranted in assuming that they had their origin in India; and made their way to the sea by the peninsula of Malacca. They can be traced from that locality through the Pacific Isles to North and South America, if not indeed also by the Straits of Behring. Captain Cook was forcibly struck with the similarity of dialect of the South Sea Islanders and the Indian Archipelago. This is observable in particular, in Sumatra, New Guinea, the Philippine Islands and in Madagascar. It has been well ascertained that the Southern Islands on either side of the Strait of Torres have been peopled by the Malay race. The reasonable presumption is that they first occupied Malacca on the coast, and from thence passed over to Sumatra, Java, and Borneo; thence to the Celebes, thence to New Guinea, the Hebrides, Fijis, Friendly Islands, Navigator, Society, Hervey and other islands in that region, and finally reached the Sandwich group and the western continent, where they, as it would seem, established a partial system of civilization long before they became known to Europeans.

The people of the Celebes Islands have a tradition that at an early day some of the nations of that group, under a celebrated chief, formed a settlement in Sumatra, and by their intermarriage

* Natural History of Man, vol. II., p. 429.

with the natives found there, the Malays were produced. The colonists, generally slaves, obtained from the Molucca Islands, employed as wood-cutters and drudges on board the fleet of the Celebes chiefs, and hence arose the name Malay—from *Mala*, to bring, and *aya* wood. *

There is a similarity between the Malays and the Molucca family very observable; and it is said that the Malay language is spoken with more purity in the Molucca Islands than in Malacca.

The natives of Malacca before the advent of the Malays were a species of negro, much resembling those of Africa. In the thirteenth century A. D., the Malays crossed the straits, invaded Malacca, drove the natives into the mountains, and founded the city of Malacca; also that of Singapore, after which they transferred the seat of their power to Malacca.

When the Portuguese reached this region in the sixteenth century, they found Malacca a rich and flourishing city. It was so inviting to their avarice that for the sake of plunder they besieged and captured it in the year 1511 A. D., and carried off a million and a half of dollars of plunder. The Portuguese put the Malay king to death. This act of wanton barbarity so exasperated the Malays and neighboring nations, that they rose in arms against the invaders and recaptured Malacca by storm. It was retaken by the Portuguese, who occupied it until the middle of the seventeenth century, when the Dutch, supported by the King of Johore, the southern province of Malacca, became masters of the city, It finally, in 1824, by treaty, was transferred to Great Britain.

The Malays had advanced to considerable importance as a maritime people before Europeans passed the Cape of Good Hope, or anchored in the East India Seas. In 1573, the king of Archeen † appeared in the Straits of Malacca with a fleet so perfect and powerful, that in a contest with three Portuguese frigates, then in the road, as to destroy them instantly with their crews. In the year 1583 this king appeared before Malacca with a fleet of 150 sail; and in the year A. D. 1615, one of his succes-

* Goodrich's History of all Nations, Vol. I., p. 554.
† The Archenese, classed with the Malay race, are doubtless descendants of the ancient Hindoos.

sors attacked the settlement on the peninsula with an armament of 500 vessels, and an army of 60,000 men.* It is obvious that a people who could raise and man such a fleet would have but little difficulty in establishing colonies upon the most remote isles of the Pacific. It is a well-established fact that the Malays have visited New Holland on fishing expeditions for several centuries, sailing thither annually from Macassar with a fleet of two hundred prows. The Malay type is very manifest in Australia among the natives, not only in the hybrids produced by their amalgamation with the Papuan nations of the island, but in a group having the chief characteristics of this race. Two distinct races exist in New Holland. One the Malay, recognized by a brownish cast of complexion, long black hair, and flat forehead; the other having black skin, black woolly hair, long protruding jaws, and the general characteristics of the Papuan family.

The Malay race, as already stated, is found broadcast over the islands of the Pacific, and the type is so visibly displayed in the natives of these islands, that a large district of the Pacific regions has been recognized as the place of residence of a branch of this race. Mr. Prichard, in his learned work, entitled the "Natural History of Man," though calling the Malay population, the Malay Polynesian Race, admits them to be "the genuine descendants, or really cognate tribes, of the Malayan family."

There are differences among the Malays of the Pacific islands, but not any more so than appears among the European nations, and not half so much as found between the Caucasian families of Asia and Europe.

The Tahitians have been considered as the type of the Polynesian Malay nations. Mr. Lesson describes them as being a handsome people, with limbs of graceful proportions, and physiognomy having a mild, gentle and frank expression. Their skull, according to Mr. Lawrence, does not differ materially from the Caucasian.†

The natives of the Society Islands, of which Otaheite is the largest, have attracted much attention ever since their discovery

---

* Marsden's History of Sumatra, p. 431,
† Lawrence's Lectures on Physiology, p. 258.

by Captain Cook, in the month of May, 1769.* Mr. Lawrence was of opinion that the people of the Society, Marquesas, Friendly and Sandwich Islands might almost be classed with the Caucasian families; and Captain Cook described the men as being "tall, strong, well-limbed, and finely shaped." The females of the better class were described by him as being above middle stature, with complexion of clear olive, or brunette. Their hair, according to Captain Cook, was, "in general, black, but in some it was brown, in some red, and in others flaxen." He describes the natives of the Marquesas as being "the finest race of people of the Pacific Islands." "The men are tall, about five feet ten inches, or six feet. Their hair, like ours, is of many colors, except red, of which I saw none." The Spaniards, however, say that people of red hair exist among the natives of these islands.

The Otaheitans are among the most intelligent people of Polynesia; in this regard they are thought to surpass the natives of the Sandwich Islands, whom they much resemble, except that their complexion is not so dark as the latter.

The Otaheitans have a tradition that the god, Tadroa, after he had formed the world, created man out of red earth; that he put the man to sleep, and took from out his side a rib or bone, of which he made a woman, called Ive, which, in their language, means a bone.

They have also a tradition in regard to a deluge, which is, doubtless, Hindoostanic. It is related thus: that in ancient times, Tadroa, their principal deity, being angry at man, on account of his wickedness, overturned the earth into the sea, with all its inhabitants; that all sunk beneath the waves, except a few islands. Otaheite was completely submerged; no living thing remained upon its surface, except two persons, who were saved alive, and from whom the present Tahitians derive their descent.†

The natives of the Pelew Islands are about the middle size, and stout; complexion, a deep copper hue; hair, long, black and

---

* The shores of Otaheite had been touched upon by Willis, and other islands of the group been visited by Byron and Carteret, before Captain Cook reached them, but to him we are indebted for the first description of them and their inhabitants.

† Ellis, Vol. I., p. 387.

glossy. They much resemble the American Indians, and, if residing upon the continent, would be considered an Indian nation
of Tartar origin.

The natives of the Friendly Islands, known as the Tonga
group, are a handsome Malay family, of dark brown complexion.
The men are muscular, with broad shoulders. The females are
not so uniform as the latter, yet often found of perfect forms and
beauty. Though they present the serene countenance, and their
general demeanor is of marked mildness, they are capable of
committing deeds of the most barbaric character. Their wars
are carried on with the utmost ferocity. They were worship-
ping no less than three hundred deities when first visited by Europeans, and put to death some of the Christian missionaries who
went amongst them to instruct them in morals and revealed
religion. Since 1821, however, they have evinced a more
willing desire to become Christians. They have no annals, and
are as ignorant of their origin as the most savage nations of Africa Interior.

The Fiji Islands are inhabited by a people of dark brown complexion, but who are a different family from the natives of the
Friendly group. When first discovered by Europeans, they
were enjoying a partial civilization, yet indulged in the inhuman practice of eating their enemies. They were a military
people; conducted war with considerable skill and great courage. M. De Urville was forcibly struck with the resemblance
between the Fijians and Arabs. Their hair is abundant and
frizzled, but not woolly like that of the African.

They possess great physical and mental energy; in both these
respects are superior to the other natives of Polynesia. The origin of this family is yet uncertain, their place in nature not yet
having been accurately defined; but, as a nation, the weight of
authority would seem to class them with the Papuan group.*
The Fijians cultivate the ground with marked skill, and they
have made no mean advance in the arts and sciences. Almost
every Polynesian art can be traced to the Fiji islanders.

The Navigator's Islands are occupied by a people of large stature, and almost fair complexion. Their hair is long, straight
and black, which they suffer to hang down their backs and over

* Pickering's Races of Man, p. 150.

their faces, though some bind it up and fasten it around the temples. The average height of the men is five feet ten inches. The females are of proportionate stature. When young, they are as fair as the brunettes of Spanish America. These islanders, who are Malays, have made considerable progress in the arts and sciences, and are almost, if not quite, equal with the most civilized nations of Polynesia.

The natives of Easter Island are a handsome Malay tribe; the females, especially, are described as very beautiful. The males are large and active, gay and courteous, and polished in their address, but licentious, with a thievish propensity so strong that they will not scruple to commit violence in order to accomplish their ends.

These natives were not the first inhabitants of the island, as antiquities exist there of which they have no knowledge by tradition or otherwise. They consist of colossal statues of gray stone, about fourteen feet high, representing the upper portion of the human form, and composed of different stone from any existing upon the island. Captain Cook had no hesitation in pronouncing them the work of another people than those dwelling upon the island when he first visited it, and the work of a much more ancient and refined nation.

The Paumatu Archipelago, or Low Islands, are inhabited by Malays, according to Hassel; but Captain Beechy described them as more allied to the Oriental Negroes. Recently they have been classed with the Malay race.*

The Sandwich Islanders are a very prominent family of Malays. They are well formed; have large bodies; in stature equal to the Americans; have a prominent nose, high cheek bones, thick lips; hair, in some instances, long, straight, and black, in others frizzled; head erect, like that of the European; and internal capacity of the skull eighty-four cubic inches. Before the discovery of these islands, on the 18th day of January, 1778, by Captain Cook, the natives had made some advance towards civilization. Since then they have become greatly distinguished by their efforts to place themselves upon equality with European nations in the arts and refined civilization.

The native inhabitants of this group are of a dark brown

* Pickering's Races of Man, p. 47.

color. The females do not display the same delicacy and grace as the Otaheitan women; but the males surpass the Otaheitans in industry and general husbandry, though their soil is far less productive and much more difficult of cultivation.

The Mendana Archipelago, in which the Marquesas and Washington Islands are embraced, are occupied by a robust and finely-formed family of Malays. Their complexion is almost as fair as the Anglo-Saxons. The females are ill-formed, but have handsome features. When first visited by Europeans, these natives were, to a great extent, uncivilized, and did not look upon those who visited them as missionaries, for their improvement, with much favor.

The Carolines, or New Philippines, and the central Archipelago, are peopled mainly by Malays. When the Carolines were first known to Europeans, the natives were enjoying a very considerable degree of civilization. They are perfectly at home upon the waves; equip large barques with sails, and without aid of compass, guided only by the stars, pass in safety over a wide and stormy ocean to the Ladrones, where they obtain iron and other European articles, which they exchange with the more easterly nations for bread-fruit.

The natives of the Central Archipelago are described as the most friendly, courteous and amiable people of the Pacific islands.

The inhabitants of the Ladrones when discovered had made greater progress in the arts and general civilization than any other nation of the south seas, except the Otaheitans and the people of the Society, Friendly, Fiji and Sandwich Islands. They had a rude species of coin; erected houses of worship composed of sand and stone cemented together and covered with gypsum. Their females were held in the highest esteem. The complexion of these natives is light brown—very similar to that of the Sandwich Islanders.

At first it seemed as if all efforts would fail in reclaiming the Polynesians from barbarism, but it has turned out that no people have so universally and readily adopted the Christian religion and elements of civilization as the natives of the Pacific islands comprising Polynesia. The Sandwich Islanders, though guilty of the murder of Captain Cook, were the first to espouse the Christian faith as a nation, and nowhere, perhaps, upon the face

of the globe has the work of the Christian missions been more
effectual than among these islanders. The entire population
are now professors of Christianity, and to a high degree adopted
the customs and habits of Europeans. They have not only a
well regulated civil government, but also properly conducted
ecclesiastical institutions, schools and colleges.

In the midst of this seemingly prosperous condition of these
natives they are rapidly on the decrease. For example, in 1849
the deaths were 4320, and the births during the same period
only 1422.

AUSTRALASIA.

Australia is not the only island of this group occupied by the
Malay race. New Zealand, and the New Hebrides also are to
some extent peopled by them.

The New Zealanders differ materially from the natives of
Australia, especially those considered the aborigines. Crozart
ranged them into three orders by their complexion, viz: white,
brown and black. The primitive people of this group have
been considered of the same family as
the Australians; at least it is now
generally supposed the blacks are the
descendants of the primitive people of
Australia, though there seems to be no
well founded reason for such conclusion. Their language is Polynesian.

The Malays of New Zealand are tall
and well formed, and of olive complexion ; some, however, are very little, if
any, darker than the Spaniards. When
first discovered by Europeans they

NEW ZEALANDER.

were not in as low a state of savage barbarity as the other
natives of these islands. They had a system of government of
such character as held them together as communities, more as a
combination against their neighbors than to otherwise advance
their social relations. The good results of their government
generally resulted in a full display of the most savage nature of
man. Their aim seems to have been the extermination of their
neighbors, whom they not only sought on all occasions to kill

and murder, but to devour. They have made rapid advancement in the work of civilization, and are considered one of the most noble families of the Pacific.

NEW HEBRIDES.

This group has a mixed population. According to Captain Cook the natives of Tanna had the Malay complexion, and none of the Negro features. Like the New Zealanders these natives were tall and handsome; but the black population was diminutive and ugly, and they still so remain.

MALAISIA.

The Islands comprising this group are inhabited by Malays, though not exclusively so. Oriental negroes and families of other races also reside upon some of them. Borneo, the largest of the group, was first peopled by the Dejakkese, or Idaan; who are fairer than the Malays. They are tall, robust and ferocious. Their only clothing is a girdle round the middle; and they extract some of their front teeth and insert pieces of gold instead. The Horafoaras of the interior, also a primitive race of the island, occupied it before the Malays, and are of darker complexion than the Idaans. In the forests dwell dark-skinned Papuans. The interior is peopled by the Biajoos Malay colonists, who have been longer established upon the island than the Malays of the coast. They are noted for their singular custom of hanging up the skulls of their enemies at the doors of their huts.

SUMATRA.

This island is also occupied by peoples of several races, of which the Malay was the original, and is the chief. Upon this island, in the regions known as the Menang-Kabao Empire, is the place where the Malays were claimed to have originated. This is only conjecture. The natives preserved no annals, and the island being occupied by Hindoos and other families who seem as permanently located as the Malays, it is impossible at this late day to determine which is the primitive race of the island. The Battahs may be considered the representatives of the first people of Sumatra. They are of less stature than Europeans; not exceeding five feet four inches, and differ from the Malays in several respects; their limbs are handsomer, better proportioned and more muscular than the Malays. Neither history nor legend discloses the origination of the Battahs, but their tradition shows them to have been dwelling upon the island many centuries. They have ancient books and a system of writing, the invention of which dates beyond their earliest records. Their ancient writings are upon paper made of the bark of trees, written in brilliant ink.

About 2,000,000 Malays reside upon this island. The Battahs number about 1,000,000. The Achenese are reckoned at not less than 600,000. They are taller and of darker complexion than the other 'natives of Sumatra. Their kingdom is in the northern part of the island, and at one time it extended not only over its greater portion, but also included a large scope of country of the adjacent continent.

The Kubus live in a savage state, and shun intercourse with the Malayan tribes around them; go naked, and seem only desirous of gratifying their appetites and passions; and are taller and stronger than the other natives of the island. Until the year 1506, Sumatra was unknown to Europeans, except the vague notion of the Italians concerning the East Indies. At that period it was visited by the Portuguese, but it was not until the year 1600 that a footing was gained there, by the Dutch.

Before the introduction of Buddhism the natives of Sumatra had no religion or idea of the Supreme Being. This system was introduced from the continent at a very early period, but has long since given place to a great extent to Islamism, which, though prevailing, sets but lightly upon the Malay population; with them it is only in form.

JAVA.

The natives inhabiting the island of Java are principally of the Malay race; are small in size, with yellowish complexion, flattened nose, high cheek bones and thin beard. Though classed with the Malay family of the East Indies, they seem to be different from them,* especially in language, which is entirely unlike the Malay. They were once a much more flourishing people

* Natural History of Man, Vol. II, p. 434.

than they are at the present day. This was the condition of things when the Portuguese first visited them in 1510; the prosperity of the Javanese was then on the decline. In 1619 the Dutch, having conquered the native princes, made Java the center of their Indian possessions.

From a survey of the splendid ruins strewn in Java, the mind is forcibly impressed with the idea that races superior to the Malay have occupied it in ages past; and viewing the natives, it is readily discovered that in their composition are mingled the blood of the Mongolian, Malay and Aryan races. The natives in their physical aspect present the complexion of the Turanian, the skull of the Aryan and some of the general characteristics of the Hindoostanic peoples.

The Chacrelas, one of the Javanese nations, are totally different from the others, and indeed from the other indigenous peoples of Malaisia. They are of fair complexion, but their eyes are so weak they cannot endure the light of the sun. They to some extent resemble the Chinese, but are evidently of Caucasian descent.

The Javanese, though having separate governments in the interior, are under the protection of the Dutch, who control the island. The natives number over 9,000,000, the Europeans only 16,000. There are also residing in Java, besides the above, 106,033 Chinese, 31,216 Arabs and 5,111 slaves.

The smaller islands in the vicinity of Java are occupied by natives of the same family as those of the Main island, except Floris, where reside the Timuri, a dark, curly-haired race. The natives of Madura, who are probably of Hindoostanic blood, still cling to their Hindoo faith, and burn their widows on the funeral pyres with their deceased husbands.

CELEBES.

The natives of this island consist of three distinct nations: the Alfoories of the interior, Boogis, and Malays. The Alfoories are of middle stature and of fairer complexion than the Malay, and are more intelligent than the other tribes of this family inhabiting other islands. They are described by Captain Forrest as a savage and piratical people, who eat the flesh of their enemies, and drink out of their skulls. They are called Haraforas, and tribes of them are found in Borneo, New Guinea, the Moluccas, Philippines, Magindans, Sumatra, and Celebes. The Macassars were a leading tribe of the island. They and the Boogis were the most powerful tribes of the island, and when the Dutch undertook the conquest of it, held sway over the neighboring islands. The Macassars at one time fitted out a fleet of 700 vessels and 20,000 men against the Dutch.

The Boogis are supposed to have originally resided in Borneo. They are a very handsome people, much more resembling the Polynesians in their persons than the Malays proper.

The Celebean natives have no annals reaching further back than about four hundred years, and they present but little of interest, except of the wild energy, brilliant warfare of the early nations in their struggles for the mastery. The whole population of the island is about 2,000,000.

PHILIPPINES.

The natives of this group of islands are of various origin, the chief savage tribes occupying the mountain districts are the Negritos, who are doubtless of the African race, and primitive inhabitants of the Archipelago. Long before the Europeans had reached these islands, the primitive natives had been driven into the mountains by the Bisayans, and Tagalas, the leading nations of the group. They have brown complexions, and are classed with the Malay race. The total population is 5,000,000; of this number 3,700,000 are Malay Indians; 1,000,000 oriental Negroes, or of the Papuan family; the remainder being Chinese, half-cast Europeans and native whites.

The Tagalas inhabit the coast of Lucon. They are a maritime people; construct vessels of considerable tonnage with which they navigate with marked skill. One of their vessels of 600 tons has made many voyages to Spain, and is considered the best ship belonging to the port of Manilla. The Bizayans are less disposed to cultivate the ground than the Tagalas; they prefer fishing and a sea life. The Tagalas occupy the island of Luzon or Lucon, and the Bizayans inhabit the other islands. Both these tribes unite the indolence and the artistic ingenuity of the Hindoos, and the vindictiveness of the Malays. These natives have been known to Europeans since the year 1520, at which time they were discovered by Magellan. This great navigator was killed by the natives of the Island of Zebu, on the 27th day of April, 1520. Not fully understanding the prowess of the natives, who were armed only with bows and arrows, he, with his small crew landed and attacked them in force 1500 strong, and was himself slain by them in the engagement. These natives are of brown complexion, and classed with the Malays.

The island of Mindoro, though a fine body of land, is less known than any other of the group. The early navigators reported marvellous stories concerning the natives; one was that they had tails. Subsequent observation has proved them to consist of oriental negroes, who occupy the interior, and Malays residing on the coast; the latter being notorious for their piracies.

MOLUCCAS.

This group, also known as the Spice Islands, when discovered by the Portuguese in 1511, were occupied by two primitive races, the Malay and Papuan, or oriental Negroes. At that time the natives of Ternate and Tidore were contending with those of Gilolo for the mastery over the latter. The Dutch put an end to the strife by assuming supremacy over the whole group. The population now consists of Malays, Papuans, Chinese, Japanese and Europeans.

MADAGASCAR.

The natives of this island differ very materially in their physical characters. Some are almost as black and as woolly-haired as the Africans; and others are of the Malay type. Mr. Prichard asserts that the mass of the population of the island are of Malayan descent. This conclusion is no doubt based upon the idea of their language, there being but one spoken throughout the island, and that an offspring of the great Malaya-Polynesian language, bearing the nearest affinity, perhaps, to the Tagala, the language of the Philippine Islands.*

The Madecassees are of olive color, of European stature, well-shaped and of good proportions. This is only the description of the Ovahs, Ankovas and Antamayes. The Ovahs are now the ruling people of the island. Their complexion is distinguished from the other Malay nations of the island by being a light olive

Prichard's Natural History of Man, Vol. II., p. 456.

hue; and they have not the thick lips so frequently witnessed in the other native Malay tribes. The Sakalavas, occupying the west coast are quite black, and have thick lips and woolly hair; but have not the depressed features of the African, and are tall, strong, and vigorous. These two families present the two extremes of the indigenous peoples of Madagascar. The hair of the Ovahs is bushy and curly, but not woolly; and there are no indications of the Negro about them.

The other principal tribes are the Anlavarts, Bestimessaras, Betanemenes, Antaximes, Ambarivoules, Bezonzons, Amayes, Ancovesovas, Andrantsais, Antsinaxes, and Saclaves.

The Bestimessaras are the finest people of the island. They cultivate the ground, and are also pastoral to some extent. The Antaximes are a rude tribe of dark complexion with woolly hair. The Betsileo tribe are of light copper color, and have long, lank, black hair. The Antaymures have been considered by some to be Arabs. They themselves claim to be the children of Amina; they are doubtless Malays.

The Madecassees have no records of origin, and no satisfactory tradition in regard to their advent upon the island.

SIAMESE.

The Siamese in personal appearance are very homely; they have broad, flat faces, long and square lower jaws, large mouth, thick lips, small nose, broad, low forehead, prominent cheek bones, dark eyes, and a complexion of a brownish hue.

The Siamese proper are doubtless Mongolians, but there are in Siam many natives of Malay descent. By a late census there were at least 320,000 Malays residing in the country.

In stature the Siamese do not average over five feet four inches in height. Their color is darker than the Chinese, but not so dark as the western Asiatics; their hair is always coarse, black and lank. The Siamese have no history earlier than the year A. D. 638, and their authentic records only reach back to the year 1350, the time of founding their old capital Yuthia. From that time forward they have made rapid progress in civilization and the arts; they are enjoying a degree of civilization superior to the other nations residing east of Hindoostan and China; they have an alphabet of their own.

12

Their early history is unknown; the first event in their recorded history is the introduction of the religion of Buddha from
Ceylon, in the seventh century A. D.   The Siamese were first
made known to Europeans by the Portuguese in 1511.

SIAMESE TWINS.

The world-renowned Siamese Twins are true representatives
of this family.   They were born May, 1811, and brought from
Siam in April, 1829, by Captain Coffin, in the American ship
Sachem; and since then have been extensively exhibited in
Europe and America.   They claim to have been born of Chinese
parents.   However this may be, they are more Malay than
Chinese in appearance and in their general characteristics.

The Malays of Malacca occupy the coast districts, and are
much like the Sumatrans, but they are not as perfect Malays as
the latter, having tainted their blood by amalgamation.

There is a tribe inhabiting the mountain regions of the Peninsula, supposed to be descendants of the primitive people of

Malacca, who seem to be Oriental Negroes, or of the Papuan family. They have black skin, black curly hair, thick lips, flat nose, and Negro features generally. There is also a savage race inhabiting Malacca, called Maracaiboes. They do not occupy the main land, but the island ports. Their complexion is not so dark as the Malays.

The Island of Ceylon is peopled by a mixed population, divided into several tribes, viz.: Cingalese, Malabars, Tamulians, and Bedhas. The Cingalese* is the leading family or tribe of the island. They are of middle stature, of slender bodies, and of fairer complexion than the other tribes, their color being lighter than the Malays generally. They seem to occupy a position between the Malays proper and the Caucasians. The Cingalese have the Malay expression of countenance. The Malabars are of darker complexion than the Cingalese, and of the same people as those occupying the coasts of Malabar. They are Turanians. The Candians are fairer than the Cingalese, and stouter. They seem to be of the same order of people; but occupying the more elevated regions of the island, and taking more exercise, gives them more vigor; and it is well known that families of the same race, occupying the uplands, will be fairer than those living in the lowlands.

The Bedhas are a tribes of savages roaming in the forests, without houses or any place of shelter except such as nature has provided for them, and subsist on animal food taken in the chase. They are, doubtless, descendants of the dark-skinned tribes of India and the Papuan family; though they still present the physique of the Indo-Malays in a very high degree.

The Cochin-Chinese are Malays, but strongly resemble the Chinese. They are strong and active, and more refined and courteous than the Siamese, their neighbors. They are liberal and charitable, and have reached a high state of improvement in commerce, agriculture and general industry; though the discovery of gold and silver, and great prosperity, have made the people, of the higher classes, at least, indolent and effeminate.

* The Cingalese only differ from Europeans in color, which is, in most cases, brown, but varies to light black. Their features are rather handsome. They have an abundance of hair. The beard is heavy and long. The females are generally well formed, and often handsome.—Natural History of Man, Vol. I., p. 245.

The Birmans, says Dr. Betton, of Philadelphia, belong to the same class of people with the Malays of the East Indies. They are a distinct family from the Karens, a branch of the Bhotiya group, who are Turanians, also occupying a district in Birmah. Some of the Birmans are almost white, whilst others are as black as the Hindoos.

The Malay Birmans are an athletic family, more so than the Hindoos, though not so neat in person as the latter, yet are more warlike and hospitable. They are very ingenious, and have attained to great proficiency in the useful and fine mechanical arts. One of their great state carriages, which was taken by the British troops in the war of 1825, and brought to London, was nineteen feet high, fourteen feet long, and seven feet wide. It was handsomely finished, and had been devoted to the service of the gods.

The Sooloo Group of Islands, off the eastern coast of Borneo, are peopled by a family of Malays, whose chief business is piracy. Ten thousand of the islanders are constantly engaged in this very perilous business upon the high seas. They have about four hundred vessels employed in their piracies, under the sanction of their government; at the same time are actively engaged in friendly commercial intercourse with other nations. Singapore is headquarters for their traffic.

The Islands of New Britain and New Ireland are peopled by Malays and Papuans. The Malays are a fine-looking, portly people; but the Papuans are a little, ugly, black tribe of savages.

Solomon Islands, also, are populated by these two families, the Papuans being the most numerous. They are as black as the African Negroes. The Malays are less pure than in the other islands; indeed, it is doubtful if a pure-blood Malay is to be found (native) upon the island.

MALAY AMERICANS.

The California Indians are of darker complexion than the natives north of the Rocky Mountains, and in other respects are quite different. Mr. Pickering remarks, in his valuable work upon the "Races of Man:" "the first of the Californians satisfied me of their Malay affinity." The Sandwich Islanders look upon the California Indians as their kindred.*

* Pickering's Races of Man, p. 99.

The remains of large, well constructed stone* edifices, called "Casas Grandes,"† existing in California and Mexico, has led to a more full investigation into the history of the California Indians. It is very manifest that they were once enjoying a much more exalted position in civilization than they are now.

The Pimos and Coco-Maricopas, who reside on the Gila, are of a clear brown complexion, entirely different from the Indians east of the mountains. The females are of good figure, tall and graceful, with finely formed limbs, some of them models of beauty. The Pimos' language is soft and melodious; that of the Coco-Maricopas is harsh and guttural. The former bury their dead; the latter burn theirs. These tribes raise excellent cotton, which they spin into yarn by a loom of very primitive order. They also weave it into cloth by a very simple loom. Their pottery is of very superior quality, and they manufacture baskets with neatness and skill.

Their moral character is of an order not usually found among the Americans. They only engage in war as a means of self-defence. They are, doubtless, descendants of Polynesians.

The Moquis, Mohavis, Zunis, Yumas, Opates, Yaquis, and Navajos, also inhabit the same regions. Of these the Moquis are the most civilized. They cultivate the soil, raise sheep, and live in villages. The Zunis also cultivate the ground.

Differing, as these tribes do, in some respects, from each other, they are, doubtless, as to origin, referable to the Malay type, transmitted through the Polynesian family. The fact that the Mongolian race has been engrafted upon the Malay, as appears to be the case in some of the tribes, does not at all change the Malay or primitive type. As in the case of Montezuma and the Aztecs, it remained visible, and still is apparent.

The hair of the Californians is straight and black, and very abundant, which is not the case with the Northern Indians, theirs being coarse and rather scanty, and the Polynesians' generally wavy, and often curled.

* Mr. Bartlett describes the Casas Grandes as constructions of mortar and clay, as well those on the Gila as in Chihuahua.—Explorations in New Mexico, California, Sonora and Chihuahua, Vol. II., pp. 281-351.

† Prichard's Natural History of Man, Vol. II., p. 555.

The Sacramento tribes are fine, stout people, as much so as Europeans, and have the Malay complexion and countenance; but their beards do not seem so abundant.   Yet all the California tribes are more hairy than the other Indian nations of America.

The manners and customs of the Californian Indians are Polynesian; they have no tomahawks, and do no scalping, which is a Mongolian practice; they have a system of government which means more than respect for the chief, as is the case with the North American Indians generally.   With the former the chief is to be obeyed, respected and feared, and to his power they seem to be in subjection.

. In Mexico, also, the Malay type is found, especially in the Aztecs and kindred tribes.   Montezuma was a good representative of his race; he was doubtless of Malay origin.   But we shall notice the Mexicans further when we come to speak of the American race.

The nautical character of the Malays to some extent explains why they are found so broadcast over the Pacific Islands. Their first advent upon the ocean as emigrants may not have been voluntary; but they are so wide-spread as to lead to the conclusion that they were emigrants by design, even to the making of conquests of the countries they coveted.   It is not for us to say at this late day whether they passed in ships or rude canoes from their original abode to this continent and other distant regions.   It is not likely they did so in a single voyage, but step by step from Asia to Sumatra and other islands, until they reached the remotest regions of the Pacific and the western continent.

The question whether Polynesia was first peopled by Malays from America, or the latter from the former, is difficult of solution, as the state of civilization seems to have been about equal in both regions when first discovered by Europeans.   But it is very manifest that this continent in very remote ages had been more densely peopled than Polynesia.   If the works of art found in America, especially in Central America and in Mexico are those of the Malays, then this continent, doubtless, was first peopled by them.   The ruined structures of Mexico, Central and South America are of very high antiquity, and seem to have been constructed by the same order of people.

The Pacific Ocean, with its remains of land, presents the appearance of a ruined world, the islands being the only monuments of its existence. They present mountains as towering as the most majestic of the existing continents.

The islands may have been peopled since the remainder of the Pacific world became submerged, or they, as parts of the mainland, may have been occupied by the same types of mankind when the great deep passed over it.

The Polynesian Islands are separated from the main land by a wide open sea, upon the rough waves of which the daring Malay would hardly venture with his canoe, yet may have drifted to the western continent in safety. Being found in California, Mexico, and other places along the coast regions of the western continent, it is not mere conjecture to say that they reached there by water by way of the Pacific, or the Cape of Good Hope.

The northern extreme of California, says Mr. Pickering, is a favorable location to receive a direct arrival from Japan.* This is suggested by the fact that the native Californians strongly resemble the Japanese. The vessels of the Japanese are capable of conveying emigrants to California, but none have been brought thither, except that one was recently drifted to the shore near the mouth of Columbia River; one was also wrecked upon the Sandwich Islands, and another was found in the northern Pacific.

The Society and Tonga Islanders had a large canoe with which they made long and successful voyages; they visited the Fiji Islands, New Hebrides, and others even more distant. Captain Cook obtained a chart from a native of the Society Islands, showing the people to have been acquainted with the Marquesas and the islands east of Tahiti. These canoes were of sufficient strength and capacity to safely conduct the natives to the coasts of America. The enterprising spirit and native disposition of the Malays warrant the conclusion that they did at a very early period visit these shores, and planted colonies in North and South America.

The Japanese annals show them to have been in existence as a people many thousands of years, and to have been a nautical na-

* Mr. Pickering classes the Japanese with the Malays.—Pickering's Races of Man, p. 117,

tion of considerable note when first discovered by Europeans. Being such, and Malays, as supposed, they may have readily, with their large strong junks, visited the remotest parts of the world. Like all the early nations in navigation, they piloted their course by the sun, moon, and stars, which were more certain guides than the compass of the present age, to those who studied their location and phases.

TECUMSEH.

CHAPTER X.

THE AMERICAN TYPE.

The American Indians constitute the American Type.—This Race consists of
many tribes; Were two great families originally in America; One seemed
to be Mongolian, the other Malay.—The Toltecs represented the former,
Aztecs the latter.—When they first occupied this Continent.—Query:
Who were the Aborigines?—Were they Scythians?—Migrations by
Straits of Behring.—Natives of South America described.—America unknown to the ancients.—Plato's Atlantis not this Continent.—The tradition
of the Welsh.—Ancient books in possession of Indians.—White Indians of
Missouri.—Early voyages of the Danes to America (Vineland).—Mohawk
language a Tartaric dialect.—Ten lost tribes of Israel.—Land of Arsarath.—
Marco Polo, Tungusians, Coreans and Indians of same origin.—Aztalan,
Votan, Caribbe Indians, Aztecs and Toltecs.—Tumuli and Pyramids.—Incas
of Peru.—Indian tradition.—Manners and customs.—Mode of burial.

THE American type comprises the Aborigines of America.
They are divided into numerous tribes, and in many respects differ materially in their physical and mental qualities.
There seems to have been, originally,
two great families of them, one much
resembling the Mongolians, the other
the Malays, physically and mentally.
The former seem to have entered the
country by the straits of Behring,
the latter by the Pacific ocean. They
both attained to a tolerable degree of
civilization during their sojourn in
Mexico and Central America. The
Toltecs were the first in the country,* that is, entered it before the
Aztecs; but when they first migrated
to Mexico, found it, as well as Cen-

INDIAN.

tral America, occupied by natives, or peoples, of whom we have

* Natural History of Man, Vol. II., p. 509.

but little, if any, account, except their works of art, consisting of ruins, temples, pyramids and tumuli. The bas-relief from Palenque in Yucatan, now in Washington City, contains a human profile eminently characteristic of the Mongolian type.*

The Indians, in general, like the Mongolians, are a beardless race. Their complexion is not red, as generally supposed, but is of a copper color, and of a darker tinge than the Chinese, but almost identical with the Mongols and their kindred tribes of Northern and Central Asia.

The term *Indian* was first applied to the aborigines of America by Americus Vespucius, its discoverer, under the mistaken idea that he had landed on the Southern coast of India.

The Indians of North America are considered by some ethnologists to be the descendants of the Magogites, the ancestors of the Scythians; and the Scythians, the ancestors of the Tartars, Mongols and Siberians. It is worthy of note that nearly all the northern regions of Asia were colonized by the Scythians, from which a basis at least was laid, upon which to predicate a conjecture that they or their descendants, the Mongols, passed the straits of Behring to America. Strong evidence exists in favor of this theory by the nations of this type of people being found inhabiting regions along the route they would naturally travel, and on either side of the straits.

The South American Indians seem so be of two types, the Malay and Mongolian, in form, at least, if not in character.

The natives inhabiting Siberia, in the vicinity of the Straits of Behring, are Mongolians: no other race has ever resided here. It will not, therefore, seem strange that the land on the American side should be occupied by them. The straits being only about forty miles wide, and shallow, would be but little hindrance to people of less enterprise than the Mongols.

In regard to the peopling of South America, the claim is that it was done by Joctan's posterity. A province in Yucatan is called Jucton, and there being evidences of a different people than the Mongolians, inhabiting that country and also South America, it is assumed that the descendants of Shem peopled these several regions of the new world.†

† Pickering's Races of Man, p. 30.
* McIntosh's Book of Indians, p. (24) xxxiv.

We gather but little information, if indeed any of reliable character, from the people of the old world in regard to the inhabitants of the New. They did not have any definite idea of any large body of land lying beyond the pillars of Hercules; and did not seem to understand the spherical form of the globe, or how to measure its magnitude. They never seemed to look beyond the physical evidences presented to them for the balancing power of the earth—considered the pillars of Hercules were the western terminus of land, and beyond them a boundless expanse of waters, except that some supposed there was an island a short distance beyond the pillars.

Diodorus Siculus, in the time of Julius Cæsar, gives an account of some Phœnicians, at a very early date, being driven by violence of a storm at sea far beyond the pillars of Hercules into the ocean; that they discovered at the distance of a few days sail, to the west of Africa, a large fertile island, watered by large navigable rivers; that this discovery was soon made known to the Carthagenians, and Tuscans, in Italy; that the Carthagenians, sometime afterwards, passed beyond the pillars, and arrived at this island (which has been called Atlantis* by the ancient authors), where they made a settlement. This story does not in the least warrant the conclusion that the Phœnicians, or Carthagenians, had reached the American Continent; but it may reasonably be inferred, from the above narrative, that the island they visited was Ireland, as other accounts fully confirm the fact that the Phœnicians at a remote day not only visited Ireland, but England also.

Plato describes the Atlantis as situated in the western ocean opposite the west of Cadiz.† Out of this island was an easy passage to a continent which exceeded Europe in extent. If Ireland was the country referred to by Plato, its whereabouts was lost sight of until Julius Cæsar saw it from Gaul, during his conquest of that country.

The Welsh have a tradition, that they were instrumental in peopling the New World by the adventure of Madoc, son of

* It has been supposed the Guanches of the Canary Islands were the wreck of the inhabitants of the Atlantis.—Lawrence's Lectures on Physiology, p. 236.

† Atalantis, according to the information gained by Solon concerning it from an Egyptian Priest, was a body of land almost as large as a continent, but it had disappeared.—STRABO, Vol. I., p. 154.

Guymeyd, who they claim sailed thither in the year 1170 A. D., and colonized part of the country. This tradition has no foundation, except in the song of an English bard. Following up the idea, some over-anxious persons seem to think that the Welsh really did discover and occupy this continent, and seek to prove it by finding Welsh names and Welsh coin among the native Indians.

The Mnacedens tribe of Indians, of Missouri, it is said, had the manners and customs, to some extent, of the Welsh. Henry Ker, who visited them in 1810, found this tribe possessed of books they preserved with great care, having a tradition that the books were brought there by their forefathers.*

The books were very old and had evidently been printed at a time when but little progress had been made in the art of printing.†

Major Rogers, in his account of the American Indians, published in 1765, mentions White Indians west of the Mississippi river. He also describes them as the fairest Indians of the continent.‡ They lived in large towns and had commodious houses, raised corn, tamed the wild cattle, and used the milk, as well as flesh, for food, keeping great numbers of dogs, and were very expert and dexterous in hunting. These statements must be taken with a great deal of allowance, as they are not fortified by any additional facts since the Indians have become better known.

The Norwegians also claim some share of the glory of peopling America, and have much higher claims to the honor than the Welsh, as the latter were never suspected of being a maritime or nautical nation; whilst the former were noted for their commercial enterprise. They colonized Greenland and Iceland, within the historical period of Europe, and coasted the continent from Newfoundland to Brazil.§ The Northmen do not merely

* The books referred to could not have been brought to America by the Welsh, as printing was not then invented, nor until long after that period. The first book of any considerable size printed was a Latin Bible, published at Mentz in 1455, by Guttenberg, Faustus & Schaeffer.

† History and Biography of the Indians of North America, p. 55.

‡ The White Indians were doubtless a family of the Mandans. Some of them were as fair as the Welsh; had light hair and blue eyes.— *Vide* George Catlin's notes of the Mandans, on visiting their town in 1832.

§ The Natural History of the Human Species, p. 259.

give conjecture on the subject of their discovery of America, but present the authentic facts, clearly showing that they visited the northern portion of North America, even as far south as Massachusetts and Rhode Island, long before Columbus reached the West India Islands. Some historians have even claimed that the Northmen had visited the coasts of Brazil prior to Columbus reaching the western continent.

The period of their discovery was in 1002. At that time, according to an Icelandic chronicle, a Norwegian vessel, commanded by Captain Lief, sailed from Iceland for Greenland. Driven out of his course by a gale, this navigator reached land far to the south, which proved to be the country subsequently called Newfoundland. He explored the coast of Labrador, and shores of Newfoundland southward, until he reached a genial climate, and a region abounding with grapes and noble forests. This, it is supposed, was Massachusetts, and in the vicinity of Boston. Afterwards the Scandinavians seem to have extended their discoveries as far as Rhode Island, where, it is claimed, they planted a Colony, and that a child of a Scandinavian mother was born upon the shore of Mount Hope Bay.*

The Norwegians of Labrador † met with the natives, called Scraelings, a tribe of Esquimaux. The southern portions of the country discovered, owing to the abundance of grapes, they called Vineland. They kept up their voyages to the continent until the year A. D. 1321, when all communications between the Scandinavian countries and North America, seem to have been cut off. Vineland was doubtless New England—Rhode Island. The latter contains the most conclusive and convincing evidences of this portion of the country having been occupied by the Northmen.

At Newport, Rhode Island, is located a round tower, constructed of unhewn stone laid in mortar composed of sand and gravel, and lime made of oyster shells. The tower is a cylinder resting upon eight round columns twenty-three feet in diameter, and twenty-four feet high, and was originally covered with stucco. This edifice was standing erect when the country was

---

* Lossing's Hist. of the U. S., p. 35, *note* 1.

† The Norwegians have left on the coast of Labrador their *Stela*—small columns of hewed stone having neither base nor capital.—Plurality of Races, by Pouchet, p, 101.

first visited by Europeans after its discovery by Columbus. The Indians (Narragansetts) then inhabiting Rhode Island had no knowledge, even tradition, of its origin. There can be but little, if any, doubt about this structure being built by the Scandinavians, who attempted a settlement in the country.* It is not strange that no record has been preserved of the attempted settlement, other than above given, as what was done by way of settlement and discovery was transacted in the gloom of the dark ages, when great events were left unrecorded.

Some authors have gone to a vast amount of trouble to prove that the American Indians are the descendants of the Hebrews, and directly from the lost tribes of Israel. The proof for such theory is so meagre as to make it wholly improbable. No one as yet has been able to discover any relationship between the Jews and the American Indians. But to the proof of the theory.

The ten lost tribes, it is claimed, emigrated to Scythia, and there, by amalgamation, became part of that great family. There was, in point of fact, but little difference between the Jews and Scythians; their complexion about the same, as also their general features.

The Israelites, who were carried away by Salmanaser to the land of Assyria, went in a northerly direction to the land of Arsarath, is evident from the book of Esdras. The author of that record was not apprised of the existence of the western continent, and hence would not undertake its description. The Arsarath of Esdras, it may safely be affirmed, was not America. The Israelites left Syria about one hundred years after they were carried thither, and were a year and a half in their journey to Arsarath. The route they must have taken, had the point of destination been this continent, would have been over high mountains, deep rivers, through a cold, dreary wilderness region, the distance of over six thousand miles to the Straits of Behring, and in addition, their way must have been blocked up by impenetrable snows.

The Arsarath of Esdras was, in all probability, Norway. It is described as a "land where no man can dwell." Norway was as little known to the ancients as America.

The ten tribes were not lost as has been generally supposed;

* Lossing's Field Book of the Revolution, Vol. I., p. 633.

their descendants are found at the present day in Persia, Media, Iran, Touran, Hindoostan and China.

Had they come to America, the arts and sciences would have been preserved, as they were advanced in refined civilization when they left Assyria, and in all the above countries where they have been scattered, as supposed, the arts and sciences have been preserved. Not so with the aborigines of America; they were, with few exceptions, savages when it was first visited by Europeans.

Though the Northmen had reached America several hundred years prior to its discovery by Columbus, their discoveries were unknown to the people of the European continent until long after the adventures of the distinguished navigator of Genoa.

Columbus himself did not suppose the land he was in pursuit of was a new continent, but an extension of Asia. Marco Polo had given such a graphic description of India and Eastern Asia as to induce the belief that it extended far eastward toward the shores of Spain; hence the great zeal of Columbus in his discoveries.

It has been claimed for Columbus, by some of his chief admirers, that he did not know of the discoveries or adventures of Polo when the former went upon his mission in search of the New World. This is hardly probable, when discovery was the sole object of his daring and perilous adventure upon the unknown ocean. He as a prudent navigator, as he was, would search every avenue for information before entering upon his great undertaking; and by such means he had satisfied himself, and to a moral certainty convinced his patrons that he would reach a large body of land by sailing westward. He was so well convinced of it that he was willing to risk his life in establishing the reality of his theory; and so powerful were his arguments, and convincing his logic, that he not only won to his interest the king and queen of Portugal, but quelled the mutiny of his crew who, despairing of success, had resolved to abandon the enterprise and return to Spain.

The North American Indians, as a general rule, have a striking similarity and sameness of features; generally tall, spare and straight, yet in some tribes the middle stature prevails; their color is almost universally the same. The fact that no other races existed upon the continent is a potent reason why the primitive type is so well preserved.*

The chief exceptions to the general rule above stated, is in the case of the white Indians already noticed; the Mowkeys, of Mexico, represented as being very fair with flaxen hair and blue eyes; also the Nobbeshaes of the same region, of the same complexion; and other tribes of the north-west on the Pacific coast.

Though the remarkable similarity of the families of the American race does exist, there is no doubt but peoples of the Caucasian, Mongolian and Malay races have also in very remote ages been inhabitants of America. The northern portion of the country was doubtless first peopled by Mongolians, and the South and west by Malays.

There are three different languages spoken by the North American Indians, besides that of the Esquimaux, viz.: Lenape, Iroquois and Floridan. The former is the most universal east of the Mississippi; and there is no perceivable affinity in these several languages. The Lenape is the language of the Miamis, Potawatomies, Mississagoas, Algonquins, Chippewas, Shawnees, Mohicans, Kickapoos, Conestagoes, and lesser tribes. The Iroquois was spoken by the six nations; the Wyandots, and Hurons, and the tribes generally beyond the St. Lawrence, except Esquimaux. The Floridan was the language of the Creeks, Chickesaws, Cherokees, Choctaws, Muscogees, Seminoles, and Pascagoulas.

There are many tribes in the great west who have dialects of their own, yet having the true American characteristics otherwise fully displayed.

Language and customs, after all, are not the best tests to discover the origin and relationship of the families of mankind; are not important in the case of the Americans, as they have preserved their original type so well that any one can identify them by their physical development.

The difficulty in regard to this race seems to be in tracing it to its original source. One great reason consists in an over anxiety on the part of zealous persons seeking to make the Americans

* The primitive people of Central America were doubtless a different race. They are now wholly extinct, and considered a lost race. Their works of art alone remain as the evidence of their existence.—Plurality of Races, by Pouchet, p. 81.

descendants of almost every prominent nation of the Old World.
Some claim them to be descendants of the Phœnicians, others of
the Carthagenians, Israelites, Arabs, Egyptians, Celts, Hindoos,
Tartars, Scythians, and others of the Coreans, Samoieds and
Tungusians. There is a strong resemblance between the Americans
and the Tungusians, Coreans, Samoieds, and Tartars proper, and
the resemblance is so marked as to impress the mind with the
belief that they are of the same family of people.

The Tungusians are like the leading tribes of Indians, tall,
straight, and athletic, and have the same complexion.* Were
the Tungusians, Kamtchatdales or Tartars to reside in America,
they would be classed with the Indian tribes. The three former
are of the same origin, as has been fully shown by the learned
Padre Sontini, of Italy, who was for a long period a missionary
in Chinese Tartary and Siberia. They do not speak the same
languages, but in all respects are of the same type as the American Indians; having the same tumid lips, small piercing black
eyes, high cheek bones, large ears, white vertical teeth, and long,
coarse black hair.

The Indians themselves have only a vague idea of their
origin, or from whence they came. Some of the tribes say they
are descendants of ancestors who came from the north; others
say from the north-west; others again say their ancestors came
from the east; and others again claim theirs came from the regions of the air. They have no annals except among the Mexicans, and no reliable traditions. All they seem to know is of
the present generation, except that some nations have preserved
same important event in characters recorded upon skins, but they
are altogether unreliable as records, and give no light as regards
the origin of the race, or its advent upon the American continent.

The Mexicans seem to have preserved the idea of the deluge in
becoming characters, and the most intelligent relic of the
American race. It consists of a painting representing an ark in
the midst of water, in which Tezpi, or Noah, is safe, whilst others
are perishing around him by the flood. It also represents a high

* The Osages are tall and well made, resembling the Tungusians. Hamilton
Smith gives their height at six and a half feet.—Natural History of the Human Species, p. 193.

13

mound of rock, upon the top of which is growing an olive tree, whereon is perched a dove, with a twig or branch of olive in its beak. Humboldt says this character of painting was found among the different Indian tribes of Mexico.

The tradition preserved in these paintings goes far to prove the truthfulness of the Book of Genesis, as no one will charge the Mexicans with priestcraft, their religion not being of the Christian character, but a gross idolatry. It is a waif in the probability of America being one day connected with Asia and Africa by land, and the people during that period passing and repassing from one country to another at will. By these connections the early people of Mexico might have readily passed from Asia to Aztalan, supposed by Humboldt to be in the region of the United States. The picture above referred to represents fifteen individuals of Caucasian type, all in a nude state, except one, who has an open cloak about his shoulders.

They have no resemblance to the Indians, but seem to be a transcript of a group of ancient Celts, Greeks and Romans. This picture, in the presentation of a group of Caucasians, is strong presumptive evidence that the Indians were not the first people who occupied the continent.

Clavigero, in his History of Mexico, reveals the fact that the Chiapanese Indians had a manuscript in their language, made by the Indians themselves, in which it was said, according to tradition, "that a person named Votan was present at the building (of the Tower of Babel), which was made by the direction of his uncle, in order to mount to heaven; that then every people was given its language; and that Votan himself was charged by God to make division of the lands of Anahuac; so he divided the land among his sons. Votan may have been Noah.*

The ancient Indians of Cuba (the Caribs), when enquired of by the Spaniards concerning their origin, answered, that they heard from their ancestors that God created heaven and earth and all things; that an old man, having foreseen the deluge, built a canoe, and embarked in it, with his family and many animals. When the waters abated, he sent forth a raven, which never returned; he then sent out a pigeon, which soon returned, with a branch of the hoba tree in its mouth. The old man, with

* American Antiquities, p. 203.

his family, disembarked, and, having made wine of the grapes produced after the flood, became intoxicated; that, whilst in that condition, one of his sons exposed his nakedness, and another covered him; upon awaking, he blessed the latter, and cursed the former. These Indians held they were the descendants of the cursed son, and hence their nakedness and degraded condition.

The Toltecs, who entered the plains of Mexico about the close of the seventh century A. D., went thither from the north, but from what country they emigrated to Anahuac is unknown, except by conjecture. They have left no written history, except their picture and hieroglyphic paintings, which are so uncertain as to be almost useless as authentic records; and their history is otherwise only presented to us in legendary story, preserved by the nations who have succeeded them. They were well instructed in agriculture and many of the most useful mechanical arts, and were skillful workers in metals. They invented the complex arrangement of time adopted by the Aztecs, and were the source of the refined civilization of Mexico before the conquest of Cortez. Their capital was located at Tula, north of the Mexican Valley. The splendid ruins of Mexico and Central America are considered by historians the work of the Toltecs. This can hardly be, as they are doubtless of a much earlier date than the seventh century, and these ruins seem to be the workmanship of a more refined people than even the Toltecs. They occupied the country only about four hundred years, then silently and mysteriously disappeared from it. After the departure of the Toltecs, in the course of a hundred years, the rude Chichemeces entered the plains of Mexico from the west. They were speedily followed by others more civilized, supposed to have been of the Toltec family. Then came the Aztecs and Acolhuans (Tezcucans). The former occupied the country, and were its rulers until the Spanish conquest. The Tezcucans were a powerful ally of the Aztecs, and their equals in all things. Their governments were identical, being elective monarchies.

Montezuma, in his first interview with Cortez, said: "We know by our books that myself and those who inhabit this country are not natives, but strangers, who came from a great distance. We know, also, that the chief who led our ancestors hither, to Aztalan, returned for a certain time to his own country, and thence came back again to seek those who were here established. We always believed his descendants one day would come to the possession of this country. Since your arrival from that country where the sun rises, I cannot doubt but that the king who sends you is our natural master."

The chief to whom Montezuma had reference was called Tecpaltzin. He, it appears, returned to the land from whence he came, where the sun rises. Taking this narrative in connection with the account of the deluge, before related, and it may from them be reasonably inferred that the Aztecs derive their origin from people beyond the bounds of Mexico, and, as we shall presently show, beyond the limits of this continent. The Aztecs were evidently of Malay origin, and we have classed them with that race.

The customs of some of the Eastern peoples of Asia, and the adjacent islands, are so similar to those of some of the tribes of the American Indians as to induce the belief that they are of the same family of mankind. In one of the islands of Japan a religious sect is found abstaining from animal food, and refusing to shed blood of man or animals; so in South America is a whole nation of Indians who eat nothing but vegetables, and abhor bloodshed and animal food.

The idea of the Indians entering Mexico from the west raises the strong presumption that they crossed the Straits of Behring; but the Aztecs did not, in all probability, enter Mexico in that direction; yet they may have done so; the better theory, however, is, that they came by the way of the Pacific, and from Polynesia or from India.

The Toltecs and Aztecs had a tradition among them, that a wonderful personage, whom they called Quetzalcate, appeared among them, who was a white-bearded man; that he acted the part of a legislator and priest; introduced the custom of piercing the lips and ears, and lacerating the rest of the body. Humboldt, in this personage and customs introduced by him, seemed to recognize one of the Rishi hermits of the Ganges, celebrated in the books of the Hindoos.

The peculiar doctrines of the Hindoos were first taught in the

East about the time of Abraham, 1449 years before the age of Confucius. Zoroaster was the author of the Hindoo faith.

The tumuli found in India are so similar to those of America, as to induce the belief that they are the work of the same type of people.

The islands in the vicinity of the Straits of Behring are peopled with Tartars. When first visited, they were found enjoying a civil government, and had attained to considerable proficiency in the useful arts. The Japanese, occupying contiguous islands, were civilized, and enjoying the arts, before the Christian era.

The Indians of South America are less uniform than those of North America; and, though in general resembling those of the north, there is evidently quite a difference in the leading families of these two regions. The most prominent family of South America claim to be children of the Sun. They have a tradition that, at an early period of their history, a white-bearded man advanced from the shore of Lake Titicaca, established an ascendancy over the natives, and imparted to them the blessings of civilization.

On the shores of this lake are extensive ruins, which were in existence long before the advent of the Incas. These ruins had an architectural grandeur about them equal to those of Egypt and Central America. The Indians admit they did not construct these ancient buildings. They are the work of a refined people, who, doubtless, occupied the country long before the advent of the children of the Sun.*

Who were the first people of South America, and when did they first possess it? is a perplexing subject of inquiry. Their works, and the slight evidence gathered from other sources, lead to the conclusion that some civilized Caucasians occupied this continent long before the Mongolians or Malays possessed it. The Peruvians admit that they got their architectural notions from the ruined buildings found in the vicinity of Lake Titicaca.†

Fort Cuzco, "Holy City," of Peru, and the great temple of the Sun, were the most magnificent structures of this continent. The

* They were, doubtless, the Paltas, considered the earliest semi-civilized people of Peru.—Natural History of the Human Species, pp. 190 and 263.
† Prichard's Natural History of Man, Vol. II., p. 601.

fortress is built of hewed stone; some of the blocks were thirty-eight feet long, eighteen feet wide, and six feet thick, and were brought from quarries fifty miles distant. Twenty thousand men were employed fifty years in rearing this great building. What is most wonderful in the achievement is its construction by peoples ignorant of the use of iron.

The Incas were the ruling family of South America, Peru being their central seat; they were a noble race, resembling the Aztecs though evidently not of the same type; they had large brains and much better developed than the other tribes of the country, as a general rule. Attained to a high state of civilization, even greater in some respects than the Aztecs; and their worship of the Sun was on a much grander scale than that of the Mexicans; they kept flocks and herds, cultivated the soil, had post roads, and well organized postal regulations. In many particulars the Peruvians resembled the Hindoos and Chinese, having the same tenacity of purpose, and cling to their country and institutions with an equal desire, preferring to remain independent of the rest of mankind.

The division into castes, the worship of the heavenly bodies, and their acquaintance with the scientific principles of husbandry, all go to establish a close affinity between them and the Hindoos.

One remarkable feature about their institutions and civilization and the Mexicans, consists in the sameness between them; yet neither knew of the existence of the other before the conquest of Cortez and Pizarro.

In the vicinity of the Straits of Behring is a group of islands inhabited by a distinct tribe of Indians, resembling the Mongols,* dwelling in houses built under ground. They are in all probability a portion of the great horde of Mongols who crossed the straits when America was first peopled by this race from Asia. They retain the features and habits of the Tartars. †

---

* The obliquity of eyes, so peculiar to the Mongolians, have been found to exist among the nations of Brazil and on the Orinoco.—Natural History of Man, Vol. II., p. 504.

† Professor Carl Newman, a German linguist of Munich, has recently discovered from the China year books, that a company of Buddhist priests entered the continent of America via Alaska, a thousand years before the discovery of Columbus, and explored the Pacific borders, penetrating into the Aztec terri-'· ·v. or the "land of Fusang," so called after the Chinese name of the Mexican

The inhabitants of Prince William's Island are a peculiar people; have flat, broad faces, large heads, and hooked noses, resembling in some degree the Samoieds.

The early people of America being of nomadic character, it is difficult to tell at this remote age the various phases through which they may have passed before they became sufficiently attached to the soil to cultivate it. There, of course, would be strife among the tribes and families for pasturage and hunting-grounds, as in the Old World; the stronger tribes always dwelling and roving at will, the lesser and weaker nations, in course of time, would be compelled to resort to agriculture to gain subsistence; hence villages and cities would be reared by them, and governments established.

The Palta people of Peru, * instinctively a family of mechanics and builders, have left many relics of huge walls, equal to, if not surpassing in artistic skill and grandeur the structures of the old world, except those in Egypt.

The great hordes of nomadic peoples, who swept over the country, drove out the industrious inhabitants living in towns and cities, cultivating the ground, and engaged in the general business of husbandry. Thus they were left uninhabited, and suffered to go to ruin, whilst the cultivated fields became wastes. They were entirely useless to the nomadic tribes who lived in the forests, despising civilization; hence the ruined cities and towns strewn throughout the western continent.

Similar scenes have been enacted in Asia and Europe. Intestine wars forced the Yuchi from Chinese Tartary westward, and the Hyatili, the White Huns, became invaders and conquerors of Cabul and Bactria; they were followed by the Mongols, who extended themselves beyond the Danube and Vistula.

The very restive spirit of these two leading types warrants the conclusion that they found their way to this continent by the Straits of Behring, or by the Pacific, and hence the reason several distinct types, such as Caucasian, Mongolian and Malay, are existing among the American Indians. We do not wish to be understood that there are Indians of pure Caucasian, Mongolian, or Malay blood, but that individuals and tribes are found bearing the impress of these several races very strongly marked.

* The Natural History of the Human Species, p. 190.

Though the Indians are divided into many tribes and nations, seemingly independent of each other, they frequently form extensive empires and submit to some great chief or sachem. The Mexicans formed an extensive empire in Anahuac, which extended over Central America also; they established and maintained a civil government, and supported a system of civilization not inferior perhaps to that now maintained by the Japanese and Chinese. They stood a beacon light to the barbarous Indian tribes of the north, who had begun to draw from that great fountain civilization and refinement, when the Spaniards destroyed the Aztec government, and the Aztecs, the ruling people, were dispersed, and disappeared as a nation and people.

Powhatan, of Virginia, was the emperor over an extensive region containing numerous tribes. Though he had a system of rules tending to civilization, they fell far short of those of Montezuma, and could hardly be considered but little, if anything, in advance of barbarism.

The five nations, or Iroquois, also called Mengwe, were the strongest Indian confederacy perhaps of North America, and when joined by the Tuscaroras in 1714, made them more powerful still; they were very warlike, and brought into subjection many of the neighboring tribes; the five nations consisted of the Senecas, Cayugas, Onondagas, Oneidas and Mohawks. The Tuscaroras, who were their kindred by language, made the sixth nation. After their union with the confederacy it was called the confederacy of the six nations. The Iroquois occupied almost the whole of Canada, south-west of the Ottawa River between Lakes Ontario, Erie and Huron, the greater part of New York, a goodly portion of Pennsylvania and part of Ohio. They were known by the name of Mengwes as well as Iroquois.

The five nations in 1649 made war upon the Wyandots, whom they defeated and dispersed; they killed many of them besides taking a great number prisoners. The Wyandots were not wholly destroyed, but seem to have held their lands, which comprised nearly the whole of the State of Ohio, as appears by the cession made by the Wyandot chiefs at Greenville in 1795. Some twenty odd years ago they sold their reserve lands in Ohio to the United States, and emigrated to the west, and now occupy the territory on the Neosho River, a tributary of the Arkansas; they are fast passing away, there being only now remaining of them about five hundred souls.

The five nations also made war upon the New England tribes, also the Eries, Andastes and Miamis, and invaded the dominions of the Catawbas and Cherokees; they subdued the Eries, * and Andastes, and conquered the Miamis and Ottawas in 1657.

After being joined by the Tuscaroras, they made war upon the Creeks and Catawbas; the latter they almost exterminated. When the confederacy first became composed of the six nations, it numbered not less than forty thousand souls; but now, all the fragments combined do not count over five thousand.

The confederacy has long since been dissolved, and the remains of the several tribes generally have taken up their abode beyond the Mississippi River, and in Canada.

The Algonquins, though not properly a confederacy, was composed of several powerful tribes, among which the Athapascas, Ottawas, Chippewas, Sacs and Foxes, Miamis, Menomonees, Piankeshaws, Potawatamies, Kickapoos, Illinois, Shawnees, Powhatans, Corees, Nanticokes, Lenni-Lenape, or Delaware, Mohegans, Abenakes, Susquehannahs, Knistenaux, and New England nations; and besides these there were other tribes of less distinction belonging to this family.

All the aborigines seem to have been, as they yet are, similar in their moral sentiment, physical character and religious belief. They spoke a great variety of dialects, but there was no written language among all the tribes, except the rude hieroglyphic system of picture representation, which was very limited in meaning and incomprehensible, and not in general use.

The chief business of the men was war, the pursuit of game and fish. The women bore the burdens, and did the drudgery; Their associations with the whites have not in the least alleviated the women in this regard; they are still imposed upon by the males, and looked upon as inferior beings.

They are all believers—no infidels among them. Their religious faith is a dualism; they believe in two spirits, one good, the other evil; worship the sun, moon and stars, and have a mysterious veneration for fire, water, wind and thunder.†

* The Eries were entirely extirpated by the five nations in 1653.—History and Biography of the Indians of North America, p. 500,

† Esquimaux, when first discovered by Europeans, had no knowledge of

They have no laws but public opinion, and well established usages. Public opinion alone sustains the chief, but while in power his word is law if the tribes confide in him. He is raised to power and driven from it by public opinion, though in some instances the chiefs have been permitted to rule as hereditary monarchs, yet none can rule without merit.

Nearly all the Indian tribes have been disturbed in their lands and hunting-grounds by the progress of civilization, which is rapidly spreading from the Atlantic to the Pacific. In fifty years hence they will be left no forests to lurk in, or places of retreat or safety. They are fast passing westward. The great mass are now beyond the " Father of Waters," and only find places of safety in the Rocky Mountains and the wilds beyond them.

There are several tribes inhabiting the country north of the mouth of the Columbia river, who are savages, and appear to belong to the same family. They live by fishing and hunting. The chief tribes are the Chinooks, Clot-Sops, Chilluckittequaws, Cathlamsahs, and Skilluts.

East of the coast chain of mountains in the northwest are located the following tribes, viz: Esheloots, Eneshures, Walla-Wallahs, Sokulks, Chimnapumes, and others of less distinction, all resembling one another in manners, customs, and physical aspect. They are all called Flat Heads, which term does not properly apply to them, but to the Chinooks, and others dwelling along the coast.

The Chinooks are more advanced in civilization than the other tribes, having the art of preparing soft leather, and weaving wool blankets from the clip of the mountain goat. In personal appearance they differ from the other tribes. Some have almost the European complexion; have the oblique eye, which is not an Indian characteristic; the arched nose is very common among them; and there is not the absence of beard, as in other tribes. Frequently beards are seen, but not so heavy as that of the Europeans.

The natives of Nootka Sound have regular features, and a tolerably fair complexion. They resemble Europeans more than Mongolians.

New California has several tribes; some have the features of the coast tribes, and others resemble those dwelling upon the

God, nor idea of any Supreme intelligence; and lived without any form of civil government.—Plurality of Races, by George Pouchet, p. 69.

plains east of the Rocky Mountains. Many tribes reside in California, Oregon, and the country east of the Rocky Mountains, and west of the Missouri river.* Those of California and the coast, with few exceptions, are of the Malay type, with which they have in this work been classed. They are, in general, fine stout men, fully equal to the European standard, with the Malay expression of countenance, and considerable beard. Their complexion is not copper color, but of the hue of the Polynesians. They have no tomahawks, and do not indulge in the business of scalping, as do the Mongolian savages and other tribes. As a general rule, the same Malay features are observable in all the coast tribes and native Indians of Central America; the same may be said of some of the families of the United States, and also of South America. The Creeks, Cherokees and Chippewas, and their kindred tribes, are, in all probability, of Malay descent; at least they do not seem to be of Mongolian origin.

When the new world was discovered, it was inhabited throughout by the native American race. Columbus met them upon the islands as well as upon the continent. They were met at Plymouth, Jamestown and Augusta, and every other locality where the whites sought to make a settlement.

The advance of Caucasian civilization has confined the Indians to much narrower limits, in consequence of which they are rapidly becoming extinct. The great tribes of New England have passed away—only live in history. The same may be said of those of New York, Pennsylvania and Virginia, and indeed of all the Colonial districts. The terror of the scalping knife is no more felt east of the Mississippi; wigwams and council-fires have disappeared, and in their places towns and cities have been reared, and a polished civilization established.

The Indians, as a general rule, are unreliable and treacherous. At first they did not seem to be so, but when they thought they discovered that the whites were intending to interfere with their rights to the soil, they seem to have resolved upon their extermination. This appears to be the desire even yet among the

---

* The Dacotahs, doubtless, occupied the west bank of the Mississippi river when it was discovered by De Soto in 1541. In his adventures in Kansas and Missouri, he found the natives dwelling in towns, and sustaining a tolerable degree of civilization, being devoted to agriculture and averse to war.—Bancroft's History U. S., Vol. I., p. 54.

savages of the west, who avail themselves of every opportunity
to murder the emigrants and settlers.

The Indians have much to complain of against the whites,
who have driven them from the Atlantic to the Pacific, at the
point of the bayonet, and inflicted upon them most cruel and relentless wars, to compel them to relinquish their homes and the
graves of their ancestors. Their history will never be written.
They cannot write it, and white men dare not publish it—dare
not submit to paper the egregious wrongs they have inflicted
upon the American Indians.

The Indians are, among themselves, less disposed to conten-
tions than peoples of refinement; are more disposed to abide by
the will of their chiefs than the most submissive subjects of the
most refined Caucasian monarch. They all seem to act from
like motives; first, provide for the sustenance of life; next, engage in war for self-defence and revenge, and then for conquest.
They are national and more clannish than any other race.
Their minds are capable of a high degree of cultivation; their
perceptive faculties are very acute, and their apprehension remarkably quick. Their general expression of countenance is
sedate and thoughtful, with an air of indifference which is manifested in their general demeanor. They are brave in war, and
under all circumstances meet death with fortitude; and the in-
fliction of the most cruel torture and death upon an enemy is
with them a pleasant pastime.

The men are grave, and, as a general rule, gloomy and silent,
except in council and in war; they never speak unless what is
considered important, and their tone of voice in private conver-
sation is low, and language simple. They have a natural dignity and circumspection about them not enjoyed by any other
race. They are of good stature, many of the nations being
above the European standard. Bartram says the "Cherokees,
Muscogees, Seminoles, Chickasaws and Choctaws are tall, erect
and moderately robust," with well-shaped limbs, and of perfect
human figure. The Osages are also tall, well made, and of Caucasian mould of body.

The squaws, or females, are generally small, low-set, and have
short bodies; in their demeanor are the reverse of the men—
sprightly. Their countenances are enlivened by pleasant smiles,

and often there is a remarkable mildness and sweetness of expression in their looks. Some of them are attractive and handsome.

The habits and dress of the native Americans are very similar; all adopting the same mode of life, have moulded themselves to the surroundings. Their clothing consists of moccasins for the feet, leggins of deer-skin or cloth for the lower limbs, and a breech-cloth extending round the loins and thighs; a blanket covers the upper part of the body, which is thrown aside in warm weather. In the warm climate the dress is much less cumbersome, the almost entirely nude state being preferred. Such was the condition of nearly all the tribes when the country was first visited by Europeans. On the northwest coast the natives wear a single robe over the shoulders, made of the bark of the cedar tree spun like hemp.

The females are industrious, and watch with very tender and affectionate care over their children, who are never chastised, especially the boys, lest their love of independence might be checked. On the death of a child, the mother laments the loss in the most affecting manner possible.

Their mode of burial is not uniform. Some deposit their dead in graves, in which are placed favorite implements of the warrior; over the grave a mound is raised, the size being regulated by the dignity or standing of the deceased. Some of the tribes on the Columbia river construct narrow sheds in which they deposit the dead, wrapped in skins. The Patagonians dry the bones of their dead, and place them in huts in the desert, surrounded by the skeletons of their horses.

The Killamucks, a tribe living on the coast south of the Columbia, enclose their dead in a wooden box, which they deposit in an open canoe on the shore, alongside of which they place a paddle and some other articles of the deceased. Other tribes, among whom are the Chinooks, place their dead in canoes elevated on posts six feet from the ground, over which another canoe is placed reversed; over the canoes are wrapped mats with cords of the bark of white cedar. The bodies, before being deposited in the canoes, are rolled carefully in dressed skins. Vancouver even reports that he saw canoes, containing corpses, suspended from the branches of trees twelve feet from the ground.

CHAPTER XI.

HAVING, in the preceding chapter briefly referred to the
American Indians, we propose now to notice them in detail; and first the Algonquin group of nations.

The French applied this term to an extensive Indian nation residing upon the banks of the Ottawa River in Canada when
they first discovered them. Subsequently the nations who spoke
dialects of the same language, were also called Algonquins. The
chief Algonquin nations were the Crees, or Knisteneans, Ottawas, Chippewas, Miamis, Potawatomies, Menomonees, Sacs and
Foxes, Piankershaws, Kickapoos, Illinois, Shawnees, Corees,
Powhatans, Nauticocks, Delawares, Mohegans, Abenakes, New
England Indians, Susquehannahs, Mannahoaks and Monocans.
Besides these there were smaller independent tribes who spoke
dialects of the Algonquin language. The Athapascas or Chepe-
wayns of British America, are considered a branch of this
family.

The Athapascas formerly occupied the country from the
western shore of Hudson Bay to the Rocky Mountains, south to
Churchill river, and north to the dominions of the Esquimaux.

The northern Beaver Mountain, Carrier, and Sussees tribes belong to this family.

The Athapascas, according to Mackenzie, were not originally native Americans, but Asiatics. By their own account of their original place of residence, they came from Siberia—at least from Asia by the Straits of Behring. Their tradition is that they "came originally from another country inhabited by a very wicked people, and had traversed a great lake which was narrow, shallow, and full of islands; where was perpetual winter with ice and deep snow." They describe a great deluge when the whole earth except the top of a high mountain was deeply covered by water. On the top of this mountain they were preserved until the waters returned to the rivers and seas. They are a quiet, peaceable people, of medium stature; some of the men have very heavy beards. Their complexion is of a lighter shade than Algonquins generally.

The Chippewas, or Ojibways, and Potawatomies, originally constituted one nation, but separated from each other at Michilimacinac,* before they became known to Europeans. The French missionaries considered the Chippewas and Ottawas one people; they occupied then an extensive empire lying between the St. Lawrence on the east and the Rocky Mountains on the west; their northern boundaries being the southern extremity of Hudson Bay, Lake Winnepeg and the head waters of the Mississippi; and their southern dominions extending south of Lakes Superior, Huron and Erie. They were a very numerous people when they first become known to the French, but many of their braves before that period had been cut off by a bloody and cruel war which had taken place between them and the Menomones; the latter having as their allies during the conflict the Sacs and Foxes, Potawatomies, Kickapoos, Winnebagoes, Sioux, Opanangoes, Shawnees, Algonquins, Nautowas, and Wabonokees; but the combined powers were forced to yield to the superior skill of the great chief Nabanois, and his associates who pursued the enemy to the Atlantic.

When the Chippewas and Ottawas first made their entrance into the northern lake regions, they found dwelling therein a

* S. G. Drake's History and Biography of the Indians of North America, p. 637.

primitive people to whom they gave the name of Mushkodoins. After several battles, the latter were forced to abandon their homes to the invading Chippewas. The latter admitted that the Mushkodoins were superior to themselves in all things except numbers. The Chippewas considered the Mushkodoins the authors of the antiquities of the country. The name of these primitive Indians only reaches us through the traditions of the Chippewas; they have disappeared from the country. Schoolcraft seems to think they may have been the workers of the copper mines of Lake Superior, and to have passed south by Chicago. They may have been the authors of the wonderful copper and brass relics, sculpture and sarcophagi recently discovered in the cave of Rock Island, Illinois, noticed in another place.

The Chippewas seem now to be a quiet, peaceable people, preferring to engage in the civil pursuits of life rather than in the business of war; they will, however, readily defend themselves against the Crow and Blackfeet Indians, their deadly enemies, and also against the Sioux. They display great skill and ingenuity in the construction of their canoes, are erratic in their habits, and much more skilled in hunting and fishing than agriculture.

The Ottawas, though early settlers in the lake basins and on the St. Lawrence, were not the primitive occupants of these localities but had been preceded by other Indian nations, especially the Miscalins and Assigunaigs now extinct. When the French first visited the Canadas, the Ottawas were living upon the banks of the Ottawa River; but after the war between the Huron and the five nations in 1649, in which they participated as the allies of the Hurons, they and the Chippewas passed to the lake regions where, in 1680, they resumed their former place of residence in the northern part of Michigan. They suffered heavy losses in the war with the Iroquois, and in which conflict the Hurons were almost destroyed.

They were the allies of the French against the English in the long and bloody war between these two European powers. They did not recognize the rights of the English after the treaty of peace between them and the French, ratified between these two powers in 1760; and when the French yielded the several stations to the British, the Indians, under the renowned Pontiac, the sachem of the Ottawas, Miamis, Chippewas, Wyandots, Potawatomies, Winnebagoes, Shawnees, Ottagamies and Mississagas, resolved to rid the country of the intruders—such they considered the English. Pontiac was an Ottawa chief, and next to King Philip was the most distinguished warrior of North America. Pontiac, having secretly completed all his plans, set apart the 3th day of June, 1763, as the time for the consummation of the conspiracy. On that day Fort Michilimackinac was captured by the Indians, and seventy of the English garrison murdered and scalped. Only twenty men escaped alive. In the course of ten days all the French posts except Detroit fell into the hands of the Indians. Pontiac, looking upon Detroit as of incalculable value to him, invested and besieged it, but without success, except the surprise of the British at the battle of Bloody Ridge. He kept up the siege for nearly a year, when, seeing no hope of ultimate success against the British, proposed terms of peace which were accepted by the English.

During the war of the Revolution, Pontiac felt disposed to assist the colonists, and would have done so had not General Hamilton, of Detroit, won him to the British interest. During the war Pontiac attended a council in Illinois. The English, suspecting him, employed a Peori Indian spy to watch over the renowned sachem, and after he had made a speech in the council unfavorable to the British, this spy murdered Pontiac by stabbing him to the heart.

He was buried where the city of St. Louis now stands. No monument marks the place where his ashes rest. He needs none to perpetuate his fame; his great deeds are part of the country's history, and more enduring than if carved in stone or engraven on brass. Pontiac was great in war, great in peace, and great in council and wisdom—won nations to his standard by his superior intelligence, dignified demeanor and courteous address, and was far in advance of his people in civilization. During the war of 1763 he appointed a commissary and issued bills of credit on bark, on each of which was pictured the commodity he desired, with the figure of the otter, the symbol of his tribe.*

The Ottawas were the allies of the French against the hostile Indians, and assisted in the extirpation of the Ottagamies and

* S. G. Drake's History and Biography of the Indians of North America, p. 546

14

Mascontins, two bold and savage tribes, who, under the influence of the English, had laid siege to the French fort at Detroit. After the death of Pontiac, his people sought refuge with the French in Canada, where some of their descendants still remain.

Remnants of this family are also in Michigan and in the Indian Territory west of the Mississippi River.

The Knistenaux, also called Crees, occupy the regions extending from Labrador to the Rocky Mountains. They well preserved the chief characteristics of the Algonquin Lenape. They were formerly a warlike people, and kept up almost constant war with the Esquimaux until Great Britain interfered and brought about a treaty of peace with the belligerents. Under the influence of the French and English (more especially the latter), the Knistenaux turned their attention to agriculture; and in which they have made very creditable advancements. They not only cultivate the ground successfully, but raise stock and reside in villages. They are described as being of moderate stature and well proportioned, sprightly and active; they have long, coarse black hair, copper-colored complexion, black, piercing eyes, and an open, agreeable countenance; the women are of good figure, well proportioned, and their feature so regular, and expression of countenance so agreeable, that they have been considered handsome.

The Knistenaux have no plausible theory concerning their origin, and have no annals or traditions of reliable character. They are, doubtless, descendants of the primitive red race of this continent, as they have retained all their chief characteristics, and may be considered as pure Indian as any of the American nations.

The Potawatomies when first known to Europeans as a distinct nation occupied the western shores of Green Bay; but about the beginning of the eighteenth century, settled themselves on the southern shores of Lake Michigan, and subsequently occupied the northern part of Ohio and Indiana.

They were known to the French missionaries in 1668. At that period a delegation visited Father Allonez upon an island in Lake Superior. They were a numerous people. In 1820 their number was estimated to be 3,400. No doubt this was the true number, as they had to be enumerated in order to receive the $5,700 annuity then being paid to them by the United States.

The great mass of this nation disposed of their lands to the Federal Government, and emigrated to the country watered by the Osage river, where they now reside; and are perhaps the most numerous of the remnants of the Algonquin nations. They had many distinguished chiefs, of whom Black-bird was the most noted warrior.

The Potawatomies are in stature about five feet eight inches, and well proportioned, with great muscular strength and considerable agility. Their complexion is darker than the usual hue of the red race; this is only the case with those parts of the body exposed to the sun and wind, as where the skin is protected by garments, the color is the same as that of the American race.

The Sacs and Foxes when first discovered by the French, in 1680, were residing at the southern extremity of Green Bay. About the year 1770, they seated themselves west of the Potawatamies, between the Illinois and Mississippi rivers. They are a warlike nation. In 1712 they made an assault upon the French Garrison at Detroit, but were repulsed with heavy loss by the French and Ottawas. In 1722 they united with the Kickapoos in hostilities against the Illinois Indians with the view of driving the latter from their lands on the Illinois river, and virtually succeeded, leaving the Kickapoos in their possession, whilst the Illinois were forced to take refuge with the French. The Sacs and Foxes sold their lands to the United States in 1830. At that time they constituted but one nation, but had two distinguished chiefs, Blackhawk and Keokuké; the former was the sachem of the Sacs, the latter of the Foxes, but each had equal power over the whole nation. Keokuké and minor chiefs engaged in the treaty of sale of their lands. Blackhawk repudiated it, and as a consequence lost his power over his nation. His repudiation of the sale and rupture with Keokuké produced the Border war, known as the "Blackhawk war," in which this distinguished chief had marshaled under his banner against the United States and the Indian forces under Keokuké, a large force of Sacs, Winnebagoes, Kickapoos, and Potawatomies. In the spring of the year 1831, Black Hawk, at the head of the Sacs crossed the Mississippi, and in a defiant and menacing manner took possession of their cabins and their old cornfields, which

had been surrendered the year before to the United States under
the treaty, and by which treaty the Sacs and Foxes had been
placed under the protection of the Federal Government. This
hostile movement brought the Federal troops into the field to
enforce the treaty. They met and defeated the Indians in several battles. Black Hawk and many of his warriors were made
prisoners. His defeat and capture placed Keokuké as the undis-
puted Sachem of the Sacs and Foxes; though humiliating to
Black Hawk, he was compelled to listen to the counsel of Keokuké, who was his inferior in military prowess, but perhaps his
superior in wisdom and honesty. Black Hawk was always at
heart an enemy of the United States. During the war of 1812
he aided the British against the Federal Government.

Black Hawk was no ordinary man. Considering the disadvantages under which he labored, he will be looked upon by
coming generations as having been one
of the most remarkable characters of the
American race. He was about medium
size, with a head of Grecian mould, a
Roman style of face, and a prepossessing
countenance. He was born of Potawat-
amie parents in 1767, but reared a Sac.
His death occurred in his wigwam on the
Des Moines river, on October 3, 1838.

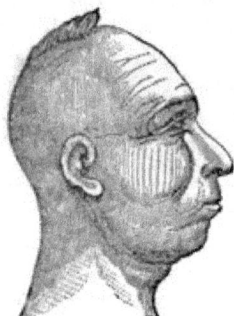

The Foxes were called Ottagamies, and
by the French, "Renards." They united
with the Sauke, or Sacs, on the Mississippi, about the year 1805. About 2400
Sacs and Foxes reside west of the Mississippi.

BLACK HAWK.

The Menemonees, when first discovered by the French in 1699,
resided upon the shores of Green Bay; their principal seat being
upon the river of that name, about one degree north of the dominions of the Winnebagoes. A portion of the tribe still occupies their ancient lands.

The Miamis and Piankeshaws occupied the country lying between the Maumee river, and the Wabash; and the latter tribe
resided upon the head waters of the latter river. Whilst on the
Wabash they numbered 3000, but in 1780 they had been reduced
to less than 1000. They have been driven west and do not now

seem to have a tribal existence. The Miamis were originally confined within the limits of Ohio, mainly upon the Miami river, and in the great Miami valley; if their story is to be believed, they were created. Their head-quarters for a long time was at Piqua. After the French war, in which they were engaged on behalf of the French, they abandoned the Miami Valley and took up their residence on the head waters of the Maumee. They were called Twigbetweens by the Iroquois, and of all the Indian tribes were the most hostile towards the United States. They have disposed of their lands and passed west beyond the Mississippi, where the great body of them now reside. Little Turtle was their most distinguished chief. He successfully contended with General Harmer and St. Clair, but was defeated by General Wayne. His better judgment dictated that it was dangerous to risk a battle with Wayne; but his associates taking issue with him, he had to consent to go into battle or be branded a coward. He reluctantly led his braves in the battle of Presque Isle, where the Indians sustained a most disastrous defeat. Before the battle he told his warriors to look well to it; that they were about to contend with (General Wayne) "a man who never sleeps." He was a man of great wisdom, extraordinary prowess, and withal was more humane and generous than was usual with his race. After this defeat he became convinced that it was useless longer to contend with the whites, and resolved to turn his attention to the civil pursuits of life, and in the guidance of his people to a more happy destiny, and turned their attention to agriculture.

He was not born a chief, but rose to that exalted position by merit. His father was a Miami chief, but his mother was a Mohican woman.

M. Volney, who had an interview with Little Turtle at Philadelphia, says, that he was as white as he himself was. He died at Fort Wayne, July 14, 1812, aged sixty-five years, and was buried there with the honors of war, under the directions of the agent of Indian affairs of that district.

According to the eighth census, 674 Indians, consisting of Miamis, Eel-river tribes and Potawatomies, resided in the State of Indiana, and receive annual annuities from the Federal Government.

The Illinois were a numerous people. The nation was divided into five tribes, namely: Kaskias, Cahokias, Towarouas, Michigamas, and Peories. Their residence when first discovered by Europeans, was upon the banks of the Illinois river. In 1670 this nation numbered 12,000, and as late as 1700 they had sixty towns; but by intestine wars and bloody contests with neighboring nations they became reduced to a few families compared with former numbers. In 1722, though yet a strong nation, by the combined power of the Sacs and Foxes and Kickapoos, they were driven from their ancient lands on the banks of the Illinois. In 1818 they ceded their lands to the United States, and emigrated to the westward of the Mississippi, where a few still remain. At the time of the sale of their lands they numbered only three hundred souls.

The Illinois had no annals, and no reliable traditions. Jesuits gathered from them and other sources the idea that they had, at an early period, come from a distant country to the west side of the Mississippi.

At Rock Island, within the limits of the country occupied by the Illinois Indians, have been recently found in a cave wonderful relics of the aborigines of high antiquity, consisting of copper statues, obelisks of solid brass, and other curious specimens of art; among which a copper sarcophagus, nine feet long and three feet in width, minutely sculptured within and without, with several hundred figures representing an immense funeral procession. On removing the lid, bones and javelins were found within. This seems to be the richest treasure of American antiquities yet discovered.

The Kickapoos, when they first became known, were residing in the State of Illinois. In 1722 they, with the assistance of the Sacs and Foxes, drove the Illinois tribe from the lands of the latter on the banks of the river of that name, and on which they continued to reside until 1819, when they emigrated to the west bank of the Missouri river in the vicinity of Fort Leavenworth.

During the Florida war one hundred of them were engaged by the Federal Government to assist in driving out and subjecting the Seminoles. They were a brave nation, and, though few in numbers compared with their neighbors, sustained their independence. They do not differ in any respect to the Algonquins, generally. They are now peaceable and well disposed towards the United States, and number now about six hundred souls.

SHAWNEES.—This distinguished nation at one time occupied the country from Pittsburg, Pennsylvania, to the Mississippi, on both sides of the Ohio river. Their great central seat was in the basin of the Cumberland river. They originally resided in the South, near Savannah, in Georgia. Though fierce and war-like, they were unable to successfully contend with the Southern nations. About the period of the location of the Jamestown colony in Virginia, the Shawnees were driven from the South by the Creeks. They came North in several bodies. One branch settled in Ohio on the Sciota river, near Chillicothe. They joined the Eries and Andastes in a war against the Iroquois. Being defeated, they fled to the South in the dominions of the Catawbas; not finding safety there, they took shelter with the Creeks. When first driven from the South, a large body of them settled in Pennsylvania. Pittsburg seems to have been their head-quarters. The Southern division about the year 1760 returned to Ohio, and uniting with their brethren of Pennsylvania, the united nation formed an alliance with the French against the English. Colonel Boquet, a distinguished British officer, was sent out with a considerable force from Philadelphia to the relief of the garrisons at Ligoneer and Pittsburg. The Shaw-nees hearing of the approach of the British, thought to meet them in ambush and destroy them at a blow, as they had done with the forces under General Braddock, a short time previous. With that view they marched out in strong force and met Col-onel Boquet with the British troops near a place called Bushy Run, between Fort Ligoneer and Pittsburg, where in two en-gagements the Indians were defeated with considerable loss. The British commander having been with Washington in his contests with the Indians, had learned their mode of fighting sufficiently well to meet them in their own game of ambush and surprise.

These defeats relieved the garrison at Fort Pitt, the Indians considering it prudent to abandon the siege before the arrival of the British. The battles of Bushy Run were fought in August, 1763. In 1774 they were again defeated by the Virginians at Point Pleasant, at the mouth of the Great Kanawha. In the war of 1812 they sided with the British; but after their defeat at the battle of the Thames, fully realized that their best policy was to come to terms of amity with the people of the United States.

The Shawnees had a tradition that tended to show they were of foreign origin, and that their ancestors had crossed the sea For a long time after the country was settled by Europeans they kept up yearly sacrifices for their safe arrival in this country. From where they came, or at what period, they have no account. Their first location was in Florida, but they did not pretend to claim they were the first people of that region, saying that Florida had been occupied by white people before they entered it. Black-Hoof, a celebrated Shawnee chief, affirms that he had often heard it spoken of by old people of his nation that stumps of trees covered with earth were frequently found which had been cut down by edged tools.*

The Shawnees for a long time had their head quarters at Piqua, on the north side of Mad river in Clark County, Ohio, about five miles west of Springfield, where the Village of West Boston is at present situated. Here, their great Chief Tecumseh was born—about the year 1768. His father, Puckeshinwa, was a chief of some distinction, having gained his title by his own merits. He fell at the battle of Point Pleasant, in 1774. His mother was of the Turtle tribe of the Shawnee nation. After the death of his father, Tecumseh was taken south, but returned in his youth to his native village. He fought his first battle on the site of Dayton, when his people engaged the Kentuckians under Colonel Benjamin Logan. At the age of 17 years he began to manifest his wonderful superiority over the most distinguished chiefs and braves of his nation. He was engaged in the battle of Fort Recovery, and also in that of Fallen Timbers. He became chief in 1795. He then for a time resided on Deer Creek, near Urbana, Ohio, and from thence removed to Piqua, where he remained until 1798, when he accepted an invitation of the Delawares to take up his residence on White River, in Indiana. In 1805, through the influence of the brother of Tecumseh, Lanlewasikam, who afterwards assumed the office of a prophet, a large number of Shawnees took up their residence at Greenville, in Darke County, Ohio. Here Tecumseh joined the prophet, who was by his wonderful dreams, and supernatural

* Schoolcraft's History of the Indian tribes of the United States, Part I., p. 19.

presentations, then creating considerable alarm among the whites who feared an outbreak. Learning the condition of things Gov. Harrison issued an address to the head chiefs of the nation to send away the Prophet. In the spring of 1808 the Prophet and Tecumseh removed to a tract of land on the Tippecanoe. Here they consummated their schemes for a general war upon the whites, which resulted in their defeat in a general battle between them and the Federal troops under General Harrison in November, 1811. TECUMSEH was not engaged in this battle, it having been conducted by the Prophet. Tecumseh was a Brigadier General in the British Army in the war of 1812, and was killed by Col. Richard M. Johnson at the battle of the Thames. This renowned chief had no superior in point of prowess and military skill. His mien was dignified; his eye penetrating; his countenance, even in death, betrayed the indications of a lofty spirit. He was among the most eloquent of American orators; humane toward his captives, never permitting them to undergo the tortures usual among the savage Indians.

The Delawares, called Lenni-Lenapes, comprised two powerful families—the Minsi, and Delawares proper. The term Lenni-Lenape, signifies original people, and according to tradition, well applies to the Delawares. Heckwelder learned from their traditional history, that their ancestors in very remote ages dwelt in the western part of the American Continent, from whence they emigrated centuries ago, eastward, in a body. After many nights' encampment (nights meaning years) they arrived at the Mississippi river, where they first met the Iroquois, who also had come from the west or some distant country, with whom they formed a confederacy against the Alligewi, a powerful nation residing eastward of the Mississippi.

The Alligewis were a tall stout people, dwelling in large towns located along the rivers watering their country, between the Mississippi and the Alleghenies. The Allegheny river is called after this nation by the Delawares; as also the Apalachian chain of mountains. After a long and bloody contest, the Alligewi were subdued by the combined forces of the Delawares and Iroquois, and forced to quit the country. They fled down the Mississippi river and never returned; and since that time the Alligewi have been lost to history and tradition. After the expulsion of the Alligewi, the Delawares and Iroquois made a mutual partition of the country eastward of the Mississippi among themselves. The Lenape, took possession of the southern portion, and spread themselves over the country along the Potomac, Delaware, Susquehannah, and Hudson rivers and their tributaries. The Iroquois, then called Mengwe, occupied the northern portion of the country; principally along the lakes and their tributaries. This division of territory, according to Indian tradition, caused the Delawares to separate into three tribes, namely: the Turkey, Turtle, and Minsi or Wolf. From these have descended many families and tribes of the Delaware nation. The Turtle and Turkey families settled near the Atlantic from the Hudson to beyond the Potomac; and the Minsi, called Manseys, occupied New Jersey and Pennsylvania. The Delawares at the early settlement of the country by Europeans were known more particularly by the name of Minsi and Delawares proper; the latter then occupying lower New Jersey, the banks of the Delaware south of Trenton, and the valley of the Schuylkill. They also occupied the countries at the head waters of the Susquehannah and Delaware rivers. Their council fires were kindled on the Minisink flats above Water Gap, and they had a village and peach orchard within the bounds of what is now Northampton County, where the village of Nazareth is located. The Five Nations subjugated the Delawares in 1650. But in 1756, their great Sachem, Teedyuscung, extorted from the Iroquois chiefs an acknowledgment of the independence of the Delawares. After the Delawares were subdued and brought under Iroquois vassalage, they commenced to retreat westward. Some crossed the Alleghenies and located on the Muskingum; those who remained in Pennsylvania joined the Shawnees, and became allies of the French in the war of 1760, against the British. In 1768, the great body of them passed into the valley of the Mississippi and settled mainly in the State of Ohio. During the war of the Revolution, the great body of them sided with the British; and in 1794 they were at the head of the confederacy that spread such terror throughout the West after the defeat of General St. Clair. Their defeat by General Wayne brought them to a sense of their condition, and satisfied them that they were unable longer to contend against the whites.

They disposed of their lands lying along the Muskingum, to the United States, in 1795, and took up their residence on the bank of the Wabash, in the State of Indiana, where they remained until the year 1819, when they ceded their lands there to the Federal Government, and removed west of the Mississippi to the country lying north of the mouth of the Kansas river.

The Delawares occupied the greater portion of Pennsylvania, and of the country generally from the Hudson to the Potomac, when William Penn first landed upon the western shore of the Delaware. His treatment of the Indians secured their friendship, and had other early European settlers pursued the same humane course toward the natives, much treasure and many valuable lives would have been saved.

The Delawares had many noted chiefs. By themselves "Tammany," of whom we have but little account, received the most devout reverence.

> "Immortal Tammany, of Indian race,
> Great in the field, and foremost in the chase!
> No puny saint was he, with fasting pale :
> He climbed the mountain, and he swept the vale,
> Rushed through the torrent with unequaled might,
> Yon ancient saints would tremble at the sight ;
> To public views he added private ends,
> And loved his country most, and next his friends ;
> His fame let every honest tongue resound ;
> With him let every generous patriot vie,
> To live in freedom or with honor die."

This chief died, it has been supposed, between the years 1680 and 1690, though even this is to a great extent founded upon conjecture. Willian Penn made his first treaty with the Delawares, in December, 1682, under an elm tree, in Kensington Township, two miles above Chestnut street, Philadelphia.

Glikhokan was among the most noted of Delaware warriors. After successfully disputing the Catholic religion with the French priests of Canada, he was converted to Christianity, in 1769, by the United Brethren, with whom he went to reside in 1770, against the wishes of his chiefs and people. He was murdered by white savages at Gradenhutten in the month of March, 1782. The leader of the murderers was Col. David Williamson, of

Pennsylvania. He had under his command about eighty white men from the neighborhood of Pittsburg. They, with more than savage barbarity, murdered and scalped ninety-six persons; none were spared; besides the helpless women, thirty-four children were murdered in cold blood by these worse than fiends in human form. These Christian Indians were cut off under the mistaken notion that some of their number had been engaged in the murder of the Wallace family, which had been committed a short time before by some Sandusky warriors.

Pakanke, Netawatwees, White Eyes, Tadeuskund (Honest John), Captain Pipe, Kilbuck, and Shingis, were among the most distinguished Delaware chiefs. Pakanke was a man of great power, not only in council, but in the field. He resided forty miles north of Pittsburg, in 1770, and reluctantly espoused the cause of Christianity. Netawatwees was head chief of the Delawares, and used his utmost endeavors to have his people adopt the Christian religion. He died in 1778, on the Muskingum river, with small pox. He had his residence for a time on the Cuyahoga river. By his influence, King Beaver, of the Turkey tribe, settled on the Muskingum, and built a town at the mouth of Nemoschille Creek.

White-Eyes was the first captain among the Delawares. He was favorable to the spread of the Gospel among his people, and, though the other chiefs had, on several occasions, proposed to expel the missionaries from the country, White-Eyes kept the chiefs and council in awe, and would not suffer the missionaries to be molested. In his speeches in council he showed that he was convinced the Christian teachers were right, and benefiting his race.

Tadeuskund, also known as Honest John, was almost equal in prowess with White-Eyes. He, after much wavering and hesitancy, was baptized by the Moravians, and received into full fellowship in the Christian church; but his conversion, doubtless, was but a matter of form, as his subsequent conduct fully proved.

Shingis was a noted Delaware chief, residing where Pittsburg now stands, in 1753, when Washington went on his mission to the French, on the Ohio. He was the first chief Washington visited, and accompanied him to Logstown. Heckwelder, who knew Shingis, considered him the greatest Indian warrior of his time. His name was a terror during the French war.

Captain Pipe was the most noted Delaware chief of the Wolf tribe during the Revolution. He, with his braves, assisted the Iroquois, under Half-King, to force the missionaries and Christian Indians from Gradenhutten, Schoenbruner, and Salem, to Sandusky. Pipe was one of the chief leaders of the Delawares when Col. William Crawford was burnt at the stake by the savages, near Sandusky, Ohio, in May, 1782. Crawford was captured by a band of Delawares, and conducted to "Wyandot," where Captain Pipe, with his own hands, painted Colonel Crawford and Doctor Knight black, preparatory to their execution. Crawford was then taken to the place of execution, where Pipe addressed the assembled Indians. At the close of his speech the executioners commenced the work of death with demoniac yells. For three hours they kept up the torture before the unfortunate victim was relieved by death. Wingenim, another noted Delaware chief, who had been upon friendly terms with Crawford, was present when he was led to the stake, and appealed to by Crawford for mercy, which he refused to extend him, under the plea that he had no power to revoke or alter the sentence. Dr. Knight was compelled to witness the agonies and death of Col. Crawford. The same punishment awaited him; but, exerting all his powers of mind and body, he escaped from his executioners, and saved his life.

Killbuck, called Gelelemend, after the death of White-Eyes, became the leading chief of the Delaware nation by appointment, during the minority of the rightful heir to the position. He was a friend of the whites, for whom he did much valuable service in protecting them from the ravages of the hostile nations. He was baptized, and became a consistent member of the Christian church, of which he died a member, in 1811, at the age of about eighty years.

An Indian chief, by the name of Killbuck, had a village on the east bank of the river bearing this name, about nine miles south of Wooster, Ohio, about the beginning of the present century.

The Crees resided on the Atlantic coast, south of the Powhatans, in the territory occupied by the Hatteras, when the country was first visited by Europeans. In 1711, they were allies of the Tuscaroras in their attack upon the white settlers. They have been classed with the Tuscaroras, but have no existence as a nation, and have all perished or become absorbed.

The Mohegans, also called Mohicans, had their residence on the banks of the Hudson; but the term was applied to several tribes inhabiting Long Island and the country lying between the dominions of the Delawares and the New England nations. The Mohicans were very early settlers in the valley of the Hudson, though we have no reliable data of their origin, or advent upon the banks of the Hudson. They were early known as Moheakannuks, and River Indians. They were peaceable and friendly towards the whites.

The Mohegans who occupied Long Island and the country between the Delawares and New England Indians were distinct from the Mohicans of the Hudson. They comprised several tribes, the most prominent being the Pequods, Manhattans, and Tunxis. The central seat of the Mohegans was at Norwich, in Connecticut, where was also their ancient burying place. They were in no respect related to the surrounding Indian nations, with whom they were engaged in war when the whites first entered their jurisdiction. They were emigrants from the west, who had entered the country not long previous to the first landing of the Pilgrims; had no annals; but, from all we can gather of authentic character, they made their way into Connecticut from the north, from the valley of the Hudson; but, otherwise, their early history is a blank; and it is more a matter of conjecture than reliable history, that they came from the valley of the Hudson, or were of the Mohican family of that locality.

The Pequods were the most powerful of the Mohegan tribes; and, before the revolt of Uncas, a noted chief, against the great Pequod sachem, Sassacus, their nation was capable of giving law to the surrounding tribes. This revolt divided their power, and, as a consequence, the Narragansetts, by the aid of the English, subdued the Pequods; and the Mohegans, eventually, after being greatly reduced by wars, were compelled to submit to the rigor and domineering subjection of the Iroquois.

Before the revolt of Uncas, the Pequods, by their fierce, war-

like and cruel disposition, occasioned the Narragansetts, though
a more powerful nation, to stand in awe, and court their friendship as a means of safety. The name of Sassacus, said Roger
Williams, was a terror to all the neighboring tribes of Indians,
and no wonder his name should be a terror, as, at that time, he
had under him no less than twenty-six noted sachems. He
could call into the field, almost at a moment's warning, 2,000
brave warriors. Feeling his power invincible, he was thrown
off his guard; and, before he was aware of it, the English and
Narragansetts stole into his village on Mystic river, one night,
and killed more than six hundred of his people. Seven only of
the villagers escaped alive to reveal the terrible tale of death to
the haughty Sassacus. Discouraged by this and other misfortunes, the Pequod chief, with his warriors, retired to Sassacus
swamp; thither they were pursued by the enemy, and almost
exterminated. Sassacus, with a few followers, fled to the Mohawks for shelter. They were not even safe there, as Sassacus
was soon murdered, and his associates in exile sold into slavery,
or incorporated into other tribes; and since that time the Pequods have had no existence as a nation or tribe.

Uncas was the great sachem of the Mohegans in 1635, when
the Pequods first became known to the English. His revolt
from Sassacus occurred about that period, and by it a large scope
of country belonging to the Pequods, called Moheag, extending
from near the Connecticut river, on the south, to the domains
of the Narragansetts, on the north, fell under the jurisdiction of
Uncas.

In 1637, the wily Uncas, for self-protection against his Indian
neighbors, joined the English in their war against the Pequods,
though the English then feared Uncas and his nation almost as
much as they did the Pequods. He soon dispelled their fears
by his extreme barbarism committed upon the Pequods near
Saybrook, in 1637. A party of Mohegans came upon seven Pequods, near the fort, killed five of them, and took one prisoner,
whom they executed in the most inhuman manner possible, and
after he was dead tore his limbs from the body and burnt them
to ashes. Some of the Mohegan executioners cut some of the
flesh from his body, which they ate, whilst singing about the fire.*

* Drake's Indians of North America, p. 150.

Uncas's fidelity to the English proved steadfast throughout his eventful life, except he was charged with protecting Pequods after they were almost destroyed as a nation by the English and Narragansetts. This is greatly to his credit, as many of the Pequods were his kindred ; especially so when, in fact, he had engaged in all the wars of the English against his own countrymen, and all the while shielded the white settlements.

The destruction of the Pequod branch of the Mohegan family did not, it would seem, satisfy the Narragansetts and their Indian allies, especially the Nianticks ; they seemed also to desire the extirpation of the Mohegans proper. In 1644, the Narragansetts and Nianticks commenced war upon the Mohegans, and for a time compelled Uncas and his men to keep within the walls of their fort. This was precipitated by Uncas declaring war against Sequasson, a Narragansett sachem, and the capture and execution of the great Miantonomoh, head chief of the Narragansett nation. In the war between this chief and Uncas, the English of Rhode Island favored the cause of the former, whilst the latter was in favor with the English of Connecticut and Massachusetts. The Rhode Islanders, to shield Miantonomoh in battle, furnished him a heavy coat of mail, which so weighed him down that, when retreat became necessary, he was readily overtaken by the fleet Mohegans. He was captured and brought into the presence of Uncas. He remained silent and sullen until the latter addressed him and said: "If you had taken me, I would have besought you for my life."[*] Uncas took his prisoner to Hartford, and delivered him over to the English. They, in general counsel with the delegates of the United Colonies, who called to their aid five of the most judicious elders, decided that Uncas should execute his prisoner, which he did, but without torture. This was a most flagrant outrage, and a gross violation of every principal of honor. Left to himself, Uncas would not have been guilty of the diabolical deed. He was bribed by the colonists, under the guidance of the elders of the Puritan church, to commit the foul murder, under the promise that he and his people should receive protection, against the Narragansetts, from the English.

After the death of Miantonomoh, Ninigret became the head

* Drake's North American Indians, p. 128.

warrior of the Narragansetts and Nianticks. Up to that time he had been a sachem of the latter tribe of Narragansetts, residing in Rhode Island. At this time, Pessicus, a younger brother of Miantonomoh, was chief of the Narragansetts. Pessicus invaded the dominions of Uncas, and drove him into his fort on the river Thames, and would have, in all probability, reduced him by famine, had not the English rendered him timely aid; but they eventually deserted him, after finding him guilty of a "devilish falsehood"—even sent out a force against him, in consequence of his hostilities toward the Indians of Quabaconk, subjects of the English. Uncas outlived his Indian enemies, and, as would seem, triumphed over them all.* He remained friendly to the English during his life. He was their ally during King Philip's war, and died at Norwich soon after its close, in 1683. His grave is upon the plain, above the falls of the Yantic, near Norwich. A monument was erected to his memory by the citizens of the town, in 1832, the foundation-stone of which was laid by General Jackson, whilst on his eastern tour during that year.

The Manhattans occupied the island upon which New York City was built when the Hudson River was discovered by Henry Hudson in 1609. They also occupied the bank of the river in lower Westchester.

Hudson's vessel (Half-Moon) came first to anchor after passing from the mouth of the river at Verplancks Point, eight miles below. Here the natives in great numbers gathered from the highlands. One of them being caught in the act of stealing a pillow and some wearing apparel from the ship, was shot in his canoe by one of the crew of the vessel as he was escaping with his plunder. Another native who leaped into the water apparently to secure the canoe and stolen goods of the thief, on taking hold of the side of the shallop, was struck by one of Hudson's men with a sword, and his hand severed from his arm, and was suffered to drown without relief. The death of these two Indians produced intense hatred on the part of the natives against the whites ever afterwards. Bloody wars ensued between the Dutch and the Algonquins, before the former were able to hold in check and prevent their ravages upon the white settlements.

* Bancroft's History of the U. S., Vol. II., p. 100.

15

In May, 1626, Peter Minuvit, the Dutch governor of the colony, purchased Manhattan island from the Manhattans for the sum of about $25.00. After its purchase he built a strong fort at the place now called the Battery. The Manhattan and river tribes of the Mohegans have all passed away, so ere long the same may be said of the Mohegans, of whom but comparatively few of pure blood now remain. Some still occupy their ancient land on the banks of the Thames, five miles below Norwich in Connecticut. In 1864, according to recent publications, there were 400 Mohegans in Connecticut.*

The Nanticocks originally occupied the country lying between the Chesapeake and Delaware Bays. They were the leading Indian nation of Maryland before they were subdued by the Five Nations. In the year 1710 they abandoned their ancient domain and settled at Wyoming upon the Susquehannah, where they resided until about the commencement of the war of the Revolution, when they crossed the Alleghenies and joined the British against the colonists. They have no tribal existence, being distributed amongs other nations and tribes.

The Abanakes, when they first became known to Europeans, resided in Maine. They were early visited by the French Jesuits, under whose moral teachings they became nominal Christians. Until the conquest of Canada by the English in 1760 they were the allies of the French. In the year 1754 the whole nation, except the Penobscots, emigrated to Canada. According to the eighth census there were then in the State of Maine 747 Abanakes, remnants of the Penobscots and Passamaquoddy tribes.

The Susquehannocks were an independent, warlike band of natives, residing upon the banks of the Susquehannah, in Pennsylvania and Maryland; but, after a bloody conflict with the Five Nations, were forced down upon the Virginians. They ravaged Maryland and north eastern Virginia at will, with the apparent approval of Governor Berkley, who, fearing his Virginia subjects, refused to allow them to defend themselves against the Indian depredations, until the planters, in defiance of Berkley, declared Nathaniel Bacon their leader, who, at the head of

* The Indian Races of North and South America, by Charles de Wolf Brownel, p. 448.

500 men, marched out against the savage invaders. Berkley, whose conduct seems to have been more cruel than that of the real savages, declared Bacon and his companions "traitors," and sent out a body of troops to arrest Bacon, who was then successfully beating back the Indians. Berkley was made governor of Virginia by her own citizens, as Cromwell made no officials in the province, and the Virginians did not recognize the authority of his successor Richard. A popular government, with the right of universal suffrage, was inaugurated. When the news of the restoration of Charles II. as king of England reached Virginia, Berkley turned traitor to the people, and disclaimed popular sovereignty. In gratitude for this treachery of Berkley, King Charles caused the arms of Virginia to be quartered with those of England, Scotland, and Ireland, " as an independent member of the empire." From this circumstance Virginia received the name of the " Old Dominion."*

The traitors, as Bacon's men were called, not only beat back the Indians, but worsted the royalists, driving them back to the Rappahannock. The royalists and Indians were subdued, and popular liberty proclaimed by the Virginians, under their great leader, Nathaniel Bacon, on July 4, 1676.

The Susquehannocks, according to the description of them by Captain John Smith, were of gigantic stature—much greater than the English. In 1707 they resided upon the western borders of Maryland, but have long since become extinct.

The Mannahoaks, another independent tribe, occupied the country at the head waters of the Rappahannock, and the Manocans, also an independent tribe, resided in the regions south of the James River. They, as also the Mannahoaks, were very rude savages of an inferior grade of the red race. They were smaller than the Powhatans, and much inferior to them in many other respects. They are also extinct.

NEW ENGLAND INDIANS.

When the early navigators visited this continent it seems to have been their custom to seize and take back with them to Europe such of the natives as they might see proper to capture

* Lossing's Pictorial Field Book of the Revolution, Vol. II., p. 254

in the New World, without for a moment considering the evil consequences which flow from such a course of wanton violence towards the Americans, the rightful owners of this continent.

Columbus, in his voyage in 1492, captured and took to Spain several natives from the West Indies. Sebastian Cabot, in 1502, arrested and took from Newfoundland three of the natives to England, who were the first native Americans exhibited in Great Britain. The French, in 1608, arrested several natives on the St. Lawrence, and took them to Paris. In 1524 John Verazzinc, in the service of Francis I., came to the coasts of Connecticut, where twenty of his crew landed and came upon an old woman, a young girl, and two little boys. They tried to carry off the girl, but her cries induced them to release her, and captured one of the boys and took him with them. In 1577, Sir Martin Frobisher attacked a party of Indians in York Sound, and killed five or six of them, taking two women prisoners. In 1607 Hendrick Hudson's crew committed many acts of violence upon the natives residing upon the banks of the Hudson River; several of the natives were killed. In 1605 Captain George Waymouth carried off five Indians from New England to Europe. Other like wrongs had been inflicted upon the New England Indians before the landing of the Pilgrims in 1620. It could hardly be presumed by the early settlers that the natives, naturally suspicious, would at once recognize the whites as friends, however kindly they might treat them. The pious Pilgrims received no kinder reception, at first, by the natives than any other adventurers.

When the Pilgrims landed at Plymouth the natives did not greet them in friendship, and had good reasons for treating them as enemies and invaders of their country. Some sixteen of the Pilgrims, clad in heavy armor and supplied with fire-arms, proceeded from the Mayflower to make discoveries. Five or six natives appeared before them, but soon disappeared in the woods without having anything to say to the English, who pursued them many miles without overtaking them. About the 8th of December, 1610, after the reconnoitering band of English had returned to their shallop, the Indians, by a shower of arrows, made an attack upon them, but did no harm. One Indian, supposed to be the chief, was probably wounded, as, after the discharge of the Pilgrim's musket, the Indian, at whom the most deliberate aim had been taken, "gave an extraordinary cry," when all the natives retired. The trophies of this victory consisted of eighteen arrows, some of which were headed with brass, some with deer-horn, and others with eagles' claws.*

Thus stood matters when the Plymouth colony disembarked on Monday, December 21, 1620, and began the first settlement of Europeans in New England. Fortunately for this infant colony the Indians had been nearly exterminated in their vicinity a short time previous by a wasting disease. Some of the more sagacious chiefs, observing the Pilgrims meant them no harm, became friendly, and rendered the colonists important aid in the conflicts with the hostile tribes. Among the friendly chiefs Samoset and Massasoit stood most prominent.

The New England Indians comprised several powerful nations and tribes. The chief nations were the Massachusetts, Wampanoags, Pawtuckets, Narragansetts, Pokonkets, Nipmucs and Pennacooks.

The Massachusetts were once a leading power among the New England nations, but before the landing of the Pilgrims, by disease and wars, had been reduced to vassalage by neighboring nations. They, as well as the New England Indians generally, when first discovered by the whites, were in the lowest state of savage barbarity. It was their stone age; all their instruments being of stone, except occasionally some of copper and brass were found among them. They were indolent, living upon fish and game; but some attention was paid by them to the cultivation of the ground in raising corn for winter subsistence. The Massachusetts resided in the country about Boston, with head-quarters at Tchticut, in Middleborough. Here was where Chickataubut, their chief sachem had his residence. At the time of the founding of the Plymouth colony, the Massachusetts nation seemed to have no abiding place, and were so hunted and pressed by the relentless Torrotines, that they were almost daily compelled to seek a new place of safety.

In 1621 Chickataubut, with eight other sachems, by a written instrument, acknowledged themselves the subjects of King

* Mount's Relation.—1 Mass. Hist. Col. VIII., 218-219.

James. This great sachem remained friendly to the English until his death, which occurred in 1633. His son Josiah, *alias* Wampatuck, in 1665 deeded the lands in Braintree to the English; also in 1653 he sold a large tract in the vicinity of North River to Timothy Hatherly and others, and subsequently sold other tracts in the vicinity of Boston. The deed for the land upon which Boston stands was made by Josiah Wampatuck, grand-son of Chickatanbut, March 19, 1695. This nation has become extinct, and the name even not regarded by recent historians as ever having a place in the history of America. Captain Smith, in his account of New England, published in 1631, states that he had been informed that all the Massachusetts had been destroyed by the plague, except about thirty, of whom twenty-eight were killed by their neighbors, leaving only two survivors, when the English first located in their country.*

The Narragansetts were a fierce warlike nation residing in Rhode Island and south-western shores of Narraganset Bay, when they first became known to the Europeans. Canonicus was the most noted sachem of this nation. Meditating a war against the whites, Canonicus, wishing to make his purpose known to the whites, sent a bunch of arrows with a rattle-snake's skin to Governor Bradford, who filled the skin with powder and balls, and returned it to the chief.

He well understood the meaning of Bradford, and concluded to live upon terms of friendship thereafter with him. They could bring between two and three thousand warriors into the field, and had they, in the infancy state of New England, known their power, could doubtless have exterminated them. They seemed to have more hatred toward some of the Indian nations than the colonists, particularly the Pokanokets, over whom presided Massasoit, one of the most wise and noted chiefs of North America. Under the influence of King Philip, they were reconciled and became his most powerful ally. They were the avowed enemies of the Pequods, who could muster more warriors in the field than the Narragansetts. Until the English joined them they were unable to succeed against the Pequods. The combined forces of the English and Narragansetts under Captain John

* Drake's History and Biography of the Indians of North America, p. 81.

Mason, however, subjugated the Pequods, but not without very great carnage.

About sixty Pequod villages, with their women and children, were burned by the white and Narragansett savages, of which fiendish conduct the English boast as a great feat of arms in the new world, performed in 1638 by the Pilgrims and their associates.

When Roger Williams was forced by the Plymouth and Massachusetts governments to leave the country, he sought shelter with the Narragansetts, where he was kindly treated by the Indians, who became the benefactors of the Rhode Island colony. They fed and protected the colony, while the Puritans of Plymouth and Massachusetts had, without food or clothing, driven Williams and his band of Christians out into the wilderness to perish among the savages.

Through the influence of Roger Williams, Rhode Island was given to the colony by Miantonomoh, the renowned Narragansett sachem, whose tragic death is noticed in another place. Here was established, under the protection of the savage nations from the persecution of the Pilgrim Christians, the first example of civil and religious liberty in the New World.

Whilst the other great nations of New England have all virtually passed from earth, a few hundred of the Narragansett descendants of the great Canonicus and Miantonomoh still survive to witness the prosperity of the descendants of the noble white men whom their ancestors had fed and protected over two hundred years ago. About four hundred Narragansetts now reside in Rhode Island.

The Pokanokets lived on the eastern shore of Narraganset Bay, in Rhode Island, and some of their tribe were in the neighborhood of Barnstable and Plymouth. Massasoit was the sachem of the Pokanoket confederacy, which included all the tribes in the vicinity of Plymouth, and his influence was felt over the tribes far in the interior. He had his head-quarters at Mount Hope on Narraganset Bay. He was the sagamore of the Wampanoags. The Pilgrims, as soon as they learned the character of Massasoit, sought a friendly interview with him. They first gained information of this renowned chief from Samoset, a sagamore from Pawtuxet, March 16, 1621. He resided

formerly at Maratiggon, five days travel distant from Plymouth.
He was a Wampanoag, a sagamore of the tribe that had previously been cut off by the plague, and had learned a little English from the Penobscot fishermen as well as that the English
were disposed to be kind to the red men. Without standing
upon useless ceremony, or even waiting to be invited, Samoset
suddenly appeared at Plymouth, solitary and alone, almost in a
nude state, his only garment being a leather belt about his waist,
with a fringe about six or eight inches long. Having entered
the town unmolested, he boldly went to the rendezvous of the
Pilgrims, and in English exclaimed, "Welcome Englishmen."*
In the name of his nation, he welcomed the whites of the country of which he seemed to be the only survivor. The kind reception and friendly intercourse between Samoset and the Pilgrims, laid the foundation of friendship between the English and
Massasoit. Assisted by Squanto, who was one of the captives carried from Pawtuxet to England by Waymouth, and who learned
to speak English, Massasoit, who then resided at Pokanoket,
paid a visit to Plymouth. For the mutual benefit of his people
and the whites, a treaty was then formed between him and the
Plymouth colony. He desired the English as an ally against
the Narragansetts, with whom he was then at war, and the English desired his alliance for their protection against the savage
nation as well, whom they greatly feared.

This great sachem proved to be the fast friend of the colonists
during his life. He stood guard, as it were, over them, giving prompt warning of approaching danger — virtually saved
them from destruction when a plot was formed for their extirpation.

The conduct of Massasoit is the more praiseworthy, as the
Pilgrims were in fact trespassers upon his domain when they
took up their residence at Plymouth in 1620. The English gave
him full assurance of their fidelity to this chief, by assisting him
in a war with Canonicus in 1632, which was ended by the
English forces under Captain Miles Standish, without much
bloodshed. Massasoit was the father of King Philip, the most
distinguished Indian chief of North America. He had a son
named Alexander, who succeeded to the government of the Po-

* Bancroft's History of the United States, Vol. I., p. 316.

kanoket confederacy upon his father's death. This ruler, upon the mere suspicion that he was going to take up arms against the Plymouth government, was dragged from his home and family and never returned alive, having suddenly died of a fever, as was said, induced by the harsh treatment of the Pilgrims, whose prisoner he then was. At his death, Philip became the head chief of the nation.

The harsh treatment of Alexander, and other hostile demonstrations on the part of the English had, together with their growing power, awoke Philip to the true condition of the Indians, and to remedy the evil he resolved to exterminate them, as the only means of safety for the red race. With this view he united all the tribes of the Wampanoags, and the great mass of the New England tribes in a conspiracy to exterminate the English. John Sassamon, a Christian Indian, learning the purpose of the murderous conspirators, revealed it to the colonists, for which kind office his savage brethren put him to death. For his murder Pokanoket Indians were seized by the Plymouth government, tried and executed upon very doubtful evidence of only one witness, who did not see the murder committed, the dead body of Sassamon having been found under the ice a few days after he had disappeared. This precipitated the war so long contemplated by King Philip. Though having in view and preparing for war for several years, Philip refrained from striking the first blow, in order, no doubt, that the English might be considered the aggressors. In 1675 the young Indian warriors began to congregate at Mount Hope, in order to avenge the death of those executed by the Pilgrims for the murder of Sassamon. The Pokanokets were ungovernable; yet Philip was not hasty, but waited until the Colonists commenced hostilities, which was by an Englishman shooting an Indian.

The war then raged with relentless fury on both sides. King Philip was the Napoleon of the combined Indian forces, numbering several thousand; some have even supposed them 10,000 strong, and Captain Benjamin Church, seems to have been the Wellington in command of the English forces, not near so numerous as that of the Indians. Philip at first was mainly successful, which brought to his ranks many nations, who theretofore had been friendly toward the colonists, but had eventu-

ally to succumb to the superior strategy and bravery of the
English who were engaged in the struggle for life.

The war in no respect was conducted on either side with any
of the principles of humanity. Each seemed to be actuated by
the most malignant motive of revenge. The English, not satisfied with the slaughter of the natives, sold their prisoners as
slaves, thus tearing them away from their friends, home and
country, to die in foreign lands.

The Narragansetts and Nipmucks suffered the most severely
in the war, each nation having lost about 1000 men. From
June to October of 1676, Captain Church's command slaughtered about 1000 natives. Philip and his warriors fought most
bravely, but under far less advantageous circumstances than the
English. They were comparatively without arms or ammunition,
and often suffered for food and want of shelter. Philip's war
seemed to be on the defence, but though broken in spirit and
driven from his possessions, he did not surrender nor yield until
the last moment of his life.

Surrounded by a few followers, whom he advised to desert
him, as the great mass of his army had already done, he was
shot and killed by his English pursuers, two ruffians firing on
the great chief whilst he was lying down in a swamp, where he
had retired, no doubt, to mourn in silence over his fate and that
of the nation. To him it must have been sad to reflect that he
was thus pursued and persecuted by the people whom his father
had protected and cherished when they first became settlers at
Plymouth.

The Pawtuckets reside in New Hampshire and Massachusetts.
They, as well as the Pennacooks, were of the Nipmuck family.
The Pennacooks were residents of New Hampshire. Passa-
conaway was the grand Sachem of the Pawtucket confederacy
during the early history of the Plymouth Colony. Among the
Indians he was known as the "great Sagamore of Pennuhog,"
and doubtless was one of the most distinguished warriors and
statesmen of his race. He died at the advanced age of 120
years.

At first he was not disposed to look upon the Colonists as friends
of the red men, but after Massasoit had become their ally, he
and his people were less alarmed for their own safety. He, like

Massasoit, preferred peace to war, but was a more distinguished warrior than the great Pokanoket sachem. Though he acted toward the English with kindness and prevented them from being assailed by hostile natives, he, in return, received from them harsh and cruel treatment. About the year 1642 the Massachusetts government took the most summary measures possible to disarm the Pawtuckets upon the mere idle report that they were conspiring against the colonists. Not being able to arrest Passacouaway, his son, a squaw and child were seized, dragged to Boston and cast into prison. Unjust as this treatment was, the great chief, looking to the future welfare of his people, did not retaliate upon the English who then aimed at the extirpation of their benefactors. His sagacity and self-command averted an exterminating war and brought a reconciliation. His nation have long since become extinct.

The Nipmucks proper occupied a district in the central part of Massachusetts. They were an independent tribe, but had no head chief of their own. At one time they were under Massasoit, at another time under the Narragansett ruler, and at another period were subject to the Mohegan sachems. Squaw-sachem Weetamoo, the widow of Alexander, was the ruler of the tribe in 1643. At times she placed herself and people under the protection of the English. She and her tribe joined king Philip in his war against the colonists, but deserted him in the hour of his greatest peril, though it is said at Philip's request. After abandoning Philip she sought refuge in her own country, but soon fell into the hands of the English. Escaping from her captors Weetamoo was drowned in crossing a river or arm of the sea as she was seeking a place of safety. The English cut off her head and placed it upon a pole at Taunton, as a warning to the Indians. This barbarous conduct of the colonists only tended to increase the hatred of the natives towards the whites.

The brutal practice of making the heads of distinguished Indians trophies of victory was frequently indulged in by the enlightened Puritans. Captain Church cut off the head of king Philip with his sword and took it to Plymouth, where it was exposed upon a gibbet for twenty years. One of his hands was publicly exhibited in Boston, and his body was quartered and hung upon trees and there left as a monument of the shocking barbarity of the savage Puritans.*

Barbarism was not a mere individual enterprise, as the Plymouth Government gave a reward of 30 shillings per head for all Indians killed or captured. The head of the great Sassacus was cut off by the Mohawks and presented to the English of Connecticut.

* Drake's History and Biography of the North American Indians, p. 227.

RED JACKET.

MANDAN CHIEF.

THE Iroquois were a distinct people from the Algonquins in several particulars; their language was radically different, and they were superior in physical and mental development. They had large brains and well developed intellectual frontal heads. The term Iroquois was applied to them by the French, but the Dutch called them Maguas; by the Indians of Virginia they were termed Massawomeks, though they called themselves Mengwes.

The Iroquois comprised the Hurons, Mohawks, Senecas, Cayugas, Onondagas, Oneidas and Tuscaroras. The Hurons constituted the Hurons proper, Wyandotts, Attionandirones, Eries and Andastes.

The Iroquois proper, constituting the six nations, were the Mohawks, Senecas, Cayugas, Onondagas, Oneidas, and Tuscaroras. Before the other five preceding nations were joined by the Tuscaroras, they constituted the confederacy of the Five Nations, who occupied lands within the State of New York. Though the Mohawk was the leading nation of the confederacy, yet their great " council fire " was in the country of the Onon-

dagas, and their metropolis located at, or near, where the city of
Syracuse now stands. The Iroquois were a warlike and brave
people, and extended their conquests into the Carolinas, New
England, Canada, and the Mississippi valley. When the Dutch
first settled on Manhattan Island they held in subjection the
Algonquin tribes in that vicinity; also those upon the Hudson,
Delaware, Connecticut and Susquehanna rivers, upon whom
they levied an annual revenue.

When the Pilgrims took up their residence at Plymouth the
Five Nations were a rising power in North America. Had not
New England been settled by Europeans it is most likely the
Iroquois would have exterminated the inferior tribes of the red
man.

They were generally successful in all their undertakings.
"Among all the barbarous nations of this portion of the continent the Iroquois of New York stand the most prominent."*

The origin of the Iroquois is unknown. According to tradition they came from beyond the lakes a great while ago, and
subdued, or exterminated, the inhabitants residing between the
lakes and the sea. When the French located in Canada in 1611,
the Five Nations were engaged in a war with the Adirondaks;
and the French, having settled upon lands of the Adirondaks,
assisted them against the Iroquois.

The Iroquois were divided into the following clans: The
Wolf, Bear, Beaver, Tortoise, Deer, Snipe, Heron and Hawk.

At the time the French settled in Lower Canada, the Iroquois
owned the land on the banks of the St. Lawrence, where the
city of Montreal is now built. They then numbered about
25,000 souls, and could bring into the field about 2,300 fighting
men. Though a brave people, they were by no means ignorant
of the advantages of civil government and a regulated system
of morals. They sought every opportunity to learn such things
as would be beneficial to them from the French and English.
Many espoused the Christian faith and became co-workers with
the Jesuits in the promulgation of morals and religion. Their
moral teachings tended to soften the manners of the unconverted
natives.†

* The Jesuits in North America, by Parkman, p. 47.
† Parkman's Jesuits in North America, p. 319.

The Mohawks, the head tribe of the Six Nations, occupied the country along the Mohawk river in the State of New York. Their language was that of the confederate nations, and had no word in it requiring the lips to be closed in its utterance. The Mohawks were amongst the bravest of the American Race.

In the war of the Revolution they were powerful allies of the British, and inflicted much injury upon the Colonists. Joseph Brant was their great leader, and played a conspicuous part against the Colonists as a Colonel in the British army. About the close of the war they emigrated to Canada and took up their residence on Grand river, there building villages, adopted a partial civilization and enjoyed, to some degree, an organized civil government.

The Mohawks, under John Brant, the son of Joseph, took sides with the British in the war of 1812. A remnant of them still reside upon their reservation near Grand river. As regards their origin, they claim they, like the trees, sprung up in the very place they were residing when first discovered by the French.*

The Senecas were a prominent nation of the Iroquois Confederacy. Their place of residence was in the State of New York and in Ohio. In the latter State they owned 40,000 acres of choice land on the east side of the Sandusky river.

They ceded this land to the United States in 1831, and emigrated to the Neosho River country south-west of the Missouri. They were the remnant of Logan's tribe of Mingoes.

The Senecas had many distinguished chiefs and warriors, as well as renowned orators, among them. Red Jacket and Farmers' Brother, in point of eloquence, were surpassed by none of their race.

The Oneidas, Onondagas and Cayugas, were residents of New York.

The Oneidas dwelt near Oneida Lake, the Onondages and Cayugas occupied the country between the Oneida and Seneca Lakes.

The Oneidas are principally settled now upon a reservation in the vicinity of Green Bay, Wisconsin; some villages also being located near Winnebago Lake. About two thousand

* Drake's History and Biography of the American Indians, p. 500.

Iroquois are, it is supposed, now living in Canada, the main portion of whom are Cayugas and Mohawks.

The Tuscaroras' first place of residence known to the Europeans was in North Carolina upon the Neuse and Tar Rivers and the islands of that province. They were the most powerful nation of that portion of the country; were quite as numerous as the Catawbas and as brave as the Mohawks. Becoming alarmed at the rapid increase of the white settlers in the Carolinas, they formed a conspiracy for their extirpation, and commenced the bloody work September 22, 1711, on the banks of the Roanoke, and Palmico Sound. Their ravages awoke the whites to a true sense of their danger. With the friendly Cherokees, Creeks, Catawbas and Yamassees, they invaded the dominions of the Tuscaroras, besieged them in their fort on the Neuse River, and forced the garrison of eight hundred men to surrender. Thus defeated and broken in spirit the hostile portion of the Tuscaroras, in 1713, abandoned North Carolina and took up their residence with the Iroquois in New York. The next year they joined the confederacy of the Five Nations, and from that time the Iroquois were known as the Six Nations.

The early history of the Tuscaroras is unknown. No tradition or legend, points to the time when they first became a nation. They doubtless came from the westward, as traces of them were in Virginia when the Jamestown Colony was first established. The Monocans, then residing at the head waters of the James River, by some classed with the Algonquins, were Tuscaroras, and very rude savages.

The Tuscaroras had a tradition that a vessel had been wrecked upon the Atlantic coast before the discovery by Columbus, the crew of which was saved by the Indians, but afterwards, wholly destroyed and eaten up by the monster quadrupeds.*

They, as well as the Oneidas, did not unite with their brethren against the Colonists in the war of the Revolution; those of them who did not join the Colonial Army against the British, remained neutral throughout the conflict.

The Tuscaroras not only evinced a desire to cultivate friendship with the whites after they came north, but also to adopt their system of civilization. Many of them became Christians,

* Schoolcraft's History of the Indian Tribes of North America, Part I., p. 125.

some even eminent teachers of the Christian religion among their kindred, among whom was Cusic. He not only became a popular Moravian preacher, but so far versed in the English language as to write a history of the Aboriginal Tribes of America.* There was no want of mental capacity among the Iroquois nations. As regards memory they are unsurpassed by any people. They have large brains, the internal capacity of the skull being eighty-eight cubic inches,—only two inches less than of the Caucasian.† Those of them who permanently settled down in the State of New York have conclusively shown that they have the capability to successfully engage in all the ordinary pursuits of life. They have well succeeded in farming, and in the mechanic arts become quite proficient.

In the early part of the eighteenth century the Iroquois confederacy numbered over forty thousand souls, but now comparatively few remain compared with their number about the year 1715, when they were most numerous.

According to the census of 1860 there were 3,785 Indians in the State of New York, the great mass of whom were the remnants of the six nations.

Schoolcraft states the number of Iroquois in Canada and the United States to be nearly 7,000 in 1859, of whom about 5,000 were then in the United States, and 3,733 in the State of New York.

THE HURONS.

When the French navigator, Cartier, in 1535, visited the country where the city of Montreal is located, the Hurons occupied that part of Canada from Three Rivers to Lake Huron, in the vicinity of the eastern coast, their ancient seat. According to the enumeration of the Jesuites, this nation, in 1639, had thirty-two villages and 700 dwellings, occupied by 4,000 families and 1,200 adult persons, making a total population of about 20,000. By the zeal and energy of Brebeuf and other devout Jesuits, the Hurons were, in form at least, converted to Christianity. Three thousand, it is said, were baptised in one day. They, more readily than any other Indians, adopted the Christian faith. While the Hurons were thus rejoicing in the prospects of a

---

* Schoolcraft's History of the Indian Tribes of North America, Part I., p. 125.
† Dr. Martin's Crania Americana, p. 195.

16

brighter future, and abstaining from their savage practices, the relentless Mohawks and their confederates were preparing for the extirpation of the Hurons and their French moral instructors.

The fearless Father Isaac Jogues went on a religious mission to the Mohawks, and was put to death by the savages as a sorcerer, upon a charge of having blighted the Indian corn; his head was cut off and hung upon the palisades of the fort. The war then raged with all the vindictive fury possible, especially on the part of the Mohawks, who nearly annihalated the Hurons, vanquished and scattered the Wyandots and exterminated the Eries; and the six nations did not seem to rest satisfied until they had virtually destroyed the Andastes in 1672. About 300 Hurons took refuge with the French at Quebec; some reluctantly united with the victors; but the greater number sought an asylum among the nations of the Ottawas, and others still more remote.

The Iroquois being furnished with firearms purchased from the Dutch at Manhattan, sought to chastise the Ottawas for sheltering the dispersed Hurons; but the latter did not wait to give them battle; for, learning the purpose of the Iroquois, the Ottawas abandoned their country, some seeking shelter in the marches of the islands of Lake Huron, and others passing far to the southward formed a junction with the Sioux.

At their own request the Hurons, who had placed themselves under the protection of the French, united with the Iroquois.

They were tall, robust and well shaped; had black, glossy hair and the Indian complexion. The Iroquois recognized the Hurons as their ancestors, calling them "fathers;" and the Delawares considered the Wyandots as kindred, calling them "uncles." *

The Andastes resided on the lower Susquehannah. The research of Mr. Shea has shown their identity with those of the Mengwe, of the Dutch, and the Susquehannocks of the English. They were fierce warriors, and for a long time successfully defended themselves against the Iroquois. They were finally forced to yield by the Senecas; but their destruction eventually was more the work of disease than implements of war.

The Eries were located to the eastward and southward of Lake Erie, and were known as the "Nation of the Cat;" but

* Prichard's Natural History of Man, Vol. II., p. 528.

very little of their history has been recorded. From what we can gather they occupied a district in southwestern New York, as far east perhaps as the Genesee or western frontier of the Senecas. They fought with the courage and desperation of the Mohawks, and used poisoned arrows ; but were destroyed by the Iroquois about the year 1654.

The Attionandirons, called the "Neutral Nation," occupied the country on the northern coast of Lake Erie and on both sides of the Niagara River, when they were visited by the French as early as 1626. La Roche Dallion reported that at that time they had twenty-eight town, several small hamlets, and a numerous population. Several of their towns were located on the south side of the Niagara. They gained the title of "neutrals" by refusing to participate in the war between the Hurons and Iroquois, but were by no means averse to war, no nation being more ferocious and cruel than this people. In their wars with the Mascontines (Fire Indians), they evinced a barbarity in burning their female prisoners, unknown to the Huron. Their dead were kept in their houses until the flesh rotted upon the bones, when it was scraped off and the bones hung along the walls until the day of the "feast of the dead," a grand burial occasion. The men wore no clothing whatever during the summer, but kept their bodies tattooed with powdered charcoal from head to foot. They were tall, stout, athletic men—in this respect even surpassing the Hurons.

When the five nations and Hurons were at war the neutral nation erected, for each belligerent party, a fort on the Sandusky; but their neutrality did not preserve them. After the Iroquois had dispersed the Hurons they commenced an exterminating war upon the Neutrals, and in the fall of the year 1650 assaulted and took one of their principal towns, containing sixteen hundred men besides women and children. Early in the next spring they captured another of their chief villages, on the taking of which they exulted in a scene of the most barbarous butchery. Overpowered and disheartened, the Neutrals abandoned everything, and took to the forests as the only place of safety, where they perished by thousands for want of food and by reason of the hardships they had to endure ; and from that time ceased to exist as a nation.

THE WYANDOTS.

This nation is a remnant of the Hurons. In the dispersion of the Hurons, after halting for a time at Michilimackinac, being there attacked by the Iroquois, they removed to the islands at the mouth of Green Bay, where they fortified themselves on the mainland. Here they were pursued by the Iroquois, and for safety went southward to the domains of the Illinois; from thence westward to the Mississippi and country of the Sioux, where their stay was short, as the Sioux soon drove them beyond their lines. Their next place of residence was at the southern extremity of Lake Superior; this they abandoned in 1671 and emigrated to Michilimackinac. They did not locate upon the island, but settled in the northern part of Michigan. Subsequently the great mass of them made a settlement near Detroit, Michigan, and on the Sandusky River in Ohio, where, under the name of Wyandots, they wielded great influence over the neighboring tribes. The Wyandots are descendants of the "Tobacco Nation" of Hurons.

Their tradition traces them no further than the first landing of the French at Quebec and Montreal in 1535. At that time their ancestors occupied the northern side of the St. Lawrence as far down as Coon Lake and westward to the Huron. The Senecas then were settled on the southern side of the St. Lawrence. These were kindred nations, yet long and bloody wars had been waged between them, in which the Hurons were the greatest sufferers. Seeing their numbers daily decreasing, and that their extermination was sought by the Senecas, they left their ancient lands and took up their residence at Green Bay. Thither they were pursued by the Senecas, who fell upon one of their villages, and killed quite a number of the inhabitants. After the French had supplied the Senecas with guns, powder and lead, they made another attack upon the Hurons at Green Bay, and, at first, were entirely successful, but by the stratagem of the Hurons all the Senecas were cut off, not one of the war-party remaining alive to tell the sad tale of blood.

The Wyandots, thereafter, also being furnished with arms and munitions of war, resolved to return to their own country, in the vicinity of Detroit. On the way thither they encountered the Senecas on the lake in the vicinity of Long Point, where a desperate battle was fought upon the water, in which the Wyandots were the victors. Not a single Seneca escaped, and the Wyandot loss was very heavy. This was the last battle between the Wyandots and Senecas. The former took an active part on behalf of the French, in the war which resulted in the reduction of Canada by the English, and were a potent power against the English in Pontiac's war.

By the treaty of September 29, 1817, between the Wyandots and the Federal Government, there was granted to the former a body of land twelve miles square, the center of which was the Fort, now the site of Upper Sandusky, the county seat of Wyandot County, Ohio; also, at the same time, was granted them, a tract of a mile square, on Broken Sword Creek. They occupied these lands until July, 1843, when they emigrated to their present place of residence, west of the Mississippi, having disposed of their lands by treaty in 1842. At the time of their emigration they numbered about 700.

The Wyandots had many distinguished chiefs, among whom, during our own time, Round-Head and King Crane were the most prominent. The former took an active part in the war of 1812. He participated in the battle of River Raisin, where General Winchester and a large number of his command were defeated and made prisoners. King Crane was distinguished for his humanity in saving the life of Miss Flemming, whom the Wyandots had tied to the stake, and were proceeding to burn. General Hull mentioned Walk-in-the-Water as a leading spirit in the war of 1812. He took a prominent part in the battle of the Thames.

THE POWHATANS

were a confederacy of thirty tribes, whose territories, consisting of 8,000 square miles, lay south of the Potomac river, in Virginia. At the founding of Jamestown, in 1607, they numbered about 8,000 souls, and had about 2,400 warriors. Captain John Smith stated that there then were 5,000 Indians within sixty miles of Jamestown; * but, at that period, however, there were two other confederacies, those of the Mannahoacs and Monacans, besides several independent tribes, in that portion of Virginia.

* Jefferson's Notes, p. 96.

The confederacy of the Powhatans, at the founding of James-town, was under the rule of the emperor Wahunsonacock, by the English called Powhatan, whose hereditary dominions lay upon the banks of the James river, and his residence where Richmond is now built. His capital consisted of twelve wig-wams.* The emperor was then about sixty years of age, and is described as being tall, well proportioned, with vigorous body, capable of enduring great hardship. His ornamented dress consisted of a robe of raccoon skins, and his imperial crown was composed of many feathers.

At one time the Powhatans claimed all the country from the sea to the falls of the rivers, and beyond the Potomac to the Patuxent in Maryland. By the law of the empire, the succes-sion to the crown did not descend to the heirs of the emperor, but passed to his brothers and sisters, the oldest first.

The Powhatans at first received the colonists with marked friendship, but the boldness of Captain Smith made them mis-trustful, and, consequently, every opportunity was sought by the natives to place the whites in the wrong before the emperor. Smith, and his party of discoverers, were assailed, and all but himself killed, who saved his life by deliberate coolness. His captors conducted him in triumph to the Chickahominy, Rap-pahannock, Potomac, and thence to the Pamunkey, making of him a public show in the several Indian settlements. He was ushered into the presence of his imperial majesty, when his fate was to be decided, and the council determined that he should die. Two huge stones were placed before Powhatan; Smith was seized and conducted to execution, his head placed upon the stones, ready to receive the fatal blow of the war-club, already raised for the purpose, when, at this juncture, Pocahontas, the humane daughter of the emperor, a girl of twelve years, who had been entreating in tears for Smith's life, resolved, in her child-like, though womanly, sympathy, to save his life or perish with him. She threw herself upon his body, clung firmly to his neck, with his head in her arms, and laid her own upon his, where the death-blow would fall. Powhatan was unable to resist the ex-traordinary conduct of his child, and the warrior was afraid to strike. Her father annulled the sentence — Smith's life was

* Bancroft's History of the United States, Vol. I., p. 125.

saved by Pocahontas, whose heroic conduct on that occasion will ever be remembered as a tribute to her memory, and an honor to her sex.* This was the turning-point in the destiny of the Jamestown colony, as from that time forward Powhatan was the fast friend of the whites. Pocahontas stood sentinel over the infant colony, ever warning them of danger. For this, and her other noble conduct, she was rewarded in due season. John Rolf, a young Englishman of education and distinction, won the heart of the Indian maiden, and married her, which alliance secured the real friendship of Powhatan, and placed Pocahontas in the highest walks of English society. From this marriage originated some of the first families of Virginia, among whom were talents of the highest order. John Randolph, one of Virginia's most gifted orators, could boast of being a descendant of Pocahontas.

Powhatan died in the year 1618, and was buried within a few miles of Richmond, Virginia. His grave was marked by a large stone, which is pointed out at the present day as "Powhatan's grave." He was succeeded by his brother, Itopatin, a weak and decrepit chief, unable to command respect or enforce obedience, who was neither distinguished in council nor in the field, but was readily made the dupe of the great Opekankonkonough, king of the Pamunkeys, who planned and attempted to carry into execution a conspiracy to massacre all the whites of the country. On the 22d day of March, 1622, the Powhatans began the slaughter. So complete were their plans, that, in the space of an hour, three hundred and fifty-seven men, women and children were murdered by the savages. In 1644, this same ruler, when he was a hundred years of age, again sought to exterminate the colonists by a general massacre. He had to be borne upon a litter to the place of slaughter. The work commenced on the frontiers, with intention to advance to the sea. In the course of two days, his warriors had murdered three hundred whites, when they were checked by Sir William Berkley, at the head of the colonial forces.

The Indians were severely punished for their temerity and

* Some have claimed that the manner, above given, of saving the life of Captain Smith, is visionary and unauthentic. However this may be, it has passed into history as a substantial fact.

crimes, being defeated with heavy loss, and driven to great extremity. The aged king was captured, and slain at Jamestown by one of the English soldiers who was placed guard over him. Broken in power, the Powhatans were compelled to make large cessions of their lands to the English, and acknowledge allegiance to the authorities of Virginia, having virtually to surrender everything—their homes and the graves of their ancestors. Their power once broken, the confederacy soon began to dissolve, and the Powhatans to disappear. It is believed that not a solitary representative of their nation survives.

THE MANNAHOACS

comprised eight tribes, and occupied the country lying between the Rappahannock and York rivers; and the Monacans, comprising five tribes, resided between the James and York rivers, above the falls. These two confederacies were enemies of the Powhatans, with whom they waged almost constant wars. The Monacans were, as has been noted in another place, a family of the Tuscaroras, who eventually became the sixth nation of the Iroquois, the latter being called Massawomekes by the Powhatans.

The Mannahoacs and Monacans, with their kindred, were entirely distinct from the Powhatans; their language was so dissimilar that they could only communicate by an interpreter. All, however, were about equal as nations in point of intelligence.

The independent tribes of distinction were the Nottoways, Meherreeks, and Tuteloes. The former resided on the river bearing their name, on whose banks a few of them still linger, near Jerusalem, Virginia. The Meherreeks and Tuteloes resided on the Meherrin river; the former were connected with the Shawanese of North Carolina, the latter with the Iroquois, and were known as Mangoaks. Both these nations are extinct.

When Philip Amidas and Arthur Barlowe, in 1584, landed on the island of Roanoke, they received a cordial welcome from the natives, the Hatteras Indians, being even entertained by the wife of the father of Wingind, the king. This treatment seemed to warrant the location of a colony upon the island, which was accordingly done. The colonists, believing the Indians were conspiring for their destruction, decoyed Wingind, the most active chief of the country, to an audience. Lane, and other head men of the colony, having him in their power, at the proper signal fell upon and brutally murdered the chief and his attendants. Disheartened at not finding the country teeming with gold, Lane, with his colony, left their settlement and returned to England. Sir Richard Greenville, some two weeks later, finding the country deserted, and unwilling to suffer it to pass into other hands, left fifteen of his men on the island of Roanoke, but they did not long survive, all being killed by the Indians.

At that period the Hatteras were a powerful nation, mustering 3,000 bowmen; but, eighty years afterwards, when the English made permanent settlement in the country, they had been reduced to fifteen warriors; during their decline, and afterwards, their territory was occupied by the Tuscaroras and the Cheraws. The Hatteras aided the Tuscaroras in a conspiracy to massacre the whites, in 1711, but their defeat in the project so humbled them that they never afterwards rose to any distinction.

The Adirondaks, on the St. Lawrence; the Nipissens, residing near the source of the Ottawa, in Canada; the Micmacs, of Newfoundland; and the Natchitoches, of Maryland, were noted Algonquin tribes.

THE ALLEGHANIANS

The Indians who resided on the southern slope of the Appalachian chain, and around its southern extremity on the lower Mississippi river, south of the dominions of the Algonquins and Iroquois, were called "The Alleghanian Race."* This group consisted of the following leading nations, viz: Catawbas, Cherokees, Uchees, Natchez, Creeks or Muscagees, Chickasaws, Yamassees and Seminoles.

The Catawbas were an independent nation. Of their kindred were the Woccan, Cheraw and Congaree tribes, all of whom long since became extinct. The Esaws of the Pedee, once a powerful nation, were probably Catawbas. The early history of this nation, before the Europeans settled in the Carolinas, is

* Prichard's Natural History of Man, Vol. II., p. 532.

unknown; but when first discovered, they had emerged from the degraded savage state, and enjoyed a partial civilization—residing in villages and cultivating the ground. Though a warlike people, their entire forces did not exceed 1500 warriors. The Catawbas lived on the Yadkin, and the river bearing their name in the Carolinas. The introduction of ardent spirits by the colonists among this nation had a very deleterious effect upon many of them, who, as Adair said, were "much addicted to excessive drinking," in consequence of which they became impoverished, and suffered their fields to remain uncultivated and go to waste. Long and bloody wars raged between them and the Iroquois; also with the Shawnees, whom they expelled from the country in 1672; but were unable to cope successfully with the Five Nations. They were friendly toward the colonists, rendering them very important aid in the war with the Tuscaroras and confederates in 1712; but in the year 1715 they joined the Yamassees and others in this great conspiracy to massacre the whites of the Carolinas. Before the war of the Revolution in America the Catawbas had become friendly toward the colonists, and in that contest with England were the allies of the patriots. A few of this family still remain at their village on the Catawba, near the mouth of Flushing creek, where they have a reservation of lands a few miles square.

The Cherokees occupied the country to the westward of the Catawbas and Tuscaroras; and what now constitutes the States of Alabama, Mississippi, Tennessee and Georgia was within their jurisdiction. They possessed the most lovely, picturesque and productive portion of the United States; and, before the disturbing influences of European civilization reached them, seemed to have enjoyed themselves in their semi-civilized retreats to a much higher degree than generally allotted to the Americans. They were an independent nation, who for many centuries had dwelt in these fastnesses, where nature seemed to have fortified them against the encroachments of ruder barbarians. Their villages were located along the streams of the valleys, no less than fifty of which were strewn throughout the country during their greatest prosperity. Before the war of 1812 the jurisdiction of the Cherokees extended over 24,000 square miles. As early as 1735, according to Mr. Adair, the historian, they could bring into the field 6000 warriors. In 1730, when Sir Alexander Cumming visited them, the nation was governed by seven "Mother Towns," each of which chose a king from the mother line of ancestry, who presided over their respective towns and territories annexed to them. Over these seven Mother Towns presided a chief or emperor. Moytoy, a noted sachem who resided at Telligno, one of the Mother Towns, was elected emperor in April, 1730, at which time the Cherokee nation, by the emperor and other officials, was acknowledged to be under the authority of the king of Great Britain; and, as a mark of willing submission to the English king, Sir Alexander Cumming, accompanied by seven distinguished war chiefs, at the request of the Cherokee nation, took the emperor's crown to England and laid it at the feet of King George II., which, with five eagles' tails, and four scalps of Indian enemies of the Cherokees, his majesty graciously accepted as a testimony of submission.

At that time the nation was very numerous; but in 1738 nearly one half of them perished by small-pox. In 1819 the total population was only 10,000; but in 1825 it had increased to 13,563; and, in 1840, at the time of their removal to Arkansas, to 18,000.*

Before their troubles with the people of Georgia, the Cherokees had made rapid advancement in civilization; had neat and flourishing villages—manufactured woollen and cotton fabrics from the raw material of their own production; and, with good farming skill, cultivated the soil, which yielded to them bountiful harvests of grain and vegetables. They excelled in the mechanic arts, though the great mass of the population devoted their attention to agricultural pursuits and raising stock, having horses, cattle, sheep, goats and swine in great abundance. On the rivers were vessels of their own, with which their surplus cotton and produce was conveyed to market, New Orleans being the principal market for their cotton. Their public roads were kept in good condition, and the traveller was never in want of a good tavern and suitable accommodations in the Cherokee country.

* Of these 15,000 signed a petition protesting against their removal to Arkansas, to which no heed was paid.—Drake's History and Biography of American Indians, p. 440.

In 1820 the nation reorganized its general government and established a federative system after the order of that of the United States. Though compelled to leave their cherished homes and tombs of their ancestors to give place to white men and settle in the wilds of the far west, they did not for a moment lose sight of their refinement or institutions, under which they have greatly prospered in their new home.

Their language is destitute of labials, and abounds in vowels, in this respect resembling the Iroquois. A native Cherokee, named Segayoh, in English called George Guess, invented a syllabic alphabet of the language of his nation in 1826. It was so perfect that young Cherokees in three days practice could write letters to their friends intelligibly. In 1828 a newspaper called the "Cherokee Phœnix" was established and printed chiefly in Cherokee, with an English translation. This was a great triumph for the Cherokees; by it much very useful knowledge was disseminated throughout the country, and the growing prosperity of the nation given to the public at large. They have written laws, printed books in their own language, and their youth are taught in well regulated schools and institutions of learning. The Cherokees, to a high degree, enjoy the blessings of Christianity. In their semi-savage condition they worshipped the sun and fire. Their town, Echotah,* was a city of refuge similar to that of the Hebrews. Here resided the "Beloved Men," in whose presence no act of evil was tolerable. The beloved people were perhaps a tribe of Cherokees, living in their own village, and who commanded the respect and reverence of their more barbarous kindred; malefactors even found safety in this city of refuge; here the sacred fire was kept constantly burning, and thence proceeded the wise counsel throughout the country which called the attention of the Cherokees from the business of war to the civil pursuits of life. The Beloved Men were not warriors, and were, no doubt, more enlightened than the surrounding nations. Mr. Bancroft says: "The beloved people of the Cherokees were a nation by themselves."†

The Cherokees are tall, erect and moderately robust; some

---

* The village in Georgia, where the "Cherokee Phœnix" was published in 1828, was called New Echotah.—Natural History of Man, Vol. I., p. 534.

* Bancroft's History of the United States, Vol. III., p. 27.

of them perfect human figures; complexion, olive; hair, black, straight and glossy, and, in some respects resembling the Iroquois. Mr. Prichard regarded them as a branch of the same family. Some of their females are as fair as Europeans, and are quite handsome, being tall, slender and of delicate form. As a nation, their countenance is cheerful, features regular and movements dignified and graceful. Though advanced in civilization above all other American Indians, and enjoying all the blessings of a free government, they are rapidly on the decline. In 1857 they numbered not less than 25,000 souls, while now, in 1869, they do not even reach 14,000. They unwisely took some part in the late war between the Federal and Confederate States. Previous to the war the Cherokees were the wealthiest nation, in proportion to numbers, on the globe, owning about four million acres of land and large herds of cattle—some individuals possessing as many as 20,000, 15,000, 10,000 head, and others lesser numbers, yet vast herds. The Federal Government holds in trust for them about one million of dollars.

The early intercourse of the Cherokees with the white settlers of the Carolinas was of friendly character. When the Tuscaroras, in 1712, commenced their war of extermination against the whites, the Cherokees were with the Catawbas, who were allies of the colonists against the Tuscaroras; but in 1715, when the great Indian conspiracy was formed to destroy the Carolinians, the Cherokees were on the side of the conspirators.

They had long and bloody wars with the Five Nations, who aimed at their subjection. The English interfered in 1750, and brought about a permanent peace between them and the Iroquois. After that they became the allies of the English; and, in 1758, assisted then in the reduction of Fort Du Quesne. On their way home from the captured fort two of their warriors were killed by Virginians; and, as a consequence, the Cherokees sought revenge, and spread desolation along the frontiers of Virginia for several years.* In the war of the Revolution they aided the British, and remained hostile toward the colonists for eight years thereafter, when, by treaty, the difficulties between them

---

* The ancient town of Echotah was burnt by the English in 1761, with fourteen others in the middle settlement of the Cherokees. A desperate battle had been fought the day preceding between the Cherokees and English under Colonel Grant.—The Indian Races of North and South America, p. 451.

and the colonists were amicably adjusted. During the war of 1812 they assisted the United States government, and rendered very important aid in the subjugation of the Creeks in 1814.

THE UCHEES

were located south-east of the Cherokees, and claimed the country above and below Augusta, Georgia, and boasted of being the most ancient people in the southern country. Their origin, and first place of abode are concealed in the gloom of the past —no annals, or even tradition, presumes ought of their early habitation. As a people they were distinct from all other American Indians, and had a language peculiar to themselves and spoken by no other nation. Their own idea of their origin was, that they naturally grew up in the place where they dwelt when the Europeans first discovered them, at which time they appeared to be but the remnant of a nation that had once enjoyed a better condition of life, though even then their towns were of a higher order than those of the Algonquins, and their skill in agriculture much superior to that of the northern nations.

The Uchees joined the Creek confederacy, and since then have, to a considerable extent, lost their identity as a nation. About 1,000 remain with the Creeks.

The Natchez occupied a small district in the valley of the Pearl River from the east bank of the Mississippi to the head waters of the Chickasaw. They were a powerful people, and in point of intelligence considerably superior to the surrounding nations. In some'respects their institutions were similar to those of the Aztecs, having a temple dedicated to the worship of the Great Spirit, on the altar of which perpetual fire was kept burning. The chiefs, like the Incas, claimed to have derived their origin from the sun, and the one highest in authority, called the Grand Sun, tried to impress the French with the idea that he was supernatural. The great temple, so much revered by the Natchez, where the perpetual fire constantly burned, was but a rude building of oval form, a hundred feet in circumference, without a window or opening, except a single doorway, in which were the images and fetiches, with bones of the dead sacredly treasured. Near the temple stood the palace of the Grand Sun, an

insignificant hut erected on a mound, and around which circled
the cabins of the tribe. This was their chief city, not far distant from where the present city of Natchez is now located.

One hundred and thirty-two years after Ferdinand de Soto
had discovered the Mississippi, it was reached by Marquette and
Jolliet by way of the northern lakes and the Wisconsin, who explored it from the mouth of the Wisconsin to the confluence of
the Arkansas.

However refined the Natchez may have been formerly, the
French found them but little if anything more advanced in
civilization than the other nations of the country. Their sacred
temple was then polluted with trophies of war, among which the
scalps of their victims decorated the palisades of the surrounding enclosure. The Natchez and Chickasaws, in whose dominion
the French were locating and constructing fortifications, looked
upon the latter with distrust and as intruders. The French, considering themselves masters of the situation, desiring to form
an extensive agricultural establishment, and coveting the La
Pomme village of the Natchez, Chepar, the haughty commander
of Fort Rosalie, ordered the chief to vacate at once. Against
this unjust demand the Natchez protested but without avail, except that they were allowed permission to remain a sufficient time
to gather their harvest; and even for this act of grace on the
part of the French, the chief of the village was compelled to
pay a tribute of corn. This and other acts of the French toward the Natchez so enraged them that they resolved to get rid
of their cruel masters by extermination. Having completed
their plans, on the 28th day of November, 1729, they fell upon
the garrison at Fort Rosalie, murdering over 200 persons; only
about twenty French and five or six negroes escaping alive, except the women and a few children who were made captives. A
similar scene was enacted about the same time among the
Yazoos, by whom the destruction of the French was more complete, all the occupants of the fort being put to death. After
those disasters, the French, aided by the Choctaws and other
friendly Indians, almost exterminated the Natchez. The Great
Sun, with more than 400 prisoners, were shipped by the French
to Hispaniola, and sold as slaves.* Those who escaped destruc-

* Bancroft's History of the United States, vol. III., p. 363.

tion and capture remained with the Chickasaws, except a few that took shelter with the Muscogees. Thus terminated the Natchez nation; and, though once so numerous, they do not now number more than 300 souls.

THE MOBILIAN NATIONS.

The Mobilians comprised a great number of tribes and nations speaking different dialects of the same language, the chief nations being the Muscogees or Creeks, Choctaws, Chickasaws, Seminoles and Yamassees. These, with kindred tribes, were divided into the Creek, Choctaw and Chickasaw confederacies.

The Mobilians inhabited the country lying south of the Cherokees, Catawbas and Algonquins, to the Gulf of Mexico, and from the Atlantic on the east to the Mississippi on the west, except the small district occupied by the Uchees and Natchez.

It is impossible to give the early history of the Mobilian nations with any degree of accuracy prior to the time the Spaniards and French settled in Florida and Louisiana. Garcilasso de la Vega, in his history of the conquest of Florida, described a number of Indian tribes, some of which are now in existence. According to this author and other early accounts of the nation, they had attained to a much higher degree of civilization than other Mobilian nations. La Vega represented them as occupying good houses surrounded by cultivated fields, and wearing linen clothing. Florida still presents the evidences of having been occupied by people more advanced than the Mobilians were generally when discovered by Europeans. Juan Ponce de Leon, a bold Spanish cavalier, was the first white man who ventured upon the coast of Florida. In 1512 he discovered it and took possession in the name of the king of Spain. Nine years afterwards he made an attempt to establish a colony upon the peninsula, but was so fiercely assailed by the Indians as to force him to desist, and was so severely wounded by the natives that he died from the effect soon afterwards in Cuba.

Pamphilo de Narvaez, another Spanish adventurer, was more successful in the outset, but unfortunate in the end. In 1528 he landed upon the shore of Florida with 300 mounted men, and sought to overawe the natives by threatening their destruction unless they acknowledged the supremacy of the Pope and sovereignty of the king of Spain. His mission was conquest and a search for gold. He pressed forward into the forest and to the village of Apalache, where he had hopes to obtain valuable plunder, but only found a collection of mean wigwams. After marching 280 leagues, Narvaez and his famished comrades reached the Gulf of Mexico, upon which they embarked as a means of escape from famine and disease. Only four survived to tell the fate of Narvaez and his co-adventurers.

Ferdinand de Soto, a companion of Pizarro in the conquest of Peru, allured by the very marvellous stories about the wealth of the country explored by Narvaez, asked and obtained permission to conquer Florida. With 600 chosen men, among whom were twelve priests, the bold leader started upon his mission of conquest. After traversing the country now constituting Florida, Alabama, Georgia and Mississippi he reached the Mississippi River.

De Soto found Florida occupied by numerous Indian tribes, some of whom were very hostile to the whites. At the Indian village of Mobile, on the Alabama River, a battle was fought between the Indians and the Spaniards, in which the latter were victors though at great cost. About 2,500 Indians were killed or consumed in the conflagration of the town, which was fired during the engagement. The loss of De Soto was eighteen killed and 150 wounded; twelve horses killed and seventy wounded; besides these losses, a large portion of the luggage of the Spaniards was consumed by the fire.

When the French Huguenots in 1564 established themselves upon the River May in Florida, they were hospitably welcomed by the Indians. Though the colony was planted amid psalm singing and devout reverence, with promises to the natives to become their benefactors, it was not long until the Christians wholly disregarded the rights of the Indians; levied upon them unjust tribute, and robbed their granaries. Forbearance, on the part of the natives, ceased to be a virtue; they lost confidence in the French and respect for their religion.

The country at that period was occupied by numerous tribes, comprising several confederacies, with three of which, respectively called Satouriona, Thimagoa and Potanou, the French came in contact. The Thimagoas had forty villages scattered

17

among the lakes and forests of the upper waters of St. John's River, and were in a much more improved state at that time than the Algonquin nations. Around their towns were well cultivated fields of corn, beans and pumpkins. The residence of the chief, which generally occupied the center of the town, was elevated upon an artificial mound, and approached by a wide gravel avenue several hundred yards in length, traces of which are still visible.

The most remarkable feature extant of the early occupants of Florida is the public roads in the western part of the State where they can be traced fifty miles in length. Their builders are unknown, and even the natives could give no account of their construction or use. These ancient roads, together with the sun-worship of the natives, has led to the belief that Florida was occupied by the same family of natives that peopled Peru.

The Muscogee was the chief tribe of the Creeks—the nucleus of that great confederacy which was of limited power prior to the destruction of the Natchez. A few years after the overthrow of the latter the Muscogees took possession of their wasted lands; and as if by magic rose to be the most powerful confederacy of the Southern Indians. In the space of thirty years they extended their sway over a fertile country of nearly 200 miles square, including fifty considerable towns, and could then muster 2500 warriors. To this confederacy belonged the Seminoles, and Yamassees. It comprised two divisions, recognized as the upper and lower Creeks; the former was seated on the branches of the Alabama, the latter on those of the Apalachicola and Florida. In 1786 the Creeks numbered 17,000, in 1829, about 20,000, and now in 1869 about 25,000.

They were distinguished warriors. At first they met the colonists in friendship, but in 1715, when the latter began rapidly to increase and extend their borders, sought their extirpation by a conspiracy. Though unsuccessful in their schemes of massacre, they occasioned the loss of many valuable lives, and kept up their ravages along the frontiers until the year 1776, when they joined the British and considered themselves licensed to murder and exterminate the colonists. At the instance of Tecumseh the Creeks joined the British in the war of 1812, and spread general alarm throughout the south by their savage warfare.

In August, 1813, a large force of the Creeks, under their great leader Weatherford, entered Fort Mims in Alabama, and in cold blood massacred about three hundred men, women and children. For this and other acts of cruelty, the Federal troops chastised them severely in several engagements; and finally the Creek warriors were almost exterminated at the battle of Horshoe Bend by General Jackson in March, 1814. Of their whole force, supposed to have been 1000 men, not more than twenty escaped alive. Manahoe, their great prophet, who had assured his people that he was proof against all missiles of war and instruments of death, was among the slain. He had prophesied, before the battle, that the Creeks would be the victors, and when he received his death wound, was engaged in one of his mysterious acts of divination. As if to rebuke him for his presumption, the fatal shot struck him in the mouth. In 1836 the Creeks united with the Seminoles in resisting their removal to the west of the Mississippi, under the treaty of 1832; but, defeated in their schemes by Generals Jessup and Taylor, were compelled to relinquish their ancient homes, except a settlement in North Carolina, and take up their residence in the Indian Territory, one of the finest positions in the United States.

The Creeks are the most prosperous, accomplished and refined Indians of North America, though in civilization they and the Cherokees are about upon an equality.

The Choctaws occupied the country bordering upon the Gulf of Mexico, from the western boundary of the country of the Creeks to the Mississippi. Their houses and villages were of a better class than were occupied by Indians generally. They paid much attention to the cultivation of the soil, and were more domestic in their habits than their Indian neighbors. Though a powerful people, the Choctaws did not engage in war as a general rule, unless in self-defense, or for the redress of grievances. At the time the French discovered them, they could muster 4000 warriors, but left a blemish upon their fame by assisting the French in the extirpation of the Natchez. Owing to their peculiar practice of depressing the forehead the Choctaws are termed "Flat Heads." In all their intercourse with the whites they seemed to cultivate friendship and live upon terms of amity with them, but their friendship did not enable them to preserve their homes, and like other Mobilian nations they were forced to surrender them to the white man and take up their residence in the wilds of Arkansas, where the remnant of this powerful people still live, enjoying many of the benefits of civilization.   In 1820 the Choctaws numbered 25,000 souls, but now do not exceed 10,000.

When the Chickasaws were first discovered, they occupied the country on the left bank of the Mississippi, from the dominions of the Choctaws to the mouth of the Ohio river eastwardly to the boundaries of the Shawnees and Cherokees. De Soto first discovered them in 1540, and spent the winter of that year in Chicaca, one of their villages, from which the natives had retired at his approach.   In the spring he demanded of the Chickasaw chiefs two hundred men as drudges to bear the burdens of the Spaniards.   Scorning the proposed slavery with the indignation it deserved, the enraged Indians at midnight fired the village and burnt it to ashes.   All the clothing, weapons and stores of the Spaniards which had escaped the fire at Mobile were destroyed.   Had the Indians known their power the whole of the Spaniards would have been cut off. Astonished at their own success they did not follow up the victory, but allowed De Soto and his adventurers to recover from their misfortunes and proceed on their mission of discovery.   In April, 1541, the Spaniards, guided by the Indians, reached the Mississippi at the lower Chickasaw Bluff, near the thirty-fifth parallel of latitude, about twenty miles below the mouth of the Arkansas.   The honor of the discovery of the "Father of Waters," was achieved by Ferdinand de Soto, the first white man who gazed upon its turbid waters.   In 1672, one hundred and thirty-two years after his departure from the country of the Chicasaws, Marquette and Joliet, who had entered the Mississippi from the Wisconsin, explored it to the village of Arkansas below the mouth of the Arkansas river.   The Chickasaws were then in possession of guns, obtained, no doubt, from the Virginians, and occupied the northern parts of the States of Mississippi and Alabama and the western portions of Tennessee and Kentucky. The Yazoos belonged to their confederacy.

At the time of the war between the French and the Natchez, the Chickasaws commanded the Mississippi from the mouth of the Ohio to Baton Rouge. They were friendly toward the English, but avowed enemies of the French; and when the latter levied their oppressive tax of a dressed deer-skin upon each male of the Natchez, without rendering any equivalent, the Chickasaws advised them to resist the indignity, and were not slow in instigating them to the massacre of the French. The plot for the extermination of the French was well concerted, and proved partially successful, as shown in another place. Owing to the fugitive Natchez being sheltered by the Chickasaws, the French undertook their chastisement, and against them commenced an exterminating war, which resulted disastrously to the French, who lost some of their best men, among whom Vincennes and Father Senat, who, with other captives, were burnt at the stake by the Chickasaws, with all the torture usually inflicted upon the victims compelled to pass through such fiery ordeals.

The Chickasaws had frequent and bloody conflicts with the Dacotah nations, by whom they were for the first time subdued. The Arkansas or Quapaws had the honor of the achievement. Before the decisive battle was fought in which the Chickasaws were conquered, the latter, owing to a want of powder, were compelled to retreat. The Quapaw chief, learning the cause of the retreat of the enemy, ordered his warriors to empty their powder on a blanket, which having been done, he divided it into two equal parts, one of which he then distributed to his own men, the other half he sent to the Chickasaws. The battle was then renewed, and resulted in the defeat of the theretofore unconquered Chickasaws.*

The origin of this great Indian family is unknown. Their tradition reports them as coming from the west, where a part of the original tribe remained. Those who crossed the Mississippi continued their journey until they arrived in Alabama, where Huntsville is located; there they halted for a short time, and then moved on in a south-west direction and settled at a place called the "Chickasaw's Old Fields," which continued their abode until they emigrated in 1837-8 to their present residence. After they crossed the Mississippi they had wars with the Choctaws, Creeks, Cherokees, Kickapoos, Osages and other

* Marcy's Explorations of the Red River, p. 94.

nations, all of whom they defeated, except the Arkansas or Quapanes.

Their government, until they removed to where they now live, was a limited monarchy. They had a king whom they called minko, who was hereditary through the female line. The clan from which the king was taken, was the highest of rank in the confederacy. The next highest was the Sho-wa, from which the highest chief was taken; the second chief was selected from the Co-ish-to clan; the third from the Aush-pe-ne, and so on, down to the lowest clan, were head men selected as officers.

Since their removal west their system of government has been materially altered. When they purchased an interest in the country west of the Mississippi, they agreed with the Choctaws to be governed by their laws, which were then, and still are, of Republican character; yet the Choctaws take no control of their financial affairs. They have greatly improved under the Choctaw government.

The country of the Chickasaws is north of the Red river, and is well adapted to all their wants. In length it is about 225 miles, and in breadth about 150 miles. They have every advantage to become enlightened and wholly civilized, and in all their efforts to do so are supported by the Federal government. Their whole number is now about five thousand.

The Seminoles, the fiercest warriors of the Mobilian nations, are supposed to derive their descent from the early Indians of Florida, who, abandoning agriculture, devoted themselves to the pursuit of game and feats of arms.* They were leading actors with the Creeks against the United States in the war of 1812.

By the treaty of Pain's Landing they had agreed to emigrate west of the Mississippi, and as early as July, 1835, every necessary arrangement for their removal had been completed, under the guidance of their head chief, John Hast. His death at that time placed Osceola in power—a chieftain who had not previously displayed any extraordinary abilities, but one always opposed to the treaty of Pain's Landing, made by only a portion of the chiefs, and by which their lands were to be relinquished. He soon gained such influence over them as to cause open resistance to their removal. At the head of the Mecasukie tribe,

* Bancroft's History of the United States, Vol. III., page 251.

Osceola commenced hostilities. At first the Indians were successful, but although afterwards frequently defeated in battle
and finally forced to emigrate, the Federal troops throughout the
bloody contest which continued until 1843, gained no victory
over the savages, regarded as an atonement for their massacre of
Major Dade in December, 1835, near Tampa Bay, when that
officer and one hundred of his soldiers were slain without any
material loss on the part of the Indians. Our best generals and
bravest soldiers were engaged in the Seminole war; Generals Jessup, Harney, Gaines, Linch, Armstrong, McComb, Call,
Twiggs, Scott and Taylor participated. As regards numbers,
the United States had greatly the advantage, but in other respects the Indians held the vantage ground. They were broken
up into small portions, would sally from their place of conceal-
ment, strike a blow and disappear, and if a band should be
crushed, another would seem to rise in its stead.

The Seminoles were under commanders of great prowess, the
principal being Micanope, Osceola, Jumper and Alligator; and
considering with whom they had to contend, will rank with the
first warriors of their race. Jumper and Alligator, it has been
said, were among the last of the Yamassees.

Though the Federal troops, including their Indian allies of
Creeks, Uchees, Shawnees, Delawares, and Kickapoos, numbered three to one of the Seminoles, resort had to be made to
the bloodhound to trace the Indians to their camps in the everglades and marshes of Florida, and to stratagem to arrest the
chiefs, before the Seminoles were forced to yield. The capture
of Osceola, in October, 1837, by order of General Jessup, at
Fort Peyton, whither he had been induced, under the idea of
engaging in a treaty, did not have the desired effect, as able
commanders were still at large; and on the 23d of October,
Wild Cat, one of the most dashing of the Seminole chiefs, who
had been in person at St. Augustine, made his escape. General
Taylor (then Colonel), in December, 1837, fought his most bloody
battle with the Mikasaukies under Sam Jones, a distinguished
Seminole chief, in which twenty-eight Americans were killed,
and 111 were wounded. Twenty Indians were killed or died
of wounds.

Osceola died in prison at Fort Moultrie, of a catarrhal fever, on the 20th of January 1838, and was buried in the fort, where a plain marble slab now marks the place where repose the ashes of the world-renowned chieftain of the Seminoles. After their subjugation, in 1842, the great mass of the tribe removed to the Indian Territory, where they continue to reside, except a few still lingering in Southern Florida, where are also a few Creeks, Uchees, and Choctaws. Before their difficulties with the whites, the Seminoles seemed to be the most cheerful and happy nation of all the American race; they had everything heart could wish in their savage state; nature supplied them with all the necessaries of life, without toil or trouble; their country was the Paradise of the South, where the air was laden with the fragrance of perennial flowers; the grapes, like those of Eschol, clustered on the vine, and oranges grew in great abundance.

The Yamassees, or Savannahs, resided in the southwestern part of South Carolina, and in Georgia. Of their early history nothing is known, other than that they were Mobilians, and belonged to the Creek confederacy. No tribe of the confederacy was more fierce and warlike than the Yamassees. They were the leading actors in the great plot of the Indians to exterminate the Carolinians, in 1715, and received just punishment for their temerity at the hands of the whites under Governor Craven, who almost exterminated them. Those who escaped took shelter under Spanish guns at Augusta in Florida. Having no place of safety in Carolina or Georgia, they were forced to take shelter in the everglades of Florida. From them, some authors claim, descended the Seminoles. From their retreat the Yamassees made frequent incursions along the frontiers of Carolina and Georgia. In the war of the Revolution, they were, with the confederate Creeks, allies of the British. This once powerful tribe has now no existence, and it is supposed that not a solitary Yamassee survives.

The Appalachians inhabited the head-waters of the Savannah and Altamaha, and gave their name to the mountains of Appalachee. As early as 1703, the Spaniards had so wrought upon the Appalachians as to cause them to desolate some of the frontier settlements of Georgia, and threaten those of the interior. At this juncture Governor Moore, with a large force of Carolinians and friendly Indians, penetrated into the heart of the

Appalachian settlement, burnt their villages, and slew about 800 of their warriors, virtually destroying their power. Broken in spirit, they left the country, after the conspiracy of 1715, in which they were engaged against the colonists.

The early explorers of the Lower Mississippi found numerous tribes of the Indians dwelling on its banks and in their vicinity. The Chetimachas, a small tribe distinct from all others, dwelt between the Mississippi and Mobile rivers, and so much resembled the Chinese that they were supposed to have derived their descent from that people; the Chapitoulas occupied the ground where the city of New Orleans is now located; the Tunicas resided at Point Coupee; the Caddos, a powerful tribe, lived on the Red River, several hundred miles from its mouth, and had a tradition that all the world was drowned by a flood, except a family of Caddos, whom the Good Spirit placed on an eminence in the prairie near where they resided, and from the saved family of the Caddos all the Indians originated. The Natchitoches occupied a district by that name, south of the Caddos.

The Tunicas were a Mobilian nation, with whom De Soto had some intercourse whilst on his way from the regions of the White River to the Mississippi. He spent the winter at an Indian village of that region, called Autiamque, on the Washita River.

The march of De Soto and his bold adventurers through the countries west of the Mississippi, from New Madrid, through the wilderness two hundred miles northwest from New Madrid, and down to the mouth of Red River, was more notorious on account of the wrongs and cruel treatment inflicted upon the natives, than celebrated on account of discoveries. Irritated and disappointed in consequence of the Indians being unable to guide De Soto to the Eldorado, the great object of his mission in the new world, he seemed to wreak his vengeance upon the unoffending inhabitants. Such of them as he desired as menials he ordered into service; made the disobedient abject slaves; and, on the slightest suspicion, the hands of the suspected were cut off as a means of intimidation. The unsuccessful guide of the Spaniards was seized and thrown to the dogs; and sometimes natives were condemned to the flames. Yet it has been claimed for De Soto that he was a man not delighting in cruelty.*

* Bancroft's History of the United States, Vol. I., p. 55.

After traversing the country on the west of the Mississippi for over a year, De Soto died from an attack of a malignant fever. Over his remains the priests chanted the first requiem heard on the Mississippi. His body was wrapped in a mantle, placed in a rude coffin, loaded with cannon-balls, and, in the gloom of midnight, was sunk in the middle of the stream, at the mouth of Red River. There the turbid waters of the Mississippi became its discoverer's tomb.

CHAPTER XIII.

THE WESTERN INDIANS.

THE Western Indians, countries of.—Dacotas or Sioux, extensive family of.—
Met by De Soto west of the Mississippi in 1541.—Marquette and Joliet, dis-
coveries of.—Mitchigama Village visited by.—War between the French and
Natchez.—Massacre of the French and extermination of the Natchez.—Tra-
dition of the Dacotas; they comprise four divisions, Winnabagoes, Assinna-
boins, Sioux and Minetarees.—Osages, Ottoes, Omahas, Iowas, Arkansas,
Kansas.—Little Crow, his great conspiracy.—The Mandans, light complexion of.—Their supposed Welsh origin.—The Crows, Pawnees, Ricaras,
Cheyennes, Blackfeet, Gros-Ventres, Shoshones, Comanches, Kiowas, Utahs,
Apaches, Navajos, Moquis, Pimos, Maricopas, Yumas, Opates, Zunis, Lipans,
Mescaleros. — The California Indians.—Tribes of Oregon and Washington.
—Flatheads, Chinooks, their fair complexion.—Natives of Nootka Sound,
fair complexion of.—New Caledonians.—Kolushi, Alaskans, Aleuts.—In-
dians, decrease of.—Their retreat from the Atlantic to the Pacific.—Progress
of the White Man.

THE Indians of the West are very numerous, and originally
occupied the country westward of the Mississippi to the
Pacific ocean.

The Dacotas or Sioux are the most extensive family of natives
residing upon this continent. The French found them on the
west bank of the Mississippi from the Wisconsin to the southern
part of Louisiana. De Soto, in 1541, found them seated on the
upper branches of the White River and also on the banks of the
Red River. Marquette and Joliet met them near the mouth of
the Des Moines, in Iowa, and were very kindly received by
them. On arriving at their village an aged chief with upraised
hands exclaimed, "How beautiful is the sun, Frenchmen, when
thou comest to visit us? Our whole village awaits thee; thou
shalt enter in peace into all our dwellings." During the sojourn
of Marquette and Joliet at the village, the former preached to the

natives the Gospel of peace, and explained to them the attributes of the Deity. Before Marquette's departure from the residence of his kind host the Indians hung round his neck the "mysterious arbiter of peace and war, the sacred calmut, a safeguard among the natives;"* they also furnished him the pipe of peace. With these sacred emblems the pioneers again entered upon the Mississippi, which they explored down to Arkansa, an Indian village below the mouth of the Arkansas river. As they approached the village of Mitchigama, which stood on the west bank of the Mississippi near the 33° of latitude, the Indians, in great force, appeared in hostile attitude: with warclubs, axes, bows and arrows they were prepared to murder the pioneers as soon as they would be reached. At the sight of the sacred calmut and peace pipe displayed by Marquette the savages cast aside their implements of war and extended to himself and Joliet a cordial welcome. The good feeling and friendly relations between the French and Dacotas did not long continue. Some of the tribes of lower Mississippi engaged with the Natchez in their conspiracy to massacre the French, in consequence of which they, in due time, were severely punished by the Arkansas, the allies of the French, who literally exterminated the Corrois and Yazous.†

Nothing definite is known concerning the origin of the Dacotas. Their own account of themselves is, that before the Assinnaboins separated from them, or they had reached the Mississippi river, their ancestors resided near Mille Lac, or Knife Lake, in Minnesota, and at the Lake of the Woods in British America. Their traditions all show that they came from the north-east. When their ancestors first came into Minnesota and Iowa other Indian nations then occupied these several localities. It is uncertain what nations they were; however, some of the Dacotas claim they were Iowas and of their own kindred. The term Dacota signifies " allied or leagued together," and all who are not Dacotas or allies are considered enemies and treated as such.‡

Ever since the French supplied the Algonquins with fire-arms

* Bancroft's History of the United States, p. 159.
† F. H. Garneau's History of Canada, Vol. II., p. 54.
‡ Schoolcraft, Indian Tribes of the U. S., Part I., p. 248.

they have been driving the Sioux to the south-west. The Dacotas comprise four divisions, viz: Winnebagoes, Assinnaboins, Minetarees and Sioux proper. The southern division embraces the Iowas, Arkansas, (Quapows,) Kansas, Osages, Missouries, Ottoes, Omahas and Puncas, who inhabit the countries watered by the Missouri, Platte and their tributaries.

The Winnebagoes were the only Dacota nation that resided on the east side of the Mississippi. Europeans first met them in northern Illinois and Wisconsin. They were formerly a warlike nation, but on friendly terms with the Algonquins until the bloody conflict between them and the Illinois, in which the Winnebagoes were almost exterminated. They now reside in Minnesota above St. Paul, and must have increased since their conflict with the Illinois, as their present population numbers about 4000.

The Assinnaboins occupy the regions watered by the upper branches of the Mississippi. They separated from the Sioux about the time of the discovery of this continent by Columbus. Since the separation the Sioux have called them "rebels." The French first visited the Assinnaboins in the year 1660, who represented they were then inhabiting their place of origin. They have suffered much in consequence of intoxication, produced by liquors furnished them by the British. In 1837 they were almost destroyed by small-pox, before which time they numbered about 10,000 souls.

The Minetarees comprise three nations: the Mandans, Crows and Minetarees proper. The Mandans occupy a portion of the country lying between the little Missouri and Yellow Stone rivers. They are of fairer complexion than the other Indian nations, in consequence of which they have been called "white Indians." It is not unusual to find among them persons having blue eyes and fine, soft hair. It is probable the white Indians referred to by Captain Isaac Stuart,* already mentioned, were identical with the Mandans; some of them had hair of reddish color. Some authors, owing to their European features, with some other slight evidences, have considered the Mandans to be descendents of the Welsh. The main basis of this theory is the adventure of Madoc, a Welsh navigator, who, in the year

* History and Biography of the Indians of North America, p. 52.

1170, with ten ships and three hundred men, went on a voyage of discovery upon the Atlantic Ocean, and never having been afterwards heard of, the hasty conclusion is arrived at that Madoc, or some of his men, safely reached this continent. Mr. Catlin, who has given a graphic and interesting account of the Mandans, seems to have no hesitation in hazarding the assertion that they descended from Prince Madoc's Welsh army. He describes the Mandans as being generally of lighter complexion than the other Dacota nations, some of them having skins almost white, with features the most pleasing; eyes hazel, grey, and, in some instances, blue. They have every shade of hair, except red and auburn. Even silvery grey is witnessed in infancy, manhood and old age. Though this may be considered a phenomenon, or freak of nature, it is nevertheless hereditary and has become national in families; in some instances this silvery grey hair is as coarse and harsh as a horse's mane, whilst that of the nation generally is fine and soft as silk.

Lewis and Clark spent the winter of 1804 with the Mandans, whom they found to be generous and hospitable; not only kind and affectionate among themselves, but entertained strangers and guests with marked attention. In 1838 the great mass of the Mandans were destroyed by the small-pox, which was communicated to them from a steamer belonging to the fur-traders. Many of those who escaped the small-pox scourge perished in hostilities with other nations. But comparatively few of the nation remain.

The Mandans were domestic in their habits, resided in villages and engaged in agricultural pursuits.

The Crows inhabit the country adjacent to the Yellow Stone, as far westward as the Rocky Mountains. They are physically models of the American race, being above the average stature and of great bodily strength and activity. They are distinguished on account of their hair, which grows to such length as to trail the ground. The men cultivate their hair as an ornament.

The Crows are a very warlike nation and keep up almost constant hostilities with the Blackfeet tribes, but with whom they are by no means able to cope on account of numbers, the latter being by far the most numerous. They also greatly suffered by the small-pox in 1838; still about 4000 of them survive. The Indian name of this nation is Upsaroka. They are classed with the Mongolian race by a distinguished Ethnologist.*

The Minetarees proper, differ very materially from the Mandans and Crows. They occupy the country about the mouth of the Yellow Stone. Their habits, manners and customs are almost identical with those of the Mandans. As nearly as can be ascertained the Minetarees number about 3000 souls.

The Sioux proper, who call themselves Dacotas, are divided

SIOUX CHIEF.

into seven tribes or "Seven Fires." Their places of residence are on the upper Mississippi and on the St. Peters River, and

* Pickering's Races of Man, p. 36.

branches of the Missouri. Some of the tribes engage in agriculture; those residing on the banks of the Mississippi and St. Peters mainly subsist by farming.

In 1862 the Sioux, under the lead of Little Crow, a noted chief, in consequence of their annuity not having being paid to their satisfaction, waged a most cruel and exterminating war upon the whites of Minnesota; and so well concerted were their schemes, that no less than six hundred and forty-four men, women and children, and ninety-four soldiers, were killed before the massacre was stayed. As an atonement for their great crimes, in thus murdering the whites, the Federal Government allowed only thirty-eight, out of three hundred and three Indians found guilty by a proper tribunal, to be executed. This clemency, though seeming unjust, was the result of mature deliberation on the part of the authorities at Washington, who found that the Indians had been greatly wronged by some of the whites, not only in withholding their annuities, but in extorting money from them for the most trivial consideration, and in consequence of which the Indians sought revenge.

Little Crow was among the Indians slain—not in battle, however, but by ambuscade. He was killed by a young man named Lampson, who shot the chief while he and his son were picking blackberries. At the time he was shot the young man who did the deed did not know he had killed the great orator and captain of the Sioux nation. Little Crow was not favorably impressed with the idea of the massacre of the whites when first suggested to him by his aggrieved people; but seeing they were determined on avenging their wrongs, eventually entered heartily into the conspiracy. In his message to his nation he urged upon them the massacre of the whites. His conduct, and that of his associates is the more strange, when it is known that the chief, and the leading actors in the conspiracy, were daily associating with the very persons they were intending to destroy; some of them members of the same Christian church, and the most civilized of the Sioux nation.

The northern Sioux occupy a district south of the Assinnaboins, and roam at will over the country from the dominions of the Sacs, Foxes and Chippewäs to the Missouri. They have ever been a powerful tribe, and classed with the most warlike of the

American race. Their number is not definitely known, but supposed to be about 9,000.

The Pawnees and Ricaras belong to the same family, but are distinct nations, the latter, owing to their dark complexion, are called the Black Pawnees. Their language is different from that of the other western Indians. The country of the Pawnees is on the Platte River, in the vicinity of Fort Kearney, Nebraska. They are a powerful people, numbering about 17,000 souls. When Lewis and Clark visited them in 1803 they were residing in villages and conducting a rude system of farming, and in which they still much engage, but in a very much improved mode.

When the Ricaras separated from the Pawnees, they established themselves on the Missouri below the Cheyenne; but eventually settled near the Mandans. They reside in villages and cultivate the ground, or rather compel their women to do so. They are tall and well-proportioned, their females handsome and sprightly.

The Ottoes were once a powerful people, having their residence on the southern bank of the Missouri, about twenty miles from the Platte; but, being reduced, they emigrated to their present residence on the south side of the Platte, in the neighborhood of the Pawnees. Catlin describes the Ottoes, Osages and Mahas (Omahas) as one nation.

The Cheyennes were a numerous people, formerly residing on the river bearing their name, which is a branch of Red River, and flows into Lake Winnipeg. Driven from there by the Sioux they went to the southern side of the Missouri River, below the Warreconne, where they erected fortifications to protect themselves against the Dacotas. Forced from this position, they emigrated to the head waters of the South Platte, where they at present live. Their places of retreat, for a time, were in the Black Mountains, from which they issued in bands to pirate upon their neighbors; even making incursions into the Mexican settlements, stealing horses with impunity. They now number about 1,500 souls.

The country lying between the Minetarees and Rocky Mountains is occupied by the Blackfeet and Rapid, or Fall, Indians. The Blackfeet are very numerous, presumed at this time to con-

18

sist of 13,000. In 1834 they numbered 30,000;* but in 1836 more than one half perished by the small pox. The Blackfeet are good representatives of the American race—are tall, erect, and of manly proportion, fully displaying all the characteristics of the aboriginals. The Arapahoes, living about the head waters of the Platte and Arkansas rivers belong to this nation. The Rapids are also known by the name of Gros-Ventres, calling themselves Aghnenin, and occupy the eastern slope of the Rocky Mountains.

The Shoshones, or Smoke Indians, reside upon both sides of the Cordilleras. Captain Lewis first met them on the dividing ridge between the Atlantic and Pacific where he was received by the natives with marked kindness. In stature the Shoshones are diminutive compared with the Dacotas and Blackfeet.

The Digger Indians are the most degraded and miserable of the Shoshone nation, if not, indeed, of all the western Indians. This more readily refers to the mountain savages, as the valley hunters of the Digger tribe are bold, active men, and nearly equal to the Sioux. Fremont gives graphic description of the Root Digger tribes.

Southward of the Shoshones, on the Platte and Arkansas, are the Paducas, consisting of several nations, viz.: Comanches, Kiowas and Utahs. The Comanches have a wide range over the plains, where for an unknown period they have been pursuing the buffalo and wild horses. They almost live on horseback, and their feats of horsemanship are most extraordinary. They descended into the plains of Texas before the country was known to Europeans, and the Indians themselves have no knowledge of when they made their advent into that country. The Comanches are a fierce and warlike nation, frequently spreading terror and alarm along the border by their assaults upon the whites. Their dwellings are of temporary character, consisting of buffalo skins, and so constructed as to be readily removed. Owing to their language being cognate with that of the Shoshones the Comanches are supposed to belong to that family. The Kiowas occupy the regions about the source of the Platte, possessing immense herds of horses that have pasturage on the lands abounding the north fork of the Red River during the

* Gallatin — Archæologia Americana, p. 133.

winter months. Like the Comanches the Kiowas seem to roam at will over the grazing portions of the country from the source of the Platte to the Red River.

The Utahs inhabit the northern part of New Mexico and southern portion of Utah. Their country is rough, yet abounds with elk, deer, bear and other game, the flesh of which constitutes their main subsistence. By nature they are warlike, and before the Federal Government extended military protection over the white settlers, made frequent forays into the settlements, killing many of the inhabitants and driving off large amounts of stock. The whole number of the Utahs at the present time is 5,000.

The Apaches range through the Rio Grande and Gila valleys in pursuit of plunder and subsistence, and are almost constantly on horseback. As a nation the Apaches are among the most widely disseminated of the American race. The Navajos, one of the largest tribes west of the Rocky Mountains, belong to this family. * They do not compare with the natives of Missouri and Mississippi, being ill-formed and emaciated and undignified, lacking those ennobling traits of character witnessed in the Iroquois and Mobilians.

In a former chapter the following nations, inhabiting New Mexico and California, were classed with the Malays, viz.: Navajos, Moquis, Pimos, Coco-Maricopas, Yumas, Mohavis, Zunis, Opates and Yaquis.

The Navajos, though classed by Bartlett with the Apache family, seem to be an entirely different people in their habits and other marked differences, and are intelligent, industrious, with an agricultural disposition and warlike habits. Though producing sufficient grain, fruits and vegetables for their own consumption, they have no permanent villages; remove from place to place as circumstances require. They occupy the country watered by the southern branches of the San Juan River in New Mexico.

The Moquis live at the head waters of the Gila; are an intelligent and industrious people occupying permanent villages, and extensively cultivate the soil. Among the Pueblos the Moquis stand prominent.

* Explorations in New Mexico, etc., by Bartlett, vol. I., p. 325.

Residing in the valley of the Gila, where they have dwelt from time immemorial, are the Pimos and Coco-Maricopas. The latter about fifty years ago, owing to frequent wars waged against them by the Apaches, abandoned their ancient homes and settled near the Pimos, whose semi-civilization they adopted; and, though in many respects distinct nations, it is difficult to trace the dividing line between them except by their languages and a few customs peculiar to each. Their languages are radically different, but complexion the same—a clear, dark brown, very different from that of the red-skins east of the Rocky mountains, and the olive color of southern Californians. Their females have good figures, with finely-formed limbs. In the disposition of the dead there is a great difference between these two nations. The Pimos bury the dead, while the Coco-Maricopas burn theirs to ashes. The former exhibit great simplicity of character, and are much inclined to live on terms of amity with their neighbors. They, as well as the Coco-Maricopas, dwell in villages and engage largely in agriculture, raising good cotton, from which they manufacture blankets and other fabrics of lesser account. Their lands are well irrigated by means of canals to conduct the water from the Gila, and in this regard seem to be only imitating a more enlightened people who had preceded them, as many traces of ancient irrigating canoes can still be seen in the country. The massive, ruined adobe buildings found existing in New Mexico, together with the fragments of pottery thickly strewn throughout the country, fully attest that, in ages past, a more civilized people dwelt in the Gila valley.*

The Yumas, also called Cuchans, reside on the left bank of the Colorado, north of the confluence of the Gila, which has been their dwelling-place since they were first known by the whites. They are partially civilized, and devote much of their time to farming the productive bottom lands in the vicinity of Fort Yuma. Though naturally fond of strife, they have been inclined to peace since the Federal Government established a military force in their midst. The Yumas are a distinct nation from the Pimas, though their languages are almost identical.

* The Indians of New Mexico are so far civilized as to freely associate with the white people. They occupy seventeen villages and support themselves by their industry. These nations are honest, frugal, and virtuous. To them has been applied the term Pueblo. They number about 7,000 souls.

On the banks of the Mohavi river dwell a nation bearing that name, representing a fine athletic people of fierce character, and superior to neighboring tribes.

The Opates of Sonora live in villages, and devote much of their time to farming—are a nation of warriors, and the only one capable of successfully contending with the Apaches.

The Yaquis, also of Sonora, though once a warlike people, are now peaceful and quiet, and, as a class, the most industrious natives of the country. They were among the first to be converted by the Jesuits, for whom they did drudgery, built churches and sustained the priests.

The Zunis live on the Little Colorado, according to the account given by Major Emory, who called them Soonees. The majority of them are Albinos.

The Lipans of Texas are, next to the Comanches, the most noted tribe of the country, and are even more for war than the latter. They have affinity with the Seraticks and Muscalaroes. Combined, these three tribes are more numerous than the Comanches, and have made some progress in civilization. The Seraticks live on the Rio Grande; the Muscalaroes on the Puerco river on the eastern branch of the former. They are of dark complexion, peaceful and industrious cultivators of the soil—raise horses, black cattle, mules, sheep and goats. The Coddoes, who formerly resided in Louisiana on the Red river and Natchitoches, have lately removed to Texas, and claim to be Texas Indians.

The California Indians have been already referred to as being of Malay origin. They differ in physical aspect as much as the nations and tribes living east of the Rocky mountains. Ida Pfeiffer describes the Indians she visited at Marysville as actually uglier than the Malays; as having short, thick necks and clumsy heads covered with short thick rough hair; the forehead low, nose flat, nostrils broad, eyes very narrow, cheek bones prominent, mouth large, and complexion yellowish brown. They live almost exclusively on fish.* Their dwellings are of the rudest kind possible. The men formerly went naked, and the females nearly so, wearing only an apron about a foot long about the loins.

The Huna nation, residing in the vicinity of Crescent city, are

* Ida Pfeiffer's Second Voyage around the World, p. 307.

similar to those at Marysville, and subsist on fish and acorns. Above this tribe, in Oregon, are the Rogue River Indians, who are larger and stronger than those of lower California, but about as low in point of culture. Before they came in contact with Europeans they had no idea of religion or a future state. These Indians neither scalp their enemies nor kill the women and children, but kill all the men falling in their hands.

The Nez-Perces, or pierced-nose Indians, occupy an extensive territory in the northern central part of Oregon in Lewis River valley above Fort Boise. They are a quiet, inoffensive people; but in self-defence evince great courage and dexterous efficiency. Captain Bonneville, who was among them, gives a vivid and graphic description of their character, stating they are benevolent, courteous and religious, and were more like a nation of saints than savages. Other travellers, however, have not spoken of them in such flattering terms.

Below the mouth of Lewis river, on the Columbia, are the Walla-Wallas, a nation very much resembling the Nez-Perces in appearance, character and habits. East of them on the head waters of the Kooskooskee river, are the Flatheads, so termed, though the Chinooks, who dwell about the lower portions of the Columbia, are the real Flatheads. They comprise several tribes—in person are diminutive compared with the Indians of Missouri; complexion lighter than that of those east of the Rocky mountains; and with other Indian nations generally, who live west of these mountains and north of California, are considered of Mongolian affinity. Lewis and Clark state that all the Indians they met west of the Rocky mountains, with the exception of the Snake tribe, were considered Flatheads; and that the greatest deformity was witnessed among the natives near the mouth of the Columbia: both sexes in that locality are Flatheads. All the Indians living on the shores of the Straits of De Fuca, and the country including the tide waters of the Columbia, are comprehended under the term Chinooks, and are inferior in stature to the natives of the interior of Oregon, with faces rounder and broader. The men and women are so much alike that strangers have difficulty in distinguishing the sex. Their eyes are oblong, and the prominent arched nose very prevalent among them. The complexion of some is fairer than any other aboriginal Americans, and in young children the color is often not strikingly deeper than among Europeans. The Chinooks and natives of Oregon and Washington territories generally pay but little attention to the cultivation of the ground, deriving their subsistence from game and fish.

The natives of Nootka Sound are of fair complexion. Captain Cook found them courteous, docile and good natured. One trait distinguishing them from other tribes is their fondness for music, their voices being so melodious as to be powerfully soothing. Captain Meares visited a dwelling of these natives, called the palace of the chief, named Wicananish, which was sufficiently large to hold eight hundred people; the rafters of the edifice were larger than the masts of a man-of-war, and carved with various figures; the huge rafters rested on blocks of wood, which were also rudely carved with images—the mouth of one of which constituted the door of the building; festoons of human skulls decorated almost every part of the interior. Mild and docile as these nations seemed to have been, Meares discovered that they were capable of inflicting the most cruel torture upon their captives, and were actual cannibals.

The natives of New Caledonia in personal appearance are less uniform than the coast tribes; some resemble the latter, while others are allied with the Chippewayn and Beaver nations east of the Rocky mountains. The Tahkali, inhabiting the northern part of New Caledonia, are distinguished for burning their dead, which of itself is strong evidence tending to show their affinity with the Hindoos.

The Kolushi nations inhabit the Russian territory north-west of New Caledonia. They are a bold, industrious and ingenious people, seeming to possess the blood of the Caucasian and Mongolian combined, though decidedly Mongolian in general appearance. Those of Alaska have a rather long visage and more prominent nose than their Esquimaux neighbors, being more after the order of the Samoieds. The Kolushi proper inhabit the coast. The territory of Alaska comprises 560,000 square miles, and contains a native population of about 70,000 souls. In 1804 they became angry at the Russians and massacred nearly all the garrison at Sitka. The Malemutes, who reside in the vicinity of the most northern Russian post, are akin of the Aleuts of the Aleutian islands. They are a tall people and of robust bodies. The Yukons, on the great river of that name, are the most numerous and warlike people of Alaska. Recent discoveries made in this region tend to show that the country has formerly been occupied by a people of much higher order of civilization than the present population. The relics, consisting of weapons of iron, stone, copper and wood, and images of carved work, lately disinterred from tombs, collected by E. G. Fast, are of such order as to strongly impress one with the idea that they were the workmanship of the same race that sculptured the images found in Central America and Yucatan. This idea is made the more impressive by the fact that there is a remote affinity between the Nootka-Columbian and the Aztec-Mexican languages; and, when these seemingly remote evidences are considered, in connection with the tradition of the Nahuatlacas that they originated in regions far to the north, and probably halted on the Gila, a strong possibility is presented that the ancient Mexicans (Toltecs) one day occupied Alaska.

The aborigines of the United States have ever been, and still are, a heavy tax upon the Federal Government. In the outset it was the aim of the Government to have the Indians live upon terms of friendship with the people of this country. With this view various treaties have been made, by which the savages yielded their hunting grounds to the white man, and passed to new retreats in the forests. But they were not safe there from the advancing steps of civilization. For a time the Alleghanies seemed to shield the red man from the encroachments of the Anglo-Saxon; but this mountain impediment was soon passed, and the wilds of the Mississippi valley converted into cultivated fields—and where lately before the Indian wigwam fire blazed, were reared towns and cities. Finally, even the barrier between the two great oceans has been scaled—where the savage lurked in apparent security amid the Rocky mountains, the only echo his war-whoop, the shrill whistle of the steam locomotive and rumbling of railroad trains are heard.

The progress of the white man has been so rapid that the red race has, comparatively, no safe places of retreat or extensive wastes wherein to lurk. They are environed by civilization.

WHEN the Spaniards first entered upon the soil of Anahuac (Mexico), they found it occupied with peoples who had emerged from the savage state, and enjoyed a semi-civilization. All the nations, however, were not thus situated, some being still in their barbarous condition. The leading nations—the Aztecs, the Cholulans and the Tlascalans—were semi-civilized—cultivated the soil, dwelt in houses, worked in mines of gold and silver, and were clad in respectable garments; and in their midst were indubitable evidences that the country in former ages had enjoyed a much higher degree of civilization than even that to which the Aztecs had attained. The splendid ruins and existing monuments of art strewn throughout the country fully attested that a highly civilized people had, centuries before, occupied Anahuac; but what race, is unknown in history, or preserved by plausible tradition. The same race had, evidently, not only peopled Mexico proper, but also Central America, and, in all probability, South America also, as traces of like civilization are found in these several localities.

The most ancient nations of Indians who inhabited Mexico, Central and South America, before the advent of the Toltecs,

(281)

were, probably, the Olmecas, Aymaras, Xicalancas, Coras, Te-
panecas, Toroscas, Mixtecas, Tzapotecas, and Othomi, with
whom, by mutual partition, the Olmecas divided the country.

The Toltecs arrived in Anahuac in the year 648 A. D., but
did not permanently settle at Tula until 670 A. D.; the Chichi-
macas became settlers in the country in 1070; the Nahuatlacas,
a family of seven tribes, of which the Aztecs were one, commenced their migrations in 1170 A. D.; the Aztecs in 1178, but
did not found their capital, Tenochtillan, afterwards called Mexico, from Mexitli, their war-god, until 1325 A. D.   The country
from whence they and their kindred nations issued was called
Azatlan, which, according to Baron Humboldt, was situated
within the forty-second degree of north latitude, and probably
in the region of what now constitutes the States of Ohio, Indiana, Illinois, Michigan, Wisconsin, Missouri and Mississippi.
Abundant evidences exist in these several localities that they
have been occupied by the human race at a very remote period,
and by peoples who enjoyed a much higher degree of civilization than the natives found inhabiting these several States when
they were first discovered by Europeans.

The Acolhuans, who were Tezcucians, next to the Aztecs were
the most distinguished nation of Indians of Mexico after the departure of the Toltecs.   They founded the great city of Tezcuco, on the eastern border of the Mexican lake, which, except
Mexico, was the largest and most splendid city of Anahuac.   It
contained three temples devoted to human sacrifice, the massive
remains of which are still strewn within its limits; each temple
measures 400 feet along the base of its front.   The Tezcucians were in advance of the Aztecs in purely intellectual progress—had the best system of laws, best histories, best poems,
and the purest dialect.*   Their system of laws was founded
upon the principles of justice; the tribunals were graded, yet
every eighty days all had to meet at the capital in a general
parliament, over which the king presided, to determine all suits
reserved for their decision by the lower courts.   Honesty and
fair dealing were required by all functionaries; to be guilty of
taking a bribe by a judge was punishable with death; the suit-
ors did not appear by counsel, but in person, and each party

* Prescott's Conquest of Mexico.

could be a witness in his own behalf; the clerk of court made a statement of the case, giving an abstract of the testimony and the proceedings of the trial in hieroglyphical painting, which was preserved by the court.

The Tezcucians excelled in poetry. Some of their poems contain sentiments of morality, and thoughts upon the mutability of human life, as lofty, eloquent, sublime, and forcibly expressed, as if the work of our most enlightened and gifted poets. The lament of one of their bards is striking:

> " Banish care, if there are bounds to pleasure,
> The saddest life must have an end.
> Then weave the chaplet of flowers, and
> Sing the song in praise of the all-powerful God:
> For the glory of this world soon fadeth away."

Agriculture, above everything else, was encouraged by the Tezcucian sovereigns and rulers; every available spot of ground was cultivated. Great attention was paid to the capital of the kingdom, which was the pride of the people. The royal palace was a magnificent structure, consisting of a group of buildings; from east to west it extended twelve hundred and thirty yards, and from north to south nine hundred and seventy-eight yards, enclosed by a wall of unburnt bricks and cement, nine feet high and six feet thick, for the one-half of the circumference, and fifteen feet high the remaining distance. The whole structure contained three hundred apartments. Two hundred thousand workmen were employed in the erection of this lordly pile.* The Tezcucians were skillful mechanics, and their style of architecture of the finest order found in Mexico.

The Tezcucians, though indulging in the heathenish practice of human sacrifice, at the same time believed in an all-powerful Creator of the Universe; and so ardent were they in this belief that they erected a temple which was dedicated "to the Unknown God, the Cause of Causes."

Nezahualcayotl, the Tezcucian king who reared this temple, was the wisest and most accomplished Indian known in history. In his declining years his mind seemed to be absorbed upon the future and his immortal destiny. The following are some of his thoughts, translated from the Othomic tongue by Galvez:

" The great, the wise, the valiant, the beautiful,
   Alas! where are they now?
   They are all mingled with the clod;
   And that which has befallen them shall happen to us,
   And to them that come after us.
   Yet, let us take courage, illustrious nobles and chieftains;
   Let us aspire to Heaven,
   Where all is eternal, and corruption cannot come.
   The horrors of the tomb are but the cradle of the sun,
   And the dark shadows of death are brilliant lights of the stars."

The Toltecs issued from a country called Huchuetapallan, supposed to be amid the Rocky Mountains, in the regions of the Gila and Colorado rivers, where traces of similar edifices to those constructed by them in Anahuac are still existing.

According to the manuscript of Don Juan Torres, grandson of the last king of the Quiches, the Toltecas descended from the house of Israel, who were released by Moses from the tyranny of Pharaoh. The story runs that, after they had fallen into idolatry, to avoid the reproofs of man, they separated from him, and, under the guidance of Tanub, their chief, passed from one continent to the other, to a place called the "Seven Caverns," a part of the kingdom of Mexico, where they founded the city of Tula. From Tanub sprang the families of the kings of Tula and Quiche, and the first monarchs of the Toltecs. Nima-quiche, the fifth king of that line, was directed by an oracle to leave Tula, with his people, and conduct them to Guatemala. After many years of suffering and hardships, they reached Lake Atitlan, near which they settled in a country they called Quiche, and there founded the city of Utatlan, which subsequently became the most noted city of Central America, a description of which is given in another place. Before the time of the conquest, after many bloody battles, the Quiches had become masters of the country, and held in subjection the powerful tribes of the Zutugiles and Kochiquels. The distracting wars left Guatemala an easy matter of conquest, though the last king, Tecum Umam, marshalled on the plains of Tzaccapa two hundred and thirty thousand warriors, in a fortified camp, against the Spaniards, but was defeated by Alvarado, and the Quiche government overthrown.*

* Travels in Central America and Yucatan, Vol. II., p. 172.

Traces, also, of a similar civilization are manifest, extending westward from the Gila to the Pacific Ocean, in the valley of the Columbia, and in Alaska. And the Chinese annals record that Foo-Sang, a Chinese navigator, visited the northwest coast of America in the fifth century A. D., and found the people inhabiting the country enjoying a degree of civilization equal to that of the Aztecs when discovered by the Europeans.

The Toltecs are said to be the builders of the great temple of Cholula, after the plan of that of Teotehuacan; this is doubted, and the Olmecas are looked upon as the founders of these great monuments. It is well established that the Toltecs were skilled in architecture, and reached a degree of civilization superior to any other single nation of Mexico. The Aztecs founded their civilization upon that of the Toltecs, and seem to have made but little, if any, improvement upon it. Their Augustan age was, perhaps, about the year 708 A. D., at which period their great astrologer, Huematzin, composed their hieroglyphical Divine Book, containing their laws, calendars and history.

The Othomi and Totonacs were barbarians who occupied the country in the vicinity of Lake Tezcuco. Their language is monosyllabic, and of the same family of languages as that of the Chinese, and unlike all other Indian nations.

The Chichimecas, a barbarous nation who dwelt about Lake Tezcuco, joined the Tezcucians and eventually became absorbed by them.

To the north of Mexico dwelt the Huaxtecas, a nation that seems to have been of the same group as the ancient nation of Yucatan, Guatemala and the West Indies.

The Tarascas, who dwelt to the north-west of Mexico, were distinct from the other natives. In the arts and civilization they were nearly equal with the Aztecs; they were an independent, bold, fearless nation, and never submitted to the Mexican powers, though repeated efforts were made to bring them under subjection.

The Tlascallans, a branch of the Aztec family, took up their residence at first on the western borders of Lake Tezcuco, and about the same time the Aztecs settled in Mexico. These two nations were very hostile towards each other and kept up bloody wars. After defeating the Aztecs in two great battles they emigrated, and took up their final residence in the valley between the lake and the Gulf of Mexico and there founded their capital, Tlascala, one of the most noted cities of Anahuac. They established a republican form of government and maintained their independence against the whole power of Montezuma.

In regard to civilization they were equal with the Aztecs. To protect their eastern border against invasion, they constructed a solid stone wall twenty feet thick and nine feet high, six miles across the valley.

The Cholulans, also a branch of the Aztec family, were among the most refined natives of Anahuac. They were well-clad, and completely astonished the Spaniards by their courteous and polite demeanor. Their great capital, Cholula, was the first city of Anahuac, and the "Mecca of the New World." It was walled, and, according to Cortez, contained 20,000 houses and a population of 150,000 at the time of the conquest. The great pyramid, bearing the name of the city, is here located. According to tradition it was built in honor of Quetzalcoate, the god of the air, and to whose worship it was dedicated. This divinity, whilst on earth, seems to have been a benefactor of his race; under his guidance the country attained to the highest prosperity; agriculture, the arts and sciences reached their zenith—the golden age of Anahuac.

Having incurred the wrath of some of the gods, this great personage was compelled to abandon the country. Taking leave of his followers, he embarked in his skiff, made of serpent's skins, on the Gulf of Mexico for Tlapallan, an unknown land, promising the Cholulans that he and his descendants would revisit them again. He was of fair complexion, tall in person, had long dark hair and a flowing beard.

The Aztecs, at first, possessed but a small portion of territory compared with what they acquired. For a long period they were confined to a district on the western shore of Lake Tezcuco, but eventually ruled over the country from the Atlantic to the Pacific, including Central America, to the farthest bounds of Guatemala and Nicaragua. Their government was monarchial, almost absolute, though elective in form; the legislative power was vested wholly with the monarch; the only relief from his bad legislation was in the judical tribunals, which were in substance the same as those of the Tezcucians.

The Aztec religion was the same as the Tezcucians. They recognized the existence of a Supreme Creator and lord of the universe. In their prayers they addressed him as "the God by whom we live." They believed in three separate states of existence in the future life; that the wicked were to expiate their sins in a place of endless darkness; those of no merit than having died of certain diseases capriciously selected were to enjoy a negative existence of indolent contentment; the highest place was reserved, as in most warlike nations, for the heroes who fell in battle or in sacrifice—these passed at once to the presence of the Sun, whom they accompanied with songs and dances in his bright progress through the heavens; after some years their spirits went to animate the clouds and singing birds of beautiful plumage, and to revel amidst the rich blossoms and odors of the gardens of paradise.* Their great error consisted in their sacrifices of human victims to their idol gods; a rite also practised by the Tezcucians, though be it said, to the great credit of the Toltecs, their altars were never stained with the blood of man.

They had made considerable advance in the sciences. In astronomy they surpassed the Romans, as their estimate of the length of the year was more accurate than the Julian calendar. By the Aztec system the year was divided into eighteen months of twenty days each, with the addition of five odd days in each year. This system was almost identical with that of the Chinese. The mode of grouping the years into cycles is still in use by the Chinese, Japanese, Mongols and some other eastern nations. This sameness of astronomical systems has led to the presumption that at a remote period they were one system used by the same family of man in Asia and America. Another fact in relation to this system is worthy of mention—which is that the lunar months, of thirteen days each, contained in a cycle of fifty-two years, with the intercalation, corresponds precisely with the number of the years in the great Sethic period of the Egyptians.

The Aztecs were acquainted with the eclipses, but to what extent is uncertain; their maps represented the eclipse of the

* Prescott's Conquest of Mexico, vol. I., p. 63

sun by the moon projected on its disk. The colossal block of stone found in the great square of the city of Mexico in the year A. D. 1790, buried several feet beneath the surface of the ground, shows, with some degree of accuracy in hieroglyphics, the division of time, the motion of the heavenly bodies, and the twelve signs of the zodiac. The stone upon which these hieroglyphics were carved in relief was of basalt, and was twelve feet square, three feet thick, and weighed twenty-four tons. The quarry from which it was taken was more than thirty miles distant from the place where it was discovered. Before it was wrought it must have weighed fifty tons. Ten thousand men were employed in bringing this block from the mountain beyond Lake Chalco to the capital.

They rivaled the other nations of Mexico in their splendor of living and the magnificence of their architecture; their paintings and sculpture seemed rather to present the idea desired to be conveyed—not so much by the execution of the design, as the certainty of the character of the symbols. Their characters were generally simple and readily understood. For instance, a tongue denoted talking, a foot-print traveling, a man sitting on the ground an earthquake. Names also had meaning annexed to each in idea; as example, "Anahuac" signifies "near the water," "Tlascallan" meant "the place of bread." Their manuscripts consisted of different materials. Some were made of cotton cloth, others of skins, and others of silk and gum; but the most common article was composed of the leaves of the aloe, and was a sort of paper resembling the Egyptian papyrus. This paper was as soft as parchment, and retained the colors of the paintings as well. The parchments contained the history of the country and all the transactions of the Aztecs from the earliest period of their semi-civilization, as well the events daily transpiring as those of ancient ages and were sacredly kept by the Aztecs; but the Spanish archbishop of Mexico, Don Juan de Zumarrago, committed them to the flames. This destructive act concealed from the world the ancient history of the Mexicans, and no doubt also the nations who had preceded them in the country. It was a great feat of superstitious bigotry, a triumph of barbarism equal to the destruction of the Arabic manuscripts in Grenada, or the Serapian library by

the Christian barbarians under Theodosius. The destruction of
these Indian manuscripts is a great loss to the literary world as
well as the ethnologist. The few that remain give but a faint
idea of the early history of the Indian nation of Anahuac. With
their destruction was lost the key by which what remains could
have been deciphered.

The agriculture of the Aztecs was closely interwoven with
their civil and religious institutions, and was in the same advanced state as the other features of their civilization. The
farming labor was done by the males, the females never doing
the drudgery as now imposed upon them, but protected by the
Aztecs with the same respect and care that is now practised by
many of the nations of Europe, though considered inferior beings
to the males.

The detestable feature of their institutions was their cruel
human sacrifices and cannibalism. Feeding upon human flesh
with them was not a matter of appetite, as with the real cannibals, but was prompted as a religious duty. The sacrifice was
ennobled by being offered to the gods, and the death upon the
altar considered by them the most glorious and sure passport to
Paradise. These features in their institutions was a great departure from those of the Toltecs, and more particularly marks
the difference between them, tending to show they were not of
the same race of mankind. In the former may be recognized
the institutions of the Malay and African, and in the latter those
of the Caucasian and Mongolian. In everything but these revolting spectacles the Aztecs seem to have been mere imitators
of the Toltecs and Olmecas.

The Aztecs were devout idol worshippers; their idols were of
the most hideous form possible; nothing of mildness or sublimity
appearing about them, except the sun, an object of worship,
which was carved on circular plates of gold "as large as carriage
wheels."*

The statues of the sun and moon, crowning the Great Pyramids in the temples at Teotihuacan were not originally considered
the idols of the Aztecs, nor of their invention, but of some earlier
nation. Upon the summit of the large mound was reared a colossal statue, consisting of a single block of stone representing the

* Prescott's Conquest of Mexico, Vol. I., p. 320.
19

human figure; on the breast was placed a plate of burnished gold and silver, facing the East, upon which the rays of the sun were brilliantly reflected over the surrounding objects, shedding upon them a dazzling lustre. This object of worship, by the cruel hand of the Christian despoilers, has entirely disappeared, and Time, the great obliterator of human events, has blotted from history the age of its dedication and the name and character of the people who first worshipped at its shrine. The Aztecs do not pretend to give their origin or destiny. It is very evident that a whole peculiar people, differing from the Aztecs and Toltecs, the founders of the antique monuments, have perished or become absorbed in the Aztec nations, who seem to have ruled the entire empire for about two hundred years before the conquest, which, from the name of the capital, was denominated Mexico.

The City of Mexico, as found when entered by Cortez in the 16th century, though a place of much note among Mexicans, was greatly over-estimated by the enthusiastic Spaniards, when compared with the then existing cities of Europe. Yet it was far in advance, in the scale of civilization, of all others theretofore found upon this continent. Considering the many disadvantages under which the Mexicans labored without the aid of the mechanic arts of enlightened Christendom, and no rules or guides but their own genius and moral qualities to direct them in the path of civilization, they may properly be distinguished as a great nation, and their capital, Mexico, a wonderful city. Like ancient Venice, it was built amid the water. The houses were generally low and of one story, and composed mostly of stone— especially these of the nobility; those of the common people were of stone foundation, and walls of unburnt bricks. The streets were narrow generally, except the principal avenue leading from the southern causeway, which was wide and extended the whole length of the city. The main streets were coated with cement and lime. The people had no domestic beasts of burden nor wheel-carriages; their pavements were kept smooth, being trodden only by the feet of man.

At the time of the capture of the city of Mexico by the Spaniards, it contained about 60,000 houses and 500,000 of a population. The streets were kept clean—a thousand persons being daily employed in watering and sweeping them. Water, fresh and pure, was brought in earthen pipes from Chapultapec, sufficient to supply the whole population.

The royal residence and public buildings were constructed upon an extensive scale. Montezuma was the great patron of architectural taste, and did much in the way of embellishing the Capital. Not satisfied with the royal residence of his father, he erected another on a far more magnificent design. It was constructed—as were all the public buildings—of stone dragged by files of men with ropes, over huge wooden rollers from the quarries, after the manner the Egyptians conveyed their huge masses of rock. Their public buildings consisted of the temples, places of sacrifice and worship, royal palace, armory, granary, aviary, menagerie, also a building appropriated as an asylum for deformed humanity, monsters and dwarfs. At Chapultapee the emperor had a most luxurious residence. Here was located his extensive garden stretching for miles around, in which stood gigantic cypresses more than fifty feet in circumference and centuries old at the time of the conquest; one of which, described by Humboldt, is noticed in another place.

The emperor, Montezuma, when the Spanish invasion commenced was living in splendid style; fully equal to the barbaric institutions of the country. He could boast of more wives than the Turkish Sultan, or the great Mormon prophet, Brigham Young. His palace was handsomely decorated and he attended by a large retinue of nobles, none being permitted to appear in his palace except his females.

The great teocalli of the city of Mexico was the pride, admiration and wonder of the Aztecs, and though considered a holy and sacred place, was one of murder, thousands of mortals being yearly sacrificed there by the superstitious priests, in reverence and honor of the god of war, Huitzilopotchli, and the "supreme god," Tezcatlipaca, who created the world. Diaz, who visited these sacred places, describes them as being stained with human blood, and their "stench more intolerable than a slaughter house in Castile." Montezuma, in great apparent kindness, conducted Cortez through the various departments of this religious edifice. The disgusting and revolting spectacle there presented hastened the downfall of the power capable of sustaining such debasing religious pretentions; yet no one justifies the Spaniards in their cruel manner of disposing of the evil. The overthrow of the Mexican government by Cortez, changed the whole character of the institutions of the country.

Whatever may have been the faults and follies of Montezuma, it cannot be denied that he was the greatest Indian ruler of the continent, and one held in greater reverence and awe than any other prince of the American race. With him terminated the royal line of the Aztec princes. He was great in war and great in peace, and his death was lamented by all his subjects; but not more so than his overthrow, as their dread sovereign master, by the Spaniards.

Montezuma was tall and well made—his hair straight, beard thin, and his complexion paler than the usual color of the Indian race. He moved with dignity, and his whole demeanor was that of a great and worthy prince. He, in his first interview with the Spaniards, wore the girdle and square cloak of the nation. It was made of the finest cotton and his sandal soles were of gold; both his cloak and sandals were sprinkled with pearls and precious stones; his head-dress consisted of a plume of royal green which floated down his back.

The portraits of the ancient Aztecs and some of their gods represented them as having had a depression of the forehead to the same extent as the nations of Indians of North America known as the Flat Heads. Aymaras, of Peru, in early times, also practiced this strange and unnatural custom, as the many skulls found in their ancient places of burial fully show. The portraits do not present the features of the Aztecs as found to exist in the days of Montezuma. They represent a high nose and long visaged people of the same order as those of like deformity existing in Central America and Peru.

The general description of the Aztecs, as given by Clavigero, represents them as having been of "good stature, generally rather exceeding than falling short of the middle size, and well proportioned in all their limbs. They have a good complexion, narrow foreheads, black eyes, clean, firm, regular white teeth; thick, black, coarse, greasy hair; their beards and skin are of an olive color."

Among the women many were found beautiful and of fair

complexion, with sweetness of temper; and general demeanor of the same order as the most amiable females of the Caucasian race. The Aztecs, if the above description is correct, were a different race from the American Indians, and of a different origin, having in remote ages reached this continent by the Pacific Ocean. Many places of temporary abode of the Aztecs are found to exist between the sea-coast and the Cordilleras eastward of the Gulf of California, and as far northward as the Gila and Colorado rivers.

The works in ruins on the Gila, called the " Cassas Grandes," are evidently of Aztec origin, being of the same character as those constructed by them in Mexico, and show their constructors to have been advanced in the arts.

Yucatan seems to have been a focal point of early civilization of Mexico. Within its limits are found some of the most splendid ruins of the western continent. The Spaniards were astonished at the seeming refinement of the natives of this and the Tobascian province; along the coast they met what seemed to them different peoples from those they had found dwelling on the islands; they dwelt in well-constructed stone houses, and were respectably clothed, and their temples were large and of considerable architectural taste. They cultivated the ground with much care, dwelt in towns, and had a well-regulated system of civil government. The natives spoke the Maya language. The Mayas were natural mechanics. Their system of architecture being of the same order as that of the Toltecs, they have been considered as the genuine descendants of that family.

The ruins of Uxmal are of very high antiquity and of extraordinary character. When first discovered by Europeans, they were overgrown with an ancient forest. The pavement of the court of one of the temples was of stone, upon which were carved, in relief, figures of tortoises, to the number of 34,000. The figures were much worn, as if they had been long trod upon before the temple was deserted and went to ruin. These structures are doubtless as ancient as any in Mexico.

Central America is virtually the old kingdom of Guatemala. It was peopled, as is generally supposed, by the Toltecs. A tradition is preserved, which relates that a noted Toltec chief, named Nimaquiche, led a colony thither from Tula. Tecum Umam, a descendant of Nimaquiche, was the ruling prince of Guatemala at the time of the conquest of Central America by Alvarado, in 1523. He invaded the country at the head of the Spanish forces, consisting of a few Spaniards and a large army of Mexicans, Tlascalans, and Cholulan Indians. At the very threshold he encountered the Quiches, in vast hosts, in battle array, under their sovereign. Some six desperate battles were fought between the natives and the Spanish forces, near the river Zamala, which, in consequence of the vast amount of blood shed, was thereafter called the " River of Blood." The chief city of the Quiches was Utallan, hardly surpassed by Mexico and Cuzco in point of magnitude and splendor. It was walled, and had only two ways of entrance, one by a causeway, and the other by a flight of steps. After the city was captured by Alvarado, or, rather, surrendered to him by the Quiches, they, purposing the destruction of the Spaniards, fired the city, but, by the treachery of other Indians, the scheme was discovered and prevented. The Spaniards, after much bloodshed, finally subdued the Quiches, and established the Spanish power at Guatemala. The Quiches, Mayas, and Kachiqueles were the chief nations and families of Central America.

About twelve miles from the village of Palenque, in the Province of Chiapa, are the ruins of Huethuetlapallan. Otolum was probably the original name of the city. These remarkable ruins are extended seventeen miles in length, and about four in breadth, along the summit and declivity of a chain of hills. A group of fourteen large ruined buildings forms the chief remains of the city. They were temples, and have a wonderful resemblance to similar institutions found existing in Egypt and Nubia. Altars, statues of deities, ornamental stones, and other works of sculpture are found amid these ruins. The sculpture and architectural ornaments are executed with skill and taste, showing the inhabitants of this ancient city to have enjoyed, to a degree at least equal with the Egyptians, a refined civilization.

At Ocasingo, in the same regions, are similar ruins, but not so great, although seeming to be about as ancient. In the ad-joining State of Oaxaca, of Mexico, are the celebrated ruins of Mitla, consisting of tombs and buildings, differing from all other Mexican ruins by having columns supporting the roof. These monuments, in point of execution, were, in design and workmanship, superior to the works of the Aztecs. These buildings were, most probably, constructed by the Mixtecas, or Tzapotecas, both which nations occupied those regions in remote ages, and during the same era as the Olmecas regimen, as they divided Mexico with them and the Xecalancas, Coras, Tepaneccas, Tarascas, and Othomi. Similar monuments exist in ruins in the valley of Copan, in Honduras. They extend along the Copan river for the distance of two miles, and comprise the walls of a supposed temple, 624 feet long, and many pyramidal structures, with sculptured idols, resembling the Egyptian or Hindoo art. They also have the evidences of a high antiquity, and were probably constructed before even the Olmecas inhabited the country.

At the time of the conquest, numerous Indian tribes inhabited Central America, besides the Quiches, Mayas, and Kochiquiles, of whose origin we have no knowledge other than the vague stories that they were Toltecs and Caribs. Among these tribes were the Moscas, or Mosquitos, who remained independent until 1824, when their territory was, by act of the United States Congress, declared to be a part of Columbia. The Poyais, also inhabiting the country on the Mosquito shore, have remained independent, and under Sir George MacGregor, a Scotch adventurer, whom they made their cacique, made great advance in civilization, and have now considerable commerce.

When the Spaniards first visited the Isthmus of Darien, they found it densely peopled with native Indians, enjoying a degree of civilization about equal to those of Guatemala. They were supposed to be of the same race as the Quiches, though divided into tribes, and differing in appearance as much as the different nations of Mexico from one another.

CHAPTER XV.

INDIANS OF AMERICA.

THE origin of the aborigines of South America is unknown to history; yet, like those of North America, they have some characteristics tending to establish that they did not originate upon this continent, though now considered indigenous. They have been divided into three physical types, and consist of thirty-nine distinct nations. The physical types are the Andians, Mediterraneans and Brasilio-Guarani. The nations classed under the Andian group are the Quichua, or Inca, Aymara, Chango, and Atacama, considered the Peruvian branch; Yuracares, Mocéténes, Tocana, Moropa, and Apolista, constitute the Antisian branch; and the Anca, or Araucona, and Fuegian, comprise the Araucanian branch.

The Mediterranean group is composed of the following nations; Patagon, or Tehuelche Puelche, Charrua, Mbocobi, or Toba, Mataguayo, Abipones and Lengua, comprise the Patagonian, or Pampéan branch; the Semucu, Chiquito, Saravéca, Otuké Curuminaca, Covaréca, Curavés, Tapus, Curucaneca, Paiconéca and Corabeca, constitute the Chiquitian branch. The Moxean branch consists of the following nations: Moxos, Chapacura, Itonoma, Canichana, Movima, Cayuvara, Pacaguava and Iténés.

(296)

The Caribi, Guarani, Tupi and Botocudo are the nations of the Brasilio-Guarani group.*

The above is the classification of the South American tribes as made by M. d'Orbigny, and generally approved, though there are other nations besides those above named.

The Andian group are the nations of the department of the Cordilleras, and seem to have been the leading peoples of the country, holding in subjection the mountain tribes from Quito to Chili, and to the borders of the dominions of the Araucanos. The leading spirits of this vast empire were the Quichuas or Incas.

The central portion of the country is occupied by the Mediterranean group, in which the peoples of the Pampas, the plains of Paraguay and Patagonians are included; also the nations in the valleys of the Chiquitos, and the low lands of the Los Moxos provinces.

The Brasilio-Guarani group occupy the country from the foot of the Peruvian Andes to the Atlantic, the plains of the Orinoco, Maragnon, Amazon and their tributary streams. Among this group the Caribs, Tupi and Guarani are the leading nations. These several localities have been in some respects materially changed since the country became known to the Europeans, by conquests and other disturbing influences; the Caribs, even before that era, passing from the islands, had driven the native tribes from the coast of the Atlantic far into the interior. The Incas, and kindred peoples, after a gallant resistance, passed off the stage as dominant nations, and the Araucanos, scorning to submit to the Spanish yoke, abandoned their lands in Chili and passed into the Pampas.

Other nations, such as the Mbocobis and Lenguas, remain in their ancient homes; also, the Chiquitos and Moxos occupy their former dominions.

The nations generally of South America have been noted for their fixed habitations and local character, except the Quichuas, Guarani and Araucanos, who have been celebrated for their migratory disposition.

The Guarani seem to have been as restive as the Gallo-celts. Under the name of Caribbees their savage hordes advanced along

* Natural History of Man, Vol. II., p. 587.

the Antilles, ascended the Orinoco and Amazon and their tributaries, descended to Buenos Ayres, passed over the plains of Chaco and settled themselves at the eastern base of the Peruvian Andes.

The Spanish conquest and the introduction of Christianity among the South American Indians have wrought a more salutary influence upon the savage nature than is generally supposed, much more, indeed, in proportion to the means employed, than in North America.   More than a million and a half of the pure aboriginal race have embraced Christianity.*

The Eastern Guarani are called the Tupi, a title they received in consequence of being the first natives who were converted to Christianity.   The nation was divided into several tribes, among which the Cariyi, Tamoyi, Tupinaqui, Timmimions, Tobayari, Tupinambe, Apanti and Tapigoas.   When the coast of Brazil was first visited by Vincente Pizarro he found the country occupied by natives of this family, who resisted the encroachments of the Spaniards and killed eight of the crew, evincing a courage equal to the bravest of the brave natives of the continent. The Tapuyas were the chief actors in this and subsequent bloody rencontres with the Spaniards.   The Tupi who occupied the coast when first visited by Europeans, have been greatly reduced in numbers, but they still are quite numerous in the interior.

The general appearance of the natives of South America does not materially differ from that of the Indians of North America. Their complexions are of two different shades: one an olive brown, the other yellow.   They are not properly "red men," though having their general characteristics.

The physical conformation of the Quichua group is marked and peculiar.   Their elevated location upon the Andes, where they breathe the thin air, causes a remarkable development of the chest; much out of proportion to the rest of the body, except the head, which is generally in tolerable proportion, but the feet and hands are always small.   Their hair is soft, thick and flowing; yet they are almost destitute of beards.   They have a prominent aquiline nose, large mouth, short, strong and well developed chin, large nostrils, retreating forehead, oblong, and generally well developed skull; complexion olive brown, having

* Natural History of Man, Vol. II., p. 592.

none of the reddish hue of the North American Indians; have features resembling the Aztecs, but lower in stature, their main height being about four feet nine inches. They constituted the ancient Peruvians, from whom proceeded the lights of civilization when the country was first made known to Europeans: dwelt in towns and cities, cultivated the soil, produced potatoes, maize and the oxalis; manufactured woollen fabrics, equal to the finest of Europe, worked in gold, silver, copper and lead; domesticated the useful animals, constructed post roads, and enjoyed a civil government almost, if not quite, equal to the Aztecs. They were a people of mental culture, no way inferior to those of the ancient world; had calculated the duration of the solar year with accuracy, recorded the events of history by signs and symbols, cultivated poetry, music and oratory, and greatly excelled in sculpture and mechanics.

The Aymaras much resemble the Quichuas, but have a different language, and doubtless were a more ancient people, as well as much more numerous. They seem to be the descendants of the ancient race who constructed the vast and singular monuments and buildings now in ruins in the vicinity of Lake Titicaca, but have no record of their ancient history. The Incas admitted that their arts and civilization were derived from the Aymaras, upon which they seem to have made no improvement. Of the Aymaras' great monuments of art we shall presently speak.

The Changos and Alacoamas resemble the Quichuas in physical aspect, though the former (Changos) are of darker hue, their complexion approaching to black. They occupy the country along the sea coast of the Pacific, the Atacama inhabiting the western declivity of the Peruvian Andes. The Antisian nation occupy the forests along the banks of the mountain streams on the eastern declivity of the Bolivian and Peruvian Andes, from the 13° to the 17° of south latitude. Their complexion is generally fair, but slightly tawny, mixed with yellow; stature much greater than the Peruvians; their forms vigorous and robust. They have but a limited civilization. Some of the tribes live in villages, cultivate the ground, and make a cotton fabric; others wander from place to place, without any fixed residence; whilst others reside in the rudest tents in a condition little elevated above the lower animals.

The Araucanians comprehend the several Indian tribes inhabiting the southern region of the Cordillera and its declivities, from the extremity of the "Land of Fire" to the 30° of south latitude. They constitute two nations: the Araucans and Pesherais. The former are a warlike race, of indomitable courageous heroism. They are similar in their physical type. Their heads are large, faces round with projecting cheek bones, large mouth, thick lips, short nose, wide nostrils, narrow receding forehead, short broad chin, scanty beard, hair black, dense and straight; complexion of this branch is about the same as the Peruvians, but generally of lighter shade. Some of the tribes, among which are the Boroanos, are almost white. Some of these natives are represented as of a swarthy complexion, with large eyes, oblong face, narrow and well-arched eyebrows, and in general appearance much more resembling the Caucasian than American type. In some instances the aquiline nose, well-formed lips, and lively expressive countenances are witnessed in this family.

The Pesherais inhabit Terra del Fuego and both borders of the straits of Magellan, from the island of Elizabeth and Port Famin towards the east as far as the group of islands which spread out to the northward and southward of the straits of Magellan. Their complexion is olive, but paler than that of the Peruvians: have huge forms and large chests, though otherwise well formed. They are a nomadic people, only subsist by the chase and fishing, and move from place to place as their desires or appetites may lead them.

The Mediterraneans occupy the regions lying between the Alpine nations of the Cordillera and the Brazilians of the western regions. They comprise three leading nations, viz: the Patagonian, the Chiquitian and the Moxian. The Patagonians consist of several tribes—are the nomadics of the continent; and like the Tartars, seem to live upon horseback, or under tents covered with skins. They are native warriors, despising agriculture, the arts and civilization.

The stature of the Patagonians is above the usual height of the natives; some are even looked upon as giants. Their average height is about six feet six inches; but this does not apply to all the tribes, some of which are much below this standard.

Las Casas relates that Catubamand,* the chief of a Patagonian tribe, inhabiting the island of Higuey, was three feet across the shoulders, and otherwise in proportion; he must have been twelve feet high.† Their complexion is darker than the other native Indians, being an olive brown; their hair, lank, long and black, beard scanty, lips thick and prominent, chin short, eyebrows arched, and the general expression of countenance cold, sullen and often fierce. They have no annals, nor any reliable traditions in regard to their origin or early history. It is thought, however, that they are the descendants of the primitive gigantic peoples of Yucatan and Southern Mexico.

PATAGONIAN.

The Chiquitians differ materially from the Patagonians; are smaller in stature, their average height being about five feet; heads large and nearly round; forehead low; nose short; eyes

* This chief was captured by the Spaniards in his native island, carried to St. Domingo and brutally hanged.—Irving's Life of Columbus, Vol. III., p. 159.

† American Antiquities, p. 154.

sunken, but horizontal; eyebrows thin and well defined; complexion bronze or pale brown. They are domestic in their habits, residing in small villages, and engage in the cultivation of the soil. They are of lively disposition, sociable nature, and remarkable for their kindness and hospitality. They are not a beardless people, though the beard is scanty and does not become developed until advanced age. The hair of the head is long, black and glossy, and never becomes gray; but in extreme old age grows a yellowish hue.

The Moxians resemble the Chiquitians, but larger in stature, and in features materially differ. Though the head is equally large, the face is less full, and rather long; forehead low and arched, nose short and flat, mouth small, lips thin, eyes small and horizontal, eyebrows arched and narrow; scanty beard, which only appears on the chin and upper lip; the hair black, long and sleek.

The Moxians dwell upon the plains and along the rivers. Fishing is their chief pursuit.

The Chiquitians and Moxians are divided into numerous tribes, recognized by the general characteristics above noted. The former are devoted to agriculture, peace and quietude; the latter to war and strife. One of the tribes, the Canichana, are cannibals, eating their prisoners of war.

The Chiquitians bury their dead in graves, depositing with the bodies arms and provisions for journey in future life, which they believe will be enjoyed after death.

Very great improvement has been made in the condition of these groups since the conquest. Of the Moxians, about 23,750 have become Christians out of about 28,000 natives; and, out of a population of 19,235 Chiquitians, 17,735 have been converted to Christianity.

The Brasilio-Guarani consists of two great families of nations, viz: Guarani and Carib, which comprise many tribes.

The Guarani are the most interesting peoples of South America. They surpass all others in the adoption of the Christian religion and European civilization; not only espousing the Christian religion and refined civilization, but enforcing these blessings upon their savage neighbors. Their complexion is coppery, or brown color, eyes black, hair jet black, long and straight, though there are some tribes whose general appearance differ but little from Europeans. They are generally well formed; some stout and tall, others under size, though well proportioned, but, like the peoples of other countries, there are differences in stature, complexion and mode of life, where there are numerous nations and tribes. There is a general tendency among all the Guarani nations and tribes to agriculture, though hunting and fishing is much engaged in.

The Cobeus are cannibals—even eat their kindred, and make war for the purpose of gratifying their unnatural appetites; even dry the flesh of human beings over fire, and preserve it for food.*

The Caribs are a numerous people. Two hundred years ago they were spread out over South America from the mouth of the Amazon to the Orinoco and Porto Rico. They consist of many tribes and nations, and were the original inhabitants of the Caribbee Islands. Formerly they dwelt in Florida, North America; but, in consequence of the difficulties between them and other natives of that country, emigrated to the Islands, and to Guinea in South America. They are à noble looking people, tall, commanding in appearance, with dark piercing eyes, and olive-brown complexion.

The Botocudas have been long considered the most savage nation of the continent. Before the introduction of Christianity among them, they were cannibals, wearing ornaments of human bones, and strings of human teeth about their necks. They are taller than the other Indian nations; but their lower limbs are very slim compared to their bodies. The color of their skin is of a yellowish tinge; the hair black and coarse, the features regular, and really more Caucasian than Indian. They go unclad and live upon fruits and game, which they take by their bows and arrows. They have a singular custom of ornamenting their ears and lips with plugs of wood; the men pierce their ears and hang clogs of wood ornaments therefrom, as also do the women; but the latter, in addition, also pierce their under lip, attaching to it a wooden ornament. They are a war-like nation, keeping up almost constant wars with the neighboring nations, and have been greatly scourged by the Tupi. It is reported that some of the more savage tribes still indulge in cannibalism.

* Natural History of Man, Vol. II., p. 63.

The Island Caribs, unlike the other natives, refused to submit to the vassalage sought to be imposed upon them by the Spaniards; boldly resisted the aggressions of the Europeans, and, when overpowered, preferred rather to die than submit to wrong.* The consequence of their subjection was their almost entire expulsion and extirpation from the islands in the 18th century.

The Caribs are partially civilized; reside to some extent in villages, and cultivate the ground. They have a system of civil government of elective character, the governor, or ruling chief, being chosen by the voice of the nation. Their language is one of the most sonorous and soft in the world, containing about thirty dialects.

The country now comprising Venezuela, New Granada and Equador before the arrival of the Spaniards was inhabited by numerous tribes of native Indians, refined savages, who were enjoying a semi-barbaric civilization. Of these the Muyscas were the most numerous and enjoyed the highest degree of civilization. They had a tradition, that whilst the nation was disputing about the choice of a king, a great legislator, a white man by the name of Bochica the offspring of the sun, mysteriously appeared among them. He was clothed in a long garment, and had a noble beard. He advised them to choose as their king or chief, Huncohua, which they did. Bochica was considered a deity, and into whose face the people dare not look.

The king selected became very distinguished as a warrior, having subdued the country from the plains of San Juan to the mountains of Opon. They treated this monarch with great reverence and respect, even carried him about in a palanquin, and strewed flowers along his pathway.

The Muyscas had an organized government recognizing the rights of individuals to hold and enjoy property, subject to taxation to support the state. Laws were regularly enacted and officers appointed to execute them. They occupied villages and dwellings in the country, and paid great attention to the cultivation of the soil.

When Chili was invaded by the Spaniards they found it thick-

* The white and black races will submit to slavery, but the red men never.
—Plurality of Races, p. 74.

ly populated by the native Indians, of whom the Araucanians seem to have been the most powerful and war-like. They resisted the invaders with great skill and bravery. Their great chief Caupolican, displayed a courage and military prowess which would be creditable to civilized commanders. In the skillful display of his forces upon the field he astonished and won the admiration of the Spanish commanders. He defeated the great Spanish General Valdivia, who was captured and put to death by Caupolican's soldiers.

Being captured during the war by the Spanish soldiers, he, in retaliation for the murder of Valdivia, was most barbarously burnt at the stake. In the province of La Platte reside the Gauchos, a most singular group of Indians. They almost live upon horseback, but have mud cottages, each containing a single room, wherein they take shelter when not engaged in the chase, at war, or in search of plunder. Beef is their principal food, which they cook by roasting over the fire on a stick.

There is a group of natives on the Pampas represented as most terrible savages, and who refuse to become reconciled to any degree of civilization, preferring to remain in their savage state and hostile to every other people. "They appear to be of the genuine Aranco breed;" are generally on horseback, and noted for their equestrianism. They keep up almost constant wars with the Gauchos, upon whom they make night assaults, murder the males and carry off the young females, of whom they make wives. They were severely punished by the colonists, who not only defeated and slaughtered large numbers of them, but drove the survivors beyond the Colorado. The interior Indians of Brazil, with some exceptions, have made less progress in the adoption of refined civilization than any other portion of South America. This is owing mainly to the introduction of negro slavery by the European colonists, and efforts to bring the natives into like vassalage. Refusing to become serfs to the white man, as long as 'they found a forest wherein to lurk or roam, kept them aloof from civilized communities; yet by slow degrees they are being reached even in their wild and savage retreat.

The Guaycurus, a numerous people of the interior, have reared all the domestic animals, but they neither sow nor reap, their

20

subsistence being chiefly the flesh of their herds and the spontaneous productions of the country.

The Vaupes, residing along the Uacaiari River, consist of about thirty tribes, are tall, stout and well formed, with a reddish brown complexion. The men wear their hair long, extending often half way down their backs; are beardless and have no eyebrows—these, both males and females pluck out. The men decorate their heads with combs—the women let their hair hang loosely over the shoulders.

This nation cultivates the soil, manufactures many useful articles, and resides in permanent houses, which are built to contain several families. One of these dwellings, upon actual measurement, was found to be 115 feet long by 75 feet broad and thirty feet high. The men wear a small piece of cloth as their only dress; the females are entirely naked, but paint their bodies in various colors in imitation of garments. The women cultivate the soil—the men engage in hunting and fishing.

There dwelt in Chaco, and the countries west of Paraguay, when the country was first visited by the Spaniards, more than forty nations of native Indians, many of whom are now extinct.

One of these nations, the Abipones, still exists in Chaco, and described by Azard as being well formed, with handsome faces, much like Europeans except in color. They have aquiline noses; color fair, if not even whiter than the Spaniards; thick, black, glossy hair, and scanty beards.

Like the tribes and nations of North America, those of the southern portion of the continent exhibit marked differences in nations, families and tribes, presenting the features and characteristics of the Mongolian and Malay types in strong resemblance. They are not all evidently indigenous. The Tartar element seems to be strongly preserved in some of the nations, and in the Nomadic tribes of the Brazilian-Guarani group, in which in some tribes the eyes are obliquely placed and raised at the outer angles, strongly indicate that they belong to the same stock or race as the Nomads of High Asia. Their complexion is the same, being yellowish, whilst that of the other native Indians is reddish-brown.

The Araucans, some of whom as already noticed, of the Pesherais group or family, are in physical aspect, very much like Caucasians. They have the aquiline nose, well formed lips, and their whole features less Indian than any other family of the natives, and in many respects act like Caucasians. Their nature is kind, hospitality liberal, earnest, highly formal, and have a religion which recognizes a future state of existence.

The natives of Paria, according to Ferdinand Columbus, were better made and whiter than the other people he had met with in South America. Other writers also give similar accounts of them, some even stating them to be nearly white and clothed with long flowing hair of yellowish or auburn hue. The Botocndos already referred to were similar to those of Paria, though more resembling the Mongols.

None of the Indians or aborigines of South America have any annals; and their traditions are of doubtful character; but the story of Manco Capac, and his sister, and his wife Mama Oello Huaco, two children of the sun, settling in the Valley of Cuzco and introducing the arts and civilization among the savage natives, has the evidences of probability about it. At all events the Peruvians when first discovered by Europeans, were enjoying a civilization equal with the Aztecs. They however were a distinct people from the Aztecs, and until the Spanish conquest neither knew of the existence of the other.

The Peruvians had a well-regulated civil government — a theocracy, of very despotic character. The Incas exercised spiritual and temporal power over the empire. In one respect they were considered spiritually supreme, and, indeed, with celestial power, over the " children of earth," their subjects. The people submitted in fear, rather than from any love of country.

The Peruvians were less skilled in picture-writing and the computation of time than the Aztecs. This is not at all remarkable, as the calendar of the latter was more accurate than that of the Greeks and Romans. The Peruvians, however, far surpassed the Aztecs in mechanical skill. They constructed roads, built suspension bridges and massive buildings with a skill and architectural symmetry almost equal with those constructed by our most skillful and enlightened mechanics. Without the knowledge of the use of iron, they substituted an alloy of copper and tin, which they prepared of such consistency and hardness as to be capable of chiseling the hardest stone. The Peruvians were not a nation of warriors, but civilians, living in tranquil subjection to their dreaded rulers. They were attentive cultivators of the soil throughout the empire, which extended more than two thousand miles along the Pacific, and back from the coast about five hundred miles.* Every inhabitant was known to the Incas. A register of deaths and births was kept by means of a curious invention called the "Quipus."†

Equality was a cardinal principle of the fundamental law of the Peruvians; no one could become rich, and no one could become poor; all were upon an equality as to property and human rights, and all were equal before the law, however exalted his intellect, or refined his taste. Every one was taught industry; each labored for the good of all and the maintenance of the government.

Though the Peruvians were a nation of civilians, they kept up an army for defensive purposes, which was sometimes converted into an army of conquest.

The Peruvians admitted the existence of the soul after death, and connected with it the resurrection of the body; they designated the place of the wicked in the center of the earth, where they should expiate their crimes by ages of wearisome toil; the good, they supposed, would pass a luxurious life of tranquillity and ease. Their belief in the resurrection of the body prompted them to preserve the dead with much care.

The Peruvians fully believed in a Supreme Creator of the Universe, whom they worshipped. The sun was the great object of adoration, though they also revered the moon and stars, thunder, lightning, and the rainbow, to which they dedicated temples. The worship of the sun was allotted to the Incas, who dedicated to this divinity superb and gorgeous temples. The most renowned one they erected was located at Cuzco, and was the pride and boast of the empire; its interior was literally a mine of gold; on the western wall was a massive plate of gold, upon which was engraved the representation of the deity, consisting of a human countenance looking forth from the midst of innumerable rays of light, which emanated from it in every direction.‡ Gold seems to have been lavishly bestowed upon every portion of this temple, where it could be ornamental;

* Prescott's Conquest of Peru, Vol. I., pp. 50–58.
† Ibid, pp. 55–118.   ‡ Ibid, p. 96.

even the cornices which surrounded the walls of the sanctuary were of gold; and a broad belt of gold, set in frieze of stonework, encompassed the whole exterior of the temple. The structure was composed of stone similar in character to that of which the great fortress of Cuzco (noticed in another place) was constructed.

The early history of the Peruvians is involved in fabulous uncertainty, though it is tolerably well established that the empire of the Incas had been in existence about four hundred years before the Spanish invasion. It is equally, if not better established, that they were not the first inhabitants of the country, as the many monuments of art, now in ruins, found in various portions of the empire, fully show. By whom these buildings were erected is unknown, unless by the Aymaras, who are claimed by some authors to be the descendants of the constructors of the ancient ruins found in the vicinity of the lake of Titicaca, and elsewhere in Peru and Bolivia. These ruins show their builders to have been equally advanced in civilization with the constructors of the buildings of Palenque, and are superior in architectural design to any subsequently built by the Incas.

Recent discoveries have shown that the Aturian Paltas, people of flattened skulls, were the constructors of the splendid edifices now in ruins in South and Central America. Whether they are of the same family of man as the Aymaras has not been ascertained. The skulls and bones of this peculiar people have been dug up near the shores of Lake Titicaca, and in the interior of Brazil. The same form of head and high nose is represented in bas-reliefs in sculpture in the ancient temples and buildings of Yucatan and Southern Mexico. Those of Palenque are peculiarly striking.*

These works of art, and bones and skulls, above referred to, are the only evidences of the existence of the now extinct Paltas. The builders of these edifices would most likely preserve the likeness of themselves, or some of their own kindred, in preference to those of strangers. The flat head seems to have been a form of head divine, as it is represented in statuary of idols as well as of heroes.†

---

* Travels in Central America, Chiapas and Yucatan, Vol. II., p. 311.

† " If the typical flat-heads were not a distinct species of man, they were at least the oldest and first wanderers that reached the American continent."— The Natural History of the Human Species, p. 257.

Late discoveries in Peru, as now claimed, show that the heads of the Peruvians were not depressed before the era of the Incas. The custom, it would seem, was cotemporaneous with the reign of the Incas. This is more than probable, as the mechanics, generally, who construct such huge works of art, are the slaves of superiors.

There were evidently different people from the Incas in power in Peru, before their era, as shown by other works of art, among which stand prominent the so called Aymaran tombs, consisting of square buildings, with monolithic doorways, through which the corpses were conducted. The bodies were ranged around in the interior, in a sitting posture, in their clothes. Some of the tombs were built of unburnt bricks, and several stories high; others were constructed of dressed stone.

The Peruvians displayed great courage in defending themselves against the invading Spaniards, but did not seem to realize their danger of subjugation until too late in the contest to retrieve their lost fortunes. They had delayed their proper defence until the enemy had become their masters. Had they displayed such prowess in the beginning of the war, they would have defied the invaders.

The Incas were the superior people of South America, in point of intellectual endowments, when they first became known to Europeans. They did not attain to their great preëminence by merely imitating others, but by force of their own mental powers. They had large and well-developed frames, to a greater extent than the other Indian nations of South America.*

From the character of the monuments and implements of the lost race of Peru and Central America, they were, doubtless, civil and inoffensive, averse to war, and devoted their energies to the civil pursuits of life. The vast ruins, which are credited to them, show they must have been extensively devoted to agriculture; otherwise such populous cities as then existed there could not have been sustained, or supplied with the necessaries of life.

* Prescott's Conquest of Peru, Vol. I., p. 39.

CHAPTER XVI.

THE AFRICAN RACE.

THE African race comprises several groups and numerous
tribes of dark complexion, chief of which being the Negroes proper, Paupan, Negrillo, Ethiopian, M'kuafe and Mussel.

The Negro is no new subject, everybody can describe him by
his black skin, black crisped woolly hair, pouched lips, flat nose,
wide mouth, curved legs and protruding jaws.

This race occupies two-
thirds of Africa, part of
the East Indies, Australia,
and numerous islands of
the Pacific Ocean; besides
are found in the West In-
dies and in North and
South America, whither
they have been carried
from their native Africa,
as slaves, by Europeans.
From present indications
the Negro is destined to
fill an important page in
American history. This
race is as old, if not more
ancient, than any of the
others. As far back as any

AFRICAN.

(311)

types are found of record the Negro is represented, and in the condition of a slave.

In the age of Rameses III., the twentieth Egyptian dynasty, which dates 1300 years B. C., the African is represented on a bas-relief tied by the neck to an Asiatic prisoner, of which Mr. Gliddon remarks: "This head is remarkable, furthermore, as the natural type of two-thirds of the Negroes of Egypt at the present day." The profile referred to is a good likeness of the African of the Southern States, and this has been the cast of the Negro race above Egypt for over three thousand years.

In the age of Seti-Meneptha I., 1500 years B. C., the Negro is fully represented upon his tomb, also the red, white and yellow races. Here we have these four types plainly represented by the Egyptians before the days of Moses; but in tenth Genesis only the three heads of families are given, without any allusion to their complexion or physical differences, if any then existed.

The Egyptian representations show the above several types to have been in existence as distinct orders of mankind 3,300 years ago. Slavery then was an institution of Egypt, and was not alone confined to the Negro race; other types were likewise enslaved, though the African seems to have been doomed to a degraded condition of servitude by the Egyptians. Their monuments, as far back as the seventeenth dynasty, which dates 1600 years B. C., shows the distinctive character and position of the Negro in Egypt. But history does not mention them as a distinct race until long after that period. Even the Greeks did not know of their existence until about 700 years B. C.

Among the ruined sculpture of Nineveh, existing in the reign of Sargon, which dates 710 years B. C., the figure of an African is represented, wounded, and in the act of imploring mercy from the Assyrians. The Romans did not become acquainted with the Negro type until the second century A. D.; at least we find no description of the African by the Roman authors before that era.

The topography of the country is such as to preclude the idea of the Negro being brought north without their having first been introduced into Egypt. They could not have been transported across the great desert, nor to Carthage, as no means of transit was then in existence, camels not being introduced in Barbary until after the fall of Carthage, and it is well known the Carthagenians never held Negro slaves. If the African was at all known to the Carthagenians, it was as the Ethiopian; which term was applied to the dark-skinned nations by the ancients, whether Negroes or Caucasians. It is recorded that Hanno, the navigator, and his contemporaries visited the Negro regions of Africa about 600 years B. C. Whatever discoveries they may have made, no other description of the people they met with, other than that they were "Ethiopians," is given.

About the same period of Hanno's discoveries, "Pharaoh Horus," of the eighteenth dynasty, records, at Hagar Silintis, his return from victories over Nigritian families of the Upper Nile.*

Among the captives of this conqueror is presented a Negress, clad about the loins with a leopard skin. This likeness of the African type is preserved in the bas-relief of Egyptian sculpture, and in the paintings dating about 1550 years B. C. This effigy shows no change in the Negro type in a period of about 3,600 years, as the figure there represented is a perfect image of the present Negro race. The Negro had then the black, woolly, crisped hair, flat nose, thick and pouched lips, long, protruding jaws, elongated heel, flat shin bone and black skin.

But there are other proofs of the existence of the Negro race of earlier date than the above. Lepsius, by his researches in Egypt, has fully shown that during the twelfth dynasty they existed as slaves. This learned author says: "Mention is often made on monuments of this period of the victories gained by the kings over the Ethiopians and Negroes; wherefore, we must not be surprised to see black slaves and servants." †

Recent researches in the Valley of the Nile fully demonstrate that the Egyptians were acquainted with the African races, and had established intercourse with them as early as 2400 years B. C.; and there is nothing to refute the conclusion that the Negroes were in Africa when the Egyptians first established themselves upon the banks of the Nile. When they first appear in history they are represented as a wide-spread and numerous people.

The truthfulness of the paintings and sculpture of the Egyp-

* Types of Mankind, p. 255. † Lepsius, p. 174.

tians, as presentations of the several races of man is very apparent, the red, white, black, and yellow are as perfectly represented by the Egyptian artists in that remote age as they could possibly be to-day.

The representation of thr Abyssinian (cinnamon-colored subject), in the grand procession of Thotmes III., of the seventeenth dynasty, which dates about 1600 years B. C., is very lifelike—the same as he is found to-day in form, features and complexion. Mr. Pickering, in his "Races of Men," uses this forcible language in reference to the Abyssinian alluded to: "It seems, however, that the true Abyssinian (as first pointed out to me by Mr. Gliddon), has been separately and distinctly figured on the Egyptian monuments, in the two men leading the cameleopard in the tribute procession of Thoatmosis III., and this opinion was confirmed by an examination of the original painting at Thebes." *

It is fully established by the Egyptian monuments and paintings, that the term "Ethiopian" does not simply refer to the African Negroes, but is applied to the leading peoples of Ethiopia, who were not Negroes, having darker complexions than the Egyptians. The Cushite king mentioned in 2 Kings xix. 9, who ruled in Egypt during the reign of Sennacherib in Assyria, was not a Negro as has been supposed, and had none of the African features.

Among the embalmed subjects of Egypt, it is remarkable that not a solitary mummified African is found until about the fourth century B. C., and then only one subject, a female, was discovered in the sacred isle of Beghl. Whether this Negress was a subject of distinction or a slave does not appear. This fact is an important landmark in the history of the African race. It shows that the black, woolly haired type did not rule in Egypt, as has been claimed by some ethnologists, and also that the African was not of sufficient note or standing in Egypt to entitle them to that sacred mode of burial. Other foreigners were embalmed by hundreds and thousands in Egypt, either out of respect or by the custom of the country.

In the reign of Sesourtesen I., the second king of the twelfth dynasty, which dates about 2348 years B. C., the African race is

* Pickering's Races of Men, p. 231.

represented on tablets as captives. This date is about the time of the deluge. The Egyptians had thus early extended their conquest to the second cataract of the Nile at Wadee Halfa. In speaking of the Negro race, the Egyptians used the epithet " Nahs ;" which signifies barbarian, and whose country they eventually became possessed of as far as the third cataract, where a marked stone was recognized as the boundaries of the Egyptian empire. The Nigritian race was forced to the south of that point by the Egyptians before the boundary was established.

The idea that the Egyptian kings, Sabaco, Sevechus, and Torkaka, of the thirtieth dynasty, 719 years B. C., were Africans, is quite erroneous. They were not of that race ; had none of the Negro features, and were not tainted with Negro blood, as their well-preserved portraits fully attest.

BISHAREE WOMAN.

The color of the skin, as found in the Egyptian paintings, is not a sure test of the types, unless accompanied with the other peculiarities of the races, as it has been discovered that the Negroes are painted in all shades, whilst the Egyptians are painted red, the color of honor amongst them. But the sculpture always shows the type to which the subject belongs. Every rational mind must, therefore, readily conclude that the African race has been in existence, as a distinct people, over 4,200 years ; and how long before that period is a matter of conjecture only, there being no reliable data upon which to predicate any reliable opinion.

Though this type was for so many ages confined to the African continent, they eventually seem to have become as widespread over the globe almost as the other races ; not, however, voluntarily, as in many instances they were carried to other regions as slaves, especially to this continent. From the earliest period of authentic history they were treated by the Caucasian race as if they had no rights they were bound to respect.

The Ethiopian family differ materially from the Negro. They are not so dark-skinned, the hair is finer, the nose more prominent, the jaws less elongated, and their features more refined and uniform. They resemble the Hindoos, and seem to be derived from them and the Negroes. They occupy the tropical regions of Africa, and in the main are pastoral in their habits. The Nubians, however, engage in agriculture, as do also some of the tribes further east along the borders of the table lands of Abyssinia.

Ethiopia occupies a prominent position in ancient history, and the people of that classic country by some of the, learned have been considered more ancient than the Egyptians, and it has even been claimed that the first inhabitants of Egypt were Ethiopians. There is very strong evidence tending to show that the Ethiopians occupied Nubia before the Lower Nile was known to the Egyptians; at all events, Nubia was the rival of Egypt, and frequently held that power in subjection, occasionally furnishing the latter with kings. They have left imperishable monuments of art; and, though not quite as extensive as those of Egypt, are very astonishing in magnitude, and grand in architectural display. Whilst the Egyptians were forced to yield obedience to the conquering legions of Cambyses, the Ethiopians bid the invaders defiance. Nor were the Romans, Saracens or Turks able to subdue or conquer them.

Ethiopia and Nubia are one and the same. Among the ancients, this region was known as Libya.* Homer mentions the Ethiopians in his poems, and Herodotus speaks of them as inhabiting the whole of Southern Africa. They have existed as a distinct people as long as any known nation. Their origin is unknown, and it is not ascertained from what region they came into the Valley of the Nile. The Berbers are a Libyan family.†

The modern Ethiopians, or Nubians, are descended from the ancient Ethiopians and Bedouin Arabs.‡ The original type has been considerably modified by amalgamation. Before the advent of Mahomet, the country had been enjoying Christianity, but the doctrines of the Saviour were soon cast aside, and the new faith adopted instead.

* They were a tawny-colored people, occupying an extensive district in Southern Egypt.—Anthon's Classical Dictionary, p. 70.
† Natural History of Man, Vol. I., p. 267.
‡ The Barabra, or Berberines, are descendants of the Nubians.—Natural History of Man, Vol. I., p. 286.

There are several tribes inhabiting the country at the present day who seem to be different from the Ethiopians in many particulars. The Mahas, living in South Nubia, have very thick hair, but not woolly. The Sheygya tribe are strictly Arabs. The Berberas, considered Arabs, are tall and handsome, having a dark-brown complexion, oval face, Grecian nose, and thick, bushy hair. A true representation of this family is witnessed on the rock at Abu-Simbal, where the likenesses of Egyptian kings are carved and painted. They are a distinct people from the Berbers of Northern Africa,* of whom we shall presently speak. The ancient Nubians, by their own tradition, were colonists from the banks of the Indus. This tradition comports well with the idea of the first peopling of the Valley of the Nile by way of Abyssinia and Nubia, the people of which, and also of Egypt, being of the same type before they amalgamated with the African.

It is claimed that a branch of the Cushite peoples, at a very remote age, had fought their way, by sea and land, and established a great political power in Arabia Felix, where they remained until the Arabians compelled them to cross the straits of Babel-mandeb. They returned from Africa more than once to hold dominion in Yemen, and kept up the prosperity of the country until the time of the Hegira. The Nubians and Abyssinians are of the same origin, though mixed with Arab blood of the Rebah tribe.

The original abode of the Ethiopians, in all probability, was on the Indus and Punjab. There the Caucasians came in contact with the black race; and hence the production of the several subordinate varieties of mankind found in India. These deductions are sustained, to some extent, by the dialects of the various families scattered over the above regions and in the valleys of the Helmund and Kauble; also in Abyssinia, Nubia and Egypt. The Sanscrit language is visible in all their dialects.

The Ethiopic family also figured in Persia at a very remote period, and a portion of them (Arabs), who were driven from Yemen to Abyssinia, doubtless constituted the Cushites of Ethi-

* The Berbers are the descendants of the Nobatæ, who were brought by Diocletian from an oasis in the western part of Africa, to inhabit the Valley of the Nile, fifteen centuries ago. They, according to Lepsius, have shining, reddish-brown hair.—Prichard's Natural History of Man, Vol. I., pp. 284-5.

opia. Tribes of this group eventually founded the Aurite of Upper Egypt. Others, less swarthy, were colonists of Lower Egypt. Some hordes preceded them across the Nile, and founded the Mourthwan and Nubian populations. The Berberas belong to this group.

The Abyssinians, though generally classed with the African type, are not Negroes, have none of the African features, and should be classed with the Caucasians, having European features; yet seem to have crisped hair. Their complexion is light, but never becomes florid; they are tall and well formed; in general appearance present the Hindoostanic family, though their complexion is not darker than that of the Arabs, if, indeed, even so dark. The females are generally fair, and pass for Europeans. They are, doubtless, Semitic.*

The ancients classed the Abyssinians with the Europeans, and gave very indefinite boundaries to their empire. Axum, a noted city on the Red Sea, and the capital of Axumitæ, was within its limits. The Abyssinians themselves claim their country was the Sheba of Scripture, and that they were converted to Judaism several centuries before the Christian era. They were converted to Christianity in the fourth century A. D., by the efforts of Frumentius, an Egyptian. They refused the adoption of the Mahometan faith, and still hold to Christianity. The natives, though partially civilized, cling to some of their barbarous customs. They eat raw flesh whilst it is warm and almost pulsating, carving slices from the living animal, which they eat as a sweet morsel, whilst the beast from which it was cut walks about the street.

There are many native tribes in Abyssinia, some of whom, such as the Shangalla, are savage Negroes. Bruce considered them the same peoples who, under the name of Funje, inhabit the regions of the river Bahr-el-Abiad, and who are masters of Sennair. Ptolemy classed the Shangalla family under the general appellation of Troglodytes, "dwellers in caves." They were noted as elephant eaters, upon the flesh of which, and that of the rhinoceros, they principally subsisted.

* The recent war between the British and Abyssinians has fully developed their Semitic character. They claim their descent from Solomon.—Phrenological Journal of 1868, May and June, pp. 191 and 229.

The Galla is the most distinguished native family, next to the Abyssinian, of this portion of Africa. Their origin is involved in obscurity. From the best information, we can, perhaps, safely say, they came from the unknown regions of the southern interior of the continent, from whence they wandered north in search of a more fruitful region than their native district. They were first seen about two hundred and thirty years ago, by Lobo, near Melinda. They are generally pastoral in their habits; but some of the tribes bordering on the Abyssinian highlands cultivate the soil. In their persons the Gallas are smaller than Europeans, and neither in hair nor features resemble the Negroes. Their complexion is of a deep brown, but those who have dwelt long upon the plains are of a darker hue. The Gallas are much fairer than the Abyssinians. Their hair is longer and more silky, and features more delicate. They have already conquered forty-two kingdoms of Abyssinia, and, since the fall of Theodore, the liberal king or emperor, are rapidly grasping the power of the whole country. Their females are handsome, and, when educated, become intelligent. There are two classes of Gallas, Northern and Southern. The Northern deal largely in slaves, principally women and children. The Southern Gallas even sell some of their own kindred as slaves. They dwell in the region called "Bararata," which is located about eight days' journey from Potta. They have a civil government, in which the rights of the people are protected, though little regard is paid to the rights of those not of their own kindred. Every eight years they elect a king, who, in addition to his civil duties, performs the religious rite of circumcising his subjects. The Southern Gallas are tall, resembling the M'kuafi, with whom they keep up almost constant war. The Gallas have strong, heavy beards, which they closely clip. They have no annals, and their origin is unknown; but they belong to the Ethiopian family.

The M'kuafi dwell in the interior, to the south of the Gallas. They do not cultivate the ground, but live upon meat and milk; keep cattle in common pasturage, each family having its own stock; also keep donkeys, sheep, goats and dogs. Their villages consist of tents, covered with bullock-skins. They do not bury their dead, but convey the bodies to the forest, to be eaten by the wild beasts. They have no religion or prayers, but own a deity they call "Augayai." They, also, are a branch of the Ethiopic family. West of them dwell the Mussai, a pastoral tribe, who speak the same language as the M'kuafi, a kindred nation, and whose habits and manners they imitate.

The Somali, an Ethiopian nation, dwell in that portion of Africa opposite the southern angle of Arabia, along the coast, in the vicinity of the straits of Babel-mandeb, and, in the interior, to the river Juba. They are, to some extent, pastoral, and engage in maritime pursuits. Their features are regular, hair flowing and of flaxen color (made so by staining), and of a dark-brown complexion. They are of Semitic stock, and are said to be possessors of books; but no account is given concerning their annals or literature. North of the Somali dwell the Danakil tribe, who are a barbarous people, with dark skin, and, usually, long, crisped hair. Their features are regular, though not African. They belong to the Ethiopian group. Those residing in the neighborhood of Angola have smooth hair, and their general features and language give strong indications of a Semitic origin.

THE HOTTENTOTS.

The Hottentots comprise three nations—the Bosjesmans, Corannos, and Nomascuas. They are well formed, but rather under the average height, especially some of the Bosjesman tribes; have high cheek bones, flat nose, prominent chin, eyes of chestnut color, long and narrow, wide apart, the inner angle being rounded, like the Chinese, whom they much resemble, though Dr. Knox says they look much like the Calmucks, and sets them down as a branch of the Mongolian race. Their complexion is of a yellowish brown; their hair black and crisped, like that of the Negroes, but grows in tufts. They

HOTTENTOT.

are kind and affectionate toward one another, and are harmless, honest and faithful, but, when under a leader, exhibit great bravery, and endure pain and hardship with great fortitude.

The Hottentots are reputed the most ancient nations of Southern Africa, though it is quite evident that they did not there originate, as traces of them appear further north, even far in the interior. Of their origin nothing definite is known; they have not even a plausible conjecture concerning it, but are in all probability of Asiatic descent. Little advance has been made by them in civilization, though having had ample opportunities to become enlightened and refined. They, however, carry on various manufactures upon a small scale, such as tanning and dressing skins, moulding iron into knives, forming mats of flags and bulrushes, and bow-strings of the sinews of animals. They are evidently now a different people from what they were several hundred years ago. At that period they were an independent nation in the enjoyment of a republican form of government, but at present are mere outcasts, and, like the American Indians, robbed of their homes and graves of their ancestors by a superior race. They are not slaves in the literal sense of the term, but seem to have no national freedom or rights their superiors, in any particular, regard with respect.

THE BOSJESMANS, (BUSHMEN).

The Bosjesmans, though a family of Hottentots, have been so long separated from them as to have to some extent lost their identity. They are called Bushmen, and considered among the lowest and most degraded of the human race, though not deficient in mental faculties. Their complexion is a yellowish-brown, have a prominent forehead, flat nose, thick lips and narrow chin. Mr. Moffat, in speaking of their barbarous customs says, among other things, that when the mother dies her infant is buried alive with her corpse.

The earliest account we have of the Bushmen is found in the narrative of Simon Von der Stell, the governor of the Dutch Colony, who undertook an expedition to the country of the Amoquas in the year 1685. They were called Sonquas, and were robbers to a great extent, subsisting upon honey and game. Their only dwellings were such as nature provided, consisting

21

of the rocky caverns of the forests.* Some of the tribes construct huts of circular form upon the open plain. In this the Bushman with his family take shelter from the winds, but not from the rain, as they have no covering.

Their weapons are the bow and arrow, with which they take game for food. In war they use poisoned arrows, which they discharge with surprising accuracy and force.

They have no settled residence; wander from place to place, often almost in a state of starvation, and seem to delight in this degradation—pay no attention to family ties; have no personal names, and when they first became known to Europeans had no morals or religion, and were too indolent to be dangerous. All they seem to desire is food, drink, sleep and the gratification of their animal passions.

THE CORANNAS.

The Corannas are a well disposed people, residing in villages. They are very much like the Hottentots, though their cheek-bones are not so prominent, and their faces more oval; in other respects they are Hottentots. Their origin, like that of the Hottentots, is unknown, except that they are descendants of the earliest people of the country.

THE DOKAS.

The Dokas, according to Professor Ritter and Dr. Krapf, are a nation of pigmies who occupy a district in the vicinity of the Juba River south-west of Kaffa, but distant from it a month's journey. They are described as being only of the stature of a boy ten years old; as going naked, and living upon ants, snakes, mice and other things not usually eaten for food; and as having no laws or government, but live together like animals. The marriage relation has no binding force upon any one. No ranks or orders exist among them; all are upon equality. They have some idea of the Supreme Being, but of very indefinite character. Their language is unlike all others. Though barbarous they are by no means wholly animals, but have fair intellects. They make the most submissive and trusty slaves of any of the Negro race. Their complexion is as black as that of the Shangal-

* Moffat's Southern Africa, p. 46.

las. If the whole story concerning them is not a fabrication, they are in all probability the same nation spoken of by Herodotus.

The belief in a Pigmy race is as ancient as Homer. He, however, located them in India. Pliny and Strabo also believed in their existence.

THE FOULAHS.

The Foulahs are a numerous people who have spread themselves over the countries watered by the Senegal and Gambia, and also the great kingdom of Foata Jalleo to the south. They are not Africans, having none of the Negro features. Their color is an olive tint, and physiognomy agreeable. The early authors entertained the belief that the Foulahs came from Fooladoo on the upper Senegal; but it has been well ascertained that they are of foreign origin, and constitute a branch of the Fellatah family. They are a robust people with strong minds, and in many respects resemble the Arabs. Their manners are courteous and gentle—no people being more hospitable; are pastoral in their habits, but cultivate the ground, and have cities and towns, mosques and schools. Timbu is their capital, which contains about 10,000 population. Their internal government is republican, and their religion Mahometan. Thus far they have not been assigned their place in nature with definite certainty, but recently have been considered a family of the Polynesian group. Richard Lander thought them a Kaffir family. They are doubtless of the same stock as the Fellahs of Egypt.

THE JAGAS.

When the Portuguese first visited the southern portion of Africa they found the inhabitants comprehended in the Mani-Kongo empire, and considered the people one nation. Subsequent discoveries show this to have been an error, and that there were several distinct nations incorporated in what was then presumed to be the empire. Of these several nations the Jagas seem to have been the most distinguished. They, according to the description given of them by the Portuguese, may be, as Prichard said: The "prototypes of the present Kaffir tribes" and other nations of Eastern Kaffir land. The Jagas were described as wandering barbarians, who fed on human flesh, eating the captives taken in war, and also the bodies of the slain.

In general appearance and habits they resemble the Kaffirs. Their complexion is a dark brown of reddish tinge. They had a system of religious worship, according to Andrew Battel, of singular paganism. In the middle of a town was erected an image, as large as a man, elevated twelve feet high, at the feet of the image was a circle of elephant teeth driven into the ground; upon these teeth were placed human skulls of persons killed in battle, and also of those offered as sacrifices to the image, which was called Quesango.

In 1542 the Jagas, under a great chief called Zimbo, made a furious attack on the people of the Batta provinces; and in the following year in vast numbers overrun the whole kingdom of Kongo, from which they were not expelled until after a bloody war of four years duration. They are still recognized as a distinct people, though of no formidable character.

PEOPLES OF KONGO.

The nations inhabiting the vast regions known as the empire of Kongo present a variety of physical differences in their aspects and characteristics. According to Lopez and Cavazzi, some are of dark-brown complexion, others of an olive hue, whilst others are of blackish-red. Some even are much better representatives of the Arabs than of Negroes. Though differing so materially, as these several nations seem to do, they, nevertheless, are all branches of the great Kaffir family, presently noticed. The Amakosah and Amazuhuh nations are tall and handsome, with a brown copper-colored skin, and in general appearance much more resemble the American than the African race.

The Kongoes are of all grades. Whilst some nations are partially civilized and refined, others are barbarians and cannibals. Some of the tribes even kill their parents and relatives, never suffering them to live beyond a certain age.

The Namacquas inhabit the banks of Orange River near its confluence. In many respects they resemble the Hottentots, though taller and more active, as well as more advanced in civil-

ization. Their dwellings are of conical form, covered with
sedge matting; they are very superstitious, believing in witch-
craft and supernatural things generally; but, latterly, the missionaries have made good progress in dispelling these absurd notions from their minds and instructing them in morals and useful
knowledge. They have strong ties of friendship, and old age is
respected among them. On the death of the father his whole
estate descends to the eldest son.

The Kaffirs occupy the country lying eastward of the colony
of the Cape along the coast called Caffraria. They are a distinct family from the Hottentots, and call themselves Kousis;
are a tall, robust, muscular, and handsome family of man. Their
complexion is almost jet black, yet have none of the Negro linea-
ments either in countenance or person, and are Caucasians in
everything but color of the skin. By some they have been considered of Semitic stock, doubtless from their features and the
Jewish custom of circumcision, which they practice; they have
no annals nor any tradition in regard to their ancestors or the
place from whence they came; they cultivate the ground to a
much greater extent than the Hottentots, and raise black cattle,
but have no other stock. The oxen are trained to do the work
of horses under the saddle as well as the other duties of the
horse. Since the Christian mission was established among them
in 1821, they have made good progress in civilization; before
that they had no idea of the Deity.

There are three leading branches of the Kaffirs, namely: Kaffirs proper, above described, Zulus and Fingoes, to each of which
families belong several tribes. The hair of all of them is woolly,
but they vary in complexion, the leading color being dark
brown.

The Matchappers, the main family of the Boshuanas, are a
tall and well-shaped people of dark complexion, though not Negroes, who cultivate the ground and engage in manufacturing
articles of iron and copper; mostly consisting of axes, adzes,
knives, spears, and bodkins. Of copper they make rings for
the arms, legs, fingers and ears. They have houses and towns of
some considerable note, among which Lattakoo, their capital, and
more than a thousand places called outposts, where they have
people and cattle. Traditions relate that their ancestors came

from a region to them unknown, though supposed to have been India, as they practice the Jewish rite of circumcision, but have no annals; and, until so advised by the Christian missionaries to the contrary, had no idea of the Supreme Being.

The Tamahas, Mashones, Morootzees, Morolonges and Maguanas stand prominent as Boshuana nations. They occupy an extensive region of the interior of Southern Africa, and have several large towns in which manufacture is carried on.

To the eastward of the Boshuanas is an extensive region of coast, inhabited by numerous tribes of natives, of whom but little is known except the Monjon and Makoa. The Monjou are Negroes of deep shining black color, are savages, and the ugliest people yet discovered. Their residence is south-west of Mozambique.

The Makoa comprise a number of powerful tribes who live in the regions behind Mozambique, extending northward as far as Melinda and southward to the Zambee River; they are a strong, athletic nation of Negroes of fierce disposition, presenting in their general aspect a ferociousness which is heightened by their natural deformity of visage; they file their teeth to a point, giving to the whole the appearance of a coarse saw. Though wild and savage in their native state, they make very docile and tractable slaves.

The country in the western part of Africa, known as Senegambia, is inhabited by three distinct families, namely: Fellatahs, Iolofs and Mandingoes. The Fellatahs are a powerful nation, wielding an important influence in Western Africa, and have erected an empire for themselves of vast extent.

Their power extends from the Atlantic and Senegambia, on the west, to the bounds of the kingdom of Bornu and Adamawaon, on the east; the Great Desert bounds it on the north, and it extends southward to the mountains of Kong, embracing a district equal to one-tenth of the continent, and as large as one quarter of Europe.

The Fellatahs are not Negroes, but bear the form and features of Caucasians. Their history is remarkable. When known to the other nations of Central Africa, they occupied the country of Melli, and lived like the wandering Arabs, whom they seem to have imitated in their habits—having their home in the desert and forest, the feeding of cattle their only care. London was overrun by them; and there, as elsewhere, they were disregarded and despised. Adopting the Mahometan faith they entered upon a more successful career. Othman, one of their sheiks, a man of great enterprise and learned in the Arabic literature and religion of Africa, succeeded in making the Fellatahs believe he was a prophet. He emerged from the forest of Tadela, and built a town in the province of Guber. Being compelled to abandon this place by the people of Guber, he, with his followers, retired to the woods of Ader Tadela, and there built a town called Soccatu. This was their Mecca. The prophet commissioned many leaders, with instructions to go forth, in the name of God and the prophet, and tell the nations of the country that God had given the Fellatahs the lands and all the riches of the Kaffirs. Their power was extended as if by magic; they overran Guber, conquered Kano, subdued Haussa, Cubbe, Youri, and parts of Nyffe, Bornu and Yorriba. The prophet, who was called Danfodio, was the terror of the Negro race. He died in the year 1816. His death did not materially alter the bounds of their empire or change the character of the government. Their complexion is tawny, or red—often no darker than that of Spaniards or Portuguese, though some tribes are quite dark; their hair is, in general, smooth and black, but in some instances is found of grayish black, and again almost as dark as that of the Negro. They are pastoral in their habits, but have lately made some progress in domestic manufactures, and are considered the most intelligent family in this portion of Africa. Their origin is unknown; they are not Malays, as some have supposed; but there is reason to believe that this is the great Phout nation mentioned in the Genesis, of which all traces have been lost.* Dr. Barth was of opinion that they were originally from the East, and Egypt their original place of abode. They are identical with the Fellahs of Senegambia.†

The Mandingoes are a tall, strong, active family of Negroes. They seem to possess the capacity of self government to a much higher degree than any other African nation, and have made greater progress in the adoption of the useful arts than the other

* Read's Savage Africa, p. 354.
† Prichard's Natural History of Man, Vol. I., p. 328.

Negro nations. They are keeping up a tolerably well regulated government, and supporting good public schools. All their leading men can read and write. Their dominions are the mountainous regions about the source of the Senegal, six hundred miles from the coast. It was among them that Mungo Park met with such marked kindness. Of their origin nothing certain has been discovered; they have a tradition that they are of Egyptian origin. Efforts have been made to trace them to the Coptic, but, as yet, no conclusive evidences have been presented tending to show their Hamitic descent.

The Iolofs occupy the delta of the Senegal and Gambia. They are a mild, hospitable and trust-worthy people, and very numerous, being not less than a million souls. Their complexion is dark, hair woolly, nose flat and lips protuberant. They are acquainted with some of the useful arts, especially manufacturing and dyeing cotton, though, in common with the rest of their race, shun work as much as possible, preferring rather to steal what they require than work for it.

The Veys, one of the tribes allied to the Mandingoes, have lately become distinguished above all others of their race by the invention of an alphabet, and are generally a highly developed family, having large and well formed heads, and possess an unusual degree of native genius.

Congo, or Lower Guinea, comprises several states, all inhabited by the same stock of people. The males are about the middle size; their features not strongly African, their color being a dark-brown. They have evidently some affinity to the Semitic family, but as to their origin nothing is known.

In Northern Guinea the inhabitants seem to be the lowest order of the Negro type; this being generally the case, though some of the tribes compare favorably with the Fellatahs and Iolofs. They live in strongly built houses or tents of circular form, and are, in some measure, engaged in agriculture. They have an immense population—supposed to number twelve millions.

The natives of the Gold and Slave coasts consist of several tribes who have attained to a much higher grade of civilization than those above described, dwelling in superior houses, of square form, two and even three stories high; go much better clad also, and have made considerable advance in the useful arts and agriculture.

The ethnographical divisions of these nations are in families, as follows: The Grebo, Avekwom, Ashanti, Efik and Yebu. The Timanis and Susus, kindred of the Mandingoes, who reside in the vicinity of Sierra Leone, may also be considered in these dominions.

All these several families, with their sub-divisions, are classed with the African race, though they present every shade of complexion, from the light mulatto to the dark-skinned Negro; in their physical aspects there are differences quite as apparent.

The Timanis and Susus are in a low condition—presenting the Negro type in a very degraded state, though not of the lowest order, as they pay some attention to agriculture and commerce.

The Krus group, and sub-divisions of the family, live on the coast from St. Andrew's to Cape Mesurado. They are represented as people of athletic bodies, vigorous constitutions, but degraded in morals and possessing all the characteristics of the Negro, though by no means of the lowest order of the race, and comparatively intelligent, noted for their open, frank bearing. They have an organized civil government, cultivate the ground and engage in commercial pursuits. Lands are held in common by all classes, and the rights of all protected by their system of laws. Slavery is not tolerated among them; and, to their great credit be it said, they have never engaged in the slave-trade. They have no annals, and of their origin nothing is known; but have been classed with the Mandingoes. Amongst them all shades of color are presented—from light-brown to the dark hue of the African.

The Fanti tribe belong to the Ashantis family. They are Negroes, and have suffered perhaps more than any other of the coast tribes from New England rum and American slave-traders. Being apt at learning, and of sprightly disposition, they have made rapid advancement in general civilization—a large portion of them having learned to read and write English. They are skilled in manufacturing cotton cloth, musical instruments, iron tools and gold ornaments, and seem to have native mechanical genius of superior order. Those of them who are educated make expert clerks and teachers, in which capacity many are employed by Europeans.

The Yebus and Efiks are only celebrated as slave-dealers. The former reside in the country watered by the Lagos; the latter not far distant from the Island of Fernando Po.

The Avekwoms dwell on the coast between St. Andrews and Dicks Cave—their principal settlement being at Cape Lahu.

The Eboes reside on the high lands near the mouth of the Niger, and are distinguished from other tribes along the coast by their complexion, which is much lighter than that of the Negroes. They seem to be a distinct tribe, having no relationship with the coast nations; but their language and general peculiarities would lead to the conclusion that they are of Semitic stock, though now ranked with the Negroes.

The Ashantis occupy an extensive country back of the Gold coast; are very numerous—supposed to be about 3,000,000 population. Except the Fellatahs they are the only natives of Western Africa who have had a history, but which only extends back to the beginning of the 18th century.

Their government is of military character of the most despotic kind possible, yet not so degrading as that of Dahomey, presently noticed. Their language is the most refined of the Guinea dialects; oratory is much cultivated by the natives, in which some of them excel; as also in music, for which they have a great taste. They have attained to considerable proficiency in the useful arts, especially in weaving, spinning, dyeing, in the manufacture of pottery, and works of metal. They are fond of war, in which they frequently indulge as pleasant past-time.

The men are well-made, though less muscular than their neighbors, the Fanties. They have dark skin, woolly hair, thick protruding lips, and, generally, flat nose and wide mouth. The females are generally handsome, especially those exempt from hardships, having fine figures and Grecian features; eyes brilliant, though set rather obliquely; are remarkably cleanly in their habits—wash themselves daily from head to foot, wearing always clean clothing. Their houses are constructed of stakes for walls, filled in with mud or gravel, the outside of which are plastered over with the same kind of mortar; the roofs consist of thatch of palm leaves; the doors of an entire piece of cottonwood, cut out of the trunk of the tree; the windows open, woodwork generally painted red, some of the wealthy class having their window-frames cased with gold.

The Ashantis' grand festivals are riots and debauchery upon a gigantic scale. On such occasions each individual is free from restraint to act as his passions may dictate. Neither theft, intrigue, nor assault, committed during the festivals, are punished by law. Both sexes seem to abandon themselves to the full desires of all their depraved passions.

On the death of an Ashantee of distinction a slave or two are immediately sacrificed at the door of his late residence, and others are immolated at the funeral. On such occasions it is usual also to sprinkle the grave of the deceased with the blood of a free man of respectability. This is done by calling several such to assist in placing the body in its final resting place in the ground, and whilst thus engaged one of the number is struck upon the back of the neck and killed, and his body thrown into the grave upon the coffin of the deceased, and buried with it.

The Dahomey kingdom is situated to the east of that of Ashantee. It is a barbaric despotism. The king has absolute power over his subjects. The highest noble is on the level of the meanest slave before the king; each must approach his majesty by crawling on his belly with his forehead in the dust. The king is all powerful. His august presence awes his subjects whose lives are in his hands. None are allowed to rise to a sitting posture in his presence, except women, and they must kiss the ground when they deliver or receive a message. It is high treason for any one to suppose that the king eats, drinks, sleeps or performs any of the functions of ordinary life.

The Dahomans are very superstitious — idol worshippers. They worship beasts of prey, and even serpents. But in the Fetich worship they seem to reverence the unknown, unseen God.

They are licentious, and give full scope to their passions. Polygamy is allowed without restraint: as in other parts of Africa, wives are purchased. All the first-born females of the kingdom belong to the king, who keeps a trained band of Amazons as a guard about his regal presence. His wives are numerous, and may be counted by scores.

The king's festivals, held in the beginning of harvest, and usually kept up about six weeks, are splendid institutions of murder. The king, on such occasions, steeps the groves of his ancestors with human blood.* The whole festival is one continued scene of horror. Thousands of victims are sacrificed every year by these superstitious natives to gratify their fanatical whims and depraved passions.

When the king of Dahomey dies, his wives exhibit the utmost grief. As if completely deranged, they destroy everything belonging to them, and then fall upon each other with fiendish fury, which is only stayed by order of the new sovereign, who stops the massacre when he finds sufficient widows have been put out of the way.

The Dahomans are a nation of warriors. The king always keeps a standing army, ready to march in defence of his kingdom, or to invade that of some other, as he may see proper. The name of the king produces the most powerful stimulating effect upon his troops. Though a tyrant, in every sense of the term, no people are more devoted to their sovereign than those of Dahomey. They are Negroes, and good representatives of the African race; are not only savages, but have made some advance in civilization, though not having kept pace with the advantages presented to them for improvement. They consist of several tribes brought under subjection to the more powerful families.

This has been considered the most cruel and savage government on the globe, which is owing to their bloody customs, and savage disposition of the bodies of the dead. Instead of burying the corpses of the victims, they are hung upon the walls and allowed to putrify. Human skulls are the favorite ornaments of the palaces and temples, and the king has his sleeping apartment paved with them.

The Damaras, a branch of the Kaffir family, wander over an extensive region in the western interior of Africa, between the seventeenth and twenty-fifth degrees of south latitude. They, about a hundred years ago, issued from the interior of the continent, and fought their way to the coast, and, by the aid of the Ovampas, have maintained their ground, but suffered severely

* Read's Savage Africa, p. 53.

in their wars with the Hottentots, who seem to desire their extirpation. They are a pastoral people, and live almost entirely upon their flocks and herds. The Damaras, in their general features and characteristics, are very similar to the nations of the interior described by Dr. Barth and Livingstone, and, like them, are divided into many tribes, and governed by chiefs, who are subject to others above them in authority. They have no definite idea of the Supreme Being, but practice circumcision, without any idea of the import of the ordinance.

They offer sacrifices of animals, and seem to reverence the spirits of their dead. They have no annals, nor any account of their origin, but entertain the strange belief that they originated from a tree.

The Ovampas, also a branch of the Kaffir family, residing to the north of the Damaras, are much more civilized than the latter. They are skillful cultivators of the ground, have well laid-out farms, and evince considerable proficiency in working metals. Their features are regular, hair black and crisped, and their complexion as dark as the Damaras.

Du Chaillu, who visited the Fan natives, on the Gamboon river, considers them as not belonging to the same family as the coast tribes; though of limited mental capacity, they display considerable ingenuity in making iron from the ore, and manufacturing weapons of war. They are most ravenous cannibals. Incredible as it may seem, the Fan nations buy and eat the bodies of their neighbors and kindred, and even relish the carcases of those who have died with sickness.* Where they hail from has not been ascertained, but they themselves say, from the northeast. Their complexion is dark brown, but they have the black, curly hair peculiar to the African. Though cannibals, the Fans are kind, hospitable and courteous; and none of the natives of Africa treated Du Chaillu with greater kindness than the Fans.†

The recent explorations of Livingstone, Barth and others have discovered many new nations and tribes of people dwelling in the interior of Africa, some of whom are Negroes, and others of the Kaffir group, the latter, though of dark skin, having none of

* Adventures in Equatorial Africa—P. B. Du Chaillu, p. 118.
† Du Chaillu, p. 129.

the Negro features, but a strong resemblance of Europeans, as
have the Kaffir tribes generally, except their complexion, which
varies from almost jet black to light brown, though Livingstone
found some of this family whose skin under their garments was
as fair as his own.   He particularly describes the Makololo tribe,
a branch of the Kaffir group, belonging to the Bechuanos family, as having a light yellow complexion.

Livingstone describes the Matiamoo empire, the capital of
which is situated about eight degrees twenty minutes south latitude, and twenty-two degrees thirty-two minutes east longitude,
as extending south to the thirteenth degree of latitude, and
stretching westward to the Loange, and northward to the upper
branches of the Liambia.   The people inhabiting this vast district, he says, "are full-blooded Negroes," the great mass of
whom being of the Balonda family.   They cultivate the soil,
breed flocks and herds, and are somewhat skilled in the mechanical arts.   The government of the Matiamoo is a mild but absolute despotism.

In alliance with the Matiamoos are several tribes dwelling
between Angola and Londa, among whom are the Kasabi, Bas-
chinge and Kasan.

North of Tete, the northwestern boundary of the Portuguese
dominions, are a number of black tribes, known as the Maravi
and Babisa; and west of them, on the right bank of the Zam-
bezi river, are located the Bambiri.   South of this river are several tribes, among whom are the Sofala, Juhamane and Quili-
mane, all of whom are Kaffirs.

The Wanika peoples, dwelling between the coast and the
lakes, are of Semitic origin, but much degenerated, and to some
extent having lost their identity by mingling with the black
race.   They are of chocolate color, having pyramidal heads, low
in front, face wide and flat, the "forehead broad and prominent,
and the nose and chin of the low Negro type."   They practice
circumcision, without understanding its import, having really no
religious belief, yet sacrifice upon the graves of their ancestors
from a religious instinct.   They cultivate the ground, but have
no regularly established government.

The Sumali nations dwell along the east coast of the continent, from Juba river to the Gulf of Aden.   They are consid-

ered as belonging to the Galla family,* but present a great variety of complexions, from olive to black; also, marked differences are observable in their physique, some resembling Arabs, and others the Negroes.

The Wakamba reside in Zanguebar. They are a powerful people, not in numbers, as they do not exceed over 70,000 souls, but in their physical and mental qualities. "Their lips are somewhat large, eyes full, chin pointed, teeth white, beard scanty, and the hair either shaved or curled with a wire." They are of dark complexion, but belong to the Kaffir family.

The Suhaili nations occupy the coast of Zanguebar. Though all the coast nations have to a greater or less extent become semi-civilized, yet the Suhaili are less advanced than the Sumali; the latter are addicted to commerce and navigation, though to a great extent pastoral in their habits. The Suhaili are virtually Kaffirs, but have woolly hair, and jet-black complexion; whilst the Sumali have flowing, soft hair, reaching over their shoulders, regular features, of Caucasian mould, and olive complexion.

Westward of the coast nations dwell the M'kuafi, a savage people, who have not yet so far advanced above their native barbarism as to bury or properly care for their dead, but leave them to be devoured by wild beasts.

The Siboo, who inhabit the eastern part of the Great Desert, are noted for their handsome features, which are purely European, though their complexion is black. They are not savages, having made some little progress in the useful arts. Their villages consist of meanly constructed houses. Bilma, their capital, is a disgrace to civilization, being mainly rude cottages constructed of mud.

The Haussa, a black nation, of Semitic origin, occupy the interior of Africa, southwest of Lake Tchad, and are a sprightly people, with pleasing and regular features, and graceful forms. They have a prominent nose, and expressive black eyes.

Until the Mohammedan invasion of the Fellatah empire, the Haussa held sway over an extensive district. Since that time they have been scattered throughout the regions of their former dominions.

* Prichard's Natural History of Man, Vol. II.

The Tuaricks occupy a vast region of the Great Desert west of Fezzan along the route of Kano and Rassina. They are a race of warriors, at least they have been so considered in times past, and by their fearless, daring and bold enterprise spread terror throughout half of the continent, though their gentle character and mild disposition does not entitle them to be considered barbarous or savage. They are by no means savages, except the dealing in slaves be considered such, yet pay no attention to the cultivation of the ground; subsisting solely by pasturage, commerce and plunder, holding in contempt those living in houses, and farming. They have written characters said to be very ancient, of which they make little use except to inscribe them upon the rocks along their trails in the desert.

Their complexion is not dark, except when exposed to the sun, and they have no negro features. The chief Tuarick tribes are the Ghraat, Tagama, and Rolluvi. They possess the kingdom of Asben, the capital of which, Agadez, even, it is said, rivalled Tripoli as a commercial emporium. The Tuaricks are called the "Berbers of the Desert." They dwell in communities and in permanently established houses. The Tuaricks are virtually Caucasians.

The ruling family of Bornu, though called Berbers, have amongst them peoples possessing the negro features and the general characteristics of the African race. The Kanuri, especially with their black skin, thick pouched lips, broad face, flat nose, wide nostrils and woolly hair, fully represent the Negro type; and not alone in their physical aspect, this mode of life and general bearing is in unison with that of the degraded African, though they are by no means of the lowest order of this type. They are partially civilized, professing the Mohammedan religious faith without understanding its import, or observing its injunctions.

The people of the kingdom of Fezzan are quite black. Their cheek-bones are high, face fleshy and nose somewhat prominent, eyes small, mouth wide, and for the most part the hair woolly. Their features differ from the genuine African type, though they are called negroes.

The natives of the kingdom of Timbuctoo, originally were Negroes, but now the population consists of Negroes and Moors and their offspring; but the latter and the Moors constitute but a small proportion of the population. The natives are a stout healthy people. Their females are said to be quite handsome. They have no temples or churches, nor any religious ceremonies; and, though emerged from the savage state, sustain a very low order of civilization. Their commerce consists principally of slaves.

The natives of the African islands do not seem to belong to the same stock as those of the continent. Those of Fernando Po are represented by Lander to be the filthiest people in the world; as stout, athletic and well-made; as having long, straight hair and a complexion of copper-color.

Mr. Read speaks of them as being savages of low order, living in rude huts, and literally opposed to civilization.* They are not the original people of the island. The original inhabitants doubtless were of the same origin as the Ompizee of Madagascar and the Guanches of the Canaries. Their general appearance and characteristics present them as of Caucasian origin, and as Indians, kindred of those found inhabiting the East and West India islands, when they first became known to Europeans. But it is now claimed that the present natives are the same type as the mountaineers of the neighboring part of the continent.

Madagascar was originally peopled by the Ompizee, a family having a brown or dirty yellow complexion. The Ovahs, who have established their sway over the greater portion of the island, are distinguished over the other natives by their light olive complexion and absence of the negro features. They are well-made, but rather under middle size.

The natives of Formosa are of the same family, and described as "Red Men." They are a large, portly people of copper-color complexion, much resembling the American Indians. †

The Sakalavas, residing on the west coast of Madagascar, are quite black, with thick lips and crisped woolly hair. They are tall, strong and vigorous. Though inferior to the Ovahs, in general, in many noble qualities they are their superiors. These two nations present the extremes of the fair and black races of the island.

* Savage Africa, p. 59.
† Indigenous Races of the Earth, p. 21.
22

The Betsileo tribe have long hair, thick lips, and are of a light copper-color. The Antaymur of like complexion claim to be of Arabian origin. Some families of this group call themselves the children of Amina. Marco Polo, the first European who visited this island, (in the 13th century,) found it occupied by Saracens, who, under four sheiks, ruled the whole country.

Though there is a large preponderance of Caucasian, Mongolian and Malay blood presented by the present Madecasses, the African type is also fully represented. This race at a very remote period settled upon the island, and for a time were dominant people on its west coast, where their descendants still retain jurisdiction.

PAPUAN.

The oriental Negroes consist of several leading families, among which are the Papuans, Australians, Semangas, and the Negritos.

Though they have been designated under these general names in various localities where they are found to exist, they may properly be called Negrillos. It is difficult to classify them as one family, their peculiarities and physical aspect being so dissimilar. One portion of them have been, by some ethnologists, considered a distinct race of blacks not possessing all the negro characteristics; but it is not probable they are a distinct type of mankind. They are doubtless cognate Africans, in whom the Negro, Malay, Mongolian and Caucasian blood is communicated: the Negro generally predominating.

The Papuans, or Melanesians, are considered the most demented and lowest of the human races. Though human, they are in some respects not many degrees in advance above the

NORTH AUSTRALIAN.

brutes. They have no history or tradition. Some of the tribes, such as the Andamans, go naked without shame, and wives are held in common. They have no idea of the Deity, or a future state. They are diminutive in stature, and make a nearer approach to the Chimpanzee than any other branch of the human family.

The Papuans proper have black, twisted, frizzled hair; in texture very coarse and bushy. They are a robust family, of dark complexion, having a thick, hard skin, the chief distinguishing feature showing them to be a different people from the Negroes proper. The natives of the Feejee Islands are good representatives of this group, and doubtless the offspring of Negroes and Malays. They are found inhabiting New Guinea, New Caledonia and other islands of the Pacific, as well as Borneo, Malacca and Philippines.

The Black Australians and natives of Van Dieman's Land, are classed with the lowest and most degraded of mankind. Their minds, however, are by no means deficient, but they only seem to exercise their perceptive faculties, which are even stronger than Caucasians. They are not uniform in physical conformation, but in general resemble the Africans. Their foreheads are narrow, lips thick, mouth large, nose depressed and wide at the base; thick beards, and long fine hair resembling the wavy hair of Europeans.*

The Negrillo family, according to Pickering, compared with the Negro, have a red rather than black complexion, and diminutive in stature compared with the Papuan. Their hair is woolly, more so than the Papuan, but less thick than the Negroes, presenting, however, the same general appearance; and having thick pouched lips, retreating forehead, and the lower part of the face very prominent, eyes generally small and deeply sunk, limbs slender with the calf of the leg high. They occupy the New Georgia Islands, New Guinea, Luzon, Sooloo, Aramanga, Sumatra, and Malacca.

The Pelew, Ladrone, Banabe, and other islands in their vicinity are occupied by natives having a reddish-brown complexion, and black curled hair. They resemble the Malays in some respects, but have a rough skin and prominent features. The district occupied by this family is called Microwsia, and some authors have considered the native Microwsians as a distinct type; but

* The Races of the Old World, p. 221.

they are not any more so than the other oriental Negroes. They are ingenious in the arts, and seem to be the vestiges of a more refined civilization, which is indicated by architectural ruins found upon some of their islands, their knowledge of navigation, and the elementary principles of civil government. Their origin may be referred to India, where similar peoples are found, though dissimilar in leading characteristics. They, as well as the native islanders, have undergone very marked changes by amalgamation since these islands were torn from the continent —as they evidently were in very remote ages a part of Asia, as was also the East Indies and Australia.

As a general rule the Microwsians are, in point of intellectual endowments, superior to the Melawsians, which results from a closer relationship with the Caucasian type than the latter.

The oriental Negroes are doubtless the remnants or fragments of an extensive family inhabiting the East Indies, Polynesia, Australia, and the Islands of the Northern Pacific, before the advent of the Malays in these regions. This branch of the Negro type was also earlier upon the continent than the Malays; indeed the Negro seems to have existed here coeval with the Caucasian and Mongolian, and from whence they and the several varieties of mankind seem to have issued.

It would be an endless undertaking to attempt to classify the families and nations of mankind of mixed origin, or those having Negro affinities. As remarked in another place, all are not of Negro origin who have a sallow or dark skin. In some instances where Negro blood exists, the skin may be fair, the hair crisped, and jaws projecting; whilst in other cases the Negro peculiarities are only presented in the shape of the skull, face, and general appearance. The Gypsies and Txchingones have some Negro peculiarities, though not sufficient to be classed with even the Microwsians. They are doubtless connected with the Laubes of Africa.

The Guanches, who occupied the Canaries and Fernando Po, were partially a civilized people when they first became known to the people of the continent. The Canary Islands were first peopled by the Phœnicians; and owing to the salubrity of this climate and beautiful scenery, were called by the ancients the "Isles of the Blessed," and "Elysian Fields." The Guanches

have been considered a branch of the Tuarick family.   The first
account of these islands, of reliable character, we gather from the
writing of the younger Pliny, who gives an account of their discovery by Juba, king of Mauritania, a profound historian and
celebrated navigator.   The Guanches were a tawny, black-eyed,
flat-nosed people, believing in a Supreme Being, a future state,
and an evil genius; they fattened their girls for marriage, with
the belief that such were the most fruitful.   When they died the
priests dried their bodies in the sun and embalmed them;* the
embalmed subjects were sewed up in goat-skins and placed in coffins consisting of one piece of wood.   These mummies seem to be
very ancient and fall to pieces when taken out of their goat-skin
coverings.

The Guanches resemble the Carribbes in several particulars,
though possessing more of the Caucasian blood than the latter;†
they were extirpated by the Spaniards in the sixteenth century.

The Berbers, a sallow-skinned people of Semitic origin, occupy
the Atlas mountain districts; they were the original people of
Barbary, and seem to have taken shelter in the strongholds from
which no power has been capable of dislodging them; they are
a distinct family from the Arabs, and, unlike the latter, are wed-
ded to the soil which they cultivate, and dwell in cities and villages.   Though their dominions are within the boundaries of the
Moorish empire, and other kingdoms into which they extend,‡
they do not submit themselves the willing subjects of any foreign
power; their only homage consisting of an uncertain, meagre
tribute; they have a republican form of government; and by
well-regulated rules make and unmake their own rulers (sheiks)
without interference by any other power; they occupied the
country before the Phœnicians colonized it, and survived all the
ravages of the Romans, Vandals, and Arabs; and the French,
even with all their skill and bravery, proved unequal to the task
of subduing them.   Though pressed by the Arabs with every

---

* Read's Savage Africa, p. 20.

† The Vegneris of the West Indies, who were partially civilized, were of the
same stock as the Guanches, though of fairer complexion.—Indigenous Races
of the Earth, p. 516.

‡ Within their dominions, at the ancient city of Lixas, south of the Straits of
Gibraltar, was the residence of Antæos, where he had the combat with Her-
cules; and also were located here the Gardens of Hesperides.—Vol. I., Pliny,
Natural History, p. 375.—Grecian and Roman Mythology, by Dwight, p. 324.

means within their power, they still remain masters of the desert and mountain districts, holding indeed a more extensive territory than is occupied by any other nation of Africa.

In ancient history the Berbers were called Libyans,* but the name by which they are generally known in modern history is Tawarek. Aside from the general title they are known as Shuluh in Northern Morocco, and in Algeria and Tunis as Kabyls. The Shuluh are a lively, intelligent people of light complexion ; the latter claim to be the descendants of the ancient Vandals ; they have long, fair hair and blonde complexion. † The Imghod tribe of this family are almost as black as the Negro, but having none other of his features ; the pure Berber has no Negro blood, and such look upon the offspring of Berbers and Negroes with contempt. The Tawareks are divided into numerous tribes varying in color from blonde to black ; some of them, such as the Kelowi, possessing other Negro features besides complexion.

Those of the Berbers considered of Semitic origin are supposed to be descendants of the Canaanites expelled from the Holy Land by Joshua ; this, however, is only surmise, there being no authentic record of the fact.

There is no portion of the globe where the human race is presented with more complexity than in Northern Africa, including the States of Barbary, except, perhaps, that of India. Almost every variety of man is here represented, as well in his savage as civilized condition. ‡

We have thus given all the leading families of the African race, and also those of this order of mankind ; and though it is manifest that the Negro is the lowest order of the human race, it by no means follows that the African is not susceptible of improvement. The Negroes are, as a general rule, good imitators, and some nations have attained to considerable eminence in the

* The ancient Libyans possessed all Northern Africa from Egypt to the Straits of Gibraltar, and southward as far as the country was known to the Greeks and Romans. They were the only people occupying the country when the Phœnicians first colonized the coast districts. The Berbers, Shilhas, and Kabyles are their decendants.—Natural History of Man, Vol. I., p. 267.

† One family of Kabyls, in Algiers, have not only a fair and ruddy complexion, but hair of deep yellow.—Indigenous Races of the Earth, p. 543.

‡ Strabo says, "It was said that the Mauritamans were Indians who accompanied Hercules hither.—Strabo, Vol. III., p. 280.

arts and general civilization by virtue of their own genius and forecast; but in no instance have they, in these respects, reached the standard of the other races, or even made a respectable approximation thereto. We speak this of the Africans in general without intending to detract aught from those nations who have attained higher in the work of civilization.

CHAPTER XVII.

THE SOCIAL NATURE OF MAN.

THE social nature of mankind is, at best, to a great degree, based upon selfishness, as it is questionable whether any one will act, in anything, without some purely selfish motive. Man is a philosopher—always considering what will best advance his own interest. All act upon this principle—savage and civilized. The savage regards the state of nature the best condition in life for individual happiness, and is, to all appearances, as happy in his barbarism as the most enlightened citizen of the world.

Happiness is but a mere matter of opinion—personal to every human being, and something only to be determined by themselves. The question of morals and social order, in this view of the subject, is not considered.

The abstract question of natural right for man to do as he may see proper is not controlled by any system of morals or political economy; but each individual, in this regard, is governed by his own natural inclination, for good or evil. Every person, in the abstract, by the law of nature, has the undoubted right to do as he pleases—not, however, interfering with the rights of others. This was the condition before mankind assumed any political supremacy. Such a state of things is considered hardly

(345)

possible; yet it is well known that the savages do so live, and have enjoyed these natural rights from their earliest existence—doing so from choice, as by this method they can have freedom better than in any other condition. It is not strange that such a government cannot exist where the strong and feeble dwell together. It is doubtless only on the principle of equity that these things are tolerated. The moment natural right is violated the laws of society must be resorted to, in order to enforce redress of grievances, as the weak cannot right the wrongs of the strong by physical force.

It would seem to be only in consequence of the depravity of the human heart that government is resorted to at all. If all were disposed to do right, laws would be useless and government a work of supererogation. The natural inclination to protect the feeble against the strong induced organization of civil government as the only means of protection against the vicious.

The affinity between the races and families of man constitutes the great binding links by which communities, families and nations keep up social order and political intercourse. When this does not exist there cannot be social order, or willing subjection to political power. It is a family tie not confined to the mere circle of consanguinity, but ramifies amid families, communities, nations and kingdoms. It is not only the basis of social order, but the momentum of international law. Without affinity there would be no harmony in society; it will not subsist where any discordant element exists in the family or government. Every community will purge itself of excrescence, where the majority constitute the ruling power; and, where they are not, the discordant element will ever be active and vigilant.

The history of nations has taught that this is the case. Egypt, not only in the case of the Hebrews, but also of the Copts and Mamelukes, presents this sad picture. Ireland, Poland and Hungary are all striking examples of the want of affinity. And such has been the condition of things also between the white and black races ever since they first came in contact with each other.

Nations and races are graded according to the degrees of intellectual endowments—the greater the development of mind, the more capable they are to enjoy political freedom. Though freedom is a natural right, flowing to every individual, it requires intellect to enjoy it properly and consistent with the rights of others. The greater the development of thought, the higher will man rise in the scale of being. Without intelligence no man can enjoy real happiness, or impart it to others.

If government is the creature of intellect, as it doubtless is, it

should be under the control of the superior in point of mental endowments, otherwise it would tend to degradation and discord.

Man, whatever may be his intellectual attainments, has no right to do wrong—to inflict injury upon others; nor has the less intellectual individual any such right, nor the right to obtrude himself upon those seeking to advance the interest and welfare of the whole community.

Political and social rights, in well regulated governments, are so intimately interwoven with each other as to be inseparable. Political rights do not alone pertain to individuals, but also to nations and governments; the political right of a nation, in one sense, is peculiar to itself, the same as the personal rights of individuals; but yet there is connected with it, a paramount right of existence based upon principles consistent with the rules of civilization and the law of nations. Every nation and government has the right to regulate its own internal police, and make such rules for the government of the people as may be deemed proper. The people may change the form of their government, at will; but only when the rights of the people are to be enhanced or better secured, is a change considered advisable.

In governments of democratic form, no change can be made without the consent of the sovereign people; to do otherwise, would be a violation of the social compact, and subversion of the fundamental laws of the nation. All power being vested in the people, in such governments, they are to be first consulted before any change in the organic law is effected, or any new elements engrafted upon their political institutions. Might gives right only in a mental point of view; yet the right of conquest is recognized in international law; but it is hardly tolerable as a part of our system of national policy.

The question of right, by which one nation assumes to hold another in subjection against the will of the latter, always has been of doubtful probability, to say the least. Such assumption is a relic of barbarism; yet it is adhered to by all the nations of the old world, savage and civilized; and under the same plea, that "might gives right," this disposition is being also manifested to an alarming extent upon this continent. It seems not to be confined alone to the oppression by the superior of the inferior races, but also extends to the families of the dominant races, in which instances the rights of the weak and feeble have been disregarded, and rules and regulations for their government imposed upon them, in the name of liberty, against their consent.

The superior races, from the earliest ages, seem to have held the weaker and inferior in subjection—at first as a question of policy, with the view that subjection would tend to their advantage. By degrees the strong encroached upon the weak and feeble nations, until they, from captives taken in war, became subjects of merchandise and abject slaves.* It seems to have been looked upon as an acknowledged right, guaranteed to the victors by common consent, to enslave and make merchandise of their captives. The system was early adopted by the Israelites, and extensively indulged in by the Jews, under divine favor, as will be shown in another place. The term slave, however, was not then applied to those in bondage; "servant" expressed their degraded condition quite as well. In Judea the slaves were generally of the nations denominated "the heathen," and all

---

* There are effigies of six nations of antiquity, showing the Negro to have been enslaved by the superior race.—Cobb on Slavery, p. 135. Indigenous Races of the Earth, p. 390.

were considered such who were not of Israel. Among the Romans slaves consisted of barbarian captives taken in war; but their capture was not confined to honorable war alone. The increasing demand made unjust war the pretext for capture, which finally eventuated in the slave-trade, not alone of the inferior races, but even Jews and Gentiles became subjects of traffic. During the Jewish war above 100,000 prisoners were taken, who, according to S. Jerome, were sold as slaves, in the time of of Hadrian, as cheap as horses.*

Slaves in the Roman Empire were far more numerous than Roman citizens, or free inhabitants; and even in the days of the Emperor Claudius the whole population of the Roman Empire did not exceed twenty millions of souls, including all provincials, of which number only about seven thousand were Roman citizens.

At a later period, when civil liberty began to be better understood by the masses, slavery was measurably resisted, and, indeed, virtually abolished so far as concerned prisoners of war and conquest; but, as regards the African Negroes, they were less fortunate. From time immemorial they have been subjects of an intolerable vassalage.

The superior races, looking upon the abject condition of the Negro as being the true index of his character, and believing him totally incapable of self-government, came to his rescue—relieved his wants and made him a slave. Until recently, slavery, in the abstract, was not looked upon as sinful—only the abuse of it was considered bad in morals, and wrong upon principles of political economy. Upon this latter question, and also the broad principles of morals, the master justified his system of slavery, and, for centuries, seemed to convince the world at large that slavery was right and justifiable under the strictest rules of morals and political economy.† In justifying the system, the Sacred Scriptures were resorted to with apparent success. In that exhaustless fountain of morals the master seems to be justified in his system of bondage;‡ the Sacred Writings, how-

---

* Gibbon's Rome, Vol. I., p. 47. *Note.*

† "And consequently, that Negro slavery, as it existed in the United States, is not contrary to the law of nature."—Cobb on Slavery, p. 51.

‡ Deuteronomy xv. 12 15.

ever do not treat of slavery in the abstract sense of the term—the word "slave" only appearing in two instances in the English Bible—but of "servants," which has the same meaning in the Hebrew and Greek originals, as also "bond-men" and "bond-maidens." The distinction between bond and hired servants was kept up in the days of Hebrew slavery the same as at the present day; slavery was the same then as is now imposed upon the Negro—a servitude for life, descending upon the offspring, according to the Bible.*

This system of slavery seems to have existed in all ages, as well before as after the advent of the Saviour, who, it appears, did not in the least interfere with or condemn the system, nor did His apostles rebuke it, or denounce the slave-master. Paul, on the contrary, rather counselled and advised the runaway slave to return, and submit himself, to his master.

Slavery was not considered sinful, in the abstract, by the ancients, and if so in any sense, it was in its abuse. Abraham did not consider it sinful, or he would not have kept three hundred and eighteen bond-servants trained in his house.†

The case of his servant-girl Hagar shows the system was not then considered sinful, but recognized by the Deity himself. Hagar, having escaped from her master, was directed by the angel that appeared before her, to return and submit herself to her mistress Sarah.‡ The Ten Commandments even recognize a system of servitude. The declaration there is: "Thou shalt not covet his man-servant nor his maid-servant."

The Hebrews bought and sold servants of their own kindred, and of the heathen as well; but the latter were less favored than the former: "If thou buy an Hebrew servant, six years he shall serve; and in the seventh he shall go out free for nothing. If he came in by himself, he shall go out by himself; if he were married, then his wife shall go out with him. If his master have given him a wife, and she have borne him sons or daughters, the wife and her children shall be her master's, and he shall go out by himself." §

Here is presented a positive separation of the parent and child, and husband and wife, by the Hebrew system of slavery,

* Leviticus xxv. 45–47.   † Genesis xiv. 14; xvii. 12.
‡ Genesis xvi. 9.   § Exodus xxi. 1, 2, 3, 4, and 5.

not only tolerated, but, as would seem, established, by the direction of Jehovah. The only alternative left for the husband in such case, if he did not wish to be separated from his wife and children, was to become a slave for life.* There was a year of jubilee for Hebrew slaves, but none for the heathen; they were to continue slaves for ever.

The right of the master to chastise the servant was recognized by the Hebrew system of slavery; but, in doing so, if he should smite the slave so that he should die, the master should not be punished, for he was his money.†

The perpetual servitude of the Levitical law was based upon the idea of superior and inferior races. The heathen were considered inferior to the Hebrews; hence were made the subjects of perpetual bondage.

The equality of races was not recognized by the Deity, if the Levitical law, and the above Scripture texts, may be considered a reflex of the Divine mind.

Aside from these Bible truths, slavery has been considered intolerable under our free system of government, by virtue of the Declaration of Rights of 1776, which declares all men capable of self-government, and endowed with certain inalienable rights. This sweeping enunciation has perplexed the minds of many of the leading politicians, who seem to think that its promulgation guaranteed freedom, at least to all the slaves of the United States. They forget, however, the fact that the Federal Constitution, and not the Declaration, is the supreme law on the subject of political rights. That instrument, based, as it was, upon the principles of the Declaration, recognized the existence of slavery, as tolerated in the Colonies, before the Revolution. The great minds that guided the revolutionary contest, and framed our system of government, should be presumed to have known as much about the rights of man, and the character of the institutions they were establishing, as any subsequent legislator, however wise he may presume to be.

Among the great men of that age, who engaged in founding our national system, was George Washington, president of the Convention that formed the Federal Constitution. He held slaves before and after it was adopted; and it is a fact worthy

* Leviticus xxv. 10, 40, 46, and 55.   † Exodus xxi. 20 and 21.

of note, that the Declaration did not free a single slave, though, by its broad and liberal terms, all mankind were entitled to liberty, as well the serfs of Russia, the oppressed Irish, and enslaved Poles, as the African Negro slaves of the United States. The Declaration had reference only to the white people of the American Colonies; they alone had struck for political freedom, and, to justify themselves in the eyes of the world, promulged the principles upon which their rights as free white men—as an independent nation—were based.

The idea that all men were created (born) free and equal must also be limited to the white people of the Colonies, who were then establishing a free government for themselves. All men are not, in point of fact, born equal. The serf is not equal with the master, and the slave is the property of his master—not born to freedom, but slavery.

THOMAS JEFFERSON.

Mr. Jefferson, when he penned the Declaration of Independence, containing the expression that " all men are created equal," did not intend to include the Negro slaves, as all his subsequent conduct proves. He was then a slaveholder, and such continued to be until the close of his life. He administered the Federal Government, under the Federal Constitution, for eight years, with slavery existing the same as when he drafted the Declaration.

The Negroes of the United States were not, therefore, born equal with the white population of the country, politically or mentally, though, as a race, having had equal, if not superior advantages over them. They have lived within reach of the refined civilization of the Egyptians and other enlightened nations of Asia and Africa for over four thousand years, yet are, to a great extent, barbarians. They, as a general rule, neither receive nor dispense civilization, though occupying the finest portions of the globe. Several tribes have made some progress in the arts and general civilization, but the great mass are but little, if at all, advanced above their native savage state. Whatever of progress they have made in the arts and civilization, is to be attributed, in the main, to the other races. Being good imitators, they can be readily taught the arts of civilized life; yet, left to themselves, they soon relapse into their native barbarism.

The researches of Livingstone, Richardson, Barth, Moffat, and others, in Africa, it was hoped, would present the Negro race in a more favorable light, and discover, in the interior, civilized and refined African nations. But the travels of these distinguished individuals have brought no new tidings in this behalf. They found some very friendly and inoffensive natives, cultivators of the ground, workers in metals, but without refinement, and possessing no polite literature or annals.

It would seem that the Deity has wisely ordered that the several races shall fill their proper destiny. For some cause, unknown to the other races, the African has been placed the lowest in the scale of being, physically, mentally, and morally. To this general rule there are exceptions; though in no instance have any of this type been found rising to the exalted standard of the Caucasian in any of these qualities. Some have far excelled the generality of their race, but even they have not reached the Caucasian standard, mentally or morally.

The Negro is not to blame for being less intellectual than the European. He did not create himself, but was brought into existence by the Great Jehovah, for his own wise purpose, and to fill the sphere allotted to him.

Attempts have been made tending to show that the Negro is affiliated with the monkey tribes, to which doctrine we do not subscribe. He is human—as much so as any of the other races, though differing in many particulars from them, especially from the Caucasian, other than in complexion. Marked differences exist, between these two types, in physical conformation. The Negro is not so tall as the white man; his bones are more heavy and clumsy; they are also whiter, from the greater abundance of calcareous salt contained in their composition; their ankle is

23

shorter, the foot flatter, and the heel is long and protruding lat-
erally.   The neck is strong, but the shoulders, arms and legs are
all weak in proportion; the humerus and femur are shorter;
the face is flatter; the skull thicker, the posterior portion being
generally more largely developed, the passions predominating
over the mental faculties.   Mentally, the Negro is inferior to
the white man; and as regards morals, they may be said to be
totally deficient in their primitive state.   This seems to be their
natural condition when not under restraint.*

Van Amringe thus describes this type:

"Even after having lived centuries with the white people,
from whom they have received every possible instruction, they
are very far from having a virtue for which they are distinguished.   The Negro is indolent, careless, sensual, tyrannical,
predatory, sullen, boisterous and jovial.   It has been a favorite
theory with some visionary philanthropists that intermarriage
of the different species would be highly favorable to the race;
but we have never heard of any of them who were willing to
commence the practice in their own families.

"There is certainly no method that could possibly be devised,
which would as certainly and expeditiously degrade the whole
human family as amalgamation.   If there is any hope for the
improvement of the condition of the dark races, the history of
mankind shows it can only be found in the preservation of the
white species.   This is the only species endowed with any power
to drag the cumbrous dark races out of the slough in which they
have been wallowing for ages."

As a race, the African has made but little progress in intellectual pursuits, from the earliest historic period, and seems incapable, by his own exertions, to rise to eminence.   His position in nature is fixed by the Creator, who, in the beginning,
placed him upon the globe to fill his designed destiny.   He is
unchangeable, being the same character of creature he was at
his origin.

The effort to elevate the Negro type, by amalgamation with
higher orders of mankind, will, in the end, prove destructive to
both races.   This has ever been the result where the superior
and inferior orders of beings have amalgamated.   The same law

* Lyell's Antiquity of Man, pp. 90, 91.

does not apply in cases of the same species, but seems to be universal in cases of distinct types.

The offspring of the Anglo-Saxon and Negro, though prolific for a time, will run out when kept apart from the vital or paramount stock, the primitive type.*

The history of the races fully attests this fact, in the new as well as in the old world. The best test, perhaps, is to be found in the West Indies, where the black and white races, and native Indians, have been amalgamating for several centuries.

The issue of the white and black parent is called a mulatto; that of a black and mulatto, a sambo; a black and sambo, a mungroo; the issue of a black and the mungroo is completely black. At this point, the Negro type, even, is degraded. The issue of the white and mulatto is a quadroon; and of the latter and a white parent, a mestie; and a mestie and white produce a complete white, but imperfect in their physical constitution, with strong traces of the Negro deformities and propensities.

None of the hybrid stock has proved to be an improvement upon the primitive types.* The Ethiopian is not equal to the Caucasian parent; nor is the Hottentot, Bushman or Kaffir an improvement of the Semitic blood. And the Negroes suffer when compared with the Papuan family, as it is well known that some of the tribes of this family (Negrillo group), are the lowest order of mankind—far below the most degraded tribe of native Africans. They are not a new race, but degraded, deformed and demoralized by amalgamation.

There is no hybrid nation extant of any distinction, if, indeed, any at all in existence, that can be called such. Hybridity is confined to individuals, and does not extend to nations. Hybrids are not cognates; the latter are those springing from the same species; the former being the product of congress between different species. They are not, as a general rule, prolific; but this rule is not so universal in the case of mankind as the lower animals.

Such a propagation as hybrids is against nature; as nature marches steadily on to perfection. It would be vain to suppose

---

* Types of Mankind, p. 398.

† The crosses in Java, between the Malays and Dutch, do not produce beyond the third generation.—Plurality of Races, by Pouchet, p. 97.

that the Caucasian type would be improved by amalgamating with the Negro. The product of such union (Mulattoes) are not even an improvement upon the Negro stock, but feeble mongrels destined to become extinct in the course of a few generations. In such case, if the typical stock be cut off, the race soon becomes extinct. Natural selection forbids such debasement of the superior types of mankind.*

The hybrids of Mexico and Central America are a feeble people; in no respect rising to the standard of even the Negro parent. The same may be said of those of the West Indies.

There are instances where the crossing of the black and white races seems to improve the former. It is only temporary, however, as, in course of two or three generations, there is a relapse —the white blood disappearing, and the Negro again predominating, the natural law of hybridity having disposed of the unnatural product—the typical blood not being susceptible of successful transmission by hybrids. If the typical stock is kept up, the race will be preserved. This is manifest from the fact that no race has yet become extinct.†

Comparative anatomy fully illustrates that all the races zoologically considered, are governed by the same universal laws in regard to their preservation, and deterioration by amalgamation, and also their affinities and peculiarities of physical structure.

The anatomist finds no trouble in determining the affinity between the Jew and the Celt, the Mongolian and Iberian, the Negro and Papuan, and the Polynesian and Californian Indian. The most common observer will be ready to say that there is a close relationship existing between these several families in the above order. Each presents the primitive type unmistakably, though in some instances, as in the latter, materially modified; but still, by the above tests, each can be traced back to its original source. No case has existed where one type has been merged in another. There may be marked and minute changes in the appearance of a race, but none such as to make it a new order of mankind.

The difficulty attending the early investigation of this subject is now obviated by the new light shed abroad by the monuments of Egypt, Assyria, Greece, Rome and America, where the

* The Origin of Species.—Darwin, p. 79.   † Antiquities of Man—Lyell, p. 456

types are fully represented; especially in Egypt, executed at a
period antedating the age of Moses over two thousand years.
With them also appear represented domestic animals and birds,
such as oxen, bulls, cows, donkeys, sheep, goats, gazelles, geese,
cranes and ducks, thus proving that man had domesticated these
animals 5,300 years ago. The Assyrian monuments prove that
even the camel and elephant were domesticated 1300 years B. C.
The perfection of the Egyptian paintings and sculpture of the
fourth dynasty, which dates 3400 years B. C., not only proves the
permanency of the types of mankind, but leaves it more than
probable that Egypt was then an ancient empire; as it is reasonable to suppose they were a polished, civilized nation, prior to
the founding of their monuments.

There was no doubt a long gloom of ages before man taught
himself the art of transcribing his thoughts upon stone or parchment, or of representing himself or neighbors upon canvas.
Fortunately for our race, the Egyptians did so transcribe and represent the types of mankind then known to them, and which
ethnology shows to be the same races extant. The distinctive
conformation of the several races, and the general anatomical
structure of each of the four types the Egyptians have represented, show most clearly that no radical change has taken place
in either of them since they were thus represented.

The anatomy of the races proves the Negro brain to be less
than the Caucasian's. Its greatest development does not exceed
that of the European in his imperfectly developed state before
he arrives at maturity. Professor Agassiz says the brain of the
native African is in strong resemblance to that of the ourang-
outang. His head is flat on the crown, and his forehead low and
slanting; these marks are universal, but they, like the other
races, differ in families.

The Egyptian mummies are as living witnesses of the types of
mankind. They constitute the actual types in such condition as
to present the form and features of each, more perfectly than
they could be represented upon canvas or carved in stone.

The Egyptian tombs are an exhaustless fountain of ethnological knowledge. Ever since Belzoni unbolted their doors, the
dry bones there deposited have been unfolding, as it were, the
history of a buried ancient world. Lepsius and Dr. Morton

have made these dry bones speak in tones not to be misunderstood. Dr. Morton obtained from these tombs 140 ancient skulls, and thirty-seven of the modern race. Among them were the Egyptian, Greek, Roman and African. He referred his collection of skulls to two races—the Caucasian and Negro.

The comparison of skulls makes the Negro the inferior race; not so much in internal capacity as the character of the brain and its development. Each type may be recognized by the character of the skull alone, and though it may become modified by amalgamation, the original will not generally be destroyed. Although this may be a good test of type, the intellect, after all, is considered the proper guide by which to discover the races.

The physical history of the races is not a work of chance; they advance in proportion to the degree of intellect. In their primitive organizations of societies they display their native mental powers. Here is where the degrees of native intellect is most wonderfully displayed, and where the superior race is most prominently presented. When we, therefore, see the Caucasian emerging from barbarism by his own forecast, and then becoming the polished and refined superior, we cannot but admit that it is the result of mental endowment. And when we see the inferior races still continuing in their degraded and barbarous condition, we cannot but attribute it to a want of intellect.

The destiny of the Negro race inhabiting the United States is now being materially changed—for weal or woe is yet undetermined. The Federal Government, under the war power, having abolished slavery, is now looking to the interest of the blacks; and during the process of reconstruction in the Confederate States, is extending to the Negroes the right of suffrage, and presenting the question of the equality of races. This is a subject of great delicacy; one which should be calmly considered by all classes. It is not submitted to the people as a question of political economy in the abstract, but as a question of natural right—extending the elective franchise to all classes of American citizens without regard to color.

The claim is that, to be free men under our system of government, entitled every man to the right of suffrage, however degraded or refined his condition in life.

The first point for consideration is, as regards the fitness of the Negroes for equality with the whites of this nationality. Suffrage and equality are inseparable. Extending to the Negroes the right of suffrage is virtually placing them upon an equality with the whites, at least politically, and in reality socially. That a people may be able to retain freedom and equality, they ought to be capable of understanding fully all the principles upon which these great principles are based. All men have natural rights; but they can only expect to enjoy these rights in proportion to the degrees of intelligence they possess.

The politicians of the old world have for centuries held that mankind are not capable of self-government upon principles of equality. The government of the United States is the only power on the face of the globe where self-government has been successsfully reared or maintained. But it was not established upon the basis of equality of races, but in the very outset declared the superiority of the white man over the other inferior races of the country, Indians and Negroes, then constituting portions of the population of the country. It is not yet settled that the black and white races can sustain the same nationality upon the principles of equality of races, politically or socially. Though the fathers of the republic, in their wisdom, guarded against the introduction of any other than the European race as participants in our political institutions, an assumed greater wisdom than they seemed to possess, now dictates that equality of races, politically at least, is necessary in order to secure the permanency of the Federal Government. The fact that the white race established and maintained our free system for eighty years by no means warrants the conclusion that the black and white population, being placed upon a forced equality, will continue to maintain it intact. Such an unnatural state of things, it is to be feared, would completely disorganize our republican system.

If the white man, with his superior intelligence, is scarcely capable of self-government upon principles of equality of individuals of the same race, it is scarcely possible that he will be willing or able to do so when an inferior race is engrafted upon his institutions, especially against his consent. The history of mankind is against such a procedure; the elements are too discordant and incongruous to harmonize.

There is not a solitary case upon record where the engrafting of one people upon another politically, or socially, has proved beneficial to the united peoples or nations. This has been the result where peoples less repulsive to each other than the Negroes to the whites were incorporated in the same government. This seems to be the natural result of such a course of policy. Nature would wrong and outrage herself if it were otherwise. The law of nature cannot be changed, nor man's social qualities stultified by political coercion.

CHAPTER XVIII.

MAN MORALLY CONSIDERED.

MAN naturally morally inclined.—Born to fatality.—Spirit of evil.—Man's mission to be happy.—His desire to worship universal—Idol worship.—Human sacrifice—Aztecs sacrificed 70,000 at dedication of their great temple, in 1486.—Natural and Revealed Religion.—Immortality of the Soul—Socrates and Plato.—Worship of the Gods.—Paganism.—Homer—his eloquence and sublime moral conceptions.—Revealed Religion—safety in its belief—no safety outside the Church.—Depravity of man.—No mystery in Morals.—All systems have religious truth.—The Crucifixion of the Saviour.—Constantine's Vision.—Rise of Mahomet.—Dark Ages.—The creation of the Roman Pontiff.—Infidelity.—Church is corrupted.—Crusaders.—Population of the Globe.—The number of Christians.—The Atheist and Savage compared.

EVERY individual, to some extent, entertains sentiments of morality; and this inclination of the mind is manifested in savage as well as civilized mankind; but the former is incapable of giving proper direction to his moral conceptions, and in their development, being guided by his natural desires, is more likely to be wrong than right. This is very manifest in instances of idol worship, and cases where savages have put to death Christian teachers visiting them for the purpose of instructing them in morals and revealed religion.

Mankind, in their uncultivated state, are too apt to be distrustful in regard to their future state of existence, believing their condition indicates that they are not in favor with the Deity; hence arise the doctrines of fatalism and dualism. Those who believe in the latter doctrine, not only entertain the idea of the existence of two Gods, but also that the spirit of evil existed from eternity. This evil spirit is too much believed in at the present day, even by civilized man, in consequence of which much evil is entailed upon the human family. Owing to this belief, man gives way to his predominant desires and passions, and then, as an excuse for his rashness, contends that he was born to fatality. Man's mission in the world is to be happy; not merely to enjoy a selfish happiness, but to impart its blessings to others. The question of moral right is one of great perplexity; conscience, which dictates to savage and civilized, does not appear to produce the same moral results in both cases, though they are actuated by like motives. The heathen worships his idol, and, entertaining the belief that he is doing a moral and religious act, offers a human victim as a sacrifice to his idol god. This, in the estimation of the Christian believer, is not only a heinous sin, but revolting murder. The savage knows not God; yet his nature teaches him that there is a Supreme Author of the Universe, and an existence beyond the grave, which he is pleased to describe as a "happy hunting-ground"—a place of endless ease and pleasure. He hopes to be happy in a future state, and to be at rest, yet has no assurance that he shall be so. But the Christian looks forward with joy to the moment when his immortal spirit, freed from its earthly tenement, shall pass to heaven, and dwell with the saints and Christ forever.

Every reasonable being has a desire to reverence and worship; savage and civilized, in this respect, are equal; but the former cannot be religious, though he may be moral and happy.

The king of Dahomey, assuming to be religious, sacrifices thousands of his race every year to his idols; and the more victims he can offer, the greater he will be in favor (as he supposes) with his gods. The Hindoo, in his frenzied idol-worship, offers his children as sacrifices to the crocodile, by relentlessly throwing them into the Ganges; yet he dreads the killing of the smallest insect, lest the soul of some dead Hindoo may have taken refuge therein. And the religion of the Hindoos prompts them to burn their living widows upon the same funeral pyre with their deceased husbands.

The greatest human sacrifice upon record was perpetrated in Mexico by the Aztecs, at the dedication of their great temple, in 1486, at which time no less than 70,000 victims perished at the shrine of the terrible deity of the superstitious Aztecs. The victim to be offered was conducted to the top of the pyramid in

the temple; here he was received by six priests, who led him to
the sacrificial stone—a huge block of jasper, and on this he was
stretched; five priests secured his head and limbs, while the
sixth, clad in a scarlet mantle, emblematic of his bloody office,
dexterously opened the breast of the wretched victim with a
sharp stone instrument, and, inserting his hand in the wound,
tore out the palpitating heart, first holding it up towards the
sun, then casting it at the feet of the deity to which the temple
was dedicated.* The body was then delivered over to the party
who captured him, and in the evening was served up as a repast
to the invited guests.

The disposition to worship is not considered to be an emana-
tion of the Divine will, but a natural desire to reverence the
Author of Nature. Such is the condition of man before he is
made to realize that he is an accountable being, and has an immortal soul.†

Natural religion implies belief in a supreme authority, which
belief is considered an innateness of the mind, and is that disposition which inclines mankind to venerate and worship supreme intelligence. But, when man attains to civilization, he
realizes that he is more than mortal; that within his physical
body dwells an immortal spirit, the author of which he seeks to
discover by the philosophy of reason and works of nature.

This desire is aptly presented in the following: ‡

> " Father Supreme! O, let me climb
> That sacred seat and mark sublime.
> The essential fount of life and love !
> Fount, whence each good, each pleasure flows !
> O, to my view, thyself disclose !
> The radiant heavens thy presence strows !
> O, lose me in the light above!

---

* Prescott's Conquest of Mexico, Vol. I., p. 76.

† The Australians, the natives of Central Africa, and those inhabiting the
country around the North Pole, are yet savages, having no religious belief.—
Plurality of Races, by Pouchet, p. 66.

‡ This quotation is from Lorenzo De Medici, addressed to the Supreme Being,
at the age when the Platonic philosophy was recognized by the poets and
prose writers during the revival of literature.—The Book of Nature, by John
M. Good.

Flee, flee, ye mists! let earth depart:
Raise me, and show me what thou art,
Great sun and center of the soul!
To thee each thought in silence tends;
To thee the saints in prayer ascend;
Thou art the source, the guide, the goal:
The whole is thine, and thou the whole."

A cultivation of this desire, as in the age of Socrates, not only revealed the immortality of the soul, but discovered to man its divine author. Socrates was the revelator of natural religion and moral rectitude; and Jesus Christ the promulgator of revealed religion and the way of salvation: both suffered death for their moral and religious teachings; "Socrates died like a philosopher, but Jesus Christ died like a God."*

Before the age of Socrates the Greeks had a refined system of Paganism. Their poets, in their literary pursuits, created, out of moral persons, quite an array of Gods, who, for several ages, seem to have controlled the destiny of the Greeks and kindred nations. Homer's Iliad is replete with the exploits, power and wisdom of these deities.

At first, the living heroes were worshipped; at their death, statues and monuments were erected to their memories, around which the people gathered and worshipped; and, finally, the most magnificent temples were dedicated to their fame, some of which were so sacred, that even malefactors, seeking refuge within their sacred walls, were shielded from all harm. The system of refined paganism was not confined to the Greeks alone, though they invented it; the Romans, Egyptians, Persians, Medes, and other early nations, also adopted its leading features, though each of these nations had a system of their own also.* Among the less civilized nations, it resulted in the sacrifice of human victims to their gods, as a test of their devout reverence for their supreme authority. The leading actors in the bloody drama were the Druids: they conducted the devoted victims to the altar, presided at the solemnity, and

* Chaucer.

* The Sadducees, entertaining the refined notions of the Semitic family, though a religious sect, believed that the soul died with the body.—Josephus, p. 361.

performed the cruel office of the sacrifice with the most devout reverence.

To the genius of Homer, more than any other person, may be ascribed the refined theory of the Pagan deities. He ranked the gods as moral persons possessed of definite characters, like men performing great actions. This stimulated men to be moral and become like the gods, who, one day, like them, had been living moral persons. His great thoughts, and sublime moral conceptions, awoke the human intellect from the slumber of ages. To his Iliad has been ascribed the glory of Greece.

HOMER.

> " His countrymen came ten thousand strong,
>   To weep o'er his narrow bed;
> And tears they gave to that child of song,
>   Who had sued to them for bread."

The Oriental poets appear to have been gifted with a moral inspiration almost divine. The Rig-veda and Paranas of the Hindoos, in point of sublimity and religious veneration, are almost equal to the writings of the inspired prophets.

The idea that there can be no true religious faith without a strict observance of all the precepts of revelation, is, doubtless, in the main, correct, so far as the finite mind is capable of judging; but, perhaps, it is saying too much, when the power and wisdom of Jehovah is considered. " His ways are not our ways;" he suffers persons to live and die in the hope of a blessed immortality, who have never belonged to any religious congregation, or partaken of any of the divine ordinances. Such individuals are not merely religious in form, but live all their lives by the strictest rules of morality, with full belief that when they pass from earth they shall dwell in the world of bliss, with God and angels, throughout the ceaseless ages of eternity.

One great error of the age consists in placing too much reliance upon the mere forms of religion; and it is to be lamented that so many professing Christians are averse to reasoning upon the subject of religion, and seem to keep their adopted faith aloof from philanthropic investigation.

Such professors are selfish bigots, and very bad examples of genuine Christianity. The chief reason for this line of policy is that such persons abhor what is termed natural religion, the believers in which being generally opposed to priestcraft. Natural religion, being guided by reason, the moral sentiments of the formal professor are supposed to be debased, when compared with those believers outside the Christian church. The difference between these two classes of believers is not so great when the subject is properly understood. God recognizes every moral and religious thought of all his accountable creatures. Without divine power, man cannot be moral or religious; and when an individual is moral and religious, though he be outside the Christian church, it is charitable to believe that such a one's mind and desires are lifted up on high, and discern heavenly things by divine inspiration.

There is, however, no justification for remaining aloof from the divine ordinances, or outside of the Christian church; and, however consistent it may be with man's natural inclinations to do so, it is a dangerous experiment, as there is the place of safety for those who wish to enjoy a blessed immortality; there is where the great Jehovah has promised to be with his people, even to the end.

Religious and moral truths were appointed to carry mankind to their most happy destiny. Like all other subjects, they require investigation, and the full exercise of the mental faculties. God endowed man with reason in order that he might comprehend his divinity, and his compassion toward mankind, and to investigate the things pertaining to their moral and religious advancement.

It is to be regretted that the great intellects of the world have not, as a general rule, been devoted to moral and religious investigation; on the contrary, those things pertaining to man's happiness on earth, and the joys of heaven, in too many instances, have fallen into the hands of weak and superstitious enthusiasts, who, instead of being guided by the philosopy of reason, as revealed in the Scriptures, have taken the shadow for the substance, virtually becoming traffickers in human souls, by establishing a selfish sectarian creed, by the arbitrary rules of which but very few only dare assume to worship.

This system of selfishness and superstitious bigotry virtually ignores the teachings of the Saviour; and hence, instead of their name being an universal brotherhood of Christian believers, the world is distracted by creeds, sects, and denominations as numerous as the families of man.

It does appear as if the human mind desires to be deceived upon the subject of religion and morals. The great mass of the people seem to have abandoned all idea of reasoning upon these subjects. One class, wholly regardless of futurity, stand as unconscious and unconcerned about their future state as the beasts that perish; whilst the professors of religion, to an alarming extent, seem to desire to hand their souls over to the keeping of the clergy, under the mistaken idea that the observance of the forms of religious worship, with liberal donations to the pious minister, will be amply sufficient for their salvation. In refined society, it is too often the case that professors of religion devote only one day in seven to religious worship, the remainder of the week being dedicated to the business of the world.

Such persons console themselves with the idea that their hired pastors will take care of their spiritual affairs during the week, whilst they are serving mammon, and, perchance, advancing the business of the devil. It is a mistaken idea that the pious minister is to become the scapegoat for the sins of the congregation.

Such professors should remember the important enunciation of the Sacred Scriptures: "If the righteous scarcely be saved, where shall the ungodly and the sinner appear?" There is not, necessarily, any mystery in morals or religion. The way to happiness is so plainly marked out that, "though a man be a fool, he need not err therein." But, owing to a morbid desire on the part of those calling themselves divines, religious doctrines have been, and still are, involved in many grave contradictions; and hence it is there are so many branches of the Christian church and unbelievers.

In all systems of religious worship there are gems of divine truth, which often, like the diamond, are prevented from being properly displayed by superfluous coverings.   There is religious truth in the Vedas of the Hindoos; in the Zendevesta of the Persians; in the Gnostic system of the Orientals, and in the Koran of Mahomet; but in all these systems there is such a display of priestcraft, and mysterious idol-worship, as render them repulsive to the Christian believer.*

The process of mystifying the moral and religious sentiments of mankind produced a powerful opposition to natural religion, resulting, in the end, in rank Atheism, with other kindred sys-

THE SAVIOUR.

tems of unbelief.   These opposing influences greatly retarded the progress of Christianity, and, for a time, almost triumphed over religion.   The Jews, to whom had been committed the keeping of moral law, rejected the Saviour, with his doctrines,

---

* There are now over two millions of Buddhists on the earth, who are highly civilized; yet their system of morals and religion ignores all idea of another life, or divinity.   There is not the slightest belief in God in all Buddhaism.—Plurality of Races, p. 71.

thus turning the tide of religion into a new channel. The Messiah had come, delivered his message, and departed.

Revealed religion was inaugurated. It consisted of two grand ideas: "The love of God, and the love of our neighbor." Upon these two commandments, said the Saviour, "hang all the law and the prophets." The crucifixion of Jesus Christ did not, in the least degree, intimidate the Christians, but, if anything, made them more bold and defiant in the spread of the Gospel. The world at large readily adopted the new faith. Rome, even, espoused it, but more as a question of policy than as a conviction of duty. Constantine, seeing the prosperity of his father as an imperial ruler, and believing it resulted from his humane course toward the Christians, prayed for the protection of heaven in the wars for his empire. God, it would seem, answered his prayers; in mid-day, in view of his whole army, appeared a pillar of light, above the sun, in the form of a cross, with the inscription: "Conquer by this." Constantine, that night, in great agony of mind as to the meaning of the wonderful vision, was relieved by the Saviour appearing to him, with the same sign, commanding him to make use of such in conquering his foes. He did so, reared the golden cross, and by this ensign conquered his foes, and enforced the Christian religion by the sword throughout his empire. After the death of Constantine, the Christian world was scourged by the barbarians of the North, consisting of Goths, Vandals, Huns, and other kindred spirits, who, in successive waves, with fire and sword, overrun Italy, Greece, Asia Minor, Spain, Britain, and Northern Africa. Before they had completed their work of destruction, a more dangerous enemy to the Christian faith arose in the East.

Mahomet, assuming to be the prophet of God, promulgated his new faith, and enforced it successfully with the sword. It being a mixture of Judaism and Christianity, his new religion was well suited to the manners and passions of the age.

What of Christianity escaped the barbarians was literally swept away by the Mahometans, who not only overrun the Eastern Roman Empire, but polluted the sacred places dedicated to the worship of the Saviour. Its submergence, however, was only temporary.

24

" Truth, crushed to earth, shall rise again ;
　　The eternal years of God are hers ;
　　But Error, wounded, writhes in pain,
　　And dies among her worshippers."

The barbarians readily adopted the refined civilization and manners of the Christians, and many also espoused their religious faith ; and, by the close of the fifth century A. D., were, with very commendable zeal and patriotism, protecting the same institutions they had so recently aimed to destroy.

The success of Constantine and Mahomet, in making proselytes by the sword, induced others to adopt the system in enforcing religious faith.

Charles the Great, by this method, effected the conversion of the principal tribes of Northern Germany and Saxony ; and the same means were resorted to in the conversion of the Wends.

The conversion of the Germans, though a great triumph for the Christian church, for the time being, resulted, in the end, quite disastrously to the Christian cause. The Germans, naturally pious, and inclined to reverence their pagan priests, submitted readily to the wishes of the clergy, who, to a great extent, used their offices for selfish purposes ; hence rose the western bishops, and, finally, the Roman pontiff. By the establishment of these high religious functionaries, the simplicity of the doctrines of Christ were cast aside, and the pomp and splendor of the priests and bishops, and the ceremonies and regalia of religious exercises, adopted instead. Thus, upon the ruins of the pure Christian religion, as taught by the Saviour, rose a sophisticated, cold, scholastic theology. The Church, however, under this system, rose as by magic, and, instead of being the persecuted, became the persecutor. The infidels—all being considered such who were outside the Christian church—were treated by the Christians as if they had forfeited all the rights of man. Religious frenzy, however, did not reach its culmination until the tenth century A. D., when the Crusaders commenced their bloody work. We will not attempt to unvail their crimes. Their avowed object was the rescuing of the holy sepulchre of the Saviour, and the City of the Great King, from the pollution of the ungodly Turks. The purpose was noble and praiseworthy, but the means resorted to were so barbarous and cruel as to

leave an indelible stain upon the Christian character. Millions
of lives were sacrificed before the Crusaders entered the Holy
City; and, before it was reached, the church had become greatly
corrupted. The Pope, to add strength to his power, offered re-
mission of sins to all who would put on the cross. This decree
of universal amnesty added millions to his standard. Saints
and sinners met upon a common level in church and state.
More than six millions of enthusiastic persons put on the cross,
determined to worship at the tomb of Jesus; among them a vast
number of females. The Queen of Hungary led a whole army
of women to Palestine. Civilized Europe appeared to become
allies of the Crusaders.

There is a point where wickedness will cease; and it was the
case with the Crusaders. In the very moment of their triumph
their glory departed, and they were compelled to yield up all
they had gained to the conquering Mongols, who not only took
Jerusalem, but virtually exterminated the Christian army at
Gaza; since which time the tomb of the Saviour has been
polluted by the semi-barbarous Ishmaelites, the Mohammedan
Turks.

Though the Crusaders were a severe scourge to the nations
falling in their way, they were the means of waking up the
slumbering energies of the people from the gloom of the Dark
Ages. When they ceased to be Christian warriors in the field,
they sought to worship at their sacred altars; but their zeal in
religious affairs soon defiled the place of worship—turned them
into theatres of mysterious exhibitions; one congregation would
exhibit, as was pretended, the identical spear that pierced the
Saviour's side; another the cross upon which he was crucified;
another the vesture for which the soldiers casts lots; whilst
another would present Moses' rod. At this juncture Martin
Luther sounded the alarm. Then commenced the bloody struggle between the Protestants and the Roman Catholics which
disgraced the Christian religion, and proved that civilized man
is more relentless and savage than the rudest barbarian. Burning human beings at the stake, for opinion's sake, by both par-
ties, was not unusual, and seems to have been a pleasant pastime
for the persecuting spectators—pretended worshipers of Jesus—
during the Reformation. The population of the globe is 900,000,-

000. Of this number 260,000,000 are Christians; of whom 139,000,000 are Roman Catholics, 60,000,000 of the Greek church, and 60,000,000 of the Protestant. This appears but a small proportion of the human family to be brought under the influence of the doctrines of the Saviour in eighteen hundred years. One great reason for this is the lack of confidence in the integrity of one another, among the different nations. The Hindoo clings to his religion as his only hope; the Mohammedan relies upon the Koran; the savage upon his Pagan idols, and the Atheist lives and dies in unbelief. He is more than savage, as it requires mind to be an unbeliever. No hope of Heaven or fear of Hell for a single moment disturbs his peaceful mind; he is degraded below the most abject barbarian. The savage, even, looks beyond the veil :—

> " His soul proud science never taught to stray
> Far as the solar walk or milky way;
> Yet simple nature to his hope has given,
> Beyond the cloud-topped hill, an humble heaven;
> Some safer world in depth of wood embraced;
> Some happier island in the watery waste;
> Where slaves once more their native land behold; '
> No fiends torment, no Christians thirst for gold."

The mind of the savage is highly exalted above the cultivated intellect of the atheist, as the former believes his spirit will live beyond the grave; but the latter has no hope; he feigns to believe there is no God; with him all is a work of chance. But the Christian only lives to admire and worship the Creator of the universe. He has no fear of death or punishment, and fully realizes his true condition here, and what he shall be hereafter. When he shall have made up the number of his days on earth, and is passing from time to eternity, he feels that death hath no sting, and the grave no victory.

He meets Jehovah in all His works of creation, and, with songs of triumph, welcomes the moment when he shall pass from earth to heaven, and forever dwell with the saints, and God, and Christ.

INDEX.

373